"In this generation of evangelical scholarship, Andreas Köstenberger ranks as one of our leading New Testament scholars. I'm delighted to see this tribute to his life and ministry, and I heartily commend this book compiled in his honor."

—Jason K. Allen,
President and Professor of Preaching and Pastoral Ministry,
Midwestern Baptist Theological Seminary

"Here, leading evangelical scholars honor fellow evangelical scholar and noted Johannine specialist Andreas Köstenberger. But whereas many Festschriften are a hodgepodge of unrelated essays, that is not the case with this work. *That You May Believe* provides a splendid introduction to many issues in Johannine studies, including tracing the history and present state of Johannine scholarship and thoroughly engaging major sources for Johannine intertextuality."

—Craig S. Keener,
F. M. and Ada Thompson Professor of Biblical Studies,
Asbury Theological Seminary

"This volume is much more than a collection of essays in celebration of Andreas Köstenberger's prolific career in research and writing on the Gospel of John. It is a course in key issues in Johannine scholarship in its own right, written almost entirely by a cast of established scholars—some of them at the very top of their disciplines—who have specialized in, among other things, issues central to the Gospel of John. From up-to-date surveys of scholarship in certain areas, especially John's use of the Old Testament, to ground-breaking treatments of more specific topics, *That You May Believe* offers the reader valuable contributions on every issue it covers."

—Craig L. Blomberg,
Distinguished Professor Emeritus of New Testament,
Denver Seminary

THAT YOU MAY BELIEVE

Essays on John in Honor of

ANDREAS J. KÖSTENBERGER

QUINN R. MOSIER
T. DESMOND ALEXANDER
ROBERT W. YARBROUGH

That You May Believe: Essays on John in Honor of Andreas J. Köstenberger
© 2025 by Quinn R. Mosier, T. Desmond Alexander, Robert W. Yarbrough, editors

Published by Kregel Academic, an imprint of Kregel Publications, 2450 Oak Industrial Dr. NE, Grand Rapids, MI 49505-6020

All rights reserved. No part of this book may be reproduced, stored in a retrieval system, or transmitted in any form or by any means—electronic, mechanical, photocopy, recording, or otherwise—without written permission of the publisher, except for brief quotations in printed reviews.

Scripture quotations marked CSB have been taken from the Christian Standard Bible®, Copyright © 2017 by Holman Bible Publishers. Used by permission. Christian Standard Bible® and CSB® are federally registered trademarks of Holman Bible Publishers.

Scripture quotations marked ESV are from The ESV® Bible (The Holy Bible, English Standard Version®), © 2001 by Crossway, a publishing ministry of Good News Publishers. Used by permission. All rights reserved.

Scripture quotations marked NASB are taken from the (NASB®) New American Standard Bible®, Copyright © 1960, 1971, 1977, 1995, 2020 by The Lockman Foundation. Used by permission. All rights reserved. www.lockman.org

Quotations designated (NET) are from the NET Bible® copyright ©1996, 2019 by Biblical Studies Press, L.L.C. http://netbible.com. All rights reserved.

Scripture quotations marked NIV are taken from the Holy Bible, New International Version®, NIV®. Copyright © 1973, 1978, 1984, 2011 by Biblica, Inc.™ Used by permission of Zondervan. All rights reserved worldwide. www.zondervan.com. The "NIV" and "New International Version" are trademarks registered in the United States Patent and Trademark Office by Biblica, Inc.

Scripture quotations marked NRSVUE are taken from the New Revised Standard Version Updated Edition. Copyright © 2021 National Council of Churches of Christ in the United States of America. Used by permission. All rights reserved worldwide.

Scripture quotations marked RSV are from the Revised Standard Version of the Bible, copyright © 1946, 1952, and 1971 National Council of the Churches of Christ in the United States of America. Used by permission. All rights reserved worldwide.

The Hebrew font, NewJerusalemU, and the Greek font, GraecaU, are available from www.linguist-software.com/lgku.htm, +1-425-775-1130.

Images on pages 35, 37, and 38 are from Alexander Stewart. Used by permission.

Cataloging-in-Publication Data is available from the Library of Congress.

ISBN 978-0-8254-4838-6

Printed in the United States of America

25 26 27 28 29 / 5 4 3 2 1

Dedicated to
Andreas J. Köstenberger

contents

Editors' Preface 9

Abbreviations 13

PART 1: EXEGETING JOHN

1. The Theme of the "Sent One" in John's Gospel
   Darrell L. Bock 19

2. Παράκλητος in the Johannine Corpus in Light of Anatolian Epigraphic Evidence
   Alexander Stewart 29

3. The Covenant Texture of the Farewell Scenes (John 13–17)
   L. Scott Kellum 43

4. The Christ Hymn of John 1: From Confessional Response to Transformative Overture
   Paul N. Anderson 65

PART 2: JOHN AND THE CANON

5. John and the Pentateuch
   T. Desmond Alexander 91

6. John and the Prophets
   James A. Roh 103

7. John and the Writings
   Gregory Goswell 115

8. John and the Synoptics
   Quinn R. Mosier 131

PART 3: JOHANNINE THEOLOGY AND SCHOLARSHIP

9. The Current State of Johannine Studies
   Stanley E. Porter 155

10. John in Theologies of the New Testament Since Gabler: Critical and Canonical
    Robert W. Yarbrough 183

11. The Reception of John's Gospel in the Early Church
    Michael J. Kruger 205

12. The Eternal Procession of the Holy Spirit in the Gospel According to John
    Gregg R. Allison 221

13. "Born Again" in Johannine Thought
    Thomas R. Schreiner 241

14. God's Presence and the Absence of Tears (Rev. 7:17; 21:4)
    Eckhard J. Schnabel 255

    Bibliography of the Writings of Andreas J. Köstenberger 279

    Contributors 309

    Author Index.. 311

    Subject Index... 315

    Scripture Index 319

EDITORS' PREFACE

L est there be any confusion as to why the apostle John wrote his account of Jesus, he closed with these words: "these are written so that you may believe that Jesus is the Christ, the Son of God, and that by believing you may have life in his name" (John 20:31 ESV). Belief in Jesus is the reason John wrote his Gospel; the deepening of belief in Jesus is the reason he wrote one of his epistles (1 John 5:13); and the hope of eternal life through believing in Jesus is the reason he faithfully bore witness to all that he saw from Jesus (Rev. 1:2–3). The same aim of pointing people to the eternal life God has given in his Son is what characterizes the writing and teaching of Andreas J. Köstenberger, in honor of whom this book is written and why it seemed appropriate to entitle it *That You May Believe*.

Andreas has made a great impact on the church through countless students who have encountered him, whether through the classroom, podcasts, his website Biblical Foundations, or one of his many publications. He has published extensively at both the academic and popular levels, writing mainly on John, biblical theology, hermeneutics, and marriage and family. His entire bibliography contains the hallmarks of why his body of work continues to help so many after thirty years of teaching, researching, and writing—a careful eye for detail and accuracy, an ability to simply articulate and synthesize large amounts of information, an awareness of context, an unwillingness to drive a wedge between scholarship and faith, and an unwavering commitment to the spread of the gospel. As he recognizes himself, "My faith and my scholarship are utterly inseparable."[1]

---

1. Andreas J. Köstenberger, *Excellence: The Character of God and the Pursuit of Scholarly Virtue* (Wheaton, IL: Crossway, 2011), 17.

Though his writing spans many topics, he is perhaps best known for his affinity for John. He has published commentaries,[2] numerous monographs and articles,[3] surveys,[4] introductions,[5] and a full-length theology,[6] all on the topic of John. He himself acknowledges John as his first love. It is for this reason that this volume is a collection of essays on John.

The book has three parts. The first part, "Exegeting John," focuses on various exegetical and background matters relating to the text of John. This section features essays by Darrell L. Bock, Alexander Stewart, L. Scott Kellum, and Paul N. Anderson. The second part, "John and the Canon," looks at how John relates to each of the three divisions of the Tanakh (Pentateuch, Prophets, Writings), as well as how he engages the Synoptic Gospels. This section features essays by T. Desmond Alexander, James A. Roh, Gregory Goswell, and Quinn R. Mosier. The third part, "Johannine Theology and Scholarship," contains various essays related to John's theology, history, and Johannine studies in general. This section features essays by Stanley E. Porter, Robert W. Yarbrough, Michael J. Kruger, Gregg R. Allison, Thomas R. Schreiner, and Eckhard J. Schnabel.

The editors wish to express their gratitude to Kregel Academic for publishing this Festschrift honoring Andreas J. Köstenberger. In a day where the Festschrift is perhaps a dying genre, we are thankful for their willingness to pursue this worthwhile project alongside us.

The editors and contributors of this volume would like to express our gratitude to you, Andreas, for your tireless pursuit of excellence in scholarship, your devotion to Christ and his church, and your desire to make

---

2. Köstenberger, *John*, BECNT (Grand Rapids: Baker Academic, 2004), withdrawn from publisher; *John*, EEC (Bellingham, WA: Lexham, forthcoming); *John*, The Gospel Coalition Bible Commentary, https://www.thegospelcoalition.org/commentary/john/.

3. Some of which include, Köstenberger, *The Missions of Jesus and the Disciples in the Fourth Gospel: With Implications for the Fourth Gospel's Purpose and the Mission of the Contemporary Church* (Grand Rapids: Eerdmans, 1998); *Studies in John and Gender: A Decade of Scholarship*, Studies in Biblical Literature 38 (New York: Peter Lang, 2001); "John," in *Commentary on the New Testament Use of the Old Testament*, ed. G. K. Beale and D. A. Carson (Grand Rapids: Baker Academic, 2007), 415–512; *Father, Son, and Spirit: The Trinity and John's Gospel*, NSBT, with Scott Swain (Leicester; Downers Grove, IL: InterVarsity Press, 2008).

4. Köstenberger, *Encountering John: The Gospel in Historical, Literary, and Theological Perspective*, EBS, 2nd ed. (Grand Rapids: Baker Academic, 2013).

5. Köstenberger, *Signs of the Messiah: An Introduction to John's Gospel* (Bellingham, WA: Lexham, 2021).

6. Köstenberger, *The Theology of John's Gospel and Letters: The Word, the Christ, the Son of God*, BTNT (Grand Rapids: Zondervan, 2009).

God and the gospel known to others. We pray the Lord will sustain your efforts in the coming years, and that you and your wife, Margaret, will have many more years in faithful service to the Lord who bought you at the price of his own Son.

Soli Deo Gloria.

Quinn R. Mosier, Kansas City, Missouri
T. Desmond Alexander, Belfast, Northern Ireland
Robert W. Yarbrough, St. Louis, Missouri

ABBREVIATIONS

AB	Anchor Bible
ABG	Arbeiten zur Bibel und ihrer Geschichte
ACT	Ancient Christian Texts
AGJU	Arbeiten zur Geschichte des antiken Judentums und des Urchristentums
AJA	American Journal of Archaeology
AJEC	Ancient Judaism and Early Christianity
AnBib	Analecta Biblica
ApOTC	Apollos Old Testament Commentary
BBR	*Bulletin for Biblical Research*
BDAG	Bauer, Danker, Arndt, and Gingrich
BECNT	Baker Exegetical Commentary on the New Testament
BETL	Bibliotheca Ephemeridum Theologicarum Lovaniensium
BibInt	Biblical Interpretation Series
BIWK	Die Beichtinschriften Westkleinasiens
BJRL	*Bulletin of the John Rylands Library*
BNTC	Black's New Testament Commentaries
BSac	*Bibliotheca Sacra*
BTNT	Biblical Theology of the New Testament
BZ	*Biblische Zeitschrift*
BZNW	Beihefte zur Zeitschrift für die neutestamentliche Wissenschaft
CBC	Cornerstone Biblical Commentary
CBET	Contributions to Biblical Exegesis and Theology
CBQ	*Catholic Biblical Quarterly*
CBQMS	The Catholic Biblical Quarterly Monograph Series
EBib	Etudes Bibliques
EBS	Encountering Biblical Studies
EBTC	The Evangelical Biblical Theology Commentary

EEC	Evangelical Exegetical Commentary
EKKNT	Evangelisch-katholischer Kommentar zum Neuen Testament
EvQ	*Evangelical Quarterly*
FAT	Forschungen zum Alten Testament
HNT	Handbuch zum Neuen Testament
HTCNT	Herder's Theological Commentary on the New Testament
HTR	*The Harvard Theological Review*
HUCA	*Hebrew Union College Annual*
ICC	International Critical Commentary
IJL	Interpreting Johannine Literature
IVPNTC	IVP New Testament Commentary
JBL	*Journal of Biblical Literature*
JETS	*Journal of the Evangelical Theological Society*
JMS	Johannine Monograph Series
JOST	Johannine Studies
JSNT	*Journal for the Study of the New Testament*
JSNTSup	Journal for the Study of the New Testament Supplement
JSOTSup	Journal for the Study of the Old Testament Supplement
JTI	*Journal of Theological Interpretation*
JTS	*Journal of Theological Studies*
KEK	Kritisch-exegetischer Kommentar über das Neue Testament
LNTS	The Library of New Testament Studies
LSJ	Liddell–Scott–Jones
MThSt	Marburger Theologische Studien
NAC	The New American Commentary
NCB	New Century Bible Commentary
Neot	*Neotestamentica*
NETS	A New English Translation of the Septuagint
NICB	New Interpreter's Commentary on the Bible
NICNT	The New International Commentary on the New Testament
NICOT	The New International Commentary on the Old Testament
NIDNTTE	New International Dictionary of New Testament Theology and Exegesis

NIGTC	The New International Greek Testament Commentary
NIVAC	NIV Application Commentary
NovT	*Novum Testamentum*
NovTSup	Supplements to Novum Testamentum
NPNF	Nicene and Post-Nicene Fathers
NSBT	New Studies in Biblical Theology
NTL	The New Testament Library
NTS	*New Testament Studies*
OTL	The Old Testament Library
PNTC	Pillar New Testament Commentary
PTMS	Princeton Theological Monograph Series
RB	*Revue biblique*
RBS	Resources for Biblical Study
ResQ	*Restoration Quarterly*
SBL	Studies in Biblical Literature
SBLDS	Society of Biblical Literature Dissertation Series
SBLSymS	Society of Biblical Literature Symposium Series
SBT	Studies in Biblical Theology
SecCent	*The Second Century*
SJT	*Scottish Journal of Theology*
SNTSMS	Society for New Testament Studies Monograph Series
SSBT	Short Studies in Biblical Theology
SSEJC	Studies in Scripture in Early Judaism and Christianity
STR	Studies in Theology and Religion
SwJT	*Southwestern Journal of Theology*
TBN	Themes in Biblical Narrative
TDNT	Theological Dictionary of the New Testament
TDOT	Theological Dictionary of the Old Testament
Them	*Themelios*
THKNT	Theologischer Handkommentar zum Neuen Testament
THOTC	Two Horizons Old Testament Commentary
TJ	*Trinity Journal*
TNTC	Tyndale New Testament Commentaries
TOTC	Tyndale Old Testament Commentaries
TWQ	Theological Dictionary of the Qumran Texts
TynBul	*The Tyndale Bulletin*
VT	*Vetus Testamentum*
VTSup	Supplements to Vetus Testamentum

Abbreviations

WBC	Word Biblical Commentary
WTJ	*The Westminster Theological Journal*
WUNT	Wissenschaftliche Untersuchungen zum Neuen Testament
ZAC	*Zeitschrift für Antikes Christentum*
ZECNT	Zondervan Exegetical Commentary on the New Testament
ZNW	*Zeitschrift für die neutestamentliche Wissenschaft und die Kunde der älteren Kirche*
ZTK	*Zeitschrift für Theologie und Kirche*

PART 1
EXEGETING JOHN

CHAPTER 1

THE THEME OF THE "SENT ONE" IN JOHN'S GOSPEL

DARRELL L. BOCK

One of the most underappreciated parts of John's Gospel is his portrayal of Jesus as the "Sent One." It is more a description of Jesus than a title, but it is loaded with significance for the portrait of the Savior by the fourth evangelist. Our goal is to survey the many texts that refer to Jesus as the "Sent One," or variations of it, to grasp John's focus on this key aspect of Jesus's identity.

SURVEY OF TEXTS

John 4:34
This initial text rings the mission call of Jesus. In a context where Jesus is speaking to the disciples about food he has that they do not know, the disciples respond, thinking Jesus is speaking literally about physical food. This is one of the many such misunderstandings in John (e.g., John 2:20; 3:4). This leads into the missional statement. Jesus has come to do God's will and complete the work that he was sent to accomplish. It is in this context Jesus speaks of being sent for such a purpose. In the larger context, Jesus has just completed a conversation with the Samaritan woman about the kind of worship the Father seeks. It is an interesting juxtaposition. For while the woman is worried about true worship and the possibility of Messiah, Jesus speaks of the Father. John has used this term to refer to God only four times before this, in John 1:14 and 18 ("as the only begotten from the Father," "the one in the bosom of the Father has explained

him"),[1] 2:16 ("the house of my Father"), and 3:35 ("the Father loves the Son"). So there is an echo that one who is more than Messiah is sent.

John 5:23, 24, 30, 36–38

Again, the Sent One is placed in a context of the Father sending the Son. The Son has received judgment authority and also is to receive honor. To fail to honor the Son is to fail to honor the Father who sent him (v. 23). The one who hears Jesus's word honors the one who sent Jesus (v. 24). Jesus executes judgment, not from his own will, but from a desire to do the will of the Father who sent him (v. 30). More than this, Jesus does not bear witness to himself. Rather, the works that he performs and that the Father has granted him to accomplish bear witness that the Father has sent him (v. 36). So the Father bears witness to having sent him, and those who refuse to hear him lack God's word in them and do not believe the one whom the Father sent (v. 38). It is emerging that this expression reflects a high Christology and is part of how John connects Jesus intimately with the Father. That relationship is not only relational but functional and supportive of the mission Jesus performs.

John 6:29, 38–39, 44, 57

In a discussion asking what is the work of God that is required, Jesus replies, "This is the deed God requires—to believe in the one whom he sent" (John 6:29 NET). Faith is the one response that matters. Jesus is inseparably linked to God.

In the bread of life discourse, again it is the Father-Son relationship that is in the background of the theme of being sent. All who the Father gives to him come, and none of them are going to be cast out (vv. 35–37). Jesus has come to do the will of the one who sent him (v. 38). The will of the one who sent him is that none of those given to him will be lost (v. 39). This becomes another missional note of the Father's and Son's commitment to those who become God's redeemed children. A few verses later, Jesus notes that no one is able to come to him "unless the Father who sent me draws him" (v. 44). In verse 57 this bread that is Jesus is to be consumed: the Father sent Jesus and Jesus lives because of the Father, and those who consume Jesus will live because of Jesus. What for Paul is being "in Christ," for John is the Sent One being in us. Jesus is commis-

---

1. Translations are the author's unless otherwise noted.

sioned by the Father and carries out that commission to draw a people to the Father and Son.

John 7:16, 18, 28–29, 33

The context for this set of passages is *controversy*. Was Jesus good, or leading people astray (7:12)? As others reflect on Jesus having had no formal instruction, the Sent One notes, "My teaching is not mine, but his who sent me" (7:16).[2] Jesus speaks not out of his own authority but from God.[3] Jesus seeks the glory of the one who sent him, not his own glory. Jesus functions as a man of truth (of integrity), so what is spoken is true (7:18). A little later in the passage, a dispute about healing on the Sabbath is met with Jesus observing that circumcision also is performed on the Sabbath. Then Jesus responds to speculation about where he is from by noting he has "not come of his own accord, but the one who sent him is true and him you do not know" (7:28). Here the reference again goes back to issues raised in John's Prologue in terms of where Jesus came from. Jesus's origins are not about the locale in which he was born; he is from heaven and the one who sent him to earth. There is a deep connection here with other texts that highlight that the Sent One is also the Son. *This* is the one God sent. And God sent him as one who knows the sender (7:29). This close connection to God at the divine level leads to a desire to arrest Jesus, but it is not yet time for that. That event comes later, and when it does Jesus will "go to the one who sent me and there you cannot come" (7:33–34). The Sent One lives in, comes from, and was sent from the one above.

John 8:16, 18, 26, 29, 42; 9:4, 25

Once again the context is one of controversy as Jesus claims to be the light of the world, something the Pharisees reject (8:12–13). Jesus responds that he knows where he came from, so even if he is witnessing to himself, the testimony is true. Jesus's judgment is true because it comes from "I and the one who sent me" (8:16). The deep connection between Father

---

2.   Gary M. Burge, *John*, NIVAC (Grand Rapids: Zondervan, 2000), 223, makes it clear Jesus sees his authority as rooted in his heavenly origins.

3.   D. A. Carson, *The Gospel According to John*, PNTC (Leicester, UK; Grand Rapids: InterVarsity Press; Eerdmans, 1991), 312, says this is a claim that goes beyond the way the prophets represented God. Prophets pointed to truth with "thus says the Lord," but Jesus's words are true because of his direct heavenly connection to the Father.

and Son is what follows. It is the Father "who sent me" who bears witness to Jesus (8:18). When they ask where Jesus's Father is, Jesus responds, "You know neither me nor my Father," for if they knew him they would also know the Father (8:19). This phrase clearly says that Jesus is sent from the Father who is in heaven. Jesus's origin, home, and authority are being emphasized in the phrase. Jesus reiterates that he is going to a place they cannot come. He is from above, and they are from below. Jesus observes he has much to say and judge, but the one who sent him is true, and Jesus is declaring to the world what he has heard from him (8:26). So now it is the message from above that is being affirmed. John issues a side comment at this point that they did not understand that Jesus spoke to them about the Father. It is an interesting remark, for they probably did grasp the meaning of the words, but did not receive it as true and so did not understand.

Jesus then switches gears to discuss the lifting up of the Son of Man in a death to come, which they will not understand, probably because that death will be followed by a vindicating resurrection that will demonstrate Jesus did nothing by his own authority but spoke as the Father taught him. Again with a touch of irony, Jesus will be lifted up in death on a cross, but he will simply be in transit to heaven through that death to return to the one who sent him. This is because "he who sent me is with me" (8:29). Jesus is not left alone as he does what pleases him. In 8:42, we get the full reveal on this phrase amid this dispute. Jesus says, "If God were your Father, you would love me, for I proceeded and came forth from God; I came not of my own accord, but he sent me." Jesus was sent from God, his Father, to do the Father's will and reveal the way to God that leads to a path of love for God.

After Jesus heals a blind man on the Sabbath, he links what he is doing with what he is saying and teaching. It is important to note that there are no miracles involving healing of the blind in the Hebrew Scriptures. This is a new level of healing introduced on a most holy day. Jesus issues one word of commentary about it in 9:4: "We must work the works of him who sent me, while it is day; night comes, when no one can work." Once again there is a juxtaposition of Jesus's connection to God as Jesus does what God is doing. They work together—this kind of healing cannot take place unless God is behind it. There also is the sense of approaching death that is not an end but a transition. Interestingly, he closes that remark with the observation again that he is the light of the world. The Sent One from heaven is vindicated by this healing that takes place on this holy day. When later Jesus's opponents say to the healed man that the healer is a sinner, he responds, "Whether he is a sinner, I do not know. One thing I know, that though I was blind, now I see" (9:25). Later the man adds, "Why, this is a marvel! You do not know where he comes from, and yet he opened my eyes. We know that God does not listen to sinners, but if any one is a worshiper of God and does his will, God listens to him. Never since the world began has it been heard that any one opened the eyes of a man born blind. If this man were not from God, he could do nothing" (vv. 30–33 RSV). The formerly blind man now sees things quite clearly.

John 10:36

In this passage, we again witness disagreement. Jesus declares in 10:30 that he and the Father are one. The reaction is that some in the crowd take up stones as they believe Jesus has committed blasphemy (10:31, 33). Jesus has already contrasted the good works he had done from the Father with their judgment. Jesus also cites Psalm 82:6, where people are called gods, to raise the question of whether making oneself a god is an issue. He then uses a "how much more" argument that Jewish teachers would be familiar with: "If he called them gods to whom the word of God came—and Scripture cannot be broken—do you say of him whom the Father consecrated and sent into the world, 'You are blaspheming,' because I said 'I am the Son of God'?" (John 10:35–36 ESV). He then backs up the remark by claiming if he is doing the works of the Father, they should believe the works and understand who he is. This echoes earlier texts that tied the one sent to the Father doing the sending. As we move through these texts, the link between Father and Son tightens, with this text putting the two more explicitly together.

John 11:42, 44

In one of the few asides that John presents, Jesus says that his remarks tied to the raising of Lazarus were uttered "for the sake of the crowd standing around here, that they may believe that you sent me" (John 11:42).[4] The miracle is tied to the glory of God, so it is seen as an act of God (11:40).

---

4. Rodney A. Whitacre, *John*, IVPNTC (Downers Grove, IL: IVP Academic, 2010), 292, says, "The Father as the sender is primary. Jesus is not a wonderworker who is able to get God to do what he wants him to do. He is the obedient Son sent by the Father to do the Father's will."

Jesus is tying together his work as being a part of what God is doing through him, recalling what was said in John 5 and 9, which we examined earlier.

John 12:44–45, 49

In what is Jesus's final public word in John's Gospel, he repeats his claim that he was sent by the Father. The one who believes in him believes not him, but in the one who sent him (12:44). The one who sees him sees the one who sent him (12:45). Jesus has come as light in the world so the one who believes in him does not remain in darkness. The one who does not believe is not judged by Jesus, for he came to save people. The one rejecting Jesus is rejected by the word Jesus speaks on the last day. This is because Jesus does not speak of his own authority but from "the Father who sent him." The Father has given him commandment about what to say and speak (12:49). Jesus speaks of the commandment of eternal life as the Father has given it to him. Here he links his message of eternal life as the way to the Father to the belief in the one sent.

John 13:20

The motif tied to the Sent One receives an expansion in this passage. Now the focus is not on the Father as the one sending the Son, but on those the Sent One now sends. John 13:20 reads, "Truly, truly, I say to you, he who receives any one whom I send receives me; and he who receives me receives him who sent me" (RSV). Jesus is completing the link here between the Father himself and his own who have received his call and taken it into the world. He has also noted the slave is not greater than the master nor is the one sent as a messenger greater than the one who sent him (13:16). Notice Jesus says this during the Last Supper with his disciples after he has washed their feet and announced he would be betrayed. One of them is not clean, but the rest are commissioned to take the message out. The authority the believing disciples bear is from the Father and through the Son.

John 14:24

Jesus returns to the sourcing of his message as he announces the coming of the Spirit. Jesus is leaving but he is not going to leave the disciples isolated. He will send the Paraclete to them (14:26). Jesus tells them this after having noted the connection between love and keeping his word. John 14:24 declares, "He who does not love me does not keep my words;

and the word which you hear is not mine but the Father's who sent me" (RSV). It is this divine sourcing of the word Jesus mediates that gives the message its gravitas and has inherent within it the need to be heeded. The Sent One is connected to the Father and brings a word from him that not only shows its authority and his own authority but also reveals who loves God by their response to it.

John 15:21

This passage discusses persecution and the rejection of Jesus that causes his death. After warning that a slave is not greater than the master (cf. John 13:16), Jesus says, "But they will do all these things to you on account of my name, because they do not know the one who sent me" (John 15:21). The link is that those who reject Jesus and his message do not know the Father, though they claim to know the one true God.

John 16:5

Jesus hints about his resurrection and makes clear his origins at the same time. John 16:5 reads, "But now I am going to the one who sent me, and not one of you is asking me, 'Where are you going?'" Jesus's heavenly origin is again the point. He is going back to where he came from, the Word that was with God before he took on flesh (John 1:1, 14). The commissioned one has his calling from above.

John 17:3, 8, 18, 21, 23, 25

Here is Jesus's prayer before he faces his death. He prays for the unity and protection of the community he has formed. The prayer is framed by the remark that eternal life is to know the "only true God, and Jesus Christ whom you [the Father] have sent" (John 17:3 ESV). The remark links Jesus Christ directly to this intimate relationship with God that is unlike earlier "sent" expressions where Son and Father are the dominant referents.[5]

The disciples' reception of Jesus's message is the point in 17:8. The word Jesus brought has been received by them, "for I have given them the words which you gave me, and they have received them and know in truth I came from you; and they have believed that you did send me."

---

5. F. F. Bruce, *The Gospel of John: Introduction, Exposition and Notes* (Grand Rapids: Eerdmans, 1983), 329, says, "The Father and the Son know each other in a mutuality of love, and by the knowledge of God men and women are admitted into the mystery of this divine love, being loved by God and loving him—and one another—in return. This is the basis of the unity for which Jesus prays in verses 20–23 below."

This has marked them as a group distinct from the world as those given to Jesus by God. So Jesus asks that they be kept in God's name as he comes back to the Father (see v. 11).

These disciples are now sent into the world just as the Father sent Jesus (v. 18). Jesus's coming consecration in death and resurrection will consecrate them in truth (v. 19). He prays as well for those who believe through their word, which means all disciples of the future. This oneness is a distinct witness to the world. John 17:21 says, "that they may be one, even as you, Father, are in me, and I in you, that they also may be in us, so that the world may believe that you have sent me." He has shared the glory of the Father and the Son with them (v. 22). The goal of forming this oneness is to make them "perfectly one, so that the world may know you have sent me and have loved them even as you have loved me" (17:23). So now evidence for Jesus being the Sent One is tied up in the oneness of identification and love that God has for his own. Jesus wants these believers to sense his raised glory and be connected to him, to "be with me where I am" (v. 24). The oneness is seen in part in their shared recognition that God has sent Jesus. In John 17:25 Jesus prays, "O righteous Father, the world has not known you, but I have known you, and these know that you have sent me." These disciples have come to know God's name, and Jesus will continue to make it known to them, with Jesus in them as well, that they may experience the love of God that God has shown to Jesus (v. 26). That ending point on love and oneness with God concludes the prayer.

The Sent One has come to make the love of the Father known and to also show that to know the Father, one must know the one sent by him, Jesus Christ. This forms a bond between God and those who know Jesus as the Sent One, much like the bond Jesus has with the Father. This knowledge of the one sent and the sender, both as a concept and as an experience, is eternal life. Sharing the message with the world about the possibility of knowing God in this intimate way is the calling of these disciples. In his prayer, Jesus almost issues a Johannine form of the Great Commission, only here he also prays for it. What Jesus prays for is a testimony of life that points to the oneness disciples have with the Sent One and, by extension, with the Sender (17:21: "that they may be in us").

John 20:21

Now Jesus carries out the commission he prayed for in John 17. In John 20:21, Jesus says, "Peace be with you. As the Father has sent me, even so

I send you." This hearkens all the way back to John 4:38, as Köstenberger notes.[6] John has been building to this moment and this calling. Jesus's disciples are commissioned with a message and a call to a certain type of life that reflects love for God. The Sent One sends out others who also are sent with the same message and commission Jesus had. That message bears authority from God and points the way to life. The link in it all is the Son whom the Father sent, Jesus Christ.

CONCLUSION

The Sent One is no mere sidebar for John. The sending motif connects a series of core themes in his Gospel. In terms of origins, it points to Jesus as the incarnate Word and as Son to the Father, sent from heaven to earth. In terms of relationship, it depicts the inseverable link between the Father and Son. Regarding Jesus's message, it argues that what Jesus teaches is from the Father. In terms of authority, it shows that Jesus shares all the authority that comes from above and the judgment he gives is true. As to Jesus's works, the miracles attest to the fact that Jesus is sent. As to one's faith, it is the Sent One who is to be believed. In terms of life, it shows that what God offers, he offers through the Sent One. Regarding community, it argues that those who receive the message of the Sent One come into this intimate link to God and the Son, forming a community distinct from the world. As to our calling, the Sent One has now sent out the sent to bring that message with all its inherent authority to a needy world. Finally, in terms of experience, to know the Sent One is to know the one who did the sending in a way that shares in the experience of God's love for the one sent. Those who receive the message of the sent ones receive the message of the Sent One as well, connecting them to that very fullness of life and love as well as to the Father who sent the Son for that very purpose.

---

6.   Andreas J. Köstenberger, *John*, BECNT (Grand Rapids: Baker Academic, 2004), 163.

CHAPTER 2

ΠΑΡΑΚΛΗΤΟΣ in the Johannine Corpus in Light of Anatolian Epigraphic Evidence

ALEXANDER STEWART

I am glad for the opportunity to honor Andreas Köstenberger in this volume. I had several classes with Andreas during my studies at Southeastern Baptist Theological Seminary, but I was most impacted through serving as his research assistant for several years.[1] This not only helped, in a small way, to pay the bills, but it gave me an early peek behind the curtain of academic publishing. I am also thankful to Andreas for encouraging me in several early publishing projects; he has played an important role in my vocational journey and I am happy to honor him for a lifetime of service to the church. Although I did not turn out to be a Johannine scholar, I hope this contribution can move the discussion forward in a small but important way.

A cursory summary of English translations reveals agreement on the translation of παράκλητος as "advocate" in 1 John 2:1, but the other four occurrences of the noun in John 14:16, 26; 15:26; 16:7 reveal a stunning lack of agreement: "advocate" in the NIV, NLT, and NRSVUE translations; "helper" in the ESV, NASB, ISV, and NKJV; "comforter" in KJV and ASV; and "counselor" in HCSB.[2] The translation problem

---

1. I would like to acknowledge the excellent support from Jesse Harris, my research assistant, who supplied scans to much of the sometimes elusive, secondary literature discussed below.
2. The choice by some commentators to transliterate the word as "paraclete" in English translations solves the challenge of picking a limiting and perhaps inappropriate English gloss but seems to create a bigger problem by failing to actually provide an English translation. For this approach see Raymond E. Brown, *The Gospel According to John (xiii–xxi)*, AB 29A (Garden City, NY: Doubleday, 1970), 637; Edward W. Klink III, *John*, ZECNT (Grand Rapids: Zondervan Academic, 2016), 632.

was explicitly discussed as far back as Origen, who concludes with many modern translations that "advocate" is appropriate to 1 John 2:1, but "consoler" better fits the occurrences in John's Gospel (*De Principiis* 2.7.4).[3] The translation problem reflects, of course, the search for the meaning and significance of this title applied by John to both Jesus and the Holy Spirit. Did John mean to invoke the image of a legal advocate in the divine courtroom, a counselor, a comforter, or a generic helper or ally in the challenges of life? If "comforter" or "helper" is chosen instead of "advocate" for the occurrences in the Gospel, does this minimize the legal connotations that may have been associated with the term by John and his first hearers?

Commentators discuss the translation problem, but do not solve it, and the secondary literature advances divergent arguments.[4] Kenneth Grayston influentially surveyed the occurrences of παράκλητος in extant literature to argue that it referred to a general supporter or sponsor that could be used in legal contexts but did not derive its meaning from legal activity.[5] Lochlan Shelfer considers some new epigraphic evidence (BIWK 5, see below) and comes to the opposite conclusion: παράκλητος "is a precise calque for the Latin legal term *advocatus*, meaning a person of high social standing who speaks on behalf of a defendant in a court of law before a judge."[6] The following discussion will consider Shelfer's arguments and add some newly published, potentially relevant epigraphic evidence from western Asia Minor to the discussion. It will offer some suggestions as to how original hearers, at least in Phrygia and Lydia, may have understood Jesus's use of παράκλητος to refer to the Spirit. There is no attempt here to exegete the relevant passages in John and 1 John or exhaustively interact with secondary literature and extrabiblical occurrences of παράκλητος; that is done competently elsewhere as noted in the

---

3. Lochlan Shelfer, "The Legal Precision of the Term 'παράκλητος'," *JSNT* 32 (2009): 132.
4. For a succinct summary of key secondary literature see Andreas J. Köstenberger, *A Theology of John's Gospel and Letters*, BTNT (Grand Rapids: Zondervan Academic, 2009), 396. Important studies include M. Eugene Boring, "The Influence of Christian Prophecy on the Johannine Portrayal of the Paraclete and Jesus," *NTS* 25 (1978): 113–23; Raymond E. Brown, "The Paraclete in the Fourth Gospel," *NTS* 13 (1967): 113–32; Raymond E. Brown, "The Spirit-Paraclete in the Gospel of John," *CBQ* 33 (1971): 268–70; A. Shafaat, "Geber of the Qumran Scrolls and the Spirit-Paraclete of the Gospel of John," *NTS* 27 (1981): 263–69; Kenneth Grayston, "The Meaning of *paraklētos*," *JSNT* 13 (1981): 67–82.
5. Grayston, "The Meaning of *paraklētos*," 67.
6. Shelfer, "The Legal Precision," 131.

footnotes. The goal will rather be to introduce and evaluate some new evidence that generally supports Shelfer's conclusions.

1. ΠΑΡΑΚΛΗΤΟΣ AND *ADVOCATUS*

Lochlan Shelfer reviews the extant occurrences of παράκλητος and concludes his survey of pagan literature as follows.[7]

> Παράκλητοι are exclusively defenders, and never prosecutors. Sometimes there is not just a single one, but several present. They speak or act on behalf of someone who is in danger, and the word seems to be fairly unfamiliar, technical, and legal in nature. Moreover, as we have seen, it seems to be a calque for the Latin legal term *advocatus*.[8]

Shelfer then makes the following points regarding the occurrences of παράκλητος in John 14:16, 26; 15:26; 16:7. Since παράκλητος was a generally precise translation equivalent to *advocatus*, which pointed to "someone of elevated status, a patron, who speaks in defense of his client before a judge, and whose influence stems from that elevated status,"[9] this is the starting point, which fits with the general background of the final judgment lying behind various parts of the Farewell Discourse.[10] A legal context is also explicitly invoked by the use of ἐλέγχω in John 16:9

---

7. In "The Legal Precision" he discusses Demosthenes (*Fals. leg.* 1), Diogenes Laertius (*Lives* 4.50), Dionysius of Halicarnassus (*Ant. rom.* 11.37.1), Cassius Dio (*Historiae Romanae* 46.20.1), Heraclitus (*All.* 59), Mimus (P.Lit.Lond. 97.4–5), the papyri (BGU II 601.11; P.Oxy. 2725.10), a propitiatory inscription (BIWK 5; discussed below), various church fathers (Tertullian, Novatian, Cyprian, Jerome), Philo (*Flacc.* 13; 22; 23; 151; 181; *Opif.* 23; 165; *Ios.* 239; *Praem.* 166; *Spec.* 1.237; *Mos.* 2.134), and rabbinic literature and the Targumim which transliterate παράκλητος as פרקליט (*m. Ab.* 4.11a; *Exod. R.* 18.3; *b. B. Bat.* 10a; *Sifra* 277a; *Targ. Job* 16:20; 33:23). His inclusion of BIWK 5 is the primary advance over other exhaustive studies of the occurrences of παράκλητος in primary sources such as, David Pastorelli, *Le Paraclet dans le corpus johannique*, BZNW 142 (Berlin: Walter de Gruyter, 2006), 40–104. This connection of BIWK 5 with 1 John 2:1 has been noted by various scholars but without any in-depth discussion: H. J. Klauck, "Die kleinasi atischen Beichtinschriften und das Neue Testament," in *Geschichte – Tradition – Reflexion, Festschrift für Martin Hengel zum 70 Geburtstag*, ed. H. Cancik, H. Lichtenberger, and P. Schäfer (Tübingen: Mohr Siebeck, 1996), 63–87, 81.
8. Shelfer, "The Legal Precision," 141.
9. Shelfer, "The Legal Precision," 141.
10. Shelfer, "The Legal Precision," 146. Shelfer develops the themes of obedience related to eternal life and the judgment that will come upon those who do not abide in the vine, those who do not follow Jesus's word, and those who hate Jesus among other contextual hints which assume the reality of divine judgment lying in the background of the Farewell Discourse.

to suggest a reversal of the trial of Jesus.[11] The title παράκλητος, however, does not exhaust the duties and attributes of the Spirit, and the explicit discussion in the Gospel makes clear that the divine παράκλητος is the Spirit of Truth (14:1–7) who teaches and reminds (14:26), bears witness (15:26–27), and will convict the world (16:8–11).[12] These activities do not contradict a legal understanding of the role of the παράκλητος as similar to *advocatus*, but they do go beyond it.

Shelfer concludes as follows:

> The title παράκλητος is certainly not exhaustive in its depiction of the duties either of the Spirit or of Jesus, nor should its meaning be stretched in order to act as such. Instead, it is one more description of the Spirit's attributes, one who makes use of a precise and legal terminology.[13]

Although it is impossible to come to a definitive conclusion based on the limited evidence, I find Shelfer's discussion to be reasonable, and his conclusions point to how the evident legal aspects of παράκλητος can make sense of the occurrences in John's Gospel.[14] In the past few years, new epigraphic evidence from Phrygia and Lydia has been published that further supports Shelfer's claims regarding how a Roman legal term was translated and utilized by non-Christians in Asia Minor to describe divine figures active on behalf of supplicants in the divine council.

2. PROPITIATORY INSCRIPTIONS

Eusebius recounts that John was allotted Asia and died at Ephesus (*Hist. eccl.* 3.1.1) while Irenaeus also locates him in Asia (*Haer.* 3.1.2).

---

11. Brown, *The Gospel According to John*, 705.
12. Shelfer, "The Legal Precision," 145–46. J. A. Draper's sociological study acknowledges that the interpreter should perhaps not expect consistency in the use of παράκλητος in the Gospel ("The Sociological Function of the Spirit/Paraclete in the Farewell Discourse in the Fourth Gospel," *Neot* 26 [1992]: 13–29, 25).
13. Shelfer, "The Legal Precision," 146.
14. In particular, it is impossible to prove that παράκλητος is a calque for the Latin legal term *advocatus* although the conclusion is possible and perhaps even probable. Moisés Silva recognizes the legal meaning suggested by several extrabiblical Greek uses of the term but cautions, "that is not to say that παράκλητος was a technical legal term comparable to Lat. *advocatus*, referring to a professional legal defender (the Gk. terms for that concept were σύνδικος and συνήγορος; see J. Behm in *TDNT* 5:801). The existence of the Lat. term, however, may have led early Christian writers to use it as the equivalent of παράκλητος in the NT" (Moisés Silva, ed., NIDNTTE, vol. 3, 2nd ed. [Grand Rapids: Zondervan Academic, 2014], 628). The extant evidence is inconclusive in regard to its use as a calque, but the word certainly seems to evoke a legal context.

Although other options have been presented and are possible, the existing evidence favors the traditional authorship, provenance, and dating of John's Gospel to the latter decades of the first century.[15] This puts John's Gospel in temporal and geographical proximity to propitiatory inscriptions, a distinctive epigraphical genre of inscriptions produced between AD 57/8 and 263/4 in Lydia and Phrygia.[16] Although these inscriptions are commonly called "confession" inscriptions, there is a growing recognition that the inscriptions do not confess anything, but rather declare that the wrath of the gods has been propitiated. Some of the inscriptions record that a confession took place but they more directly give thanks and praise the power of the gods for accomplished propitiation. The inscriptions provide "public proof that the conflict between human and deity has been settled."[17] Propitiatory steles were prominently and publicly displayed and would have been known broadly throughout Asia Minor. If it is likely that John ministered in and wrote from Asia Minor, epigraphic evidence of theological beliefs from the nearby regions would provide important evidence for how John's Gospel would have been understood by the first hearers and how the Gospel sought to build on and transform their ideas of a divine

---

15. Köstenberger, *A Theology*, 53–60, 72–79, 82–84.
16. Although past collections had been published, interest in these inscriptions was reignited by Georg Petzl, *Die Beichtinschriften Westkleinasiens, Epigraphica Anatolica* 22, Bonn, 1994 (hereafter BIWK), which contains 124 inscriptions. There have been many additional publications since 1994 which include Georg Petzl, "Neue Inschriften aus Lydien (II), Addenda und Corrigenda zu '*Die Beichtinschriften Westkleinasiens*,'" *Epigraphica Anatolica* 28, (1997): 69–79; Peter Herrmann and Hasan Malay, *New Documents from Lydia*, Österreichische Akademie der Wissenschaften, Philosophisch-Historische Klasse, Denkschriften, 340, Band, Ergänzungsbände Zu Den Tituli Asiae Minoris 24 (Vienna: ÖAW, 2007); Hasan Malay and Georg Petzl, *New Religious Texts from Lydia*, Ergänzungsbände zu den Tituli Asiae Monoris 28, Denkschriften der philosophisch-historischen klasse 497 (Vienna: ÖAW, 2017). For prior discussion of this epigraphic genre in relation to the New Testament see Eckhard J. Schnabel, "Divine Tyranny and Public Humiliation: A Suggestion for the Interpretation of the Lydian and Phrygian Confession Inscriptions," *NovT* 45.2 (2003): 160–88; Clinton E. Arnold, "'I Am Astonished That You Are So Quickly Turning Away!' (Gal 1.6): Paul and Anatolian Folk Belief," *NTS* 51 (2005): 429–49; Klauck, "Die kleinasi atischen Beichtinschriften"; H. J. Klauck, "Heil ohne Heilung? Zu Metaphorik und Hermeneutik der Rede von Sünde und Vergebung im Neuen Testament," in *Sünde und Erlösung im Neuen Testament*, ed. H. Frankemölle (Freiburg: Herder, 1996), 18–52; W. Ameling, "Paränese und Ethik in den kleinasiatischen Beichtinschriften," in *Neues Testament und hellenistisch-jüdische Alltagskultur*, ed. R. Deines, J. Herzer, and K. W. Niebuhr (Tübingen: Mohr Siebeck, 2011), 241–49; M. Öhler, "Sünde, Bekenntnis und Sühne in kleinasiatischen 'Beichtinschriften' und dem 1. Johannesbrief," in *Epigraphik und Neues Testament*, WUNT 365, ed. Th. Corsten et al. (Tübingen: Mohr Siebeck, 2016), 155–84.
17. Aslak Rostad, *Human Transgression–Divine Retribution: A Study of Religious Transgressions and Punishments in Greek Cultic Regulation and Lydian-Phrygian Propitiatory Inscriptions ('Confession Inscriptions')*, Archaeopress Archaeology (Oxford: Archaeopress Publishing, 2020), 3.

παράκλητος. Most of the inscriptions discussed below postdate John's Gospel, but inscription #2, although not a propitiatory inscription, likely predates the Gospel and shows that the general picture drawn from the later propitiatory inscriptions reflects beliefs concurrent with the writing of John's Gospel.[18]

Schnabel identifies nine elements that are common to propitiatory inscriptions and can be summarized as (1) the name of the wrongdoer, (2) the offense, (3) the god's reaction, (4) the punishment, (5) the propitiatory action, (6) the public confession, (7) an acknowledgment of the god's power, (8) the erection of the stele, (9) a profession of faith or praise.[19] Not every inscription contains each element. Three inscriptions from the same cultural and religious milieu, in particular, reveal belief that a deity could function as a παράκλητος who would advocate for the supplicant in the divine council. The first inscription below was discussed by Shelfer, but the second and third were just recently published and, to my knowledge, have not yet been discussed by New Testament scholars in relation to the meaning of παράκλητος.

2.1 Inscription #1

BIWK 5, dated to AD 235/6, is a lengthy inscription that has drawn significant attention for a number of reasons. Many aspects of this fascinating inscription have been discussed in the literature, not least the way it switches back and forth between first-person divine speech and first-person human speech as follows.

> In the year 320, on the 12th of the month Panemos. In accordance with the fact that I was instructed by the gods, by Zeus and the great Mēn Artemidoros: "I have punished Theodoros on his eyes according to the transgression he committed" (κολασόμην τὰ ὄματα τὸν Θεόδωρον κατὰ τὰς ἀμαρίας). I had intercourse with Trophime, the slave of Haplokomas, wife of Eutykhes, in the *praetorium* (?). He removed the first transgression with a sheep (ἀπαίρι τὴν πρώτην

---

18. Klauck makes several arguments to demonstrate the importance of these inscriptions for the study of the New Testament despite their generally later date. They include the fact that the basic themes are evident much earlier in poetry and curse tablets, the inscriptions illustrate early Christian vocabulary in temporally close sources, and they reveal a possible reception horizon for the Christian message (Klauck, "Die kleinasiatischen Beichtinschriften," 69). He rightly rules out the idea of Christian influence on the confession inscriptions (Klauck, "Die kleinasiatischen Beichtinschriften," 69).

19. Schnabel, "Divine Tyranny," 161.

Figure 2.1. Inscription 1. BIWK 5, AD 235/236

ἁμαρτίαν προβάτω[ν]), a partridge and a mole. The second transgression (Δευτέρα ἁμαρτία): Even though I was a slave of the gods (ἀλλὰ δοῦλος ὢν τῶν θεῶν) in Nonu, I had intercourse with Ariagne, who was unmarried. He removed [the transgression] with a piglet and a tuna. At the third transgression (τρίτη ἁμαρτία) I had intercourse with Arethusa, who was unmarried. He removed the transgression with a hen (or cock), a sparrow and a pigeon; with a *kypros* of a blend of wheat and barley and one *prokhos* of wine. Being pure (καθαρός) he gave a *kypros* of wheat to the priests and one *prokhos*. As intercessor, I took Zeus (Ἔσχα παράκλητον τὸν Δείαν). (He said): Behold! (εἴδαι) I hurt his sight because of his deeds, but now he has propitiated the gods (εἰλαζομένου αυτοῦ τοὺς θεούς) and written down [the events] on a stele and paid for his transgressions. Asked by the council (Ἡρωτημαίνος ὑπὸ τῆς συνκλήτου) [the god proclaimed]: I will be merciful (εἴλεος εἴμαι), because my stele is raised on the day I appointed. You can open the prison; I will release the convict when one year and ten months has passed.[20]

Theodorus recounts being instructed by the gods regarding the cause of his eye ailment. He outlines the specific sins and the means of atonement. The gods do not elsewhere seem to be particularly concerned with sexual activity unless it took place in sacred space or the individual did not engage in proper purification before entering sacred space; the gods

---

20. Translation from Rostad, *Human Transgression–Divine Retribution*, 204. The image was originally taken by Dr. Hasan Malay and provided by Dr. Georg Petzl; used with permission.

perhaps held Theodoros to a higher standard because he was a slave of the gods, probably a temple functionary.[21] Theodorus recounts how he appealed to Zeus to be his παράκλητος and how Zeus spoke on his behalf to the divine council and proclaimed that he would be merciful because Theodorus had propitiated the gods.[22]

The key line is, "I had a παράκλητον, Zeus" (ἔσχα παράκλητον τὸν Δείαν). It has been variously translated as "As intercessor, I took Zeus,"[23] "I asked for Zeus's help,"[24] "I asked for Zeus's assistance,"[25] "I had Zeus summoned,"[26] and "Ich gewann Zeus als Parakleten."[27] In light of the legal context of the divine council, παράκλητος should probably be translated as "advocate": "As advocate, I took Zeus."

The "council" (συνκλήτος) could refer to a council of priests, although there are comparable inscriptions that point toward widespread belief in a judicial council of the gods.[28] In support of this, a propitiatory inscription from Kollyda dated to AD 205/6 is translated by Herrmann and Malay (no. 85) as follows:

> In the year 290, in the month Peritios, Ammianos and Hermogenes, sons of Tryphon, appear (at the temple) asking the gods Men Motyllites and Zeus Sabazios and Artemis Anaitis and the great Senatus and the Council of the Gods (εγάλην συνᾶτος

---

21. Öhler speculates that Theodorus was probably committed to sexual abstinence ("Sünde, Bekenntnis und Sühne," 158).

22. There is ambiguity regarding whether Zeus is both the prosecutor and advocate or whether Mēn is the prosecutor and Zeus the advocate. See E. Varinlioğlu, "Eine Gruppe von Sühneinschriften aus dem Museum von Uşak," *Epigraphica Anatolica* 13 (1989): 37–50, 38; Shelfer, "The Legal Precision," 140.

23. Rostad, *Human Transgression–Divine Retribution*, 204.

24. A. Chaniotis, "Under the Watchful Eyes of the Gods: Aspects of Divine Justice in Hellenistic and Roman Asia Minor," in *The Greco-Roman East: Politics, Culture, Society*, ed. S. Colvin [New York: Cambridge University Press, 2004], 28.

25. A. Chaniotis, "Ritual Performances of Divine Justice: The Epigraphy of Confession, Atonement, and Exaltation in Roman Asia Minor," in *From Hellenism to Islam: Cultural and Linguistic Change in the Roman Near East*, ed. Hannah M. Cotton et al. (New York: Cambridge University Press, 2009), 115–53, 133.

26. M. Ricl, "The Appeal to Divine Justice in the Lydian Confession-Inscriptions," in E. Schwertheim, ed., *Forshung in Lydien*, Asia Minor Studien 17 (Bonn: Habelt, 1995), 67–76, 72.

27. Klauck, "Heil ohne Heilung?" 34.

28. Much attention has been given to the judicial nature of the final lines and whether local priests were empowered to execute physical justice. If they were involved, it was likely only because Theodorus was a temple functionary of some sort; it is also quite possible that the language of release from captivity is metaphorical for healing (Varinlioğlu, "Eine Gruppe," 37–39). The early arguments by F. S. Steinleitner and Josef Zingerle that the priests had judicial authority to pass sentences has largely been rejected by recent scholarship (Rostad, *Human Transgression–Divine Retribution*, 45–48; Chaniotis, "Under the Watchful Eyes of the Gods," 1–43, 28–30).

καὶ σύνκλητον τῶν θεῶν), asking also the village and the Hieros Doumos in order that they will find mercy as they were punished because they overcame their father, while he was acknowledging the power of the gods (ἐξομολογούμενον τὰς δυνάμις τῶν θεῶν); and their father did not obtain pity, but after his death, on account of his first (primary) written declarations they wrote "nobody at any time should disparage the gods" on a stele and set it up praising the gods (εὐλογοῦντε[ς] τοῖς θεοῖς).[29]

The designation συνᾶτος is a Latinism related to the Roman senate and used here with no concern for gender or case;[30] it is likely joined to σύνκλητον τῶν θεῶν with an epexegetical use of καί to refer to one group and not two: "the great senate, that is, the council of the gods." Herrmann and Malay suggest that the Greek title for the assembly of the gods was simply extended with the Latin gloss for the same divine assembly.[31] They refer further to Herrmann and Malay, no. 51, an inscription dated to AD 102/3 from the area of Hamidiye-Mağazadamlari that calls Meis Ouranios Aremidorou Axiottenos an "all seeing judge in heaven" (κριτὴς ἀλάθητος ἐν οὐράνῳ); the designation "points to *divine judgments*' in heaven."[32] Herrmann and Malay conclude that "the people of Roman Lydia believed in the existence of divine Councils and that divine trials took place in heaven."[33]

2.2 Inscription #2

Although not a propitiatory inscription, a metrical dedication to Apollon Syrmaios on a marble altar found where the sanctuary of Apollon Syrmaios is located in Parloenoi, west of Saittai, in Lydia is dated to the first century

Figure 2.2. Inscription 2. Close up of metrical dedication to Apollon Syrmaios on marble altar

---

29. Herrmann and Malay, *New Documents,* 113–14.
30. Herrmann and Malay, *New Documents*, 115.
31. Herrmann and Malay, *New Documents*, 115.
32. Herrmann and Malay, *New Documents*, 75–76, italics original.
33. Herrmann and Malay, *New Documents*, 115.

BC or AD. Verlag der Österreichischen Akademie der Wissenschaften kindly provided the following images and permission for use.[34]

It reads as follows:[35]

> Lord Phoibos Apollon Syrmaios, Epichares has wrought and put up for you, (his) comforter (?, intercessor?), this censer as thanksgiving for a (fulfilled) prayer. Φοῖβ(ε), ἄναξ, Συρμαῖ(ε) Ἄπολλον, / σοὶ τόδ(ε) εὐχωλῆς χάριν / στῆσε παρκλητῆρι τεύξας / θυμίητρον Ἐπιχάρης.

Figure 2.3. Inscription 2. Metrical dedication to Apollon Syrmaois on marble altar

The editors suggest that the otherwise unattested word παρκλητήρ was shortened from παρακλ- because of the trochaic tetrameter and has the meaning of παρακλήτωρ or παράκλητος.[36] It is unlikely, however, that it

---

34. Images were originally published in Malay and Petzl, *New Religious Texts*, 119.
35. Translation and Greek text from Malay and Petzl, *New Religious Texts from Lydia*, 109, 119.
36. Malay and Petzl, *New Religious Texts from Lydia*, 120.

should be connected to παράκλήτωρ, a neologism invented to translate the *piel* of םחנ in Job 16:2 as "comforter." The fact that the LXX translator invented παρακλήτωρ suggests παράκλητος was not seen as an appropriate translation for the context in Job, possibly because of its legal connotations.[37] The inscriptions discussed above reveal religious beliefs in which deities were viewed as potential legal advocates in the divine council on behalf of the supplicant. This would suggest παράκλητος as the intended meaning of παρκλητήρ.

2.3 Inscription #3

Finally, Georg Petzl has recently published an inscription from AD 192/3 that reads "παρεκλήτεθσεν δὲ Κ[- - -]τηνός."[38] Although this is the verb παρακλητεύω instead of the noun, the cultural context behind the propitiatory inscriptions suggests the function of legal advocate and suggests that the deity "*acted as advocate* on behalf of a sinner."[39] Petzl translates the key phrase as "Κ[- - -]tenos war (mein/sein/ihr) Rechtsbeistand" (the deity was the confessor's legal counsel or legal advisor), although he notes that it is uncertain whether this legal action was thought to have taken place in the divine council or was a figurative way to describe the deity's support in securing victory in a human court case.[40]

Ricl explains the historical development of belief in the role of a divine advocate in the divine counsel through the influence of Hittite prayers that often call upon a deity to intercede with a different angered deity.[41] She notes that "Hittite prayers often resemble a judicial process conducted before a court composed of gods, where the prosecutor is an angry deity. The defendant can use the 'services' of a 'divine lawyer' requested to act as an intercessor on his behalf; the course of justice is the

---

37. Shelfer, "The Legal Precision," 132.
38. Georg Petzl, *Die Beichtinschriften Westkleinasiens: Supplement, Epigraphica Anatolica* 52 (Bonn: Habelt-Verlag, 2019): 1–105, no. 130, 25. Petzl's translation of the inscription is, "[- - -] ich (oder: er/sie) erstattete der Göttin [- - -] und schrieb (den Vorgang) auf einer Ste-le nieder. Im Jahr 277, [am x. Tag?] des Monats Artemisios. Κ[- - -]tenos war (mein/sein/ihr) Rechtsbeistand" (Petzl, *Die Beichtinschriften Westkleinasiens*, 26).
39. Marijana Ricl, "Observations on a New Corpus of Inscriptions from Lydia," *Epigraphica Anatolica* 44 (2011): 143–52, italics original. I would like to thank both Dr. Ricl and Dr. Petzl for email correspondence regarding this inscription, which was discussed as unpublished by Dr. Ricl in 2011 and published in 2019 by Dr. Petzl.
40. Petzl, *Die Beichtinschriften Westkleinasiens*, 26.
41. Ricl, "Observations on a New Corpus," 151.

assembly of gods."[42] Although it is certainly possible that Hittite influence shaped the development of these ideas in Asia Minor over the centuries, the main point here is that these inscriptions reveal ideas about a legal divine παράκλητος that were current in the first few centuries AD in Asia Minor and the surrounding regions.

CONCLUSION

Several conclusions can be drawn from the preceding discussion. First, pagan hearers or converts from a pagan background in western Asia Minor had the categories in place to immediately conceptualize the existence of a divine παράκλητος who could be induced through prayer and sacrifices to legally advocate for the supplicant in the divine council to secure acquittal and the cessation of divine wrath and punishment.

Second, John's Gospel interacts with these preexisting pagan ideas by presenting the Spirit and Jesus as divine παράκλητοι (note the expression ἄλλον παράκλητον in 14:6 which suggests Jesus is the first παράκλητος).[43]

Third, since an English translation requires a limiting English gloss, "advocate" is probably the best English word to translate παράκλητος in each of the five New Testament occurrences of the word.[44] Although John's Gospel certainly expands in various ways on the legal idea, these explicit expansions build upon the legal connotations of the term and do not nullify them. The Jewish and emerging Christian worldview communicated by John's Gospel corrects pagan conceptions at many points, but the existence of a favorable divine παράκλητος would have been a point of redemptive correspondence as Christian missionaries were able to announce favorable access by God's grace to the only true divine παράκλητος who, among many other things, could secure acquittal in the divine court (as is explicit in 1 John 2:1).[45]

---

42. Ricl, "Observations on a New Corpus," 151.

43. On Jesus, the advocate, as the model for who the παράκλητος is and what he does in John's Gospel within the broader biblical paradigm of two successive redemptive or prophetic figures, see J. Ramsey Michaels, *The Gospel of John*, NICNT (Grand Rapids: Eerdmans, 2010), 791. The polemical implications of restricting the title παράκλητος to Jesus and the Spirit is noted by Silva, NIDNTTE, vol. 3, 632.

44. Toan Do highlights the differences in the function of the παράκλητος in 1 John and the Gospel (*Re-Thinking the Death of Jesus: An Exegetical and Theological Study of Hilasmos and Agapē in 1 John 2:1–2 and 4:7–10*, Contributions to Biblical Exegesis and Theology [Leuven: Peeters, 2014], 133–46), but, as argued above, these differences do not require a significantly different contextualized meaning to παράκλητος, which would require the use of a different English word in translation.

45. Öhler does not interact with the Gospel of John, but he does outline parallels between the propitiatory inscriptions and 1 John 2:1 in terms of the forensic context ("forensische Kontext") in which the deity

In addition to being a divine παράκλητος sent by God and Jesus to aid Christians, the Gospel makes clear that the Spirit will have a variety of functions in believers' lives that are enumerated well by Köstenberger: "(1) he will bring to remembrance all that Jesus taught his disciples (14:26); (2) he will testify regarding Jesus together with his followers (15:26); (3) he will convict the world of sin, (un)righteousness, and judgment (16:8–11); and (4) he will guide Jesus's disciples in all truth and disclose what is to come (16:13)."[46] These enumerated activities expand the picture of the Spirit's role, but they do not therefore negate the main legal context evoked by the term παράκλητος. Grayson helpfully framed the lexical question as "whether parakletos is a legal word sometimes used more generally or a word of more general meaning sometimes applied in legal proceedings."[47] Although the recently published epigraphic evidence discussed above probably will not settle the debate, it seems to support the first option. Παράκλητος, as the translation equivalent of *advocatus*, is best understood as a legal word which was occasionally used more generally but would have brought to mind a legal conceptional context among readers in Western Asia Minor.

---

is the judge and sinners are the offenders ("Die Gottheit wird als richtend verstanden, Sünder als Straffällige.") and in which a deity functions as advocate ("Die Funktion der Gottheit ist dabei die eines Fürsprechers"; "Sünde, Bekenntnis und Sühne," 182). "In beiden Corpora spielen Mittlerfiguren eine wichtige Rolle. Sprachlich wird dies an der Verwendung von παράκλητος sehr deutlich, einer göttlichen Figur, die zwischen dem Sünder und der Gottheit interveniert" ("Sünde, Bekenntnis und Sühne," 183).

46. Köstenberger, *A Theology*, 397.
47. Grayston, "The Meaning of *parakletos*," 70.

CHAPTER 3

THE COVENANT TEXTURE OF THE FAREWELL SCENES (JOHN 13–17)

L. SCOTT KELLUM

I met Andreas Köstenberger in 1996 when I interviewed the NT faculty of Southeastern Baptist Theological Seminary to select a major professor in my PhD studies. Although the faculty was excellent, I quickly determined I wanted to work under Andreas's leadership. During the interview, Andreas stated, "You're going to work in John, right?" By then, I was so sure I wanted to work under his leadership that if he had offered a study on Canaanite pottery instead of John, I would have said yes! The decision to work in the Fourth Gospel under Andreas has shaped my career and benefited me more than space allows me to recount. At no point in the writing phase did I ever feel compelled to include a suggestion because I had to. Instead, Andreas's directions always made the project better and made me a better scholar. I am forever indebted to his abilities, leadership, and friendship. Furthermore, I am thrilled to offer the following essay in his honor.

The present essay explores a covenant texture in what I call the "farewell scenes." These scenes make up the time in the Fourth Gospel between Jesus's retreat to celebrate Passover with "his own" and his arrest in chapter 18. These scenes include the foot washing (John 13:1–30), the Farewell Discourse (13:31–16:33), and the final prayer (17:1–26).[1]

---

1. All English Scripture references are to the English Standard Version.

The term "new covenant" occurs only once in the Old Testament in Jeremiah 31:31. Oddly enough for a corpus carrying the title "The New Covenant" (ἡ καινὴ διαθήκη), the whole phrase is used only five times (Luke 22:20; 1 Cor. 11:25; 2 Cor. 3:6; Heb. 8:8; 9:15) in the New Testament, and only one lengthy passage (Heb. 8–10) explicates the concept. Moreover, for our investigation, the broader term "covenant" (διαθήκη) does not occur in the Fourth Gospel and occurs only four times in the fourfold gospel. It is no wonder that readers unfamiliar with a covenantal environment do not recognize it in the New Testament, particularly the Gospel of John.

Yet, none of these things should deter us from investigating the concept in John's farewell scenes. As Scott J. Hafemann noted, the covenant reality in actualization does not require saturation of the term.[2] Instead, the concept and contours of covenant may saturate and undergird a document from a covenant community.

Scholars have long recognized similarities between the Farewell Discourse and Deuteronomy (Moses's farewell).[3] Klink is largely on target when he states, "The comparisons between Deuteronomy and John's Farewell Discourse are worthy to note, especially in that both are expressions of their respective covenants between God and his people (Deuteronomy, the old covenant; John, the new covenant)."[4] I do not deny the similarities, but I would suggest that beyond similarities based on the genre of a Farewell Discourse,[5] we are looking at a *conceptual* link between John's farewell scenes and Deuteronomy rather than a direct literary link. Furthermore, that link is the covenant concept and form. Thus, the farewell scenes demonstrate a fulfillment of the prophetic oracles that promised a specific covenant: the new covenant.

1. COVENANTS IN THE ANCIENT NEAR EAST

Most agree on the general parameters of a covenant relationship arising from the ANE. T. Schreiner expresses the broad contours as relationship, election, binding promises, and obligations.[6] First, a covenant creates a rela-

---

2. Scott J. Hafemann, "The Covenant Relationship," in *Central Themes in Biblical Theology*, ed. Scott J. Hafemann and Paul R. House (Grand Rapids: Baker Academic, 2007), 24.

3. Aelred Lacomara, "Deuteronomy and the Farewell Discourse (Jn 13:31–16:33)," *CBQ* 36 (1974): 65–84.

4. Edward W. Klink, *John*, ZECNT 4 (Grand Rapids: Zondervan Academic), 845.

5. See, L. Scott Kellum, "Farewell Discourse," in *Dictionary of Jesus and the Gospels*, 2nd ed. (Downers Grove, IL: IVP Academic, 2013), 266–69.

6. Thomas R. Schreiner, *Covenant and God's Purpose for the World*, SSBT (Wheaton, IL: Crossway, 2017), 13–14.

tionship (normally with a nonrelative), making it different from a commercial contract where no such relationship exists. It creates, in theory at least, a family-type relationship by election, i.e., a relationship that one chooses to enter, in contrast to natural family relationships. Finally, some binding promises and obligations define the "familial" expectations. The agreement is then ratified with ritual elements, at times, including dramatic enactments. The definition of Gentry and Wellum expresses it well:

> A covenant is an enduring agreement that defines a relationship between two parties involving a solemn, binding obligation (or obligations) specified on the part of at least one of the parties toward the other, made by oath under threat of divine curse, and ratified by a visual ritual.[7]

In my view, the covenants defining God's relationship with humanity are to be understood as follows: There is likely a covenant at creation (see Hos. 6:7) that is renewed with Noah in Genesis 6 and ultimately fulfilled in the new creation. These two covenants provide for God's establishment of creation necessary for history itself that allows for a redemptive covenant.[8] As T. Schreiner notes, "Redemption can't occur without a created order."[9] The cosmology is marked by two ages, this age and the age to come, the former dominated by the Abrahamic covenant (narrowed through David and fulfilled in Christ). The Sinai covenant defines a holy nation and dominates the first age, working within the Abrahamic. The promised new covenant is inaugurated and accomplished by Jesus and dominates the present age. In this arrangement, the farewell scenes show what I call a texture of both common and specific covenant elements.

2. ELEMENTS IN THE FAREWELL SCENES COMMON TO ANE COVENANTS

It is common to divide the ANE treaty into two covenants: suzerain-vassal and grant treaties. The former is represented well in the Old Testament by Sinai, with its blessings and curses based on obedience to stipulations. The latter is represented best by Abraham, where the sovereign blesses the

---

7. Peter Gentry and Stephen J. Wellum, *Kingdom through Covenant: A Biblical-Theological Understanding of the Covenants*, 2nd ed. (Wheaton, IL: Crossway, 2018), 164.
8. Hafemann, "The Covenant Relationship," 19.
9. Schreiner, *Covenant and God's Purpose*, 36.

vassal without stating any stipulations. Admittedly, it is more complicated than one requires obedience and the other does not (after all, Abraham was expected to obey).[10] Whatever the specific type, some commonalities exist across all forms of the ANE treaty. Some of these commonalities can be found in the Fourth Gospel's farewell scenes.

2.1 Fictive Kinship

Covenants created a family relationship between the covenanting parties who otherwise were unrelated. The convention is to refer to it as a "fictive kinship."[11] It is "fictive" only because it is not necessarily biological but a created kinship. This is precisely the kind of relationship described in the Prologue to the Gospel. John noted in 1:12–13, "But to all who did receive him, who believed in his name, he gave the right to become children of God, who were born, not of blood nor of the will of the flesh nor of the will of man, but of God." John clearly describes a non-biological kinship. The difference between previous covenants and the present situation is that a new birth is described that makes kinship more than a mere treaty.

For our purposes, it is interesting to note that until the farewell scenes, there is a pronounced absence of familial language between Jesus and his disciples in the Gospel of John in chapters 1–12. The relationship pictured before his last Passover is a rabbi and his disciples (however unique and multidimensional that Rabbi is). As Köstenberger noted in 1998, "John portrays the relationship between Jesus and his closest followers in terms of the customary teacher-disciple relationship in first-century Judaism."[12] At the farewell scenes, the disciples no longer address Jesus as ῥαββί but in more exalted terms.[13] Köstenberger attributed the shift to Jesus's role for the disciples as now exalted Lord rather than the more human/mundane ῥαββί.[14] This is certainly correct. The exalted Lord has cut a covenant with his disciples so that he takes his rightful place as Lord. Thus, Thomas's confession Ὁ κύριός μου καὶ ὁ θεός μου (John 20:28) is the ultimate confession of believers toward Jesus. To these observations, we should also

---

10. What is implied earlier in Genesis is explicitly stated at Genesis 17:1, "walk before me and be blameless."
11. See e.g., Sandra L. Richter, *The Epic of Eden: A Christian Entry into the Old Testament* (Downers Grove, IL: IVP, 2008), 70.
12. Andreas J. Köstenberger, "Jesus as Rabbi in the Fourth Gospel," *BBR* 8 (1998): 100–101.
13. Köstenberger, "Jesus as Rabbi," 125.
14. Köstenberger, "Jesus as Rabbi," 125.

note how Jesus addresses his disciples after chapter 12. Below are some of the more prominent examples.

John's address to his readers in the epistles is well-known to be "little children" (παιδία or τεκνία). Jesus, however, only addresses his own as τεκνία ("little children") at the beginning of the Farewell Discourse (13:31—and never uses παιδία). Carson asserts that Jesus takes "the paschal role of head of the family," i.e., for ceremonial reasons.[15] But the meal is over at this point. When Judas departs (13:30), Jesus addresses his own from the vantage point of his accomplishment (glorification), including an inaugurated new covenant.

Whether one assumes futurist or realized eschatology, Jesus employs another familial allusion at 14:3. At least part of his going away is to prepare a place for the disciples in the Father's house. While I prefer a futurist explanation of the meaning of the verse, the allusion to the "Father's house" certainly conveys a familial relation since being in the house is to be family. This, too, is indicative of the non-biological kinship that is established in a covenant. My thesis is that this "kinship" is through the inauguration of the new covenant that was already part of the ANE covenant texture.

2.2 Election

Another commonality of the covenant format is the phenomenon of choice. Sherri Brown notes, "In the biblical narratives of God's covenantal interaction with humankind, God is always the primary agent: God determines to make the covenant, and God chooses the person or people through whom he will implement his plan for creation."[16] Generally, a covenant is unlike a family relationship because one does not choose his/her parents. It is more like a marriage where a couple creates a family relationship by choice.[17] In the ANE, the stronger party initiated covenants.[18] In biblical covenants, God (clearly the stronger party) chooses individuals with whom he will enter a covenant. God chooses Abraham (Gen. 12:1; 18:19), Israel (Deut. 7:6; 14:2), and David (Ps. 89:3). All of these elect

---

15. D. A. Carson, *The Gospel According to John*, PNTC (Leicester, UK: InterVarsity Press; Grand Rapids: Eerdmans, 1991), 483.

16. Sherri Brown, *Gift upon Gift: Covenant through Word in the Gospel of John*, PTMS 144 (Eugene, OR: Pickwick, 2010), 64.

17. Schreiner, *Covenant and God's Purpose*, 14.

18. Elmer A. Martens, *God's Design: A Focus on Old Testament Theology*, 4th ed. (Eugene, OR: Wipf & Stock, 2015), 71.

willfully entered into covenant with God who (more than) prompted the relationship. Dumbrell's note about Abram surely applied to all these: "God conferred greatness rather than rewarding it."[19]

The Fourth Gospel affirms divine election at several points (e.g., John 6:65). The farewell scenes include it four times. In the first three, Jesus does the electing (13:18; 15:16, 19). In the last (17:9), God has given the disciples to Jesus. As in other places in the Fourth Gospel, Jesus stands in essential unity with the Father. For our topic, the stronger party initiates the relationship. This most fundamental element of a covenant with God is evident in the farewell scenes and forms the foundation of the relationship with God through the new covenant.

2.3 Obedience Based on Love

Another foundational element of a covenant relationship involves the nature of obedience. Modern Christians are familiar with the concept of obedience to God. They are not as familiar with the grounds for that obedience. In a covenant relationship, the grounds for obedience is not fear or duty but love. The concept is introduced most powerfully in Deuteronomy 6:4–5: "Hear, O Israel: The LORD our God, the LORD is one. You shall love the LORD your God with all your heart and with all your soul and with all your might." Obedience, then, is the expression of love for God. "Love" (אהב) is often paired with "steadfast love" (חֶסֶד). See, for example, Deuteronomy 7:9: "Know therefore that the LORD your God is God, the faithful God who keeps covenant and steadfast love [חֶסֶד] with those who love [אהב] him and keep his commandments, to a thousand generations." This word is difficult to translate but has the essence of faithfulness based on love (although truly more nuanced). The latter defines the response to incorporation into the covenant. As E. A. Heath states,

> Covenant is only actualized between God and his people in the Bible where there is *hesed*/ for it is a committed, familial love that is deeper than social expectations, duties, shifting emotions or what is deserved or earned by the recipient. More than just an inclination or emotion, *hesed* incarnates itself in action.[20]

---

19. William J. Dumbrell, *Covenant and Creation: An Old Testament Covenant Theology*, revised and enlarged edition (Milton Keynes, UK: Paternoster, 2013), 65.
20. E. A. Heath, "Grace," in *The Dictionary of the Old Testament: Pentateuch*, IVP Bible Dictionary Series, 1, 371–75, ed. T. Desmond Alexander and David W. Baker (Downers Grove, IL: InterVarsity Press, 2003), 372.

In the Farewell Discourse, love and obedience are so affiliated they can be compared to two sides of the same coin. The most direct example is John 14:15: "If you love me, you will keep my commandments" (cf. 14:21–24). It is not hard to see the links to the concepts described above. Moreover, this covenantal connection is inseparably intertwined with the premier expression of sanctification in Johannine literature: abiding.

I have argued elsewhere that when we compare John 15:10 with 14:15, 21–24, we may define the essence of "abiding in me/my love":

> If "abiding in his love" is accomplished through keeping his commandments, we already have a statement on how followers of Jesus and disciples keep his commandments: through loving him (see 14:15, 21–24). So, because abiding is accomplished in obedience and obedience is accomplished through love, then abiding is loving Christ. So instead of a long list of do's and don'ts, Johannine sanctification is one major do: love Christ. This supremely positive command puts a whole new spin on how a believer approaches consecration. No longer negative and oppressive, it is, rather, positive and freeing. The essence of abiding in Christ is loving him.[21]

Using "abiding" to describe the relationship is not a Johannine innovation. Edward Malatesta argued rather convincingly that abiding language (μένειν, ἐμμένειν, εἶναι ἐν) has its roots in the Old Testament covenant relationship.[22] Two of the clearest examples he cited are Deuteronomy 27:26 and Jeremiah 31:32. In Deuteronomy 27, Moses gave Joshua instructions for a covenant renewal, famous for the antiphonal repetition of blessings and curses from Mt. Gerizim and Mt. Ebal. At the conclusion of the curses, Moses stated, "Cursed be anyone who does not confirm the words of this law by doing them" (v. 26). Thus, obedience and abiding are directly connected. Furthermore, the announcement of the new covenant in LXX Jeremiah 31:32 states the reason a new covenant is necessary: "because they did not abide [ἐνέμειναν] in my covenant."[23]

---

21. L. Scott Kellum, *Preaching the Farewell Discourse: A Homiletical Walk-through of John 13:31–17:26* (Nashville: B&H Academic, 2014), 139.

22. Edward Malatesta, *Interiority and Covenant: A Study of [Einai En] and [Menein En] in the First Letter of Saint John*, AnBib 69 (Rome: Biblical Institute, 1978), 60–61.

23. Second temple literature has some similar examples. The most direct comparison Malatesta listed was 28:6–7 where "Remember the covenant of the Most High" is parallel to "abide (ἔμμενε) in the commandments." Malatesta, *Interiority*, 60–61.

The Johannine usage of "abide" is not limited simply to the believer's obedience. The object of abiding is in Jesus, the true vine. The only Old Testament parallel to this is Isaiah 30, where the prophet upbraids Israel for seeking help outside of God. The passage concludes with "blessed are those who abide in Him" (μακάριοι οἱ ἐμμένοντες ἐν αὐτῷ). While there is a new depth of experience with the term, we see the typical Johannine association of Jesus with the Father and the covenantal aspect of love and obedience being inseparable.

The concept is also expressed when Jesus refers to his disciples as friends (φίλοι). When Jesus defined friendship as doing "what I command you" (John 15:14), he immediately connected it to abiding. Thus, C. K. Barrett correctly states, "There is no essential difference between being Christ's φίλος and abiding in his ἀγάπη."[24] The allusion to the relationship to Abraham is unmistakable, as he was the first "friend of God." The comparison is twofold: Jesus is equated with God and the disciples to Abraham. The covenantal dimensions of this statement are not distant.[25]

2.4 A Ritual Meal

The Johannine farewell scenes include a meal, but the meal is not a major part of the story (unlike the Synoptics). Even though this is the case, scholars hotly debate the meal's nature. In my opinion, Carson is correct to connect John 13:1, "Now before the Feast of the Passover," to point to the foot washing and to identify the supper (13:2, δείπνου, an evening meal) as the Passover meal.[26] In this light, John 13:1–2 identify the meal as Passover in agreement with the Synoptics. Without much debate, in the farewell scene, John wants our attention on the foot washing, not the supper itself. The scene has been recast in a way that does not deny the synoptic accounts but emphasizes a new dimension.

---

24. C. K. Barrett, *The Gospel According to St. John: An Introduction with Commentary and Notes on the Greek Text*, 2nd ed. (Philadelphia: Westminster, 1978), 477.

25. Klink, *John*, 975–76.

26. Carson, *John*, 460. Raymond Brown (*Gospel of John*, AB 29A [Garden City, NJ: Doubleday, 1966], 529) denies the meal is a Passover meal but does admit it has "Passover characteristics." See also Köstenberger's essay, "Was the Last Supper a Passover Meal?" in T. Schreiner and M. Crawford, ed., *The Lord's Supper* (Nashville: B&H, 2011), 6–30; Craig L. Blomberg, *The Historical Reliability of the Gospels,* 2nd ed. (Downers Grove, IL: IVP Academic, 2007), 221–25; and Matthew Colvin *The Lost Supper: Revisiting Passover and the Origins of the Eucharist* (New York: Lexington/Fortress Academic, 2019), 17–20.

I believe this emphasis is to make a double point: believers' greatness is in serving, and Jesus's serving is in cleansing the believer. For the present point, John notes that the event occurs at a meal. This meal is a visual ritual that accompanies a covenant.

Covenants in the ANE, especially those in the biblical text, were typically accompanied by a ceremonial meal as part of their ratification. In the Old Testament, both Abimelech and Isaac (Gen. 26:30) and Laban and Jacob (31:54) make covenants among themselves that include a meal. In Exodus 24:11, Moses, Aaron, Nadab, Abihu, and seventy of the elders of Israel ate dinner on Mt. Sinai in the presence of YHWH at the ratification of the Sinai covenant.

Not every recorded covenant ceremony is accompanied by a meal. Admittedly, biblical silence does not mean a meal did not take place. However, no covenant *renewal* of the Mosaic covenant reports an accompanying meal that is eaten because a covenant was made. Besides Deuteronomy, these renewals include Joshua 24; 2 Kings 23:1–3; 2 Chronicles 34:29–33; and Nehemiah 8–10.[27]

There are two possible exceptions. First, at the covenant renewal in Nehemiah 8:10, 12, the text contains instructions to merrily eat festival dishes (מִנַמִשְׁמַ) and notes they departed to eat them, providing for the poor (Neh. 8:12). This does not sound like a ceremonial meal but a joyful celebration. David Shepherd suggests the closest parallel is Esther 9:19–22, which describes a festal celebration.[28] Others have noted that it is possibly related to a peace offering.[29] Since a meal accompanied peace offerings,[30] neither support an understanding that it was a covenant meal.

Second, in Deuteronomy 27:7, Moses stipulates a covenant enactment ritual with the wandering generation's children. He specifically states that they should "sacrifice peace offerings and shall eat there." Because all was done following Moses's instructions in Joshua 8:30–35, we can

---

27. This enumeration is dependent upon Levi Baker, "New Covenant Documents for a New Covenant Community: Covenant as an Impetus for New Scripture in the First Century" (PhD dissertation, Southeastern Baptist Theological Seminary, 2022), 66–67. Baker disagrees with Williamson (*Sealed with an Oath*, 106–8, 111–19) who also includes Josh. 8:30–35;, 2 Chron. 14–15;, 2 Kings 11:17–18;, and Ezra 10:1–5. Baker excludes them because they do not meet all the criteria of a covenant renewal.

28. David J. Shepherd and Christopher J. H Wright, *Ezra and Nehemiah*, THOTC (Grand Rapids: Eerdmans, 2018), 84.

29. Mervin Breneman, *Ezra, Nehemiah, Esther*, NAC 10 (Nashville: Broadman & Holman, 1993), 227–28.

30. R. T. Beckwith, "Sacrifice," in *New Dictionary of Biblical Theology*, ed. T. Desmond Alexander and Brian S. Rosner, 754–62 (Downers Grove, IL: InterVarsity, 2000), 757.

assume they ate a meal, although it is not stated in Joshua. This should not be included on two grounds. First, I do not think this is a formal renewal but an act of remembrance and consecration.[31] Second, even if I am wrong, because Moses specifically mentioned peace offerings in the same sentence, it is likely that any meal was part of the peace offering. Ultimately, I contend that the Old Testament records no covenant meal accompanying any covenant renewal, only ratification of covenants.[32] Thus, the new covenant is not a renewal of a previous covenant but a new one: the promised new covenant (Jer. 31:31–34).

2.5 An Inaugural Sacrifice

Another common element of a covenant with God is an inaugural sacrifice. The writer of Hebrews clearly expresses the necessity of sacrifice and covenant in Hebrews 9:18–22:

> Therefore not even the first covenant was inaugurated without blood. For when every commandment of the law had been declared by Moses to all the people, he took the blood of calves and goats, with water and scarlet wool and hyssop, and sprinkled both the book itself and all the people, saying, "This is the blood of the covenant that God commanded for you." And in the same way he sprinkled with the blood both the tent and all the vessels used in worship. Indeed, under the law almost everything is purified with blood, and without the shedding of blood there is no forgiveness of sins.

The writer refers to Exodus 24:4–8, where the sequence is: first, God gives the covenant; second, the people agree to abide by it; third, sacrifices are offered; and fourth, the blood is sprinkled on the people. The connection to the sacrifice and covenant is seen strongly in the phrase "blood of the covenant" that is used for both the old covenant (Exod. 24:8) and

---

31. R. S. Hess, "Joshua," in *New Dictionary of Biblical Theology*, ed. T. Desmond Alexander and Brian S. Rosner, 165–71 (Downers Grove, IL: InterVarsity Press, 2000), 167.

32. Some, like Reka Chennattu, suggest the NT scene is a covenant renewal. Chennattu acknowledges the lack of a meal with the renewal in Joshua 24 is not like the farewell scene but suggests the search for exact parallels should be rejected in favor of essential elements of OT covenant traditions. Chennattu, *Johannine Discipleship as a Covenant Relationship* (Grand Rapids: Baker Academic, 2005), 69.

the new (Matt. 26:28;, Mark 14:24; Heb. 9:20; and 10:29). Neither are possible without sacrifice.

In the farewell scenes, Jesus's death is alluded to several times (e.g., John 13:3, 31–33; 14:1–4, 12, 19, 28; 16:7, 16–17; 17:1, 11). Most of these are in the context of his "going away" rather than specifically referencing his death. After all, much of the speech is about thriving in his absence (including his presence in his absence). However, the major reference to the death of Christ as a sacrifice is the foot washing. Bauckham explains it well:

> There can be no doubt that John understands the footwashing in relation to the cross, where the Jesus who in chapter 13 undertakes the role of a slave finally dies the death of a slave. The footwashing both provides an interpretation of the meaning of the cross, as Jesus's voluntary self-humiliation and service for others, and also gains its own fullest meaning when seen in the light of the cross it prefigures. In this respect, it parallels the Synoptic accounts of "the institution of the Lord's Supper," accounts whose function in these Gospels is not to record the institution as such (only the disputed verse Luke 22:19b indicates that the rite is to be repeated by the disciples), but rather to provide an interpretation of Jesus's coming death.[33]

The scene is one of the most striking of John's contributions to the Last Supper. It is an example of selfless service. Jesus applies the selfless service in two directions. First (and foremost), it represents Jesus's cleansing of the believer. Second, it demonstrates that the key to greatness in Christianity is serving others.[34] The two are not mutually exclusive. We should not be surprised that the foot washing "explains the salvific necessity of being washed by Jesus (John 13:6–11) and how it functions as a model for believers serving one another (13:12–20)."[35]

The chronological debate over "before the feast of the Passover" (Πρὸ δὲ τῆς ἑορτῆς τοῦ πάσχα) revolves around its reference.[36] Does it refer to

---

33. Richard Bauckham, *The Testimony of the Beloved Disciple: Narrative, History, and Theology in the Gospel of John* (Grand Rapids: Baker Academic, 2007), 130.

34. A topic expressly narrated in Luke 22:24–30 describing the disciples' dispute over who would be the greatest.

35. Craig Keener, *The Gospel of John: A Commentary*, 2 vols. (Peabody, MA: Hendrickson, 2003), 2:907.

36. See Köstenberger's essay, "Was the Last Supper a Passover Meal?," 20.

the entirety of the farewell scene,[37] or does it prepare the reader specifically for the foot washing? If the former, it is difficult to identify the meal as a Passover meal. If the latter, the agreement with the Synoptics is confirmed. I think the foot washing sets up both the farewell scene and the passion narrative. This is particularly true because the foot washing introduces the meaning of the crucifixion as the means for cleansing the believer. Thus, the two cannot be separated, for the former defines the meaning of the latter as an expression of Jesus's love (13:1) and the means of our cleansing (13:8). The foot washing, then, anticipates the actual death of Christ but visualizes the meaning of it ahead of the event.[38] It is his sacrifice for humanity. Thus, the sacrifice necessary for the new covenant is the death of Christ, which is the controlling theme of the Book of Glory; "having loved his own who were in the world, he loved them fully." This leads us to the matters in the farewell scenes specific to the new covenant.

3. ELEMENTS IN THE FAREWELL SCENES SPECIFIC TO THE NEW COVENANT

The farewell scenes in the Fourth Gospel not only show a covenant texture; we can also note that some of the promises only related to the new covenant are evident in these scenes. The following is not an exhaustive survey of the Old Testament or the farewell scenes. We will, however, establish the point rather securely.

3.1 The Messiah as the Embodiment of the Covenant

At least two passages related to the new covenant in the Prophets describe the Messiah as identified with the covenant. The first comes in the servant songs of Isaiah. In Isaiah 42:6, the servant is told, "I will give you as a covenant for the people, a light for the nations." It is disputed whether this refers to the new covenant. But since Isaiah 42:1–6 is alluded to by several New Testament passages to identify Jesus, we are compelled to understand the servant (perhaps complexly) referring to Jesus and "covenant" as the new covenant.[39] Malachi 3:1 is another passage that closely

---

37. See, e.g., Barrett, *John*, 435; more recently Klink, *John*, 122.
38. Carson, *John*, 465. The discussion regarding Jesus's response (v. 10) to Peter's request (v. 9) and the textual variant εἰ μὴ τοὺς πόδας is not relevant to the current topic. The foot washing remains a symbol of Jesus's death however it is interpreted.
39. See, e.g., Isaiah 42:1 and Matthew 12:18. See also Mark 1:11; Luke 3:22; 9:35; Philippians 2:7. See also T. Rata, "Covenant," in *Dictionary of the Old Testament: Prophets* (Downers Grove, IL: IVP Academic, 2012), 103–4. See also Charles L. Quarles, *Matthew*, EBTC (Bellingham, WA: Lexham Academic, 2022), 76.

identifies the Messiah and the new covenant. He is "the Lord whom you seek . . . the messenger of the covenant."

This covenant identification can be seen in the farewell scenes at several points. The first is the well-known John 14:6, "I am the way, and the truth, and the life. No one comes to the Father except through me." Schnackenburg aptly described the passage as "a culminating point in Johannine theology," in particular his doctrine of salvation as centered entirely in Jesus Christ.[40]

Finally, in John 15:1–5, the analogy of the vine and the branches demonstrates a similar identification. Jesus, as the true vine, replaces the Old Testament's vine (Israel). Accordingly, the people of God are identified through their living connection to Jesus. The result is that Jesus "applies to himself the redemptive-historical description of the people of God. He thus becomes the one who represents or embodies the people."[41] In this way, like Matthew, John identifies Jesus as the new Abraham, that is, the new Israel.[42]

In the final prayer, Jesus identifies the nature of eternal life, which is, by definition, the point of the new covenant. At 17:3, Jesus states, "And this is eternal life, that they know you, the only true God, and Jesus Christ whom you have sent."

Finally, I have already noted that love as the basis of obedience is a feature of all biblical covenants, which is obvious in the Farewell Discourse (14:15, 21; 15:9–11). For the present observation, that Jesus is the object of that obedience/love certainly puts him at the center of the new covenant as the Father is in the older. In this sense, as the Father embodies the old covenant, so, too, both the Father and the Son embody the new.

3.2 The Spirit of God and Human Transformation

The book of Ezekiel says a great deal about the Spirit of God and the transformation of human beings under the new covenant. Ezekiel 11 concludes a section describing the departure of God's presence from the temple because of Israel's abominations (8:6). Ezekiel, after seeing horrific judgment on the nation (and particularly on a leader of Israel), cries out,

---

40. Rudolf Schnackenburg, *The Gospel According to St. John*, trans. David Smith and G. A. Kon, HTCNT (New York: Crossroad Publishing Company, 1987), 3:64–65.

41. Herman Ridderbos, *The Gospel of John: A Theological Commentary*, trans. John Vrend (Grand Rapids: Eerdmans, 1997), 515.

42. See Quarles, *Matthew*, 97–100.

"Ah, Lord GOD! Will you make a full end of the remnant of Israel?" (Ezek. 11:13). God's answer describes the second exodus of Israel. He will bring Israel back from the nations. They will remove the detestable things. And, in Ezekiel 11:19–20, God states:

> I will give them one heart, and a new spirit I will put within them. I will remove the heart of stone from their flesh and give them a heart of flesh, that they may walk in my statutes and keep my rules and obey them. And they shall be my people, and I will be their God.

This is the first of several references to a spiritual indwelling and renewal in Ezekiel. Because this first reference employs the covenant formula ("they shall be my people, and I will be their God"), the reference seems to be "speaking clearly about a new covenant."[43] This makes the warning in Ezekiel 18:31 to "Cast away from you all the transgressions that you have committed, and make yourselves a new heart and a new spirit" likely a reference to the new covenant.[44]

In a similar vein, Ezekiel 36:22–36 links the transformation by the Spirit to the new covenant. After citing Israel's abandonment of the Lord, he affirms a second exodus in 36:24. And then he promises to cleanse them and give them a new heart, a heart of flesh, not stone. Upon putting the Spirit in them, they will "walk in my statutes and be careful to obey my rules" (Ezek. 36:27). This is confirmed by the covenant formula, "You shall be my people, and I will be your God" (36:28). Notably, Ezekiel's oracle of the valley of dry bones (that are brought to life again) immediately follows this passage and is linked.[45] Again, this clearly references the things accompanying the new covenant. In this case, what is highlighted are new life and transformation by the Spirit of God.

Isaiah 59:21 also promises a covenant with the people of God that features the Spirit of God being upon them and their descendants. Since Paul interprets the previous verse as a future salvation of Israel (Ezek. 11:26), the setting is clearly eschatological and new-covenant. The situation presented is similar to Joel 2:28–32.[46]

---

43. Gentry and Wellum, *Kingdom through Covenant*, 585.
44. Gentry and Wellum, *Kingdom through Covenant*, 589.
45. Lamar Eugene Cooper, *Ezekiel*, NAC 17 (Nashville: Broadman & Holman, 1994), 322.
46. It is possible that the individual upon whom the Spirit rests may be the prophet himself. However, it is not likely, for the passage speaks of the blessing being upon children and grandchildren. As Oswalt notes,

Jeremiah 31:33 (the foundational text announcing a new covenant) states, "I will put my law within them, and I will write it on their hearts." The verse introduces one of the four major differences between the old and new covenants. Anthony R. Petterson calls it "a new mode of implementation, namely, a divine initiative to internalize the law. . . . This contrasts with the old covenant directive to put it there themselves (cf. Deut. 6:6; 11:18)."[47] Western Christians tend to think of the heart as the seat of the emotions. However, in the Old Testament, about half of all the metaphorical occurrences of "heart" (לֵב) refer to the human will.[48] Although the Spirit of God is not mentioned, the use here refers to a transformation of the human desires by God as a key difference to the old covenant.

The Farewell Discourse contains several passages addressing the topic. Notably, the three paraclete passages (John 14:15–26; 15:26–27; 16:7–15) promise the sending of the Spirit and some of the benefits accompanying his arrival. These include mediating the presence of Jesus, his teaching in his absence; witness to the world (presumably through his followers); and conviction of sin (thus, the Spirit empowers witness externally and internally). Admittedly, the function of the Spirit elucidated by Jesus is not specifically the transformed heart of Ezekiel. However, the different descriptions can be linked to the Spirit's indwelling.

Moreover, if we telescope out to the larger structures of the Gospel of John, we can see the farewell scenes point to the transforming work of the Holy Spirit as indicated in Ezekiel. In John 21, commonly called the epilogue, five correspondences to the Farewell Discourse help us see the connections of the farewell scenes to the passion and resurrection of Christ.[49] First, Jesus had predicted in 13:36–38 Peter's denial. As Peter stands before Jesus at a charcoal fire (John 21:9), we are reminded of a previous charcoal fire (18:18) where he denied Christ. Second, the

---

"The idea that the prophet is being addressed is surely countered correctly by Dillmann's comment that there is no evidence of a hereditary prophetic gift" (John N. Oswalt, *The Book of Isaiah, Chapters 40–66*, NICOT [Grand Rapids: Eerdmans, 1998], 531).

47. Anthony R. Petterson, "The New Covenant in the Book of the Twelve," in *Reading the Book of the Twelve Minor Prophets*, ed. David G. Firth and Brittany N. Melton, Studies in Scripture and Biblical Theology, 103–24 (Bellingham, WA: Lexham Academic, 2022), 104. Petterson is adapting Bruce A. Ware, "The New Covenant and the People(s) of God," in *Dispensationalism, Israel and the Church*, ed. Craig A. Blaising and Darrell L. Bock (Grand Rapids: Zondervan Academic, 1992), 68–97.

48. See Hetty Lalleman, *Jeremiah and Lamentations: An Introduction and Commentary*, TOTC (Downers Grove, IL: IVP Academic, 2013), 234.

49. Much of what follows is dependent on Kellum, *Preaching the Farewell Discourse*, 222–23.

essence of discipleship in the Farewell Discourse is loving Jesus. This is precisely the question that Jesus asks of Peter (ἀγαπᾷς με; [Do you love me?]). Third, Jesus commands Peter to tend/feed his flock (21:15–17). Assuming such tending is done through love for Christ and his flock, this is closely connected to the new commandment (13:34–35; 15:13–17). Fourth, in 13:36–38, Peter (overconfidently) declares his willingness to die for Jesus. In chapter 21, the restored Peter will die for his faith (21:18–19). Finally, twice Jesus tells Peter to "follow me" (ἀκολούθει μοι, 21:19;, μοι ἀκολούθει, 21:22), precisely what Peter longed to do in John 13:37.

The larger intent of the exchange in chapter 21 seems to be to demonstrate that, while the information given in the farewell scenes was for a later time (see 13:36), that time has arrived. Essentially Jesus says, "Peter, game on." We naturally ask, "What has changed?" Jesus's death and resurrection made possible the gift of the Spirit. Since they were not able to follow Jesus before, now they are able, presumably at least in part due to the transforming work of the Spirit (cf. 20:22). So then, in the Old Testament, the long-promised indwelling of the Spirit is closely connected to the inauguration of the everlasting/new covenant and the account of the book of glory reflects this closely. This does not seem to be coincidental at all.

3.3 Gentile Inclusion

Occasionally it is thought that Jeremiah 31:31–34 is only for the Jewish nation. True, it is addressed directly to a unified Israel at an unspecified future date.[50] However, other passages dealing with the new covenant do specifically contain Gentile inclusion.[51] For example, in Isaiah 55:5, the Lord promises to make an everlasting covenant through a new and greater David. Moreover, this covenant applies to the nations. It states, "Behold, you shall call a nation that you do not know, and a nation that did not know you shall run to you, because of the LORD your God, and of the Holy One of Israel, for he has glorified you."

Another new-covenant passage with Gentile inclusion is in Isaiah 56. In this passage, both the foreigner and the eunuch will participate in "my salvation" that is yet future (56:1). Because neither could participate under the old covenant (see, e.g., Lev. 21:18, 20; 23:1–7), the covenant

---

50. Gentry and Wellum, *Kingdom through Covenant*, 539–60.
51. See Bruce A. Ware, "The New Covenant and the People(s) of God," 72–73.

referred to should be understood as the new covenant.[52] Thus, from the outset, the new covenant has a universal ambition that the New Testament writers see no need to defend.

This universal application can be seen in at least two passages in the farewell scenes. In John 16:8–9, one of the ministries of the Paraclete is to convict the world "concerning sin and righteousness and judgment." While "convict" here has the sense of "prove it guilty,"[53] we should not suggest that the conviction excludes repentance on the part of some. After all, a major role of the Paraclete is to witness to the world (John 16:26).

The second passage is found in the final prayer. In John 17:2, Jesus notes that he has authority over all flesh, "to give eternal life to all whom you have given him." In 17:18, Jesus states that he sent the disciples "into the world." Furthermore, in John 17:21 and 23, Jesus expressly states the disciples' mission is so that "the world may believe that you have sent me." Given the clear Gentile-inclusion thread in the rest of the Gospel (see, e.g., John 1:29; 3:16–17; 4:42; 6:33, 51), there can be little doubt that these allusions are to Gentile inclusion as well.

3.4 Universal Intimacy

Jeremiah 31:34 introduces universal intimacy as another distinction between the new and old covenants: "and no longer shall each one teach his neighbor and each his brother, saying, 'Know the LORD,' for they shall all know me, from the least of them to the greatest, declares the LORD." The oracle declares a promise of an entirely different relationship with God when one is in the covenant. Gentry and Wellum state it best:

> What Jeremiah 31:34 is saying, however, in contrast to 31:29–30, is that in the old covenant, people became members of the covenant community simply by being born into that community. As they grew up, some became believers in Yahweh, others did not. This pattern resulted in a situation within the covenant community where some *members* could urge other *members* to know the Lord.[54]

---

52. See Gentry and Wellum, *Kingdom through Covenant*, 501–4: "We see, then, that those who were formerly outside the people of God and excluded from worshiping in the temple are now joined to the Lord and characterized as true worshippers" (503).

53. Andreas J. Köstenberger, *John*, BECNT (Grand Rapids: Baker Academic, 2004), 470.

54. Gentry and Wellum, *Kingdom through Covenant*, 555.

Gentry and Wellum then equate knowing the Lord with believing in him. I agree with them, but modern Christians might easily confuse it with simply entering the covenant rather than an ongoing relationship. The entry into the covenant through faith leads to a continued relationship also characterized by believing.

In the first movement of the Farewell Discourse, Jesus urges belief in him as they would believe in God (John 14:1).[55] He then gives three reasons for faith in him: Jesus's veracity (14:2–4), Jesus's relationship to salvation (14:5–7), and Jesus's relationship to the Father (14:8–14).[56] Such an urging to faith echoes the old-covenant situation stated above. In John 14:7, Jesus removes all doubt that they do not really know him, "If you had known me, you would have known my Father also." They, not yet under the new covenant, do not know him and are urged to do so.[57] But the day has arrived when a different situation will arise, and Jesus quickly notes it: "From now on you do know him and have seen him."

Andreas points out that "know" is part of the covenantal framework. Thus:

> In the OT, people frequently are exhorted to know God (e.g., Pss. 46:10; 100:3), with knowledge of God generally being anticipated as a future blessing (or being urged) rather than claimed as a present possession. With Jesus's coming, however, the situation has changed dramatically.[58]

What has dramatically changed things is the inauguration of the new covenant that specifically promised the knowledge of God as a critical difference to the older covenant. This is so radically new and important that it is understood as the essence of salvation in John 17:3, "And this is eternal life, that they know you, the only true God, and Jesus Christ whom you have sent."

---

55. Assuming the first instance of πιστεύετε is an indicative, while the second is an imperative.
56. Kellum, *Preaching the Farewell Discourse*, 90.
57. The meaning here is dependent on a text critical decision. I prefer the pluperfect (ἐγνώκειτέ με) over the aorist (ἐγνώκατέ με) chosen in the eclectic text, signifying a contrary-to-fact condition. My preferred reading is based on a wide distribution, early dating, and the suspicion that the choice of the other reading is unduly influenced by its occurrence in 𝔓⁶⁶ (in my opinion, better dated to the fourth century than the second). My preferred reading is reflected in the ESV, NASB, NKJV, NIV, LEB, and RSV.
58. Köstenberger, *John*, 430.

3.5 A Better Sacrifice

We noted above the sacrifice of Christ was an inaugural sacrifice. It is also fundamentally different from the system in the old covenant. This difference is indicated in the prophecies of the new covenant. Jeremiah 31:31–34 concludes with, "For I will forgive their iniquity, and I will remember their sin no more." "For" (כִּי) provides the basis for the knowledge of God and the writing of the law on their hearts. Forgiveness itself is not a novel matter. After all, there was an elaborate system in place for the people of God to receive forgiveness through the sacrifices of Israel. Instead, the promise is to "remember their sin no more" (וּלְחַטָּאתָם לֹא אֶזְכָּר־עוֹד). This requires a more comprehensive provision.[59] Lynwood, Scalise, and Smothers write,

> The final promise in this verse will put an end to the threat in Jer. 14:10: when the LORD remembers sin, punishment follows (cf. 44:21). But the LORD's promise not to remember their sins anymore means an end to divine wrath (31:23, 28). The people of the new covenant will not bear the guilt of their ancestors' sin or their own. They will be free to make a fresh start, under no lingering threats (compare Num. 14:20–23), because of God's gracious gift of pardon. The LORD will write the *torah* ("instruction, law") on a heart polished smooth by forgiveness (cf. Jer. 5:20).[60]

The farewell scenes show a similar doctrine when Peter objects to Jesus washing his feet. It leads to an exchange that hints at the scope of the forgiveness associated with his death (I defended the sacrificial meaning of this aspect above). Jesus's response to Peter is, "If I do not wash you, you have no share with me" (John 13:8). Later in the passage, we see that washing results in cleansing. Therefore, the foot washing symbolizes Jesus's sacrifice, to be narrated in the following chapters. The result of his sacrifice will be spiritual cleansing.

Moreover, and reflecting Jeremiah 31:34, the cleansing is comprehensive. Jesus notes the one washed by Jesus is "completely clean" (John 13:10,

---

59. See Ware, "New Covenant," 81.
60. Keown, Gerald Lynwood, Pamela J. Scalise, and Thomas G. Smothers, *Jeremiah 26–52*, WBC 27 (Waco, TX: Word Books, 1995), 135.

καθαρὸς ὅλος). Although it does not deny there could be an ongoing nature/need in the individual's life, the cleansing is pictured as comprehensive.

Another verse that may reference the status of the believer is John 15:3. In the analogy of the vine and the branches, Jesus declares that his followers are "already clean" (ἤδη ὑμεῖς καθαροί ἐστε). Many suggest a direct connection between the passages.[61] It is, however, unclear that the reference is to the same experience. Given that the agency for cleansing is Jesus's word and the cognate καθαίρει describes "pruning" in the context, it may be best not to import meaning from earlier in the section.

Finally, while some deny that the Passover connections point to Jesus's salvific sacrifice,[62] the opinion here is that it is obvious. So it leads us now to address further Passover implications at the supper. Köstenberger has ably defended the view that the Last Supper was a Passover meal, including the Johannine version.[63] Even R. E. Brown, who denies the meal was Passover, must describe the meal as undoubtedly having Passover "characteristics."[64]

The difference of opinion arises from the virtual absence of the supper from John's account. At the same time, it is unthinkable that John was ignorant of the institution of the Lord's Supper.[65] That should lead us to investigate it from the vantage point of a theological recasting of the scene that passes on the report of the Synoptics' ritual institution by focusing on another aspect of the evening. That aspect is the foot washing and the example advocated by Jesus. If I am correct, the recasting focuses on the meaning of the death of Jesus as cleansing "his own."

The original Passover is best interpreted as a consecration ritual that prefigured Israel's installation as "a kingdom of priests and a holy nation" (Exod. 19:6). This can be seen in other consecration rituals in the Old Testament. As T. D. Alexander notes:

> Striking parallels exist between the Passover ritual, the ratification of the Sinai covenant (Exod. 24:1–11), and the process by which

---

61. See, e.g., J. Ramsey Michaels, *The Gospel of John*, NICNT (Grand Rapids: Eerdmans, 2010), 802–803.

62. See, e.g., Jörg Frey, *The Glory of the Crucified One: Christology and Theology in the Gospel of John*, The Baylor-Mohr Siebeck Studies in Early Christianity Series (Waco, TX: Baylor University Press, 2018), 195. Frey claims the Passover theme in the Fourth Gospel "presents no basis for a sacrificial-cultic interpretation."

63. Köstenberger, "Was the Last Supper a Passover Meal?," 17–23.

64. Brown, *John*, 2:556, 578. This begs the question: what other ritual/festival meal had such characteristics?

65. Osborne states, "Today most believe John's omissions were deliberate, and he was indeed supplementing the synoptic witness." Grant Osborne, Philip W. Comfort, and Wendell C. Hawley, *The Gospel of John, 1–3 John*, CBC 13 (Carol Stream, IL: Tyndale House Publishers, 2007), 8.

the Aaronic priests are consecrated (Exod. 29:1–37; Lev. 8:1–36). In all three cases, animal sacrifices are offered, blood is sprinkled, and a meal involving sacrificial meat is eaten. While the circumstances differ, in each context a process occurs by which people are consecrated to a holier status.[66]

Alexander further suggests that Jesus's death (that John clearly connects to the Passover) has the same three dimensions: atonement, purification, and sanctification.

> The concepts of atonement, purification (or cleansing), and sanctification are all associated in John's Gospel with Jesus's sacrificial death as the "Lamb of God, who takes away the sin of the world" (John 1:29; cf. 1:36). Additionally, John draws attention to the themes of deliverance from death and redemption from slavery to sin and the devil. All these reflect a strong Passover typology, associated with a new exodus, centered on Jesus Christ.[67]

In the farewell scenes, John does not emphasize the Supper and the ritual aspects, but he does address the sacrificial dimensions of atonement, cleansing, and sanctification as part of the spiritual life of the believer. I have already addressed the first two (atonement and cleansing). The third dimension (sanctification) is also alluded to in the farewell scenes. Regarding what Christians gain by believing in Christ, I will look particularly for sanctification as a *state*, set aside as holy, not necessarily a *process* of becoming holy, although the two domains are inseparable.[68] The former is the essence of consecration, and the latter is the outworking of it in the believer's life, addressed as "abiding" in the Farewell Discourse and "sanctify them" in John 17:17.

In terms of a state, Jesus implies sanctification when he describes the disciples as "his own" (John 13:1, τοὺς ἰδίους—"having loved his own who were in the world, he loved them to the end"). The word was previously used of the Jewish nation in 1:11, who did not receive him. Now it is used in

---

66. T. Desmond Alexander, *From Paradise to the Promised Land: An Introduction to the Pentateuch*, 4th ed. (Grand Rapids: Baker Academic, 2022), 102.

67. Alexander, *From Paradise to the Promised Land*, 108.

68. See Carson, *John*, 565: "Ideally if someone is set apart for God and God's purposes alone, that person will do only what God wants, and hate all that God hates. That is what it means to be holy, as God is holy."

distinction to those rejecting the new covenant (by rejecting the embodiment of it).[69] Thus, the Twelve represent the founding of Jesus's own community.

This new community can be seen in its privileges, instructions, and characteristics in the Farewell Discourse. The primary privilege of the new community is best seen in the ministry of the Paraclete. They will uniquely enjoy the ministry of the Paraclete, mediating the presence of Christ (John 14:15–30) and empowering their witness (15:26–27). Even the conviction of the world seems to be to build the community (16:7–11).[70]

The primary instruction for the new community is the new commandment (13:34–35; 15:12) that must assume a set-aside brotherhood. They are to love one another. This love, then, will distinguish them from others (13:35).

The new command's juxtaposition to the hatred of the world (15:18) indicates a primary characteristic of the community. Although surely not limited to it, that world chiefly includes the old covenant community. They hated Jesus without a cause (15:25), even though he had spoken to them (15:22) and did miracles in front of them (15:24). Furthermore, the disciples will be cast out of the synagogues (16:2). Thus, the contrast between the disciples and the world highlights two distinct communities (17:14). The new community is a body of individuals given to Christ by the Father, distinct from the world (17:6), set aside for his glory.

CONCLUSION

The farewell scenes of John's Gospel demonstrate a covenantal texture even though the word "covenant" is not used. Some of the texture is common to the ANE covenant form. These elements in the farewell scenes are fictive kinship, election, obedience based on love, a ritual meal, and an inaugural sacrifice. Some elements, however, would not be recognized as "covenantal" if they were not specific to the new covenant. These are the Messiah as the embodiment of the covenant, the Spirit of God and human transformation, Gentile inclusion, universal intimacy, and a better sacrifice. Thus, the covenantal texture is not only reflective of the ANE treaty form, but also indicates a fulfillment of the prophetic declaration of a new, everlasting covenant of peace for all who enter that covenant through faith in Christ.

---

69.   See Köstenberger, *John*, 402: "'His own' are now the Twelve, the representatives of the new messianic community, no longer the old covenant community, which had rejected Jesus as Messiah."

70.   See Carson, *John*, 537: "This convicting work of the Paraclete is therefore gracious: it is designed to bring men and women of the world to recognize their need, and so turn to Jesus, and thus stop being 'the world.'"

CHAPTER 4

THE CHRIST HYMN OF JOHN 1: FROM CONFESSIONAL RESPONSE TO TRANSFORMATIVE OVERTURE

PAUL N. ANDERSON

There are few more momentous and history-impacting texts in world literature than John 1:1–18.[1] It served as an engaging introduction to John's story of Jesus, which became the most widely embraced text in the history of early Christianity;[2] it contributed to the most intense of theological controversies—and their resolutions—in the first four Ecumenical Councils (325–451 CE), becoming a favorite text throughout church history of heretics and orthodox alike;[3] it became a theologized basis for the excluding the Johannine witness from the first three historical quests for Jesus in the modern era;[4] it has posed a basis for a number of diachronic theories of Johannine composition;[5] and it has offered a literary basis for synchronic interpreters to see the Johannine

---

1. This paper was presented at the Wycliffe Colloquium on Scripture and Theology in Toronto (October 2022) and at the Vienna SNTS meetings (July 2023) and is available online: https://www.youtube.com/watch?v=z-7YGA47M_Y&list=PLy0RDQNnZ7lRXChOd16li1fezFy3VNNTF&index=4.
2. Maurice F. Wiles, *The Spiritual Gospel: The Interpretation of the Fourth Gospel in the Early Church* (Cambridge: Cambridge University Press, 1960).
3. Paul N. Anderson, "The Johannine Riddles and their Place in the Development of Trinitarian Theology," *The Bible and Early Trinitarian Theology*, ed. Christopher A. Beeley and Mark E. Weedman, Studies in Early Christianity 5 (Washington, DC: Catholic University Press, 2018), 84–108.
4. Paul N. Anderson, *The Fourth Gospel and the Quest for Jesus: Modern Foundations Reconsidered*, LNTS 321 (London: T&T Clark, 2006).
5. Paul N. Anderson, *The Christology of the Fourth Gospel; Its Unity and Disunity in the Light of John*, WUNT 2/78, (Tübingen: Mohr Siebeck, 1996); 3rd ed. with a new introduction and epilogue (Eugene, OR: Cascade Books, 2010).

Gospel as a literary whole—its literary features announced and prefigured by the Johannine Overture.[6]

However, does the Johannine Overture advocate the divinity of Jesus, or the humanity of Christ, or both?[7] Were these verses the first stroke of the evangelist's quill, or do we have here a later confessional hymn added by the compiler? Does the Johannine Overture reflect John's being "a spiritual gospel" over and against "the facts" (or, more literally, "the bodily things") of the Synoptics, with the third-century mistranslated musings of Clement eclipsing John's claims to eyewitness memory?[8] Do the odd references to John the Baptist in verses 6–8 and 15 reflect their being added, or being added to? Why are some of the Overture's themes not replicated in the rest of the narrative (*Logos* as a reference to Christ, *plēroma* [fullness] as a theme, *monogenēs* [only begotten] as a reference to the Son)? And why is the language and cadence of this text so similar to 1 John 1:1–3? Finally, who are the people referenced as "we" in John 1:14 and 16, and is there some relation to the same in 21:24, as well as the prolific uses of the first-person plural pronoun in the Johannine Epistles?

In addressing issues from literary- and historical-critical perspectives within an overview of John's dialogical autonomy, most of the theologi-

---

6. Indeed, the Johannine Prologue can be seen as a microcosm of the entire Johannine Gospel. See Simon Ross Valentine, "The Johannine Prologue—a Microcosm of the Gospel," *EvQ* 68, no. 4 (1996): 291–304. See also the eight key terms in the Gospel of John featured in John 1:4–14 (Andreas J. Köstenberger, *Encountering John*, 2nd ed. [Grand Rapids: Baker Academic, 2013], 38). In my classes on John, I use Köstenberger's excellent book *Encounters with John* (2013) alongside my *Riddles of the Fourth Gospel* (Paul N. Anderson, *The Riddles of the Fourth Gospel* [Minneapolis: Fortress, 2011])—a fine combination, I believe!

7. In the view of Rudolf Bultmann, the main thrust of the Prologue was v. 14c—the Word became *flesh*—an incarnational thrust; in the view of Ernst Käsemann, the main thrust was v. 14e—and we beheld his *glory*—a form of naïve Docetism. Bultmann, "The History of Religions Background of the Prologue to the Gospel of John," trans. John Ashton in his *The Interpretation of John* (Philadelphia: Fortress, 1986), 18–35; Bultmann, *The Gospel of John: A Commentary*, trans. G. R. Beasley-Murray, R. W. N. Hoare, and J. K. Riches, JMS 1 (Eugene, OR: Wipf & Stock, 2014); Käsemann, "The Structure and Purpose of the Prologue to John's Gospel," in *New Testament Questions of Today* (Philadelphia: Fortress, 1969), 138–67; Käsemann, *The Testament of Jesus*, JMS 6, trans. Gerhard Krodel, edited and critical introduction by Paul N. Anderson (Eugene, OR: Wipf & Stock, 2017).

8. Clement mused that while the Synoptics recorded the bodily matters (*somatika*), John wrote a spiritual gospel (*evangelion pneumatikon*, Eusebius *Hist Eccles* 6.14). However, *somatika* was mistranslated as "facts" by Arthur Cushman McGiffert (1890), leading some modern scholars to explain John's differences with the Synoptics fallaciously as ethereal pneumatism versus Synoptic "facts" (Paul N. Anderson, *The Fourth Gospel*, 1–41). In the light of John's mundane features ("John: The Mundane Gospel and Its Archaeology-Related Features," *The Bible and Interpretation* (July 2020): https://bibleinterp.arizona.edu/articles/john-mundane-gospel-and-its-archaeology-related-features), note the impressive collection of more than two dozen essays illuminating connections between archaeology, John, and Jesus—the first full volume on the subject ever: Paul N. Anderson, ed., *Archaeology, John, and Jesus: What Recent Discoveries Show Us About Jesus from the Gospel of John* (Grand Rapids: Eerdmans, 2024).

cal-historical issues of previous paragraphs will thereby be clarified. And such is the goal of the present essay.

1. THE RELATION OF THE GOSPEL'S OVERTURE TO THE JOHANNINE CORPUS

Given the questions raised above, the place of the Overture to the rest of the Johannine corpus is a longtime question for scholars.[9] It clearly introduces the narrative compellingly and well, and the Gospel's main themes are laid out engagingly within a confessional, strophic prelude to what follows. Then again, the strophic-poetic features of the Christ hymn reflect a worship context, with impressive similarities to 1 John 1:1–3, and the references to John the Baptist (John 1:6–8, 15) clearly lead into verses 19–42, echoing also Mark 1:1–20. Thus, several approaches to the issue have been advanced over the last century or so.

First, in Rudolf Bultmann's view, the fact that some later Gnostics embraced John the Baptist as a prophetic figure led him to imagine a gnostic origin of the Overture and the Johannine "I am" sayings as originating in a hypothetical Revelation-Sayings Source. Thus, Bultmann saw the Christ hymn as rooted in a written document—along with the Johannine "I am" sayings—to which were added later the references to John the Baptist.[10] However, in my own analyses of Bultmann's diachronic theory of composition, there is no stylistic, contextual, or theological evidence for his inference of alien sources underlying or overlaying the evangelist's work.[11] I do believe the author of the Epistles (John the Elder) served as the final compiler of the Beloved Disciple's work, but, with Raymond Brown, his operation was conservative rather than intrusive, although the later material added (chs. 6, 15–17, 21, etc.) clearly addresses some of the disruptive issues reflected in the epistles.[12]

---

9. The question was raised pivotally by Adolf von Harnack, "Über das Verhältnis des Prologs des vierten Evangeliums zum ganzen Werk," *ZTK* 2 (1892): 189–231.

10. Bultmann, "The History of Religions Background of the Prologue to the Gospel of John," follows Wellhausen in seeing the Baptist references as added later as a means of addressing the interests of later audiences.

11. Anderson, *The Christology of the Fourth Gospel*, 70–136.

12. For an overall theory of John's composition—the first stages being gathered as an augmentation of Mark (ca. 80–85 CE) to which the compiler added the Christ hymn, the eyewitness reference of 19:34–35, chs. 6, 15–17, 21, and perhaps other material after the death of the Beloved Disciple. Paul N. Anderson, "On 'Seamless Robes' and 'Leftover Fragments'—A Theory of Johannine Composition," *Structure, Composition, and Authorship of John's Gospel*, ed. Stanley E. Porter and Hughson Ong, *The Origins of John's Gospel* (Leiden: E.J. Brill, 2015), 169–218. See also this overlooked first-century clue to

Second, in the analysis of C. K. Barrett and others, the content of the Overture can be seen as an overall unity, which also introduces perfectly well what is to follow.[13] Thus, there is no need to infer a diachronic history of the text. Further, as R. Alan Culpepper shows with a chiastic reading of John 1:1–18, the central pivot of the unit is the message that those who believe in Jesus as the Christ become children of God, welcomed into the divine family (vv. 10–13, especially v. 12).[14] This analysis also coincides perfectly with the Gospel's statement of purpose in 20:30–31: "these things are written that you might believe in Jesus as the Christ, the Son of God, and believing, have life in his name" (author's translation). Pushing the synchronicity of the narrative further, Peter J. Williams has argued that John 1:1–18 should not even be called a "Prologue," as interpreters before the modern era did not use such language but simply accorded this text as a part of the overall narrative.[15] Such a view, however, fails to take note of the strophic and hymnic features of the verses, as the full narrative begins in verse 19.

Third, some interpreters have distinguished component parts of verses 1–18, seeing some of them as poetic and others as narratival. Clearly the references to John the Baptist in verses 6–8 and 15 stand out as narrative

---

John's apostolic authorship: Paul N. Anderson, "Acts 4:19–20—An Overlooked First-Century Clue to Johannine Authorship and Luke's Dependence Upon the Johannine Tradition." *Bible and Interpretation*, September, https://bibleinterp.arizona.edu/opeds/acts357920. As I peruse Köstenberger's list of multiple "asides" in John, I wonder if some of these might also have been added by the final compiler, clarifying the work of the evangelist (Köstenberger, *Encountering John*, 231–35).

13. C. K. Barrett, *The Gospel According to St. John: An Introduction with Commentary and Notes on the Greek Text* (Philadelphia: Westminster, 1978); D. A. Carson, *The Gospel According to John*, PNTC (Leicester, UK: Inter-Varsity Press; Grand Rapids: Eerdmans, 1991); Andreas J. Köstenberger, *John*, BECNT (Grand Rapids: Baker Academic, 2004); Köstenberger, *A Theology of John's Gospel and Letters*, BTNT (Grand Rapids: Zondervan Academic, 2009); Köstenberger, *Encountering John*; Gail R. O'Day, *John*, NICB VIII (Nashville: Abingdon, 1995); Craig S. Keener, *The Gospel According to John: A Commentary*, vol. 1 (Peabody, MA: Hendrickson, 2003), and others. See also these monographs, showing how John 1:1–18 introduces fittingly the narrative that follows: Peter M. Philips, *The Prologue of the Fourth Gospel: A Sequential Reading*, LNTS 294 (London: T&T Clark, 2006); Elizabeth Harris, *Prologue and Gospel: The Theology for the Fourth Evangelist*, JSNTSup 107 (London: Bloomsbury, 1994); Edward H. Gerber, *The Scriptural Tale in the Fourth Gospel: With Particular Reference to the Prologue and a Syncretic (Oral and Written) Poetics*, BibInt 146 (Leiden: Brill, 2017).

14. R. Alan Culpepper, "The Pivot of John's Gospel," *NTS* 27 (1980): 1–31. Köstenberger concurs and also sees v. 12 as the central thrust of the Prologue (Köstenberger, *A Theology*, 180), which coheres with his and Carson's view that the main thrust of the Johannine evangel is evangelistic: calling audiences to first-time belief in Jesus as the Jewish Messiah/Christ. Indeed, the witnesses, the signs, and the fulfilled word are designed to lead hearers and readers to life-producing belief (cf. Paul N. Anderson, *Navigating the Living Waters of the Gospel of John: On Wading with Children and Swimming with Elephants*, Pendle Hill Pamphlets #352 (Wallingford: Pendle Hill Press, 2000).

15. Peter J. Williams "Not the Prologue of John," *JSNT* 33, no. 4 (2011): 375–86.

reporting (with a clarification in verse 8), leading into verse 19, where religious leaders from Jerusalem interrogate John, asking if he were Elijah, or the Prophet, or the Christ, which he denies, pointing instead to Jesus. J. Ramsey Michaels poses an interesting thesis, seeing verses 1–5 as a briefer "Preamble" and identifying 1:6–3:36 as the witness of the Baptist to Jesus as the Messiah/Christ.[16] This makes a good deal of sense, as the evangelist declares explicitly that John's ministry is presented as happening alongside that of Jesus *before* John was thrown into prison (3:24, augmenting Mark 1:14 chronologically). However, verses 9–14 and 16–18 of John 1 are also strophic and poetic in their form, so they cannot be ruled out as component parts of a confessional unit.

Most interesting, in my judgment, is the inference of John A. T. Robinson,[17] Barnabas Lindars,[18] and others, that the hymnic material of John 1 was added to the passages heralding John the Baptist's witness (vv. 6–8, 15, 19). In fact, Raymond F. Collins sees the Johannine Christ hymn as the first commentary on the Johannine narrative itself, which was added to the final edition of its composition process, as John's story of Jesus was prepared to be circulated among the churches.[19] This is also the view of Werner H. Kelber, who cites Michael Theobald's 1988 reference to John's opening stanzas as a "*Metareflexion*" upon the spiritual and cosmic meaning of Jesus and his mission, thus deservedly being seen as a "postface," rather than a "preface," in Kelber's view.[20] Or, perhaps musical genres are more fitting than literary ones, if indeed the Christ hymn was used in the worship life of early Christianity.[21] That being the case, perhaps the Johannine Christ hymn should be seen (and sung) as an overture. Also consider that an overture is composed only after all the other musical scores of a piece have been completed. Thus, rather than seeing

---

16. J. Ramsey Michaels, *The Gospel of John*, NICNT (Grand Rapids: Eerdmans, 2010). However, note also the chiastic and poetic features of vv. 9–13, as cited by Morna Hooker, "John the Baptist and the Johannine Prologue," *NTS* 16 (1970): 354–58.

17. John A. T. Robinson, "The Relation of the Prologue to the Gospel of St. John," *NTS* 9 (1963): 120–29; *The Priority of John*, ed. J. F. Coakley (London: SCM, 1985).

18. Barnabas Lindars, *The Gospel of John*, NCB (Grand Rapids: Eerdmans, 1972).

19. Raymond F. Collins, "The Oldest Commentary on the Fourth Gospel," *The Bible Today* 98 (1978): 1769–75.

20. Werner H. Kelber, "The Birth of a Beginning: John 1.1–18," *Semeia* 52 (1990): 120–44.

21. Jan du Rand suggests we might view the Johannine narrative as a symphony, with forward movement and repeated themes along the way; see du Rand, "Reading the Fourth Gospel Like a Literary Symphony," in *What Is John?*, vol. 2, ed. Fernando Segovia, SBLSymS 7 (Atlanta: Society of Biblical Literature, 1998), 5–18. This could also account, in my view, for some of the repetitions and variations in the narrative itself.

the Christ hymn as the basis for the Johannine narrative—a transcendent and cosmic tale of Jesus as the preexistent *Logos* with little to do with mundane places and times—it is best seen as a response to the evangelist's preaching and teaching over the years (as was 1 John 1:1–3), which was added to the narrative as part of its finalization and circulation.

That being the case, what do we make of the abrupt references to John the Baptist in verses 6–8 and 15? Were they added to the hymn, or was the hymn packaged around them? While others might see the references to John the Baptist as added to the Christ hymn, a more plausible inference is to envision verses 6–8 as the original beginning of the second biography of Jesus—as does Helen Bond,[22] who, along with Richard A. Burridge,[23] sees Mark as the first biography of Jesus—perhaps having heard Mark performed among the churches.[24] Morna D. Hooker has also noted telling echoes of Mark 1, suggesting their earlier function rather than later additions.[25] Thus, while John's story of Jesus reflects echoes of Mark, it is not dependent upon Mark for its content. The Fourth Gospel is independently Johannine in its character and origin. Further, as an augmentation of Mark's story of Jesus, the Johannine witness also poses a number of distinctive features, functioning as something of a dialogical corrective along the way. Thus, in beginning with the witness of the Baptist, John 1:6–8, 15, 19–42 provides a complement to Mark 1:1–15, and an alternative to the Elijah reference in Mark 9:13, seeing Jesus as fulfilling biblical typologies.[26] John indeed came announcing and preparing the way for Jesus; however, he was neither the light, nor the prophet, nor Elijah; such

---

22. Helen Bond, *The First Biography of Jesus: Genre and Meaning in Mark's Gospel* (Grand Rapids: Eerdmans, 2020).

23. Richard A. Burridge, *What Are the Gospels? A Comparison with Greco-Roman Biography* (Waco, TX: Baylor University Press, 2020).

24. With Ian D. Mackay, *John's Relationship with Mark: An Analysis of John 6 in the Light of Mark 6–8*, WUNT 2/182 (Tübingen: Mohr Siebeck, 2004), who sees the Johannine evangelist's familiarity with Mark involving hearing it performed among the churches. Thus, the Markan-Johannine relationship is not a function of text-dependency; it is more a factor of oral-aural dialectics (Paul N. Anderson, "Mark and John—the *Bi-Optic* Gospels," in *Jesus in Johannine Tradition*, ed. Robert T. Fortna and Tom Thatcher (Louisville: Westminster/John Knox Press, 2001), 175–88; Anderson, "Mark, John, and Answerability: Interfluentiality and Dialectic between the Second and Fourth Gospels," *Liber Annuus* 63 (2013): 197–245.

25. Morna D. Hooker, "John the Baptist and the Johannine Prologue," *NTS* 16 (1970): 354–58; "The Johannine Prologue and the Messianic Secret," *NTS* 21 (1974): 40–58.

26. Paul N. Anderson, "Jesus, the Eschatological Prophet in the Fourth Gospel: A Case Study in John's Dialectical Tensions," in *Reading the Gospel of John's Christology as Jewish Messianism: Royal, Prophetic, and Divine Messiahs*, ed. Ben Reynolds and Gabriele Boccaccini, AJEC 106 (Leiden: Brill, 2018), 271–99.

roles, in Johannine perspective, are reserved for Jesus. Thus, the original beginning of the Johannine narrative was likely as follows (vv. 6–8, 15, 19–23 NRSVUE):

> There was a man sent from God whose name was John. He came as a witness to testify to the light, so that all might believe through him (he himself was not the light, but he came to testify to the light). . . .

> John testified to him and cried out, "This was he of whom I said, 'He who comes after me ranks ahead of me because he was before me.'" . . .

> This is the testimony given by John when the Jews sent priests and Levites from Jerusalem to ask him, "Who are you?" **He confessed and did not deny it, but he confessed,** "I am not the Messiah."

> And they asked him, "What then? Are you Elijah?" He said, "I am not." "Are you the prophet?" He answered, "No." Then they said to him, "Who are you? Let us have an answer for those who sent us. What do you say about yourself?" He said [citing Isaiah 40:3],

>> "I am the voice of one crying out in the wilderness, 'Make straight the way of the Lord.'"

Given that Mark 1:1–5 heralds the witness of the baptizer, John 1:6–7 augments that theme, while also clarifying that John came to bear witness to the light, but he was not the light (v. 8). And, as Mark 1:7 notes John's witness that Jesus came after him, John 1:15 clarifies that while Jesus came after John *chronologically*, he was before him in terms of *prominence*. One can even imagine verses 1–3 expanding the precedence of Christ cosmologically as an ontological embellishment of that theme by the Johannine worship leaders. John's baptizing with water, versus Jesus's baptizing with the Holy Spirit in Mark 1:8 is also echoed in John 1:33 (also bolstered by Matthew 3:11 and Luke 3:16). And, while Mark's report begins *after* John has been thrown into prison (Mark 1:14), the Johannine account claims to report events that happened *before* John was thrown into prison (John 3:24). Thus, along with chapters 6, 15–17, and 21 (as well as a few clarifying insertions), the Johannine Christ hymn appears to have been packaged around the narrative's original beginning, which was designed as a dialogical complement to Mark, both chronologically and geographically.

2. THE JOHANNINE PROLOGUES AS RESPONSES TO THE EVANGELIST'S NARRATION

In terms of its content and vocabulary, the Johannine Christ hymn is most similar to the Prologue of 1 John 1:1–3, which is introduced as the Elder's edifying purpose in verse 4. That being the case, the origin and character of the epistle's opening may well suggest something similar to that of the Gospel, as both appear to have originated first as responses to the evangelist's narrative ministry. To begin with, 1 John 1:1–3 reflects the Elder's appreciation for the witness of the Johannine evangelist over the years (John 19:34–35; 21:20–24), although he may also have his own content to convey, as one claiming likewise to be among the eyewitness generation.[27] Among the dozens of contacts between the Johannine Epistles and Gospel, some of them clearly reflect familiarity with and the echoing of the evangelist's teaching ministry over the years. These include the reference to the "new commandment"—to love one another—mentioned by Jesus in John 13:34, which by the time 1 John 2:7 is written has become the "old commandment," which they have heard from the beginning; the injunction to abide in Christ in John 15:4–7 is claimed by community members in 1 John 2:6; and assertions that those who walk in the light do not walk in darkness (John 8:12; 12:35) are referenced in 1 John 1:6–7; 2:9. Thus, 1 John clearly reflects familiarity with the evangelist's witness, even if it was finalized later.[28]

Note, however the especially clear contacts between the Johannine narrative and the Elder's introduction to the first Johannine Epistle. Not only do these contacts reflect familiarity with the evangelist's narration;

---

27. Indeed, the Elder and the Beloved Disciple may well have been eyewitnesses. See Paul N. Anderson, "The Son of Zebedee and the Fourth Gospel: Some Clues on John's Authorship and the State of the Johannine Question," in *El Evangelio de Juan. Origen, Contenido, Perspectivas—The Gospel of John. Origin, Content, Perspectives*, Colección Teología Hoy No. 80, ed. Bernardo Estrada and Luis Guillermo Sarasa (Bogota: Editorial Pontificia Universidad Javeriana / Studiorum Novi Testamenti Societas, 2018), 17–82 and 241–49.

28. Building on the work of Raymond Brown, here, see Paul N. Anderson, "The Community That Raymond Brown Left Behind—Reflections on the Dialectical Johannine Situation," in *Communities in Dispute: Current Scholarship on the Johannine Epistles*, ed. Paul N. Anderson and R. Alan Culpepper, Early Christianity and its Literature 13 (Atlanta: SBL Press, 2014), 47–94.

they also connect with audiences' familiarity with the Johannine witness over the years.

- Jesus declares what he has heard from the Father, and the Spirit declares what is from Jesus → the Elder declares what was from the beginning (John 8:26, 38; 13:21; 16:13–15 → 1 John 1:1–4)
- Jesus knew things and people from the beginning → the Elder testifies to what was and what people have known from the beginning (John 6:64; 8:44; 15:27; 16:4 → 1 John 1:1; 2:7, 13–14, 24; 3:11)
- The Son testifies to what he has seen and heard → the Elder testifies to what he and others have seen and heard (John 3:32 → 1 John 1:1, 3; cf. also Acts 4:19–20, where John the apostle testifies to what he and others have seen and heard)
- Thomas demands to see and touch the fleshwounds of the risen Lord → the Elder attests to what believers have looked at and touched with their hands (John 20:24–29 → 1 John 1:1)
- The words of Jesus are life-producing → the Elder witnesses to the word of life (John 5:24; 6:63, 68 → 1 John 1:1)
- Jesus testifies to what he has seen → the Elder testifies to what has been seen—the life revealed (John 3:11 → 1 John 1:2)
- Jesus has come that people might receive eternal life → the Elder declares eternal life to his audiences (John 3:15–16, 36; 5:25; 6:40, 47; 10:28; 17:1–3 → 1 John 1:2)
- The life the Father gives is manifested to the world → the Father's eternal life is revealed to us (John 5:21, 26 → 1 John 1:2)
- Those who keep the Son's word will be loved by the Father, and the Father and the Son will make their home with them → to have fellowship with believers is to enjoy fellowship with the Father and the Son (John 14:23 → 1 John 1:3)

If the Prologue to 1 John reflects familiarity with the evangelist's witness, though, might the Christ hymn also reflect the same? Indeed, the Johannine Christ hymn introduces the completed Gospel well, but such likely does not reflect a later composition only—theologically and cosmologically oriented—over and against the more mundane features of the narrative, eclipsing Johannine historicity. Indeed, John's story of Jesus deserves to be seen as "the mundane gospel," not simply "the spiritual gospel."[29] That being the case, note how the elements of the Christ hymn echo—as well as introduce—key elements of the narrative.

- The Son is one with the Father → the Word was with God, and the Word was God (John 10:30 → 1:1–2)
- As light of the world, all who follow him will receive life → in him was life, and the life was the light of all humanity (John 8:12 → 1:4)
- Believers are liberated from darkness by the light → the light overcomes darkness (John 11:9; 12:46 → 1:5)
- Jesus is come as the light of the world → the light that enlightens all was coming into the world (John 9:5 → 1:9)
- The world does not know the Father or the Son → though he made the world, the world did not know him (John 16:3; 17:25 → 1:10)
- Jewish leaders do not receive Jesus's testimony → he came unto his own, but they did not receive him (John 3:11 → 1:11)
- Those who believe become children of light → those who believe become children of God (John 12:36 → 1:12)
- People must be born from above and of the Spirit → being born of the divine—not human—initiative is key (John 3:3, 6 → 1:13)
- In the tangible ministry of Jesus his glory is revealed → in the incarnation of the Word is God's glory revealed (John 2:11; 11:4 → 1:14)
- While Moses gave the Law, he also wrote of Jesus as the way, and the life → while the Law came from Moses, grace and truth came from Jesus (John 1:45; 5:46; 7:19; 14:6 → 1:16)
- No one has ever seen God, but the Son has revealed the Father → no one has seen God at any time, but the only begotten God at the Father's side has revealed him (John 6:46 → 1:18)

Again, these features introduce the narrative fully, but, if inquiring about their origin—assuming that the Johannine narrative developed over a period of at least five decades before being rendered in a preliminary edition or stage of development—it requires little imagination to see the Johannine Christ hymn as developing first as a confessional affirmation

---

29. Paul N. Anderson, "John: The Mundane Gospel and Its Archaelogy-Related Features," *The Bible and Interpretation* (July 2020): https://bibleinterp.arizona.edu/articles/john-mundane-gospel-and-its-archaeology-related-features.

of John's story of Jesus, which it then introduces in service to its finalization and circulation. Thus, as the Prologue of the first Johannine Epistle developed as the Elder's affirmation of the evangelist's witness, so did the Johannine Christ hymn. It also need not have been written by the Fourth Evangelist to serve as an engaging introduction to his work, finalized after his death by the Elder (John 21:20–24).

As confessional compositions, the two Johannine prologues serve experientially preparative functions. Especially if audiences are somewhat familiar with any of their features, one can imagine their joining in with reciting a familiar chorus inwardly or otherwise, taking in a participatory appetizer, enhancing receptivity to the content that follows.[30] As a stand-alone confession, of course, the Johannine Christ hymn would have been complete, in and of itself, but from a literary standpoint, its inclusion as a launchpad for the Johannine witness insured its preservation over the centuries as one of the most significant and influential compositions in world history. Note also the poetic and strophic features of both Johannine prologues.

3. CONFESSIONAL FEATURES OF THE JOHANNINE PROLOGUES

In reviewing the Prologue to the first Johannine Epistle, several things become clear. First, the first- and second-person plural references are multiple, suggesting corporate settings. What "we" have experienced, we declare to "you," so that you might have fellowship with us, whose fellowship is with the Father and his Son, Jesus Christ. Its pronouns are not singular—individualistic; they are plural and corporate. First John 1:1–3 is a confession emerging from one community, appealing to other audiences, inviting them to join them in fellowship, participating also in their embrace of the Father and the Son, so that their joy might be fulfilled (v. 4).

Second, appeals are made to firsthand encounter: what we have seen and heard—what we have seen with our eyes and touched with our hands—concerning the Word of life. Thus, the memory of what was revealed from the beginning is passed along from first generation Jesus-followers to later audiences in distant places, connecting apostolic witness with later generations as part of the Johannine legacy.

---

30. Argued more fully in Paul N. Anderson, "On Guessing Points and Naming Stars—The Epistemological Origins of John's Christological Tensions," in *The Gospel of St. John and Christian Theology*, ed. Richard Bauckham and Carl Mosser (Grand Rapids: Eerdmans, 2007), 311–45.

The Christ Hymn of John 1: From Confessional Response to Transformative Overture

Third, note the strophic character of 1 John's Prologue. Within these three verses, a lead statement is followed by four qualifying phrases, a quatrain, in which the fourth phrase introduces a new element that leads into the next verse. This reflects a strophic pattern: A, B, B, B, C (v. 1), followed by C', D, D, D, E (v. 2), followed by E', F, F, F, G (v. 3). Thus, each verse leads into the next, and the overall confession introduces the circular, leading into the Elder's characteristic hope that his audience's joy will be complete (v. 4; 2 John 12). It is also likely that this hymnic confession would have been familiar to audiences as the Elder's first epistle was circulated among the churches, whereas 2 John was written to a single community, and 3 John was written to an individual.

> We declare to you what was from the beginning:
>> what we have heard,
>> what we have seen with our eyes,
>> what we have looked at and touched with our hands,
>> concerning the word of life.
>
> This life was revealed,
>> and we have seen it
>> and testify to it
>> and declare to you the eternal life:
>> that was with the Father and was revealed to us.
>
> What we have seen and heard
>> we also declare to you
>> so that you also may have fellowship with us,
>> and truly our fellowship is with the Father
>> and with his Son Jesus Christ (NRSVUE).

The symmetry is even more pronounced in the Greek:

Ὁ ἦν ἀπ᾽ ἀρχῆς,
  ὃ ἀκηκόαμεν,
  ὃ ἑωράκαμεν τοῖς ὀφθαλμοῖς ἡμῶν,
  ὃ ἐθεασάμεθα καὶ αἱ χεῖρες ἡμῶν ἐψηλάφησαν,
  περὶ τοῦ λόγου τῆς ζωῆς—

καὶ ἡ ζωὴ ἐφανερώθη,
  καὶ ἑωράκαμεν
  καὶ μαρτυροῦμεν
  καὶ ἀπαγγέλλομεν ὑμῖν τὴν ζωὴν τὴν αἰώνιον
  ἥτις ἦν πρὸς τὸν πατέρα καὶ ἐφανερώθη ἡμῖν—

ὃ ἑωράκαμεν καὶ ἀκηκόαμεν
  ἀπαγγέλλομεν καὶ ὑμῖν,
  ἵνα καὶ ὑμεῖς κοινωνίαν ἔχητε μεθ᾽ ἡμῶν·
  καὶ ἡ κοινωνία δὲ ἡ ἡμετέρα μετὰ τοῦ πατρὸς
  καὶ μετὰ τοῦ υἱοῦ αὐτοῦ Ἰησοῦ Χριστοῦ·

Therefore, it is clear that 1 John 1:1–4 introduces the epistle from at least one community to others, serving as a circular that was read among the churches of the region. Like the letters of Christ to the churches in Revelation 2–3, the first Johannine Epistle was likely circulated and read among the house-churches of Asia Minor in the later decades of the first century CE, calling for right beliefs and right actions, as well.

The Johannine Gospel also shows evidence of being prepared for such circulation among the churches, and with Richard Bauckham on this score, the Elder has prepared John's story of Jesus to be received among the churches, not just for a single community.[31] Thus, modifying Brown's good work, the Johannine Evangel was likely written *from* at least one community, but not narrowly *for* only one community.[32] If anything, its first stages of development reflect an augmentation and modest corrective of Mark—which likely preceded the writing of the epistles chronologically—and the Elder's finalization of the Beloved Disciple's witness after his death (around 100 CE) reflects harmonization with Matthew and Luke, as well as Mark. John's first ending (20:30–31) defends its autonomy over and against Mark, and its second ending defends its selectivity over and against the other Gospels as well (21:20–25).[33]

---

31. Richard Bauckham, "John for Readers of Mark," in *The Gospel for All Christians: Rethinking the Gospel Audiences,* ed. Richard Bauckham (Grand Rapids: Eerdmans, 1998), 147–71.
32. Raymond E. Brown, *The Community of the Beloved Disciple* (New York: Paulist Press, 1979).
33. Paul N. Anderson, "On 'Seamless Robes' and 'Leftover Fragments'—A Theory of Johannine Composition," in *The Origins of John's Gospel*, ed. Stanley E. Porter and Hughson Ong, vol. 2 of Johannine Studies (Leiden: Brill, 2015), 169–218.

In comparison with the Prologue to 1 John, the Christ hymn of John 1 shows a number of similarities and differences. First, the first-person plural language as to what "we" have beheld and experienced carries over in its testimonial way, but missing is second-person plural language, addressed to specific audiences: "you" or other direct references to others. In that sense, the Johannine Gospel's crafting is designed for more general circulation among the churches—including familiar communities, but not limited to them. Thus, it is crafted to be a universal and public witness rather than a local, sectarian document.

Second, like the opening of the Epistle, the Johannine Christ hymn also appeals to firsthand encounter with the Jesus of history, not simply the Christ of faith. Even more specifically, the author claims to have encountered divine glory in the beholding of the flesh-becoming-Word, full of grace and truth (1:14). And such glory is that of the only begotten Son of the Father, which attests to the fleshly humanity of Jesus, not simply the divinity of Christ. The light of life is thus not a disembodied means of ideational illumination; it is embodied in the physical presence and ministry of Jesus, to which the Johannine leaders attest, countering those who might be claiming that Jesus was so divine that he did not come in the flesh (1 John 4:1–3).

Third, the strophic design of the Johannine Christ hymn as we have it, packaged around the witness of John the Baptist, is less uniform in its structuring than 1 John 1:1–3, although its strophic form is still pronounced, nonetheless. Instead of quatrain phrases following an assertion, however, the Johannine Christ hymn as it stands reflects lead statements that are followed by couplets and tercets, a few quatrains, and even a sestet at the end (depending on how one breaks the phrases, of course). The pattern is thus A, B, B and A, B, B, B, involving the development of themes in progressive ways. It could also be that we have here an adaptation of a fuller hymnic unit with a more consistent meter, but the strophic character of the Christ hymn is perfectly engaging as it is. Whatever the case, most likely is the possibility that regional audiences would have been familiar with the narrative's opening confession, as it clearly served as an experientially engaging worship piece designed to involve hearers transformingly in the content they were about to receive.

4. THE THREE STANZAS OF THE JOHANNINE CHRIST HYMN

As a confessional response to the Johannine witness over the years within the evolving Johannine situation, the three stanzas of the Christ hymn move from (a) broader, cosmological perspectives to (b) reflections on the movement's history to (c) an articulation of the gospel message itself. And as a revised introduction to the Johannine Gospel, it reveals a move beyond an augmentation of Mark to a larger, cross-cultural and inter-faith interest, sounding the good news of God's saving-revealing action in the works and witness of Jesus as a means of extending the blessings of Abraham and Moses to the diverse families of the Mediterranean world.[34] Thus, the Johannine Christ hymn poses a universal and inclusive appeal, inviting audiences to receive in faith the Jewish Messiah—Christ Jesus of Nazareth—as a means of being welcomed into the divine family.

Outreach, however, was not the only function of the Johannine Christ hymn; its thrust was also highly political. The christological hymns of the New Testament also served a religio-political function, in pushing back against the Roman imperial cult of the mid-to-late first century CE. As Jewish resistance literature, the hymnic confessions of John 1:1–5, 9–14, 16–18, Philippians 2:6–11, Colossians 1:15–20, and Hebrews 1:1–4, and functioned to push back in faithful solidarity against imperial hegemony.[35] Thus, it is neither the divine Julius nor Augustus, nor is it Caligula, Nero, or Domitian, who deserved veneration; it is Christ alone, who has put worldly powers under his feet. Appropriating Psalm 110:1 (the most oft-quoted Hebrew Scripture verse in the New Testament) in a number of ways, God's triumphal action in the death and resurrection of Christ Jesus asserts confidence in the eschatological, world-redeeming initiative of God, bringing hope for humanity and the dawning of the new age.

That being the case, note the progressive development of themes between the three stanzas of the Johannine Christ hymn, moving from cosmic claims, to community memories, to continued outreach.

4.1 Stanza 1: The Cosmic Advent of the Divine Word (vv. 1–5)

The opening stanza of the Johannine Christ hymn begins with the relation of the preexistent *Logos* to God. The *Logos* was with God, and the

---

34. C. H. Dodd, *The Interpretation of the Fourth Gospel* (Cambridge: Cambridge University Press, 1953) and others, John 1:1–18 clearly connects John's story of Jesus with the cosmological worldviews of Hellenistic audiences, drawing in themes from Heraclitus, Stoics, and Philo as well as such Jewish texts as Genesis 1;, Proverbs 8:22–30;, Deuteronomy 18:15–18; and Exodus 33–34.

35. See Paul N. Anderson, "The Johannine *Logos*-Hymn: A Cross-Cultural Celebration of God's Creative-Redemptive Work," in *Creation Stories in Dialogue: The Bible, Science, and Folk Traditions*, Radboud Prestige Lecture Series by Alan Culpepper, ed. R. Alan Culpepper and Jan van der Watt, BibInt 139 (Leiden: Brill, 2016), 219–42.

Logos was God. He is the creative source of all things and the originator of life and light, which darkness neither comprehends nor overtakes. In that sense, the contributions of the fifth-century BCE philosopher of Ephesus, Heraclitus, would have evoked resonance with the Johannine Prologue among audiences of Asia Minor and beyond. In the view of Heraclitus, the cosmos is in flux; the one thing certain is change. One cannot step into a moving stream twice in the same place; the water has moved on. At the origin of God's creative activity is the divine spark, which is the source of life itself. While creation involves flux, however, that which holds things together is the divine *Logos*, which as a principle of reason is available to all humanity. These teachings bolstered the love of truth in Greek philosophical traditions, and his work was especially picked up by Cicero and the Stoics, developed further by Philo of Alexandria.

In Philo's work, the character of God's creative *Logos* is not merely a philosophical construct; rather, it roots in God's creative work in Genesis 1. It is by neither violence nor force that the ordered cosmos came into being; it is by the creative Word of God that the cosmos derives both its origin and its ordering. Likewise, in Hebrew thought, the delivered word of the patriarch or the prophet—as well as the word of the Lord—changes reality as it goes forth from the speaker. In the delivery of Isaac's blessing, Jacob is irreversibly blessed rather than Esau (Gen. 27), and the prophetic word of Micaiah ben Imlah comes true, even against the designs of King Ahab and his court prophets, who assured the king falsely of success against the enemy (1 Kings 22). Thus, the Jewish background behind the advent of the Son as the divine *Logos* would have resonated with Jewish audiences as well as non-Jewish ones, and one can even imagine the ministry of Apollos of Alexandria in Ephesus advancing such christological connections with Heraclitus, Genesis, and Philo (cf. Acts 18:24–28).[36] The Christ hymn of Hebrews 1:1–4 likewise furthers such connections, linking the God who has spoken in many times and many ways with God's Son, appointed now as heir of all things.

A further point and set of connections deserve mention here as well. In addition to being the ordering source of creation, the divine *Logos* is also the source of life and light for all humanity. And indeed, the power

---

36. See, for instance, the monograph of Craig Evans, *Word and Glory: On the Exegetical and Theological Background of John's Prologue*, JSNTSup 89 (Sheffield: Sheffield Academic Press, 1993), which demonstrates the centrality of the Jewish sending-motif (*Shaliach*) in the Johannine Prologue, translated into Hellenistic-friendly terms for the benefit of Diaspora audiences.

of light speaks for itself, as darkness is extinguished by its mere glimmer. Note also the universal reach of the Light. It is availed to all people, and the darkness can neither grasp nor overcome it. These insights (vv. 4–5) set the stage well for the narrative that follows. First, all people have access to God's saving-revealing activity in the advent of the *Logos* as the life and light of God. Second, despite the throes and wiles of darkness, God's saving-revealing action will finally triumph; in the following narrative, the resurrection of Jesus has the last word. Third, those who are in the dark are exposed by their miscomprehension in the narrative. And, with Bakhtin, stupidity in narrative is always rhetorical. So, reader beware: you don't want to miscomprehend the witness of the Revealer, as do the unbelieving actants in the narrative; so be ready to get it right, both in perception and in the existential response of faith to the divine initiative in the story that follows.

Note here the strophic character of the first stanza of the Johannine Christ hymn:

"The Cosmic Advent of the Divine Word"

In the beginning was the Word,
    and the Word was with God,
    and the Word was God.
    He was in the beginning with God.
All things came into being through him,
    and without him not one thing came into being—what has come
    into being.
In him was life,
    and the life was the light of all people.
    The light shines in the darkness,
    and the darkness did not overtake it.

Ἐν ἀρχῇ ἦν ὁ λόγος,
    καὶ ὁ λόγος ἦν πρὸς τὸν θεόν,
    καὶ θεὸς ἦν ὁ λόγος.
    οὗτος ἦν ἐν ἀρχῇ πρὸς τὸν θεόν.
πάντα δι' αὐτοῦ ἐγένετο,
    καὶ χωρὶς αὐτοῦ ἐγένετο οὐδὲ ἕν.
ὃ γέγονεν ἐν αὐτῷ ζωὴ ἦν,

καὶ ἡ ζωὴ ἦν τὸ φῶς τῶν ἀνθρώπων·
καὶ τὸ φῶς ἐν τῇ σκοτίᾳ φαίνει,
καὶ ἡ σκοτία αὐτὸ οὐ κατέλαβεν.

4.2 Stanza 2: The Uneven Reception of the Divine Initiative (vv. 9–13)

In addition to declaring what has been from the beginning, the Johannine Christ hymn recounts the history of the Word's and the Light's reception, which was uneven during the ministry of Jesus and has continued to be so in the interim. Certainly, the Johannine memory rings true, that the Galilean Prophet—like John the Baptist, his forerunner—was embraced by the Jewish populace while also being rejected by threatened magistrates and leaders. An overlooked fact is that despite the Judean leaders' plotting the death of Jesus and handing him over to the Romans to be crucified, many of the Judeans (or "Jews") also believed in Jesus, as declared explicitly in John 8:31 (cf. also 2:23; 7:31; 8:31; 9:38; 10:42; 11:45; 12:42). John is *not* anti-Jewish.[37] In addition, as a corrective to Mark 6:1–6, not everyone in Galilee refused to honor the hometown prophet; indeed, even Samaritans and Galileans believed in Jesus (John 4:1–45). Thus, in addition to augmenting Mark, the Johannine evangelist also poses a dialectically alternative presentation of Jesus and his ministry rooted in historical memory, not spiritualizing flourishes overall.[38]

Still within the earlier phases of the Johannine tradition (30–70 CE), followers of John the Baptist would have been pointed to Jesus by the memory of their leader, whose joy is fulfilled by the increase of Jesus and his own diminishment (3:27–30)—a bit of friendly competition. That thrust would likely have the later phases of the Johannine situation in Asia Minor (70–100 CE) if there were still followers of the Baptist in Ephesus as referenced by Acts 18–19, and a new set of tensions likely emerged with leaders of local synagogues in post-70 Judaism. Telling are the three references to followers of Jesus being expelled from synagogues for confessing Jesus openly (John 9:22; 12:42; 16:2), and by the time

---

37. Some Judean leaders oppose Jesus (not all), and none of the general references to Judaism or Israel are negative. Paul N. Anderson, "Anti-Semitism and Religious Violence as Flawed Interpretations of the Gospel of John," in *John and Judaism: A Contested Relationship in Context*, ed. R. Alan Culpepper and Paul N. Anderson, Resources for Biblical Study 87 (Atlanta: SBL Press, 2017), 265–311. A longer edition published on *The Bible and Interpretation*, October 2017, https://bibleinterp.arizona.edu/articles/2017/10/and418017.

38. Paul N. Anderson, "Mark, John, and Answerability: Interfluentiality and Dialectic between the Second and Fourth Gospels," *Liber Annuus* 63 (2013): 197–245.

that 1 John 2:18–25 is written, it appears that some members of Johannine Christianity have departed and rejoined local synagogues. Nonetheless, the evangelist's witness points to the signifying works of Jesus, compelling testimonies, and fulfilled words showing that Jesus really is the Jewish Messiah/Christ, availing life to those who believe in his name (John 1:9–13; 20:31).[39]

Note, however, the universalism of the second stanza. The saving-revealing light of God, which is accessible to all humanity, has now come into the world. Yet revelation demands a believing response: will humans respond receptively to the divine initiative, or not? Such is the existential question that revelation precipitates. Here the universalist teaching of Heraclitus is referenced with irony, as the ordering and life-producing work of the divine *Logos* is availed to all, but not all are receptive to the gift. Despite his having created the world, the world fails to recognize its own Ground and Source of Being and Life. Nonetheless, as many as receive the Revealer receive also the gift of adoption into the divine family, born not of human initiative or schemes, but born of God. This theme in the narrative will account for receptions and rejections of Jesus alike. People who know the Father recognize also the Son; those rejecting the Son either are thus not abiding in a knowing relationship with the Father, they oppose the truth, or they love the praise of humans over the glory of God.

"The Uneven Reception of the Divine Initiative"

The true light,
> which enlightens everyone,
> was coming into the world.
He was in the world,
> and the world came into being through him,
> yet the world did not know him.
He came to what was his own,
> and his own people did not accept him.

---

39. Paul N. Anderson, "The Having-Sent-Me Father—Aspects of Agency, Encounter, and Irony in the Johannine Father-Son Relationship," *Semeia* 85 (1999), 33–57. For a longitudinal view of the Johannine dialectical situation, cf. Paul N. Anderson, "Bakhtin's Dialogism and the Corrective Rhetoric of the Johannine Misunderstanding Dialogue: Exposing Seven Crises in the Johannine Situation," in *Bakhtin and Genre Theory in Biblical Studies*, Semeia Studies 63, ed. Roland Boer (Atlanta: SBL Press, 2007), 133–59.

But to all who received him,
>who believed in his name,
>he gave power to become children of God,
>who were born, not of blood
>or of the will of the flesh
>or of the will of man,
>but of God.

ἦν τὸ φῶς τὸ ἀληθινὸν
>ὃ φωτίζει πάντα ἄνθρωπον
>ἐρχόμενον εἰς τὸν κόσμον.
Ἐν τῷ κόσμῳ ἦν,
>καὶ ὁ κόσμος δι' αὐτοῦ ἐγένετο,
>καὶ ὁ κόσμος αὐτὸν οὐκ ἔγνω.
εἰς τὰ ἴδια ἦλθεν,
>καὶ οἱ ἴδιοι αὐτὸν οὐ παρέλαβον.
ὅσοι δὲ ἔλαβον αὐτόν,
>ἔδωκεν αὐτοῖς ἐξουσίαν τέκνα θεοῦ γενέσθαι,
>τοῖς πιστεύουσιν εἰς τὸ ὄνομα αὐτοῦ,
>οἳ οὐκ ἐξ αἱμάτων
>οὐδὲ ἐκ θελήματος σαρκὸς
>οὐδὲ ἐκ θελήματος ἀνδρὸς
>ἀλλ' ἐκ θεοῦ ἐγεννήθησαν.

4.3 Stanza 3: The Father's Glory, Grace, and Truth Revealed (vv. 14, 16–18)

The third stanza of the Johannine Christ hymn attests to having encountered the Father's glory, grace, and truth in the fleshly ministry of Jesus. Here, the firsthand witness of the Beloved Disciple is also attested by communities of believers who not only embrace his witness, but now profess firsthand encounter as well. Certainly, this can happen as a factor of spiritual visitation in a meeting for worship or otherwise; but, as the Elder professes, there may be more than one eyewitness in the Johannine trajectory, and the tabernacled dwelling of the divine *Logos* among humans is professed to be the place—the eschatological *topos*—in which the shekinah glory of God is encountered. Further, in combatting traveling ministers who deny the fleshly suffering and existence of Jesus (1 John 4:1–3; 2 John 7), it is in the Word becoming flesh that God's glory is most powerfully known. Thus, the eyewitness of John 19:34–35 attests not to the divinity of Christ Jesus, but to the water-and-blood humanity of Jesus as the Christ.

And, grace upon grace is received through Christ, who, as the Eschatological Prophet predicted by Moses (Deut. 18:15–22), provides grace and truth as a means of fulfilling the Law. Within the Johannine narrative, Jesus is accused of breaking Sabbath laws by healing on the Sabbath, and yet religious leaders fail to appreciate the healing of the lame man because they do not have God's love in their hearts (John 5:42). Likewise, religious leaders fail to celebrate the healing of the blind man because in their legal ways of thinking; they claim to see, when it is actually they who are blind (9:41). When challenged as to his authorization, Jesus claims the Mosaic agency schema as the basis for his loving and grace-filled ministries, and in the evangelist's perspective, these grace-filled healings actually fulfill the gracious Law of Moses rather than breaking it. Thus, grace follows grace, as the Johannine Jesus truly puts into play a profound understanding of how God can be loved supremely and how one's neighbor is loved redemptively.

As the way, the truth, and the life (14:6), the Father's loving character is truly revealed by the ways Jesus loved his own unto the end (13:1), and indeed no one has greater love than to lay down one's life for one's friends (15:12–17). However, Jesus as the only way to the Father is not a feature of exclusivism, countering diametrically the universality of the saving light of Christ declared in John 1:9. If asked why the Son is the only way to the Father, John 1:18 and 6:44–46 provide the answer. No one has seen God at any time; it is only the Son who reveals the full truth of God's character, being, and love. Thus, no one *can* come—not *may* come—to the Father except by being drawn by God's saving-revealing initiative, which Jesus as the Christ eschatologically is and does. Human initiative cannot suffice; the only hope for humanity is the divine initiative, which Jesus declares and even embodies. Jesus therefore reveals the true character of the Father, and through that eschatological, time-changing revelation is liberating truth availed to the world (8:31–32).

"The Father's Glory, Grace, and Truth"

And the Word became flesh and lived among us,
    and we have seen his glory,
    the glory as of a father's only son,
    full of grace and truth.

From his fullness we have all received,
> grace upon grace.
> The law indeed was given through Moses;
> grace and truth came through Jesus Christ.
No one has ever seen God.
> It is the only Son, himself God,
> who is close to the Father's heart,
> who has made him known.

> Καὶ ὁ λόγος σὰρξ ἐγένετο καὶ ἐσκήνωσεν ἐν ἡμῖν,
> > καὶ ἐθεασάμεθα τὴν δόξαν αὐτοῦ,
> > δόξαν ὡς μονογενοῦς παρὰ πατρός,
> > πλήρης χάριτος καὶ ἀληθείας·
> ᴵὅτι ἐκ τοῦ πληρώματος αὐτοῦ ἡμεῖς πάντες ἐλάβομεν,
> > καὶ χάριν ἀντὶ χάριτος·
> > ὅτι ὁ νόμος διὰ Μωϋσέως ἐδόθη,
> > ἡ χάρις καὶ ἡ ἀλήθεια διὰ Ἰησοῦ Χριστοῦ ἐγένετο.
> θεὸν οὐδεὶς ἑώρακεν πώποτε·
> > μονογενὴς θεὸς
> > ὁ ὢν εἰς τὸν κόλπον τοῦ πατρὸς
> > ἐκεῖνος ἐξηγήσατο.

5. FROM TRANSFORMING ENCOUNTER TO CHRISTOLOGICAL CONFESSION, AND BACK AGAIN

While critical scholars of the modern era have discounted the historicity of Johannine witness because it is theologically imbued and distinctively presented, these represent flawed ways of conducting historical inquiry. Every memory worth retaining is pondered and reflected upon precisely because of meaning, and such is always a subjective enterprise. Further, the Johannine memory of Jesus reflects the Beloved Disciple's putting the teachings and ministry of Jesus into his own words over the years, and rather than involving a corruption of historicity, such reflects an integration of the historic past with emerging historical situations. Nor is the Johannine account founded upon alien sources (a la Bultmann and Fortna) or spiritualized expansions upon Mark or the Synoptics (a la Barrett and the Leuven School). Every contact shared between John and Mark is different, and 85 percent of the Johannine narrative has no Synoptic parallel. Thus, John's story of Jesus is rooted in an autonomous reflection upon the ministry of Jesus, developed first as a somewhat corrective augmentation of Mark, and finalized later by the Elder as a harmonized complement to and engagement of the Synoptics.[40]

The Johannine witness, though, appeals to transformative encounter with Christ on a number of levels. From the latest stages to earlier ones, the Holy Spirit—the Spirit of Truth—guides people into truth, bringing to mind in relevant ways the memory of Jesus and his teachings. Before that, the risen Christ appears to the disciples on the shore, to Thomas, to the faithful in the upper room, and to Mary Magdalene in the garden. During the reported ministry of Jesus, transformative encounter is reported by the woman at the well, by Nathanael, and by others. Might it also be a subtle reference to the Transfiguration, as is 2 Peter 1:16–18? Stranger things have happened. Whatever the case, these transformative reports in John's narrative are the sorts of encounters referenced in John 1:14, whereby God's glory is encountered in the physical deeds and presence of Jesus of Nazareth, continuing further in the ministry of the Holy Spirit. And the narration of such by the evangelist has provided the basis for the composition of the Johannine Christ hymn, as the witness to how Jesus has been encountered in the past becomes the basis for christological confessions in the future.

In that sense, transformative spiritual encounter in the Johannine teaching has led to the articulation of faith-based confessions, leading up to the development of a three-stanza Christ hymn. And, like the first Johannine Epistle, the Johannine Overture prepares hearers and readers experientially to be receptive to the content of the narrative that follows. That being the case, transformative encounter has led to the opening christological confession of the finalized Johannine Gospel, which is designed to lead audiences back into the essence of firsthand religious experience, whence the Johannine narrative originated. Thus, from transformative encounter, to hymnic christological confession, and back again reflects the origin, character, and design of the Johannine Christ hymn. And, if embraced accordingly, transformative encounter continues—the essence of salvific and redemptive faith itself.

---

40. For an overall theory of Johannine composition, see Anderson, "On Guessing Points and Naming Stars," 311–45.

CONCLUSION

Like the Prologue of 1 John, the Christ hymn of John 1 developed first as a confessional response by Johannine believers to the evangelist's teachings and witness over the years. The Johannine Christ hymn, though, was not the first stroke of the evangelist's quill—eclipsing all grounded and historical elements in the Johannine narrative because of an all-consuming cosmic and theological perspective. No. Such relates to the later reflections of Johannine believers upon the Beloved Disciple's witness over the years, as well as other reports, whereby a confessional affirmation of the Johannine account has developed as a three-stanza hymnic overture packaged around the Gospel's original beginning, citing the witness of John the Baptist as an augmentation and alternative presentation in relation to Mark, the first biography of Jesus. That being the case, the earlier Johannine narrative emerged as the second biography of Jesus, presenting two signs before those narrated in Mark 1, and three signs in Judea, augmenting Mark chronologically and geographically. Added as an engaging and familiar confession, the Johannine Christ hymn prepares hearers and readers to be receptive and responsive to the narrative that follows. Thus, the Johannine Prologue, or Overture, serves as an engaging and transformative opening to the faith-evoking narrative that follows—moving from encounter, to confession, and back again—inviting likewise a transformative reading and hearing of the Johannine witness. And, with the Elder and his associates, later audiences are drawn experientially into the final exclamation (21:24 italics added): "We *know* his testimony is true!"

PART 2
JOHN AND THE CANON

CHAPTER 5

JOHN AND THE PENTATEUCH

T. DESMOND ALEXANDER

It is a pleasure to contribute to this Festschrift in honor of Andreas Köstenberger, with whom I have had the privilege of partnering on several projects and from whose writings I have benefited greatly.

1. QUOTATIONS AND ALLUSIONS IN JOHN

Like the authors of the Synoptic Gospels, the author of the Fourth Gospel, by tradition identified as the apostle John, draws heavily on the Old Testament in narrating his account of the life of Jesus. The author's familiarity with the Old Testament is reflected not merely through the use of quotations that are drawn from a small number of different books, but from numerous allusions to Old Testament passages. John's use of quotations is relatively easy to tie down,[1] but his use of allusions leaves greater room for subjectivity on the part of the reader. Nestle-Aland[28] provides a list of more than 230 Old Testament texts that have been associated with John's Gospel. Although this list includes items that some scholars would

---

1. According to S. Moyise, *The Old Testament in the New: An Introduction*, 2nd ed. (London: Bloomsbury T&T Clark, 2015), 93–102, there are seven quotations from the book of Psalms, four from the book of Isaiah, two from Zachariah, and one from Exodus. These quotations are found in John 1:23; 2:17; 6:31, 45; 10:34; 12:14–15, 38, 39–40; 13:18; 15:25; 19:24, 28, 36, 37. See also Andreas J. Köstenberger, "John," in *Commentary on the New Testament Use of the Old Testament*, ed. G. K. Beale and D. A. Carson (Grand Rapids: Baker Academic; Downers Grove, IL: IVP Academic, 2007), 415–19. B. G. Schuchard, "Form Versus Function: Citation Technique and Authorial Intention in the Gospel of John," in *Abiding Words: The Use of Scripture in the Gospel of John*, ed. B. G. Schuchard and A. D. Myers, RBS 81 (Atlanta: Society of Biblical Literature, 2015), 23–45, finds 13 quotations. J. Clark-Soles, "Israel's Scriptures in John," in *Israel's Scriptures in Early Christian Writings: The Use of the Old Testament in the New*, ed. M. Henze and D. Lincicum (Grand Rapids: Eerdmans, 2023), 286–87, presents a list of eighteen quotations, adding to those of Moyise four composite quotations found in John 7:38;, 7:42;, 8:17; and 17:12. He also suggests that there are three unmarked quotations in John 1:51; 12:3; and 12:27.

omit and omits items that others would include, it nevertheless highlights the importance of John's familiarity with the Old Testament.

According to Steve Moyise, "Some have deduced . . . that quotations are more important to John than allusions."[2] We will contend in this essay, however, that allusions have a significant role in demonstrating John's dependence on the Pentateuch, with quotations playing only a minor part. The same may also be true for John's dependence on other parts of the Old Testament, but no attempt is made in this essay to demonstrate this. Strikingly, John possibly employs only one quotation from the Pentateuch, referencing Exodus 12:46 (or possibly Num. 9:12) in the context of Jesus's bones not being broken at his execution (John 19:36). While the context strongly suggests that John 19:36 associates Jesus with the paschal sacrifice mentioned in Exodus 12, the source of the quotation is disputed. Some argue that it derives from Psalm 34:20 (33:21 in LXX).[3] Despite the lack of consensus over the source of the quotation in John 19:36, there are solid grounds for believing that the Fourth Gospel is profoundly influenced by imagery taken from the book of Exodus, centered especially on the concept of Passover.[4]

Given the flexible nature of John's quotations,[5] it may be more appropriate to describe them as "explicit allusions," being the tip of an iceberg as regards John's dependence on the Old Testament. While quotations are somewhat easier to identify in the narrative, we ought to avoid jumping to the conclusion that John's use of "proof texts" is more significant than his use of less explicit allusions. The visibility of the former does not necessarily imply that they should be given more weight than other allusions for understanding John's use of the Old Testament.

---

2.   Moyise, The Old Testament in the New: An Introduction, 102.

3.   A. T. Hanson, The Prophetic Gospel: A Study of John and the Old Testament (Edinburgh: T&T Clark, 1991), 218–22.

4.   If this broader picture is considered, it favors linking John 19:36 with Exodus 12:46. See Stanley E. Porter, "Can Traditional Exegesis Enlighten Literary Analysis of the Gospel? An Examination of the Old Testament Fulfilment Motif and the Passover Theme," in The Gospels and the Scriptures of Israel, ed. C. A. Evans and W. R. Stegner, JSNTSup 104 (Sheffield: Sheffield Academic Press, 1994), 403–5. For a revised version of this essay, see his chapter "Exodus 12 and the Passover Theme in John" in Stanley E. Porter, Sacred Tradition in the New Testament: Tracing Old Testament Themes in the Gospels and Epistles (Grand Rapids: Baker Academic, 2016), 127–52.

5.   According to M. J. J. Menken, Old Testament Quotations in the Fourth Gospel: Studies in Textual Form, CBET 15 (Kampen: Kok Pharos, 1996), 207, John appears to follow the text of the LXX, but he has "added, omitted, or changed elements on the basis of analogous OT passages."

Given the practical challenge of listing and discussing in a relatively short essay all Pentateuch allusions in the Fourth Gospel, we shall adopt a more limited, alternative approach, which hopefully may prove to be fruitful. We shall address the question, How do allusions to the Pentateuch serve the declared purpose of John's Gospel, when he states, "Jesus performed many other signs in the presence of his disciples, which are not recorded in this book. But these are written that you may believe that Jesus is the Messiah, the Son of God, and that by believing you may have life in his name" (John 20:30–31 NIV)?[6]

2. SIGNS IN EXODUS AND JOHN

In this brief statement regarding the book's purpose, John highlights a number of concepts that are important throughout the Gospel. He recalls the series of "signs" that he has recorded in the first half of his account, all of which point to Jesus's miraculous and divine power. These begin with Jesus turning water into wine at Cana in Galilee (John 2:1–11) and end with Jesus raising Lazarus to life (11:1–45).[7] Apart from the feeding of more than 5,000 people, these miraculous signs are unique to John's Gospel. These signs are grounds for believing that Jesus Christ has been sent by God. As John records after the first sign, "What Jesus did here in Cana of Galilee was the first of the signs through which he revealed his glory; and his disciples believed in him" (2:11 NIV). Importantly, John draws attention to how the first sign caused Jesus's disciples to believe. Soon after this, he writes, "Now while he was in Jerusalem at the Passover Festival, many people saw the signs he was performing and believed in his name" (2:23 NIV). Following up on this connection between "signs" and "believing," John reveals that Jesus himself was of the opinion that without "signs" the people would not believe. Addressing a royal official with a sick son, Jesus states, "Unless you people see signs and wonders . . . you will never believe" (4:48 NIV). The link between "signs" and "believing" is also highlighted in John 7:31: "Still, many in the crowd believed in him. They said, 'When the Messiah comes, will he perform more signs than this man?'" (NIV, cf. John 9:16). Since the prominence given to

---

6. Clark-Soles, "Israel's Scriptures in John," 292–93, observes that in the textual tradition of John 20:30–31 the verb "to believe" in verse 31a is sometimes preserved in the present tense πιστεύητε "continue to believe" and sometimes in the aorist tense πιστεύσητε "come to believe."

7. The other signs are the healing of an official's son (4:46–54); the healing of paralyzed man (5:1–15); the feeding of 5,000 men (6:1–14); Jesus's walking on water (6:15–21); the healing of a blind man (9:1–41).

"signs" is a distinctive and unique feature of John's Gospel, we should ask the question, What may have inspired John to focus on "signs" in describing the life of Jesus?

The most obvious answer is to be found in the book of Exodus. John was possibly influenced by the description of how God provides Moses with a series of signs that are intended to persuade the Israelites to believe (see Exod. 4:1; cf. 4:5). After the Lord reveals two miraculous signs to Moses, he states, "But if they do not believe these two signs or listen to you, take some water from the Nile and pour it on the dry ground. The water you take from the river will become blood on the ground" (Exod. 4:9 NIV). Subsequently, when Moses and Aaron performed these three signs before the people, "they believed" (Exod. 4:31 NIV). Further signs follow as Moses and Aaron confront the Egyptian king. While the miraculous events that are recorded in Exodus 7–12 are frequently referred to as the "ten plagues," this is an unfortunate designation that distracts from the true nature of what happens in Exodus.[8] In Exodus 7:3, the Lord refers to them as "signs and wonders" and these terms continue to be used in chapters 7–11.[9] Additionally, whereas the expression "ten plagues" is never found in the Bible, the phrase "signs and wonders" comes on a number of occasions to denote the events recorded in Exodus 7–12 (see Deut. 4:34; 6:22; 7:19; 26:8; 29:3; 34:11; Neh. 9:10; Pss. 105:27; 135:9; Jer. 32:20–21; cf. Deut. 4:34; 7:19). Most likely John's interest in signs derives from the exodus story. As Nicholas Piotrowski observes, "In the Fourth Gospel Jesus's miracles are inversely parallel to the plagues of Egypt. In the exodus the signs spelled death for the Egyptians; now Jesus's signs are sources of life."[10] Of particular note is the transformation of water into blood in Egypt and into wine at Cana in Galilee (Exod. 7:14–25; John 2:1–12).

John's purpose statement in 20:30–31 also highlights the concept of Jesus being the source of life. This is a theme that runs throughout the Gospel, appearing first in the Prologue when John states, "In him was life, and that life was the light of all mankind" (John 1:4 NIV). While all the

---

8. See T. D. Alexander, "Translation or Tradition: A Brief Survey of Some Translational Issues in the Book of Exodus," *The Bible Translator* 74 (2023): 179–91.

9. See Exodus 7:9; 8:23; 10:1–2; 11:9–10.

10. N. G. Piotrowski, "Exodus, The," in *Dictionary of the New Testament Use of the Old Testament*, ed. G. K. Beale, et al. (Grand Rapids: Baker Academic, 2023), 240; cf. T. D. Alexander, *From Paradise to the Promised Land: An Introduction to the Pentateuch*, 4th ed. (Grand Rapids: Baker Academic, 2022), 95.

signs in John's Gospel may be associated with life, the idea that Jesus is the source of life is prominently illustrated in the story of Lazarus being raised to life, the last of the signs in the first half of the Gospel. In his encounter with Martha, Jesus states, "I am the resurrection and the life. The one who believes in me will live, even though they die; and whoever lives by believing in me will never die. Do you believe this?" (John 11:25–26 NIV). Importantly, Martha responds by saying, "Yes, Lord, . . . I believe that you are the Messiah, the Son of God, who is to come into the world" (v. 27 NIV). If John's purpose in writing, as stated in John 20:30–31, is to convince his readers that Jesus is the "Messiah, the son of God," who brings life, Jesus's words and Martha's response are a fitting illustration of what John wishes to communicate to his readers.

3. THE PASSOVER AND JESUS'S DEATH

Paradoxically, the idea that Jesus brings life is intimately connected to his death, which is the focus of the second half of the Fourth Gospel. Attention is drawn to this in chapters 11 and 12 in developments associated with the resurrection of Lazarus.[11] Remarkably, Lazarus's resurrection becomes the reason for Jesus's death. John 11:45–53 records how the Sanhedrin determines that Jesus must die, with Caiaphas, the high priest, proclaiming, "You know nothing at all! You do not realize that it is better for you that one man die for the people than that the whole nation perish" (11:49–50 NIV). As Marianne Meye Thompson remarks, "What brings life to Lazarus brings death to Jesus—but what brings death to Jesus brings life to the world."[12]

Following on from Caiaphas's pronouncement, after a brief mention of the forthcoming Passover (11:55–57), John records how Mary, Lazarus's sister, anoints Jesus's feet with expensive perfume (12:1–8). In the face of criticism directed against her extravagant expression of thankfulness to Jesus for restoring her brother to life, Jesus speaks of his forthcoming death (12:7–8). Remarkably, the one who had previously said "I am

---

11. According to Andrew T. Lincoln, "The Lazarus Story: A Literary Perspective," in *The Gospel of John and Christian Theology*, ed. R. Bauckham and C. Mosser (Grand Rapids: Eerdmans, 2008), the Lazarus story is both "a pivot" (211) and "the Fourth Gospel in miniature" (232).

12. M. M. Thompson, "The Raising of Lazarus in John 11: A Theological Reading," in *The Gospel of John and Christian Theology*, 237. In a similar vein, Lincoln, "The Lazarus Story: A Literary Perspective," 223, observes, "The protagonist who is the giver of life is moving toward his own death. . . . Life for Lazarus will mean death for Jesus." Thompson also notes that "the conflict between life and death shapes the narrative of John 11, as it shapes the entire Gospel" (236).

the resurrection and the life" (11:25 NIV) expects that very soon he will be dead. Beginning with these references to Jesus's death, chapters 12–19 detail events that lead up to and include his crucifixion. Importantly, for John, Jesus's death coincides with the remembrance of Passover in Jerusalem. This is no mere coincidence. Passover provides John with the key to understanding how Jesus's death can bring eternal life to others. The movement from signs to Passover reflects the narrative sequence in Exodus 3–12.

Passover enjoys a special prominence in the Fourth Gospel. The noun πάσχα "Passover" comes in John 2:13, 23; 6:4; 11:55 (twice); 12:1; 13:1; 18:28, 39; 19:14. The term ἑορτή "feast" is used with reference to the Passover in 2:23; 4:45; 5:1; 6:4; 11:56; 12:12, 20; 13:1, 29. Of the four canonical Gospels, the Gospel of John uniquely mentions three annual Passover celebrations (John 2:13; 6:4; 11:55) and, significantly, places the crucifixion of Jesus at Passover (John 18:28, 39; 19:14). Moreover, John highlights the fact that Jesus's bones, like those of the Passover sacrifice, are not broken. This detail is specific to Passover. With this in view, the quotation in John 19:36 probably alludes to Exodus 12:46 and/or Numbers 9:12.

John's special interest in Passover permeates the whole of his Gospel. Despite the objections of some scholars, there is good reason to believe that John the Baptist has Passover in view when he speaks of Jesus Christ being the "Lamb of God, who takes away the sin of the world" (John 1:29; cf. 1:36). On its own, John's statement is ambiguous; too little is said to tie his remark to one specific Old Testament sacrifice.[13] However, in the context of the whole of the Fourth Gospel, a Passover understanding seems to be implied. John the Baptist's use of the Greek term ἀμνός "lamb" points specifically to a young sheep. This is in keeping with Passover, for which the sacrificial animals are to be "year-old males without defect" (Exodus 12:5 NIV). While the LXX of Exodus 12 consistently uses the term πρόβατον "sheep" to translate the Hebrew term שֶׂה, Exodus 12 qualifies the use of πρόβατον by noting that the animals were to be year-old males. John's use of ἀμνός avoids the need for any qualification; unlike πρόβατον, which John uses elsewhere, ἀμνός denotes a younger animal.

Scholars who are reluctant to associate John the Baptist's remarks with Passover usually contend that there is no soteriological dimension to

---

13.   For a survey of different proposals regarding the identity of the lamb, see C. W. Skinner, "Another Look at 'the Lamb of God'," *Bibliotheca Sacra* 161 (2004): 89–104.

Passover. It is not unusual to find statements affirming that the Passover sacrifice "did not . . . deal with sin."[14] C. K. Barrett writes, "The reference cannot have been drawn directly from Judaism, since in Judaism the lamb sacrificed at Passover does not take away sins."[15] According to John Collins, "The Passover is not an atoning sacrifice."[16] In a similar vein, but not rejecting the possibility that Jesus is a Passover sacrifice, Clark-Soles comments, "When John depicts Jesus as the Passover lamb, he emphasizes Jesus as liberator (not as an atoning sacrifice as construed in penal substitutionary atonement theories)."[17]

The grounds for denying a soteriological dimension to the Passover sacrifice may be traced back to a claim made by George Buchanan Gray in 1925. Drawing on customs from Syria, Gray maintained that the blood ritual associated with Passover warded off a hostile power.[18] Those in the house were protected by the blood on the doorframe, which "re-inforced" the already closed door. In the light of this understanding of the Passover ritual, Gray claimed that "the Paschal victim was not a sin-offering or regarded as a means of expiating or removing sin."[19] Viewed from this perspective, it is difficult to see how Passover can form the basis of John the Baptist's comment about the Lamb of God taking away the sin of the world. However, Gray's proposal regarding the Passover sacrifice is open to challenge.

According to the Pentateuch, Passover plays an important role in making holy the firstborn Israelite males. This is summarized in Numbers 3:13 when the Lord says to Moses: "On the day that I struck down all the firstborn in the land of Egypt, I consecrated for my own all the firstborn in Israel, both of man and of beast. They shall be mine: I am the LORD" (ESV). A similar statement linking Passover to the sanctification of the firstborn is made in Numbers 8:7. The concept of

---

14. Andrew T. Lincoln, *The Gospel According to Saint John*, BNTC 4 (Peabody, MA: Hendrickson; London: Continuum, 2005), 113.

15. C. K. Barrett, The Gospel According to St. John: An Introduction with Commentary and Notes on the Greek Text, 2nd ed. (London: SPCK, 1978), 176.

16. C. J. Collins, "Numbers, Book of," in *Dictionary of the New Testament Use of the Old Testament*, ed. G. K. Beale, et al. (Grand Rapids: Baker Academic, 2023), 573; cf. C. J. Collins, "The Eucharist as Christian Sacrifice: How Patristic Authors Can Help Us Read the Bible," *WTJ* 66 (2004): 21–23.

17. Clark-Soles, "Israel's Scriptures in John," 305.

18. G. B. Gray, *Sacrifice in the Old Testament: Its Theory and Practice* (Oxford: Clarendon Press, 1925), 362–63. Gray claims that Passover had an apotropaic purpose. See J. K. Howard, "Passover and Eucharist in the Fourth Gospel," *SJT* 20 (1967): 331–32.

19. Gray, Sacrifice in the Old Testament, 397.

"consecration/sanctification" is also highlighted in Exodus 13:2 when God instructs Moses to make holy all firstborn males. According to instructions for recalling Passover when the Israelites enter the land of Canaan, given in Exodus 13:11–13, all new firstborn males that are not sacrificed must be ransomed (Hebrew הדפ) from death by the offering of a הֶשׂ "sheep/goat." This process reflects what happened in Egypt at the first Passover; year-old animals were sacrificed as substitutes for the firstborn Israelite males in order to ransom them from death.[20] In addition, at the first Passover the application of blood to the doorframes of the houses and the eating of the sacrificial meat with unleavened bread contribute toward the cleansing and sanctification of the firstborn males.[21] In the light of how Passover consecrates the firstborn so that they belong to God, there can be little doubt that it has a substantial soteriological dimension that addresses human sinfulness.[22]

When Passover is understood as a consecration ritual, it is perhaps easier to appreciate the significance of other passages in the Fourth Gospel. A knowledge of Passover sheds light on Jesus's remarks about eating his flesh and drinking his blood in John 6:53–58. At the Passover in Egypt, the eating of the sacrifice is an important component of the ritual (Exod. 12:8–11).[23] The sacrificial meat is holy and its consumption sanctifies those who eat it. Jesus's comments in John 6:53–58 suggest that those who metaphorically eat and drink his flesh and blood benefit from his death.[24]

The concept of Jesus Christ sanctifying others is picked up in John 17:17–19. As Paul Hoskins notes,

---

20. One of the unexpected features of the first Passover account in Exodus 12 is the death threat pronounced on the Israelite firstborn males. On previous occasions when God struck Egypt, he distinguished between the Israelites and the Egyptians. No harm befell the Israelites. The introduction of a death threat is best understood in the light of Passover being a consecration ritual. To be made holy, the firstborn Israelite males must be delivered from death through the offering of a substitutionary sacrifice.

21. For a fuller discussion, see T. D. Alexander, *Exodus*, ApOTC 2 (London: Apollos, 2017), 230–34; cf. T. D. Alexander, "The Passover Sacrifice," in *Sacrifice in the Bible*, ed. R. T. Beckwith and M. Selman (Carlisle: Paternoster; Grand Rapids: Baker, 1995), 1–24.

22. Howard, "Passover and Eucharist in the Fourth Gospel," 332, cites Numbers 28:22 and Ezekiel 45:21–25 as evidence that the Passover sacrifice dealt with sin.

23. A process similar to the Passover ritual occurs when the high priest is sanctified for service in the tent of meeting. See Exodus 29:31–34; Leviticus 8:31–32.

24. See P. M. Hoskins, "Deliverance from Death by the True Passover Lamb: A Significant Aspect of the Fulfillment of the Passover in the Gospel of John," *JETS* 52 (2009): 296–97; cf. Porter, "Traditional Exegesis," 413–14.

At the last Passover in John, Jesus sanctifies himself for his disciples so that they might be sanctified by the truth (17:19). Jesus's sanctification is probably sanctification of himself as a sacrifice in light of "for them" (ὑπὲρ αὐτῶν). Jesus therefore appears to be saying that one of the purposes of his sacrificial death is to sanctify his disciples. Thus, his sacrifice sanctifies them like the Passover lamb sanctified the firstborn sons of Israel.[25]

As part of the first Passover ritual, blood was applied to the doorframes of the Israelite houses. This appears to have had a cleansing effect.[26] Observing this connection between blood and cleansing at Passover, Hoskins writes,

> It is fairly common for interpreters to see John 13:8–10 as anticipating the efficacy of the sacrificial death of Jesus for completing the cleansing of the disciples of Jesus from sin. The setting for this teaching is the Passover (13:1). As with sanctification, cleansing from sin recalls one of the aspects of the Passover lamb that points to its value as a sacrifice of atonement.[27]

In a gospel centered on how the substitutionary death of Jesus Christ gives eternal life to others, Passover as a consecration ritual offers an excellent paradigm to explain how Christ sanctifies sinful people so that they may eventually dwell in God's presence (see John 14:1–6; cf. Exod. 15:17). In line with this, Jesus's remarks in John 8:31–36 about setting free those who are enslaved to sin may be another allusion to the events associated with the first Passover.[28]

John's interest in Jesus as the ultimate Passover sacrifice comes to a climax in John 19:13–42. As Stanley E. Porter observes,

> Many commentators are willing to concede Passover elements in this scene but have failed to realize the force such a depiction

---

25. Hoskins, "Deliverance from Death by the True Passover Lamb," 294.
26. Josephus, *Ant.* 2.312, states briefly that the Israelites purified their houses with the blood from the Passover sacrifice using bunches of hyssop.
27. Hoskins, "Deliverance from Death by the True Passover Lamb," 295.
28. See P. M. Hoskins, "Freedom from Slavery to Sin and the Devil: John 8:31–47 and the Passover Theme of the Gospel of John," *TJ* 31 (2010): 47–63.

would have, because they have failed to see how the theme has been developed throughout the Gospel. This passage is not a simple equation of Jesus with the Passover victim on the basis of only the points of correlation mentioned in this particular passage but actually a climactic scene that brings to a decisive conclusion a major thematic element developed throughout John's Gospel.[29]

Porter highlights various ways in which events linked to Jesus's death correspond with aspects of the Passover celebration. The timing of Jesus's death coincides with the slaughter of the Passover animals. The mention of hyssop in John 19:29 recalls its use in Exodus 12:22. Importantly, John 19:36–37 "brings the Passion Narrative to a close by citing in double, emphatic fashion OT quotations that make the sacrificial Passover death not only specific but also virtually undeniable."[30] According to Porter, in John 19, Jesus Christ "is seen in a final and summative way as the fulfilment of the Old Testament and as the true and perfect Passover lamb."[31]

From his reading of the Fourth Gospel, Porter concludes that the plot of John's Gospel centers on the idea that Jesus's death is "a substitute and replacement for the Passover sacrifice."[32] Interestingly, he arrives at this conclusion without referring to John's use of signs and without viewing Passover as a consecration ritual. Yet, as we have observed, the narrative movement of the Fourth Gospel appears to be modeled on the book of Exodus, moving from signs to Passover. Moreover, John's account of the life of Jesus appears to be influenced by the idea that Passover is a consecration ritual, which involves being ransomed from death, being purified from the defilement of sin, and being sanctified through the eating of the sacrificial offering. Viewed from this perspective, as the ultimate Passover sacrifice, Jesus Christ is the source of the eternal life that will be experienced by those who believe that he is the Messiah, the Son of

---

29. Porter, *Sacred Tradition in the New Testament*, 144; cf. Porter, "Traditional Exegesis," 418.

30. Porter, *Sacred Tradition in the New Testament*, 151; cf. Porter, "Traditional Exegesis," 421. Porter comments that these quotations "are . . . to be recognized as final fulfillment statements, bringing the entire course of plot development to a close" (151).

31. Porter, "Traditional Exegesis," 427. Cf. M. W. G. Stibbe, *John*, Readings: A New Biblical Commentary (Sheffield: Sheffield Academic Press, 1993), 35, who writes, "The whole of the Gospel could be described as a *Passover plot* in that it moves through the three Passover festivals in 2.13, 6.4 and 13.1."

32. Porter, "Traditional Exegesis," 421. Elsewhere he writes, "The evidence of a Passover theme in the Fourth Gospel, it seems to me, is stronger than many recognize. The Passover theme essentially states that Jesus is seen by the author of the Fourth Gospel as the suitable and in fact ideal or perfect Passover victim" (406).

God. In a Gospel that emphasizes how Jesus Christ is the source of life, his portrayal as the perfect and ultimate Passover sacrifice is exceptionally appropriate.[33]

4. THE DIVINE NAME IN EXODUS AND JOHN

In the light of how the Fourth Gospel draws on the book of Exodus as regards both signs and Passover, it is surely no coincidence that it also gives prominence to the "I am" sayings of Jesus. Scholars have long recognized the possibility that the "I am" statements recorded in John allude to Exodus 3:14 and God's use of "I am" in this context. Strong parallels exist between what God achieves for the Israelites in Egypt and what Jesus Christ as the Son of God does in bringing eternal life to those who believe in him. Since John presents Jesus as the source of life, it is noteworthy that the "I am" sayings associate Jesus with life. As W. Ross Blackburn observes:

> In the seven well-known "I am" statements Jesus speaks of himself as "bread of life" (6:48), "the light of the world" who brings life to those who follow him (8:12), "the door" through which leads to abundant life (10:9–10), "the good shepherd" who lays down his life so that his sheep may be protected and live (10:11–15), "the way, the truth, and the life" (14:6), and "the vine" to whom the disciples must be connected if they are to live and bear fruit (15:1–6).[34]

By associating Jesus Christ with God's designation of himself as "I am," the author of the Fourth Gospel lends weight to his presentation of Jesus Christ as the unique Son of God. Jesus Christ is not merely an exceptional human being who offers his life as a Passover sacrifice. He is the divine Son of God and, as such, has come to bring about a greater exodus that involves delivering people from enslavement to the evil powers of this world.

---

33. While John's Gospel offers the fullest articulation of this idea, we find it embedded in other New Testament writings (e.g., 1 Cor. 5:7; 1 Peter 1:18–19).

34. W. R. Blackburn, *The God Who Makes Himself Known: The Missionary Heart of the Book of Exodus*, NSBT 28 (Downers Grove, IL: IVP Academic, 2012), 59. In addition to the expressions noted by Blackburn, Jesus sometimes uses "I am" without a predicate (John 8:24, 28, 58; 13:19).

CONCLUSION

Given that the Exodus narrative recounts the greatest salvation event in the Old Testament,[35] it is perhaps no surprise that John's account of the life of Jesus Christ abounds in allusions to Exodus 1–13. Recalling John's purpose in writing his Gospel, it is hardly coincidental that three of the Gospel's most distinctive features are all found together in the book of Exodus. By focusing on John's allusions to the book of Exodus, our study goes some way toward confirming Clark-Soles's observation regarding John's use of the Old Testament: "The more the reader is familiar with Scripture, the more resonances she will hear and the more layers she will uncover."[36] We have not exhausted the topic. Other allusions to the Pentateuch are plainly evident in the Fourth Gospel but space does not allow for a detailed discussion of these at this stage.[37] With this in view, the present essay has deliberately explored allusions that have received less attention yet have the appearance of being highly significant for understanding the rhetoric of John's narrative. A close reading of the Fourth Gospel strongly suggests that its structure and content have been heavily influenced by the Pentateuchal account of how God redeemed the Israelites from slavery in Egypt. The exodus story provides the perfect paradigm to encapsulate all that Jesus Christ achieves in bringing life to those who believe in him. As the ultimate, perfect Passover sacrifice, Jesus Christ ransoms from death, cleanses, and sanctifies everyone who trusts in him. As the great I AM he redeems from bondage those who are enslaved by the evil powers of this world. When these allusions in John to the book of Exodus are recognized, there can be little doubt that as regards his use of the Pentateuch, the author of John gives greater weight to allusions than quotations.

---

35. B. D. Estelle (*Echoes of Exodus: Tracing a Biblical Motif* [Downers Grove, IL: IVP Academic, 2018], 184) describes the exodus as "the foundational salvific event of the Old Testament." C. J. H. Wright ("Reading the Old Testament Missionally," in *Reading the Bible Missionally*, ed. M. W. Goheen, The Gospel and Our Culture [Grand Rapids: Eerdmans, 2016], 116) refers to the exodus as the "primary model of redemption in the Old Testament (primary both chronologically and theologically)."

36. Clark-Soles, "Israel's Scriptures in John," 312. He also writes, "From the very first words, 'in the beginning,' John tells a story whose structure and content depend upon Scripture as it has been written, spoken, digested, and lived by scriptural ancestors and followers of Jesus."

37. See, e.g., Köstenberger, "John," 419–20; M. J. J. Menken, "Genesis in John's Gospel and 1 John," in *Genesis in the New Testament*, ed. M. J. J. Menken and S. Moyise, LNTS 466 (London: Bloomsbury T&T Clark, 2012), 88–95; K. H. Jobes and A. T. Le Peau, *John through Old Testament Eyes: A Background and Application Commentary*, Through Old Testament Eyes: New Testament Commentaries (Grand Rapids: Kregel Academic, 2021). Other ways in which the Fourth Gospel alludes to the Pentateuch include: echoes of Genesis 1 in the Prologue; references to the patriarchs, Abraham and Jacob; Moses's association with grace and truth; the revelation of God's glory; the raising up of the serpent in the wilderness, and more.

CHAPTER 6

JOHN AND THE PROPHETS

JAMES A. ROH

It is a tremendous privilege to contribute a chapter to this volume in honor of Andreas Köstenberger and his contributions to biblical scholarship, particularly in the fields of Johannine studies and biblical theology. I am especially indebted to Dr. Köstenberger's mentorship throughout my doctoral studies and beyond. To begin our discussion on John and the Prophets, I would like to highlight his specific contributions in the area of the New Testament use of the Old Testament, and, specifically, John's use of the Old Testament.[1] Köstenberger helpfully situates John's use of Scripture as an essential element of his worldview.[2] With this in mind, John draws upon the witness of Scripture as a whole, in which the prophetic texts play a crucial role, to present Jesus as the fulfillment of prophetic hopes and expectations. In this chapter, we will survey John's use of the prophets by first examining explicit quotations, and then, key allusions and motifs.

1. QUOTATIONS OF THE PROPHETS

John's Gospel contains six quotations from the Prophets, four of which are drawn from Isaiah and two from Zechariah: John 1:23/Isaiah 40:3; John 6:45/Isaiah 54:13a; John 12:15/Zechariah 9:9; John 12:38/Isaiah 53:1; John 12:40/Isaiah 6:10; John 19:37/Zechariah 12:10. In terms of

---

1. Andreas J. Köstenberger, "John," in *Commentary on the New Testament Use of the Old Testament*, ed. G. K. Beale and D. A. Carson (Grand Rapids: Baker Academic, 2007), 415–512. See more recently, Andreas J. Köstenberger, "The Use of the Old Testament in the Gospel of John and the Johannine Epistles," *SwJT* 64:1 (2021): 41–55.
2. See Andreas J. Köstenberger, *A Theology of John's Gospel and Letters*, BTNT (Grand Rapids: Zondervan Academic, 2009), 275–310.

frequency, John's use of Isaiah is rivaled only by his use of the Psalms.[3] Notably, Isaiah is the only prophet (or Old Testament source) specifically named within John's scriptural citations. With regard to the structure of the Johannine narrative, the quotations of Isaiah are located at the beginning and end of Jesus's public ministry, effectively serving to frame John's presentation of Jesus around the prophet's testimony.[4] The final set of Isaianic quotations (John 12:38–40) is introduced by a fulfillment formula ("so that the word of the prophet Isaiah might be fulfilled [πληρωθῇ]") and cues a distinctive pattern of introductory formulae in the second half of the Gospel, which depicts Jesus's passion in terms of scriptural fulfillment (13:18; 15:25; 19:24, 36; cf. 18:9, 32).[5] The final quotation of Zechariah 12:10 (John 19:37) concludes this pattern and draws the account of Jesus's crucifixion to a close.[6]

The first quotation of the prophets occurs in John 1:23 in the opening scene with the Baptist (Isa. 40:3): "He [the Baptist] said, 'I am the voice of one crying out in the wilderness, "Make straight the way of the Lord," as the prophet Isaiah said'" (ESV).[7] The use of Isaiah 40:3 in connection with the Baptist is likely drawn from earlier Synoptic tradition (Matt. 3:3; Mark 1:2–3; Luke 3:4–6).[8] In contrast with the Synoptic presen-

---

3. The Psalms are quoted seven times in the Gospel of John, and the NA[28] identifies more than thirty potential allusions.

4. Some have suggested that the quotation formulas that are specifically ascribed to Isaiah (1:23: "as the prophet Isaiah said"; 12:38: "so that the word spoken by the prophet Isaiah might be fulfilled") form a deliberate *inclusio* to frame the beginning and end of Jesus's public ministry; see Michael A. Daise, *Quotations in John: Studies on Jewish Scripture in the Fourth Gospel*, LNTS 610 (London: T&T Clark, 2019), 9–11; Catrin H. Williams, "Isaiah in John's Gospel," in *Isaiah in the New Testament*, ed. Steve Moyise and Maarten J. J. Menken (London: T&T Clark, 2005), 101–2; Jorg Frëy, "'Dass sie meine Herrlichkeit schauen' (John 17.24): Zu Hintergrund, Sinn und Funktion der johanneischen Rede von der δόξα Jesu," *NTS* 54 (2008): 375–97.

5. See Craig A. Evans, "On the Quotation Formulas in the Fourth Gospel," *BZ* 26 (1982): 79–83; Craig A. Evans, *Word and Glory: On the Exegetical and Theological Background of John's Prologue*, JSNTSup 89 (Sheffield: Sheffield Academic, 1993), 176: "Whereas in the first half of the Gospel Jesus performs his many 'signs' and conducts his ministry 'just as it is written,' in the second half of the Gospel Jesus's rejection and crucifixion take place 'in order that Scripture be fulfilled.'" On John's use of "fulfillment" language, see Brian J. Tabb, "Johannine Fulfillment of Scripture: Continuity and Escalation," *BBR* 21:4 (2011): 495–505, italics are added by the author.

6. See William Randolph Bynum, "Quotations of Zechariah in the Fourth Gospel," in *Abiding Words: The Use of Scripture in the Gospel of John*, ed. Alicia D. Myers and Bruce G. Schuchard, RBS 81 (Atlanta: SBL Press, 2015), 47–74, who proposes a Zecharian *inclusio* to frame the account of Jesus's passion. Also note John's use of a double quotation in 12:38–40 (Isa. 53:1 and 6:10) and 19:36–37 (Exod. 12:46; Num. 9:12; and Zech. 12:10).

7. All Scripture references are taken from the English Standard Version, unless otherwise stated.

8. Maarten J. J. Menken, *Old Testament Quotations in the Fourth Gospel: Studies in Textual Form*, CBET 15 (Kampen: Kok Pharos, 1996), 71.

tation, however, the Fourth Gospel specifically identifies the Baptist as the Isaianic voice and integrates the quotation into John's speech (ἐγὼ φωνή). Most commentators favor John's citation of the LXX rendering, but the differences in form are well documented.[9] The main distinction between John's text and the LXX is that John appears to conflate "prepare" (ἑτοιμάσατε) and "make straight" (εὐθείας ποιεῖτε) in the LXX with the single term "make straight" (εὐθύνατε).[10] As elsewhere in his use of Scripture, John likely adapts his scriptural source to align with his presentation of Jesus. In this case, "make straight" (εὐθύνατε) places the emphasis squarely on the Baptist's witnessing function. The Baptist is not presented in terms of "preparing the way" for the Messiah as a forerunner, but rather as one who sees and testifies to Jesus's messianic identity as a contemporary.[11] This reading aligns with John's characterization of the Baptist as a major "witness" to the Messiah (1:6–8, 15, 19–28). Along these lines, the Baptist is included in a host of witnesses to Jesus's messianic identity in the first of many trial scenes.[12] Other witnesses include Moses (5:46), Abraham (8:56), Isaiah (12:41), and the beloved disciple himself (21:24). Additionally, the quotation of Isaiah 40:3 frames Jesus's public ministry around the manifestation of God's glory in Jesus, particularly in his signs (2:11).[13] In John's summary reflections in 12:37, he comments, "Though he [Jesus] had done so many signs before them [the Jewish crowd] they still did not believe in him."

The second quotation occurs in the "Bread of Life" discourse (6:22–59) and comprises the first occasion in which Jesus quotes Scripture in

---

9. Andreas Obermann, *Die Christologische Erfüllung der Schrift im Johannesevangelium: Eine Untersuchung zur Johanneischen Hermeneutik anhand der Schriftzitate*, WUNT 2/83 (Tübingen: Mohr Siebeck, 1996), 93–94; Bruce G. Schuchard, *Scripture within Scripture: The Interrelationship of Form and Function in the Explicit Old Testament Citations in the Gospel of John*, SBLDS 133 (Atlanta: Scholars Press, 1992), 1–15; Williams, "Isaiah in John's Gospel," in *Isaiah in the New Testament*, ed. Steve Moyise and Marten J. J. Menken (London: T&T Clark, 2005), 103; Menken, *Old Testament Quotations*, 1–35; Köstenberger, "John," 480–81; Daise, *Quotations in John*, 31–66.

10. Aside from identifying the Baptist as the "voice in the wilderness," John also excludes the phrase "the paths of our God" (τὰς τρίβους τοῦ θεοῦ ἡμῶν).

11. Menken, *Old Testament Quotations*, 26–35. As evidence, Menken cites John's denial of being Elijah (John 1:21), who was likely viewed as the precursor of the Messiah.

12. On the cosmic lawsuit motif, see A. E. Harvey, *Jesus on Trial: A Study in the Fourth Gospel* (London: SPCK, 1976); Andrew T. Lincoln, *Truth on Trial: The Lawsuit Motif in the Fourth Gospel* (Peabody, MA: Hendrickson, 2000).

13. Catrin H. Williams, "The Voice in the Wilderness and the Way of the Lord: A Scriptural Frame for John's Witness to Jesus," in *The Opening of John's Narrative (1:19–2:22): Historical, Literary, and Theological Readings from the Colloquium Ioanneum 2015 in Ephesus*, ed. R. Alan Culpepper and Jörg Frey, WUNT 385 (Tübingen: Mohr Siebeck, 2017), 39–57.

his response to his Jewish detractors (6:45): "It is written in the Prophets, 'And they will all be taught by God'" (Isa. 54:13). Jesus's citation likely follows the LXX rendering[14] and the appeal to Isaiah's prophecy is reinforced by additional resonances between John 6 and Isaiah 54–55.[15] Interestingly, Jesus adds the intertext of Isaiah 54:13 to the prominent references of the exodus narrative throughout John 6 (e.g., "manna in the wilderness," cf. Ps. 78(77):24; Num. 11:7–9; Neh. 9:15). By citing Isaiah 54:13, Jesus interprets the "bread from heaven" (6:31–33) as a symbolic precursor of the Torah, in which the giving of this "bread" is set in eschatological terms: Jesus himself is the divine teaching promised by Isaiah.[16] This episode sheds some light on Jesus's own use of Scripture, according to John. Jesus identifies himself as the "bread of life" not only in relation to the manna in the wilderness but also with respect to the salvific provision promised in Isaiah 54–55. Jesus, thus, demonstrates a knowledge of Scripture that draws upon "its entirety as a witness for him."[17] In a prior episode, he indicts his Jewish opponents on this very point: "You search the Scriptures because you think that in them you have eternal life; and it is they that bear witness about me" (John 5:39). John's use of Isaiah, from this standpoint, accentuates Jesus's own pattern of scriptural engagement

---

14. As indicated by the use of θεός rather than κύριος (MT: יהוה), and compresses "all your sons" (MT: וכל בניך; LXX: καὶ πάντας τοὺς υἱούς σου) to "all" (πάντες). Commentators who favor this reading include Menken, *Old Testament Quotations*, 67–77; Williams, "Isaiah in John's Gospel," 106. See also Schuchard, *Scripture within Scripture*, 51, who concludes more cautiously: "What little evidence there is for the influence of a specific textual tradition points tentatively in the direction of the OG."

15. Additional resonances include: (1) instructions to "come" (ἐρχόμαι), "buy" (ἀγοράζω), and "eat" (φάγω) (John 6:5–7, 26–27; cf. Isa. 55:1–3); (2) the occurrence of the word βρῶσιν (John 6:27, 55; cf. Isa. 55:10); and (3) Jesus's self-description using the language of descent (καταβαίνω) (John 6:33, 38–44; cf. Isa. 55:10–11). See Alicia D. Myers, *Characterizing Jesus: A Rhetorical Analysis on the Fourth Gospel's Use of Scripture in Its Presentation of Jesus*, LNTS 458 (London: T&T Clark, 2012), 111; cf. Diane M. Swancutt, "Hungers Assuaged by the Bread from Heaven: 'Eating Jesus' as Isaian Call to Belief: The Confluence of Isaiah 55 and Psalm 78(77) in John 6.22–71," in *Early Christian Interpretation of the Scriptures of Israel: Investigations and Proposals*, ed. Craig A. Evans and James A. Sanders, JSNTSup 148; SSEJC 5 (Sheffield: JSOT Press, 1997), 218–51.

16. Joshua J. Coutts, "Revelation, Provision, and Deliverance: The Reception of Exodus in Johannine Literature," in *The Reception of Exodus Motifs in Jewish and Christian Literature: "Let My People Go,"* ed. Beate Kowalski and Susan E. Docherty, TBN 30 (Leiden: Brill, 2021), 279. Later rabbinic traditions interpreted Isaiah 54:13 as indicating God himself teaching the Torah in the eschatological future (cf. *Pes. R.* 32:3–4; *Pes. K.* 12:21).

17. See Myers, *Characterizing Jesus*, 111–12, who adds: "As a result, the Gospel audience is shown a Jesus who is only properly understood in light of all of Scripture, and whose authority allows him to interpret Scripture in new ways, bringing together separate texts in order to offer a fuller presentation of his own identity" (112).

by bringing the full testimony of Scripture, and particularly the prophetic witness, to bear on the explication of his identity and mission.

The third quotation occurs during Jesus's triumphal entry into Jerusalem, where his arrival on a donkey as the "King of Israel" is interpreted in accordance with Scripture: "Fear not, daughter of Zion; behold, your king is coming, sitting on a donkey's colt!" (John 12:15). Most commentators propose Zechariah 9:9 as the primary source text, but the form of the quotation is compressed and contains features that do not align precisely with either Hebrew or Greek versions.[18] Many suggest that John's quotation in 12:15 combines elements from other source texts including Isaiah 40:9 or Zephaniah 3:16 ("fear not"), and Genesis 49:11 ("donkey's colt").[19] As we will see in John 12:38–40 and 19:36–37, several of John's quotations can be traced to two or more scriptural sources.[20] In his use of Zechariah 9:9, John depicts Jesus as actively fulfilling the promise of a Davidic king spoken by the prophet. The phrase, "do not fear," announces God's presence and salvation.[21] By reenacting Zechariah 9, moreover, Jesus accepts the royal messianic title without affirming the crowd's

---

18. Differences in textual form include (1) the replacement of χαῖρε with the phrase μὴ φοβοῦ ("fear not"); (2) the omission of the line, "righteous and having salvation is he, humble" (MT: צדיק ונושע הוא עני; LXX: δίκαιος καὶ σῴζων αὐτός πραΰς); (3) the occurrence of καθήμενος (MT: רכב; LXX: ἐπιβεβηκὼς); (4) the occurrence of πῶλον ὄνου (MT: בן־אתנות; LXX: πῶλον νέον). On the textual form of John's citation in 12:15, see Adam Kubiś, *The Book of Zechariah in the Gospel of John*, EBib 64 (Pendé: Gabalda, 2012), 27–114; Ruth Sheridan, *Retelling Scripture: "The Jews" and the Scriptural Citations in John 1:19–12:15*, BibInt 110 (Leiden; Boston: Brill, 2012), 222–32; Edwin D. Freed, *Old Testament Quotations in the Gospel of John*, NovTSup 11 (Leiden: Brill, 1965), 66–81; Günter Reim, *Studien zum Alttestamentlichen Hintergrund des Johannesevangeliums*, SNTSMS 22 (Cambridge: Cambridge University Press, 1974), 30; Daise, *Quotations in John*, 157–99; Bynum, "Quotations of Zechariah," 55–59; Menken, *Old Testament Quotations*, 79–97; Schuchard, *Scripture within Scripture*, 71–84; Köstenberger, "John," 473.

19. See C. K. Barrett, *The Gospel According to St. John*, 2nd ed. (Philadelphia: Westminster John Knox, 1978), 418–19; Raymond E. Brown, *The Gospel According to John*, 2 vols., AB 29–29A (Garden City, NY: Doubleday, 1966–70), 1:458; Reim, *Studien*, 30; Kubiś, *Zechariah*, 84–85; Menken, *Old Testament Quotations*, 95–96; Schuchard, *Scripture within Scripture*, 74–83; Bynum, "Quotations of Zechariah," 59; Köstenberger, "John," 473.

20. See Catrin H. Williams, "Composite Citations in the Gospel of John," in *Composite Citations in Antiquity: Volume Two: New Testament Uses*, ed. Sean A. Adams and Seth M. Ehorn, LNTS 593 (London: T&T Clark, 2018), 94–127, esp. 124–25, who distinguishes between "composite citations" and "conflated citations." The former refers to two or more scriptural sources fused together to form a single quotation; the latter indicates two or more elements woven into a quotation as a substitute or in addition to the primary source text. See also Bynum, "Quotations of Zechariah," 59, who notes: "[John's] substitution of a fitting and well-known phrase, 'Do not fear,' could reflect his interaction with other passages in addition to the cited verse from Zechariah, such as Isaiah 40:9; 41:10; 44:2; or Zephaniah 3:16. However, such a substitution would not have been offensive to his audience, and would have been quite in keeping with first-century quotation of sacred works."

21. Williams, "Composite Citations," 109.

political expectations of him.[22] The quotation is followed by a remembrance formula in verse 16 ("[his disciples] remembered [ἐμνήσθησαν]," cf. 2:17, 22), which underscores the initial misunderstanding of Jesus's actions on the part of the crowd and even the disciples.[23] The issue of unbelief comes to the fore in Jesus's indictment of his Jewish opponents at the end of chapter 12, where we find the next two prophetic quotations.

The fourth and fifth quotations occur in tandem at the close of Jesus's public ministry: Isaiah 53:1 in John 12:38 and Isaiah 6:10 in John 12:40. In unparalleled fashion, John links together two quotations widely attested in early Christian literature to offer scriptural rationale for Jewish unbelief.[24] The form of John's citation of Isaiah 53:1 agrees verbatim with the LXX and picks up on the preceding comment concerning the unbelief of "the crowd" (12:37).[25] John assesses Jewish unbelief as a fulfillment of Isaiah 53:1, where the "arm of the Lord" (ὁ βραχίων κυρίου), in its new Johannine context, is understood as Jesus's ministry of signs.[26] Likewise, the referent of "Lord" (κύριος) is Jesus, which recalls the Baptist's citation of Isaiah 40:3 in John 1:23. The form of John's citation of Isaiah 6:10, however, does not agree with either the MT or LXX, and the differences have been thoroughly discussed.[27] The notion of fulfillment in 12:38 extends to John's citation of Isaiah 6:10 in John 12:40, where the evangelist recasts the prophetic rebuke as a failure to *see* with the omission of hearing and the addition of the verb τυφλόω ("to blind"): "He has *blinded their eyes* [τετύφλωκεν αὐτῶν τοὺς ὀφθαλμοὺς] and hardened their heart, lest *they should see with [their] eyes* [ἴδωσιν τοῖς ὀφθαλμοῖς] and understand with the heart and

---

22. Bynum, "Quotations of Zechariah," 61–62.

23. Herman Ridderbos, *The Gospel of John: A Theological Commentary*, trans. John Vriend (Grand Rapids: Eerdmans, 1992), 424.

24. Isa. 53:1 in Rom. 10:16; Isa. 6:9–10 in Matt. 13:14–15; Mark 4:12; Luke 8:10; Acts 28:26–27; Rom. 11:8.

25. See Daise, *Quotations in John*, 70–71, who underscores the dependence on the LXX through its use of the vocative κύριε, which is a departure from any known Hebrew tradition; cf. J. Ross Wagner, *Heralds of the Good News: Isaiah and Paul "in Concert" in the Letter to the Romans*, NovTSup 101 (Leiden: Brill, 2002), 179n181, who draws the same conclusion in Paul's citation of Isa. 53:1a in Rom. 10:16.

26. Williams, "Isaiah in John's Gospel," 108; Daise, *Quotations in John*, 106.

27. Craig A. Evans, *To See and Not Perceive: Isaiah 6.9–10 in Early Jewish and Christian Interpretation*, JSOTSup 64 (Sheffield: JSOT, 1989), 129–35; Rudolf Schnackenburg, "John 12, 39–41: Zur christologischen Schriftauslegung des vierten Evangelisten," in *Das Johannesevangelium IV*, 2nd ed. (Freiburg: Herder, 1990), 143–50; Menken, *Old Testament Quotations*, 99–122; Obermann, *Die christologische Erfüllung der Schrift*, 235–55; Schuchard, *Scripture within Scripture*, 91–106; Daise, *Quotations in John*, 72–97. See also Köstenberger, "John," 479–83, where he cautions that "it is hard to settle this issue with any degree of certainty" (480).

turn and I heal them."[28] Most commentators suggest that the omission of hearing is the result of John's emphasis on the Jews' failure to believe in response to Jesus's visible signs.[29] Nevertheless, the choice of τυφλόω may betray traces of additional Isaianic influence, especially LXX Isaiah 42:18–19; 43:8; 56:10.[30] The focus on sight also has an important literary function related to John's use of the term in the episode of the healing of the blind man in chapter 9, which includes Jesus's indictment of the Pharisees: "that those who do not see may see [οἱ μὴ βλέποντες βλέπωσιν] and those who see may become blind [οἱ βλέποντες τυφλοὶ γένωται]" (9:41).[31] Jesus's words in this instance constitute a probable allusion to Isaiah 6:9.[32] The stinging indictment of the Pharisees, then, presented in terms of "blindness," anticipates the fulfillment of Isaiah 6:10 in John 12:40.[33] The correlation between "seeing" and "believing" comes to the forefront in John 12, where the evangelist ties these themes together in summary fashion by bringing the two Isaianic quotations in concert with one another.[34] The Jews did not believe in Jesus's signs (12:37), the revelation of the "arm of the Lord" (12:38), because they were blinded by God as foretold by Isaiah (12:40). The response of Jesus's Jewish opponents is even contrasted by the witness of Isaiah himself: "Isaiah said these things because he saw his glory and spoke of him" (12:41). We will comment on this text further below.

The final quotation occurs in the passion narrative and constitutes John's last scriptural citation: Zechariah 12:10 in John 19:37. This quotation brings the arrangement of fulfillment formulae found

---

28. In the MT, the movement is from heart to ears to eyes, back to eyes to ears to heart in a concentric structure, which is preserved in the LXX. As opposed to the chiastic structure found in the MT and retained in the LXX, John arranges the lines in a parallel structure. Note the use of καμμύω (not τυφλόω) in Matt. 13:15 and Acts 28:27.

29. Schnackenburg, "John 12, 39–41," 143–50; Menken, *Old Testament Quotations*, 99–122; Schuchard, *Scripture within Scripture*, 91–106; Williams, "Isaiah in John's Gospel," 109–10; Köstenberger, "John," 481.

30. Freed, *Old Testament Quotations*, 87; Schuchard, *Scripture within Scripture*, 102–3; Williams, "Composite Citations," 112–13. See the usage of τύφλος as it pertains to God's people in LXX Isa. 42:18–20; 43:8.

31. Note the additional parallel between chapters 9 and 12 concerning the fear of being cast out of the synagogue (ἀποσυνάγωγος in 9:22 and 12:42).

32. See Judith M. Lieu, "Blindness in the Johannine Tradition," *NTS* 34 (1988): 83–95. "The quotation [John 12:40] is based on Isa 6.10 and thus seems to continue an allusion to Isa 6.9 in Jesus's words in John 9.39" (85).

33. See Evans, *To See and Not Perceive*, 134, who points out that "the explanation of obduracy in ch. 12 has been illustrated by at least one of the specific 'signs.'"

34. Köstenberger, "John," 481.

in the second half of the narrative to a close, which portrays Jesus's rejection and crucifixion as conforming to the pattern found in the Jewish Scriptures. John's use of Zechariah 12:10 in 19:37 occurs in the context of a double quotation where a composite of texts (Exod. 12:46; Num. 9:12; Ps. 34:20) is cited in 19:36. Similar to 12:38–40, the two quotations are linked together: "And again another Scripture says. . ." (19:37). In this way, John portrays the details of Jesus's death, that both his legs were not broken and his side was pierced, not simply as "spontaneous superficial human actions of the moment," but rather, as "the fulfillment of ancient divinely spoken words."[35] The form of the citation conforms more closely with the MT but is not exact.[36] Several commentators favor John's adaption of the Hebrew text.[37] One of the key issues concerning the form is John's use of ὄψονται ("*they will look* on him whom they have pierced") against the LXX reading (ἐπιβλέψονται). Given the combined source material in the preceding quotation (Exod. 12:46; Num. 9:12; Ps. 34:20), this may be an additional case where John is employing composite elements in a single quotation. If so, LXX Isaiah 52:15 ("because those to whom it was not reported about him shall see [ὄψονται]") emerges as a likely source, given the intratextual links with Isaiah 52:13–53:12 elsewhere in the Gospel (e.g., the "lifted up" sayings in 3:14; 8:28; 12:32, 34).[38] John's emphasis on sight also recalls the allusion to Isaiah 6:10 in 12:40. In keeping with John's inaugurated-eschatological outlook, John depicts God's salvation in Jesus as a present reality realized through a proper vision of Jesus on the cross.[39] In other words, those who have eyes to see God's glory in the Son being "lifted up" on the cross are those who believe and receive eternal life.

---

35. Bynum, "Quotations of Zechariah," 66.
36. On the textual form of John's citation, see Kubiś, *Zechariah*, 171–80; Bynum, *Fourth Gospel*, 2–5, 163–67.
37. Rudolf Schnackenburg, *The Gospel According to St. John*, 3 vols (New York: Crossroad, 1982; 1987), 3:293; Leon Morris, *The Gospel According to John*, rev. ed., NICNT (Grand Rapids: Eerdmans, 1995), 727n109; Paul Miller, "'They Saw His Glory and Spoke of Him': The Gospel of John and the Old Testament," in *Hearing the Old Testament in the New Testament*, ed. Stanley E. Porter (Grand Rapids: Eerdmans, 2006), 128.
38. The affinities between Isaiah 52–53 and Zechariah 12:9–13 are well documented. See Martin Hengel with Daniel P. Bailey, "The Effective History of Isaiah 53 in the Pre-Christian Period," in *The Suffering Servant: Isaiah 53 in Jewish and Christian Sources*, ed. Bernd Janowski and Peter Stuhlmacher, trans. Daniel P. Bailey (Grand Rapids: Eerdmans, 2004), 85–90.
39. Köstenberger, "John," 505.

2. PROPHETIC ALLUSIONS AND MOTIFS

Although John contains a fewer number of Old Testament quotations than the Synoptic Gospels, the numerous allusions to the Old Testament demonstrate the embedded character of John's use of Scripture. Along these lines, John alludes to the prophets extensively. Köstenberger identifies thirty potential allusions to the prophets.[40] A number of Johannine motifs, moreover, are drawn not from a single scriptural source but from a configuration of texts from the prophetic literature. For example, the image of Jesus as the "good shepherd" (John 10:7–18) recalls a number of prophetic texts including Jeremiah 23:1–4; Zechariah 11:4–17; and especially Ezekiel 34.[41] Similarly, the "vine" is a frequent symbol throughout the prophets (John 15:1; cf. LXX Jer. 2:21).[42] Our present investigation does not permit exhaustive research into every potential allusion or motif. We will highlight a few of the most significant ones below.

The Baptist's declaration of Jesus as the "Lamb of God" (1:29, 36: ὁ ἀμνὸς τοῦ θεοῦ) has generated substantial discussion around John's exact scriptural source.[43] Most scholars contend that John's language is likely drawn from the Passover lamb (Exod. 12) given the abundance of paschal references throughout the Gospel (2:13, 23; 6:4; 11:55; 12:1; 13:1; 19:14, 36).[44] Given his preceding citation of Isaiah 40:3, however, the Baptist's reference may indicate an additional scriptural element, in which the "lamb" (ἀμνός) of Isaiah 53:7 serves as another source drawn from the prophets.[45] We see this connection more clearly in the Lamb's

---

40. Köstenberger, "John," 420.

41. On John's allusions to Ezekiel, see Gary T. Manning, *Echoes of a Prophet: The Use of Ezekiel in the Gospel of John and in Literature of the Second Temple Period*, JSNTSup 270 (London: T&T Clark, 2004); Brian Neil Peterson, *John's Use of Ezekiel: Understanding the Unique Perspective of the Fourth Gospel* (Minneapolis: Fortress, 2015).

42. See also Isa. 5:1–7; 27:2–6; Jer. 6:9; 12:10–13; Ezek. 15:1–8; 17:5–10; 19:10–14; Hos. 10:1–2; 14:7.

43. For an overview, see Christopher W. Skinner, "Another Look at 'The Lamb of God,'" *BSac* 161 (2004): 89–104.

44. See e.g., Martin Hengel, "The Old Testament in the Fourth Gospel," in *The Gospels and the Scriptures of Israel*, ed. Craig A. Evans and W. Richard Stegner, JSNTSup 104 (Sheffield: Sheffield Academic, 1994), 34; Craig S. Keener, *The Gospel of John: A Commentary*, 2 vols. (Grand Rapids: Baker Academic, 2003), 1:454; Reim, *Studien*, 52, 179.

45. See the discussion on textual matters in Catrin H. Williams, "'Seeing,' Salvation, and the Use of Scripture in the Gospel of John," in *Atonement: Jewish and Christian Origins*, ed. Max Botner, Justin Duff, and Simon Durr (Grand Rapids: Eerdmans, 2020), 134–43. See also Jasper Tang Nielsen, "The Lamb of God: The Cognitive Structure of a Johannine Metaphor," in *Imagery in the Gospel of John: Terms, Forms, Themes, and Theology of Johannine Figurative Language*, ed. Jörg Frey, Jan G. van der Watt, and Ruben Zimmermann, WUNT 200 (Tübingen: Mohr Siebeck, 2006), 217–56. The Isaianic servant is further identified by the Baptist's testimony in 1:34 if one accepts the more difficult reading: "the chosen one of

soteriological implications in the second half of the statement: "who takes away [ὁ αἴρων] the sin of the world." The use of αἴρω contrasts the LXX reading of Isaiah 53:4, 11–12, which renders the Hebrew אשׂנ as [ἀνα] φέρω.[46] John may have been attracted to the Hebrew reading in Isaiah 53:12 (אשׂנ), in light of his allusion to Isaiah 52:13 (אשׂנ) in Jesus's "lifted up" sayings (3:14; 8:28; 12:32, 34).[47] In the present case, John draws upon key intertextual links through the use of shared lexical features in his appropriation of Isaianic material. In combining both scriptural elements, John presents a complex view of Jesus's death in terms of sacrifice and glory. The "Lamb of God" who takes away the sin of the world (1:29), as we proceed in the narrative, is also the one who is "lifted up" and glorified on the cross (12:32, 34).

To pick up on our previous discussion on Isaianic quotations, John also incorporates several Isaianic motifs throughout his narrative including glory (John 1:14; 2:11; 5:41; 7:18; 8:50; 12:41; 17:5, 22, 24/Isa. 6:1; 40:5; 48:11; 52:13; 60:1), light (John 1:4, 7, 9; 3:19; 8:12; 9:15; 12:35/Isa. 9:1; 49:6; 60:1), the divine name (John 1:12; 2:23; 3:18; 5:43; 10:25; 12:13, 28; 14:13–14, 26; 15:16, 21; 16:23–24, 26; 17:6, 11–12, 26; 20:31/Isa. 42:8; 43:7; 48:11; 52:6), the absolute "I am" (ἐγώ εἰμι) sayings (John 4:26; 8:24, 28, 58; 13:19; 18:5, 8/Isa. 41:4; 43:10; 46:4; 48:12; 51:12; 52:6), and the "lifted up" sayings (John 3:14; 8:28; 12:32, 34/Isa. 6:1; 52:13).[48] Significantly, a number of Isaianic quotations and motifs

---

God" (ὁ ἐκλεκτὸς τοῦ θεοῦ; cf. LXX Isa. 42:1: ὁ ἐκλεκτός μου). This reading is supported by John's use of Isaiah within the context of the Baptist's testimony (e.g., the bestowal of God's Spirit on Jesus also fits the context of the servant in Isaiah 42:1 but may also allude to Isaiah 11:2).

46. See J. Terence Forestell, *The Word of the Cross: Salvation as Revelation in the Fourth Gospel*, AnBib 57 (Rome: Biblical Institute, 1974), 160, who notes that αἴρω is never used in the LXX to denote the bearing of sin(s). Bauckham, *Gospel of Glory*, 154, contends that the phrase "he bore the sin of many" (Isa. 53:12) "makes it certain that the Gospel is here dependent on the Hebrew text of Isaiah."

47. See Richard Bauckham, *Gospel of Glory: Major Themes in Johannine Theology* (Grand Rapids: Baker Academic, 2015), 157, who suggests that by rendering אשׂנ as αἴρω, John is "exploiting the range of meaning of both verbs" to coordinate the "lifting up" of Jesus and the "taking away" of sin by the Lamb of God.

48. See Nicole Chibici-Revneanu, *Die Herrlichkeit des Verherrlichten: Das Verständnis der δόξa im Johannesevangelium*, WUNT 2/231 (Tübingen: Mohr Siebeck, 2007); Kai Akagi, "The Light from Galilee: The Narrative Function of Isaiah 8:23–9:6 in John 8:12." *NovT* 58 (2016): 380–93; Joshua J. F. Coutts, *The Divine Name in the Gospel of John*, WUNT 2/447 (Tübingen: Mohr Siebeck, 2017); Catrin H. Williams, *I Am He: The Interpretation of 'Anî Hû' in Jewish and Early Christian Literature*, WUNT 2/113 (Tübingen: Mohr Siebeck, 2000); Catrin H. Williams, "Johannine Christology and Prophetic Traditions: The Case of Isaiah," in *Reading the Gospel of John's Christology as Jewish Messianism: Royal, Prophetic, and Divine Messiahs*, ed. Benjamin Reynolds and Gabriele Boccaccini, AJEC 106 (Leiden; Boston: Brill, 2018), 92–123.

are intertwined at crucial points within the narrative. For example, John 8:28, "When you have *lifted up* the Son of Man, then you will know that *I am he*." John 12 serves as the tip of the iceberg in this respect, where two key quotations and several motifs are thoroughly integrated.[49]

The focal point of John's use of Isaiah is his commentary on the prophet's witness to Jesus in 12:41: "Isaiah said these things because he saw his glory and spoke of him." John's comment likely alludes to both Isaiah's temple vision (Isa. 6:1) and the glorification of the Servant (52:13).[50] The two texts are linked together through shared lexical features: Isaiah 6:1, the Lord's throne is "high and lifted up" (MT: אִשֵּׂא רָם; LXX: ὑψηλοῦ καὶ ἐπηρμένου); and Isaiah 52:13, the Servant is "high and lifted up" (MT: רִי אִשֵּׂא רֹם; LXX: ὑψωθήσεται καὶ δοξασθήσεται).[51] In this way, John presents Jesus in conjunction with both the glory of the Lord in Isaiah 6:1 and the rejection and ultimate glorification of the Servant in Isaiah 52:13–53:12.[52] And in so doing, John fuses two seemingly incongruent visions of Isaiah together: The "glory" of the enthroned Lord is combined with the Servant whose appearance was without "glory" (LXX Isa. 52:14; 53:2).[53] On the flip side, Jesus's Jewish opponents are unable to perceive his glory "for they loved the glory that comes from man more than the glory that comes from God" (12:43). The convergence of Isaianic material at these points suggests a clustering pattern of thought. Joshua Coutts observes, "John regarded general concepts he derived from Isaiah as embedded in a wider network or cluster of Isaianic concepts or themes."[54] The upshot of John's

---

49. See Daniel J. Brendsel, *"Isaiah Saw His Glory": The Use of Isaiah 52–53 in John 12*, BZNW 208 (Berlin: de Gruyter, 2014).

50. Bauckham, *Gospel of Glory*, 53; Brendsel, "Isaiah Saw His Glory," 113–21; Williams, "Isaiah in John's Gospel," 110–15.

51. This practice may be related to the rabbinic rule *gezarah shavah*. See Catrin H. Williams, "John, Judaism, and 'Searching the Scriptures,'" in *John and Judaism*, ed. R. Alan Culpepper and Paul N. Anderson, RBS 87 (Atlanta: SBL Press, 2017), 77–100; Bauckham, *Gospel of Glory*, 53.

52. Jonathan Lett, "The Divine Identity of Jesus as the Reason for Israel's Unbelief in John 12:36–43," *JBL* 35:1 (2016): 159–73.

53. Lett, "The Divine Identity," 171, concludes: "The servant's humiliation informs our understanding of the glory Isaiah encountered in the temple, and vice versa. Jesus is not glorified in spite of his humiliation, nor does his glory remain hidden in his crucifixion; it is precisely *because* this is the very nature of God and God's glory that Jesus can will his own humiliation"; cf. Bauckham, *Gospel of Glory*, 54: "[Isa. 52:13 LXX] is the exegetical source of John's remarkable and distinctive way of speaking of the exaltation ('lifting up') and glorification of Jesus as taking place through his humiliating death as well as his subsequent resurrection. The point of Jesus's deepest humiliation is, paradoxically, also his glorification. Whereas the more common early Christian way of thinking envisaged humiliation followed by exaltation, suffering followed by glory, John sees exaltation and glory in the humiliation and death."

54. Coutts, *Divine Name*, 37.

113

cluster of Isaianic motifs is the presentation of Jesus as the Son who shares the Father's glory and name, even taking on the divine self-designation, "I am he," and is ultimately glorified by God by being "lifted up" on the cross.

CONCLUSION

Our survey of John and the Prophets demonstrates that John's use of the prophetic literature falls in line with his overall use of Scripture. John demonstrates a wide knowledge of the Jewish Scriptures (both Hebrew and Greek texts) and thoroughly absorbs the language, motifs, and imagery of the prophets into his presentation of Jesus. In the first half of the Gospel, John frames Jesus's public ministry around Isaiah's testimony of God's glory in Jesus through his ministry of signs. At the close of his ministry, John presents Jesus as the long-awaited Davidic king, according to Zechariah, while indicating that Jewish obduracy was also in fulfillment of prophetic testimony. The fulfillment motif dominates John's use of the prophets (and Scripture) in the second half of the Gospel, where details of Jesus's crucifixion are played out in accordance with the testimony of the prophets (along with the Psalms). Finally, drawing especially upon a network of Isaianic motifs, he recasts Jesus's crucifixion as the ultimate revelation of God's glory.

CHAPTER 7

JOHN AND THE WRITINGS

GREGORY GOSWELL

It is a great pleasure to contribute a chapter to this volume that celebrates the contribution of Andreas Köstenberger to New Testament studies and to the study of the Gospel of John in particular. My experience of coauthoring a book with Andreas was one of happy cooperation with a writing partner who was uniformly gracious, encouraging, and insightful.[1] I found it a wonderfully enriching experience. In that volume, Andreas surveyed the Old Testament quotations in John, and the present essay focuses on quotations, allusions, and themes that arguably can be attributed to the Evangelist's interaction with the Writings, the third section of the Hebrew Old Testament canon. The Psalter takes pride of place in this regard. The other key book to consider is Daniel, with a focus on the expression "the son of man." The influence and use of other books in the Writings is less tangible,[2] but I will suggest some thematic convergences with John.

1. THE SEVEN QUOTATIONS FROM THE PSALMS

The only quotations from the Writings in John's Gospel are the seven drawn from the Psalms, and these make up exactly half of the fourteen Old Testament quotations in the Gospel. The tally of seven is hardly accidental and suggests the presence of numerical symbolism as a way of underlining the importance of this Old Testament book to the author of the Fourth

---

1. Andreas J. Köstenberger and Gregory Goswell, *Biblical Theology: A Canonical, Thematic, and Ethical Approach* (Wheaton, IL: Crossway, 2023).
2. For a list of likely OT allusions and verbal parallels, see Andreas J. Köstenberger, "John," in *Commentary on the New Testament Use of the Old Testament,* eds. G. K. Beale and D. A. Carson (Grand Rapids: Baker Academic, 2007), 415–512, here 419–20.

115

Gospel.[3] The next most prominent book in terms of the number of citations, hardly surprisingly, is Isaiah, with four quotations, followed by two from Zechariah and one from the Pentateuch (if John 19:36 depends on Exod. 12:46 or Num. 9:12). As well, also giving prominence to the use of the Psalms is the fact that six out of the seven quotations are formally identified as citations of Scripture (the exception is John 12:13).

The first quotation from Psalms is in John 2:17 in the context of the cleansing of the temple (Ps. 69:9 [MT 10]: "Zeal for your house will consume [καταφάγεταί] me"). The LXX is modified by the evangelist, who changed the verb from an aorist to a future,[4] so that the quotation indicates what the zeal of Jesus will lead to and points forward to his death on the cross (the most common understanding),[5] or, as argued by Michael Daise, it points forward to Jesus's future ardor in establishing the new metaphorical temple, though it will require his death.[6] This story is the start of what becomes a pattern in the Gospel, for the temple is the setting for many of its accounts of Jesus's actions (e.g., John 5:14; 7:14, 28; 10:23; 11:56; 18:20).[7] This quotation serves to highlight the first appearance of opposition to Jesus and his mission, and the last three quotations from the Psalms have the same focus, situated as they are in the passion narrative.[8] It is not stated when the disciples "remembered" this psalmic verse and connected it to Jesus's action of cleansing the temple, but it may have been at the time of,[9] or else it was after, the resurrection, through the ministry of the Spirit-Paraclete, that they gained this perspective (cf. 2:22: "When therefore he was raised from the dead") (cf. 12:16).[10] In several of the quotations,

---

3. For the use of heptads in John's Gospel (e.g., the seven "I am" sayings), see Michael A. Daise, *Feasts in John: Jewish Festivals and Jesus's "Hour" in the Fourth Gospel*, WUNT 2/229 (Tübingen: Mohr Siebeck, 2007), 32–34.

4. Maarten J. J. Menken, *Old Testament Quotations in the Fourth Gospel: Studies in Textual Form*, CBET 15 (Kampen: Kok Pharos, 1996), 38–40.

5. E.g., Karen H. Jobes, *John Through Old Testament Eyes* (Grand Rapids: Kregel Academic, 2021), 70.

6. Michael A. Daise, *Quotations in John: Studies on Jewish Scripture in the Fourth Gospel*, LNTS 610 (London: T&T Clark, 2019), 144–55.

7. Benjamin J. Lappenga, "Whose Zeal Is It Anyway? The Citation of Psalm 69:9 in John 2:17 as a Double Entendre," in *Abiding Words: The Use of Scripture in the Gospel of John*, ed. Alicia D. Myers and Bruce G. Schuchard, RBS 81 (Atlanta: SBL, 2015), 141–59, here 145–47.

8. There is no call to deny the historicity of this event in Jesus's ministry, see Andreas J. Köstenberger, *Encountering John: The Gospel in Historical, Literary, and Theological Perspective*, 2nd ed. (Grand Rapids: Baker Academic, 2013), 62–64; Allan Chapple, "Jesus's Intervention in the Temple: Once or Twice?" *JETS* 58 (2015): 545–69.

9. Andreas J. Köstenberger, *John*, BECNT (Grand Rapids: Baker Academic, 2004), 107n24.

10. Martin Hengel, "The Old Testament in the Fourth Gospel," in *The Gospels and the Scriptures of Israel*, ed. Craig A. Evans and W. Richard Stegner, JSNTSup 104 (Sheffield: Sheffield Academic, 1994), 380–95, here 390–91; Daise, *Quotations in John*, 127–33.

including the one found in John 2:17, the words of David the chief psalmist are placed in the mouth of Jesus as a fitting expression of his feelings and experience (cf. John 13:18; 15:25; 19:24). The use of a verse from Psalm 69 in application to Jesus has been prepared for by Andrew's identification of Jesus as "the Messiah" (John 1:41). There is a dearth of explicit Davidic links in this Gospel compared to the Synoptics, though John by no means denies the messianic status of Jesus, of which there are various indicators (e.g., his birth in Bethlehem, ironically hinted at in 7:40–42).

The second quotation from Psalms is in John 6:31 (Ps. 78:24b: "He gave them bread from heaven to eat [φαγεῖν]"). The addition of the infinitive ("to eat") may be derived by the evangelist from the parallel line in 78:24a;[11] certainly, the eating motif is important in the Johannine context (John 6:35–58). The scriptural citation made by the people is more significant than they realize, for they do not see it as having any application to Jesus himself, even though he has just matched that miracle (6:26).[12] We do not need to view Jesus as rebuking the crowd for falsely elevating Moses (6:32: "it was not Moses who gave you the bread from heaven"),[13] rather, this correction is connected to the main point Jesus wishes to make, for Jesus implies that he identifies himself with God who fed the people. The importance of the feeding of the five thousand in the Gospel is signaled by the amount of narratival space allotted to it and its aftermath (the seventy-one verses of John 6) and by the citation from the Psalter at this point. In the psalm a focus is the unbelief of the wilderness generation and the judgment that fell on them (Ps. 78:21–22, 31), and the story in John 6 is in accord with the cited psalm, for both passages depict people who eat but fail to believe.[14]

The third quotation is in John 10:34 (Ps. 82:6: "I say, you are gods"). In the psalm, this exalted mode of address may be due the role assigned to those addressed to exercise God's prerogative to judge. This is the explanation of its use in application to *judges* in Psalm 82 (cf. Ps. 58:1

---

11. Bruce G. Schuchard, *Scripture within Scripture: The Interrelationship of Form and Function in the Explicit Old Testament Citations in the Gospel of John*, SBLDS 133 (Atlanta: Scholars Press, 1992), 36–37.

12. Margaret Daly-Denton, *David in the Fourth Gospel: The Johannine Reception of the Psalms*, AGJU 47 (Leiden: Brill, 2000), 131.

13. I do not agree with Menken, who argues that the crowd see Moses as the giver of the manna (*Old Testament Quotations*, 54–63). Moses is not as such mentioned in Psalm 78.

14. Ruth Sheridan, *Retelling Scripture: "The Jews" and the Scriptural Citations in John 1:19–12:50*, BibInt 110 (Leiden: Brill, 2012), 148–50.

[MT 2]),[15] and the Jewish leadership in the Gospel of John claim the right to pronounce a judgment on Jesus. Likewise, a judicial interpretation of what is said to the king in Psalm 45:6 ("Your throne, O God") is supported by mention in Psalm 45 of "throne" and "uprightness," as well as by the "[loving] righteousness . . . [hating] wickedness" contrast.[16] The citation of Psalm 82:6 is more than just a clever ploy by Jesus, for it fits the situation in more than one way. Jesus is challenging the Jews to judge and evaluate his claims fairly and properly, and there is a sense in which Jesus is on trial throughout his ministry, not just when later, he stands before Pilate.[17] The psalmic quotation is part of Jesus's defense of his claim to be the Son of God (John 10:33, 36), and Jesus as the divine Son is the ultimate judge, and, as noted by Margaret Daly-Denton, the parallel line in Psalm 82:6b ("sons of the Most High, all of you") supplies the Son of God language that Jesus uses in application to himself.[18]

The fourth quotation is in John 12:13 (Ps. 118:25–26: "Hosanna! Blessed is he who comes in the name of the Lord, even the King of Israel!").[19] It is paired with a citation from Zechariah 9:9, which includes the wording, "your king is coming." My claim is that this makes clear that Jesus enters Jerusalem as the divine King. In the severely shortened version of Zechariah 9:9 provided in John 12:15 ("Fear not, daughter of Zion; behold, your king is coming, sitting on a donkey's colt!"), the evangelist only includes elements that reflect the main features of his own presentation: Jesus's entrance into the city and his seated posture on the animal (cf. Matt. 21:5).[20] The result is that there is no emphasis on lowliness.[21] The words "even the king of Israel" are an interpretive addition to Psalm 118, perhaps under the influence of Zephaniah 3:15 or Isaiah

---

15. This is the view of Rashi; see Mayer I. Gruber, *Rashi's Commentary on Psalms* (Philadelphia: The Jewish Publication Society, 2007), 350. For other instances, see Exod. 21:6 and 22:8 (KJV, NIV). The alternate interpretation is that these verses about going *to God* refer to going to the sanctuary for judgment (cf. 1 Sam. 10:3), where the appointed judges reside; see Brevard S. Childs, *The Book of Exodus: A Critical, Theological Commentary*, OTL (Philadelphia: Westminster, 1974), 469, 475.

16. Cf. Geoffrey W. Grogan, *Psalms*, THOTC (Grand Rapids: Eerdmans, 2008), 99.

17. Cf. Sheridan, *Retelling Scripture*, 196–97.

18. Margaret Daly-Denton, "The Psalms in John's Gospel," in *The Psalms in the New Testament*, Steve Moyise and Maarten J. J. Menken (eds.), The New Testament and the Scriptures of Israel (London: T&T Clark, 2004), 119–38, here 126; Daly-Denton, *David in the Fourth Gospel*, 169–76.

19. For argument that it is, indeed, a scriptural quotation, see Daise, *Quotations in John*, 158–60.

20. Menken, *Old Testament Quotations*, 79–81.

21. As noted by Wayne A. Meeks, *The Prophet-King: Moses Traditions and the Johannine Christology*, NovTSup 14 (Leiden: Brill, 1967), 87.

44:6,[22] and this produces a segue to the quotation from Zechariah (cf. Luke 19:38: "Blessed is *the King* who comes in the name of the Lord!"). The evangelist uses the title "the king of Israel" only two times (John 1:49; 12:13), but it provides a key for understanding Johannine Christology. The Synoptic Gospels record many kingdom sayings (cf. John 3:3, 5), but the Fourth Evangelist chooses to concentrate on the person of Jesus as king. Martin Hengel goes as far as to say that "[the Fourth Evangelist] emphasizes the kingship of Jesus much more than the Synoptics."[23] The messiahship of Jesus is a prominent feature in the first three Gospels (e.g., the multiple uses of "the son of David" designation in Matthew), and Jesus is recognized as the Messiah in John as well (e.g., 1:41), but John's penchant to use the title "king" of Jesus enables the meaning of this term to slide between messianic and divine denotations. References to Jesus's identity as "king" are strategically placed at the beginning (1:49), middle (12:13), and end of the Gospel (19:21).[24] In other words, "Jesus begins his ministry as king, enters Jerusalem as king, and is crucified as king."[25]

The motif of kingship is extensively featured throughout the Johannine passion narrative. It is mainly expressed using kingly titles, that is, "king" or "the king of the Jews," whereas the title "the Christ" is absent from the trial narrative, suggesting a non-messianic understanding of Jesus's kingship. In fact, the title "king" is the only one used of Jesus in the Johannine passion narrative, except for one (negative) use of the title "the Son of God" by the Jews (19:7).[26] The title "the king of the Jews" is used of Jesus by Pilate (18:33, 37; 19:15) and by the Roman soldiers (19:3), and he is crucified as "the King of the Jews" (19:19–22). This suggests that the issue of Jesus's kingship forms the "main focus of the trial,"[27] and

---

22. Maarten J. J. Menken, "The Quotations from Zech 9:9 in Mt 21:5 and in Jn 12:15," in *John and the Synoptics*, ed. A. Denaux, BETL 101 (Leuven: Leuven University Press, 1992), 571–78, here 575.

23. Martin Hengel, *Studies in Early Christology* (Edinburgh: T&T Clark, 1995), 336; cf. Edwin D. Freed, *Old Testament Quotations in the Gospel of John*, NovTSup 11 (Leiden: Brill, 1965), 76.

24. Ruben Zimmermann, "Imagery in John: Opening up Paths in to Tangled Thicket of John's Figurative World," in *Imagery in the Gospel of John: Terms, Forms, Themes, and Theology of Johannine Figurative Language*, ed. Jörg Frey, Jan G. van der Watt, and Ruben Zimmermann, WUNT 2/200 (Tübingen: Mohr Siebeck, 2006), 1–43, here 34.

25. Andrew C. Brunson, *Psalm 118 in the Gospel of John: An Intertextual Study on the New Exodus Pattern in the Theology of John*, WUNT 2/158 (Tübingen: Mohr Siebeck, 2003), 224n135.

26. Reimund Bieringer, "'My Kingship is not of this World' (John 18:36): The Kingship of Jesus and Politics," in *The Myriad Christ: Plurality and the Quest for Unity in Contemporary Christology*, ed. Terrence Merrigan and Jacques Haers, BETL 152 (Leuven: Leuven University Press, 2000), 159–75, here 160.

27. Matthew L. Skinner, *The Trial Narrative: Conflict, Power, and Identity in the New Testament* (Louisville: Westminster John Knox, 2010), 95.

more is at stake than simply the issue of messianic kingship when Jesus is referred to as a king in the Fourth Gospel.[28] Unlike the other Gospels, there is a lack of any Davidic reference in the entry into Jerusalem. In 12:13, Jesus is designated "the King of Israel" rather than "the Son of David" (as in Matt. 21:9, 15), nor is there any mention of "the kingdom of our father David" (as in Mark 11:9–10). As noted by John Lierman, "even with its pronouncedly royal Christology, no Gospel does more to distance Jesus from Davidic expectations than John's does."[29] Andrew Brunson is correct, therefore, when he says that the title "king of Israel" primarily points to YHWH.[30] Brunson also sees the exhortation "Fear not" added by the evangelist to the quotation from Zechariah 9:9 (John 12:15) as supporting the supposition that Jesus in John 12 is identified as the divine King.[31]

As well, the expression "the coming one" (ὁ ἐρχόμενος) in the quotation from Psalm 118 (12:13) is found alongside the addition by the evangelist of the title "the King of Israel," so that the crowd's acclamation of Jesus as "the coming one" is inseparable from the title "the King of Israel" in John 12.[32] A shift of emphasis is to be noted compared to what is found in the account of Jesus's entry into Jerusalem in Matthew 21, which includes two references to Jesus as "the son of David" (21:9, 15), whereas any Davidic link is missing in the description of the entrance in John 12. There is in the Old Testament an expectation of the coming of YHWH (e.g., Pss. 96:13; 98:9) as well as of the coming of the Messiah (John 4:25; 11:27). In particular, God's coming is a leading feature of the prophecy of Zechariah (e.g., Zech. 2:10 [MT 14]; 8:3; 14:5) and Zechariah 9:9 is best interpreted as describing the coming of God, not the Messiah.[33] This language of "coming" can also be related to what is

---

28. David Rensberger, "The Politics of John: The Trial of Jesus in the Fourth Gospel," *JBL* 103 (1984): 395–411, here 406.

29. John Lierman, "The Mosaic Pattern of John's Christology," in *Challenging Perspectives on the Gospel of John*, WUNT 2/219 (Tübingen: Mohr Siebeck, 2006), 210–34, here 216–17; cf. D. Moody Smith, *The Theology of the Gospel of John* (Cambridge: Cambridge University Press, 1995), 86–87.

30. Brunson, *Psalm 118*, 234.

31. Brunson, *Psalm 118*, 237–38. If the injunction "Fear not" derives from Zephaniah 3:16, this also supports a reference to the Divine Warrior (Sheridan, *Retelling Scripture*, 226–29). Or if it comes from Isaiah 44:2, it carries the same implication (Schuchard, *Scripture within Scripture*, 77–78).

32. Brunson, *Psalm 118*, 223.

33. This is a minority view argued for by Wolter H. Rose, "Zechariah and the Ambiguity of Kingship in Postexilic Israel," in *Let Us Go Up to Zion: Essays in Honour of H. G. M. Williamson on the Occasion of His Sixty-Fifth Birthday*, ed. Iain Provan and Mark J. Boda, VTSup 153 (Leiden: Brill, 2012), 219–31; and Gregory Goswell, "A Theocratic Reading of Zechariah 9:9," *BBR* 26 (2016): 7–19.

said in the Johannine Prologue about the incarnate Word of God coming into the world (John 1:9, 14; cf. 3:31). This is where the use of Zechariah 9:9 in John 12:15 ("Your king is coming") is significant, and I am arguing that the Fourth Evangelist also understands this Old Testament text as referring to the future entrance of God into Jerusalem.

The fifth quotation is in John 13:18 (Ps. 41:9 [MT 10]: "He who ate my bread has lifted his heel against me"). The motif of personal betrayal is also found in another Davidic psalm (55:12–14 [MT 13–15]), with the figure of Ahithophel possibly in mind in both psalms.[34] In the account of the Last Supper, Jesus has Judas in view as early as John 13:10 ("but not all of you"), and he follows up his citation of Psalm 41 by staging what is, in effect, an enactment of what is described in the psalm, by giving a morsel of bread to Judas (John 13:26), who soon after leaves on his errand of betrayal.

The sixth quotation is in John 15:25 (Pss. 35:19; 69:4 [MT 5], both of which say: "They hated me without a cause"), but the use of Psalm 69 elsewhere in the Gospel favors it being the source here. As in John 10:34, the "Law" mentioned in 15:25 is not the Pentateuch, and in both Johannine texts the Jews are, in effect, accused of breaking "your/their law" that they claim to reverence and obey.[35] The quotation of Psalm 69 is within a paragraph that has six earlier mentions of the world's hatred of Jesus and his disciples (15:18 [2x], 19, 23 [2x], 24), with the quotation of the psalm forming a crescendo.[36] Just as Jesus was hated, the disciples are warned that they too will be hated.[37]

The seventh quotation is in John 19:24 (Ps. 22:18 [21:19 in LXX; MT 19]): "They divided my garments among them, and for my clothing [ἱματισμόν] they cast lots"). All four Gospels note the connection between the suffering of Jesus and the contents of Psalm 22. The actions of the soldiers (John 19:23–24a) are said to be the fulfillment of this psalm, with John choosing to take advantage of the poetic parallelism and

---

34. Menken argues that the quotation is a translation from the Hebrew by the evangelist, with the influence of the analogous passage 2 Sam. 18:28 (*Old Testament Quotations*, 125–38); see also, Schuchard, *Scripture within Scripture*, 113–17.

35. See, also, the polemically charged wording of 8:17 ("your law").

36. Daly-Denton, "The Psalms in John's Gospel," 131.

37. J. Ramsey Michaels also reads the previous psalmic citation as applying more widely than just to Judas. See "Betrayal and the Betrayer: The Uses of Scripture in John 13:18–19," in *The Gospels and the Scriptures of Israel*, ed. Craig A. Evans and W. Richard Stegner, JSNTSup 104 (Sheffield: Sheffield Academic, 1994), 459–74.

differentiate between their treatment of his garments in general and of his robe. The tearing of robes in the Old Testament can presage the loss of royal authority (1 Sam. 15:27–28; 1 Kings 11:29–31), and so the untorn robe of Christ may be intended to signal that his death on the cross represents no loss of power or prestige, but rather is his enthronement and glorification, in line with the presentation of his death as his lifting up (e.g., John 3:14; 12:32).[38]

The wording of three other passages in the Gospel may be influenced by the Psalter, as well as by other Old Testament passages: "From within him shall flow rivers of living water" (John 7:38; cf. Ps. 78:16, 20), the psalm referring to the miracle of water from the rock (Exod. 17); "I thirst" (John 19:28; cf. Ps. 69:21 [MT 22]); and "Not one of his bones will be broken" (John 19:36; cf. Ps. 34:20 [MT 21]).[39]

2. THE USE OF THE BOOK OF DANIEL

In the Gospels, Jesus makes frequent use of the expression "the son of man," indeed, it is his typical mode of self-reference. The usual view is that this usage is based on the figure in Daniel 7, and the special importance of the phrase for the self-understanding of Jesus lies in the fact that in the Gospels it is *only* found on the lips of Jesus.[40] On the basis of instances in the Synoptic Gospels where "the son of man" self-designation is used interchangeably with the first-person pronoun in parallel texts (e.g., Matt. 16:13 // Mark 8:27 and Luke 9:18), and also seeking to take into account the son of man texts unique to the Fourth Gospel, apparently generated by the author of John (e.g., John 1:51; 6:27, 53, 62), Larry Hurtado argues that the term carries no fixed or defined meaning; in other words, it "designates but does not define Jesus."[41] Hurtado is right to urge caution in assuming that every use of

---

38. Daly-Denton, "The Psalms in John's Gospel," 132–33.

39. Those scholars who foreground the link with the Psalter include Daly-Denton, "The Psalms in John's Gospel," 119, and Marianne Meye Thompson, "'They Bear Witness to Me': The Psalms in the Passion Narrative of the Gospel of John," in *The Word Leaps the Gap: Essays on Scripture and Theology in Honor of Richard B. Hays*, ed. J. Ross Wagner, C. Kavin Rowe, and A. Katherine Grieb (Grand Rapids: Eerdmans, 2008), 267–83, here 277–79.

40. Mark 2:10 is perhaps not an exception to this rule ("But that you may know that the son of man has authority on earth to forgive sins"). See Geza Vermes, *Jesus the Jew: A Historian's Reading of the Gospels* (London: Collins, 1973), 180. The expression occurs only once elsewhere in the NT on the lips of Stephen, who models his words on those of Jesus under similar circumstances (Acts 7:56; cf. Luke 22:69).

41. Larry W. Hurtado, "Summary and Concluding Observations," in *"Who Is This Son of Man?" The Latest Scholarship on the Puzzling Expression of the Historical Jesus*, ed. Larry W. Hurtado and Paul L. Owen,

the phrase means that what is said about the son of man is something inherent to the phrase. For example, Mark 8:31 ("the Son of Man must suffer many things") does not require the interpreter to try to find a *suffering* son of man figure in Daniel 7.[42] According to Hurtado, the term has no inherent christological content but is a circumlocution for "I" that originates in Jesus's distinctive way of referring to himself.[43] It is true that many uses of the expression do not appear to carry any particular nuance; however, this approach too quickly disposes of the link of the phrase with the human figure of Daniel 7, which was an important Old Testament text for Jesus, as demonstrated especially by statements made by him toward the end of his ministry (e.g., Mark 14:62),[44] and this would seem to explain why Jesus chose to use this term.

Jesus claims that he has been given authority to judge "because [ὅτι] he is the Son of Man" (John 5:27),[45] and yet it is the one who was ancient of days who judges in Daniel 7,[46] and my thesis is that this is evidence that Jesus merges the two figures and identifies himself with both. The vision of "one like a son of man" in Revelation 1:13–16 (= the risen Jesus, given Rev. 1:18) also shows the combined influence of Daniel 7:9 and 13, namely, it amalgamates the separate descriptions of "the one like a son of man" and the one who was ancient of days (e.g., his hair like white wool [Rev. 1:14; cf. Dan. 7:9]).[47] Jesus's self-referential use of "the son of man" should be understood as a shorthand way of referring to the scene of Daniel 7:13–14 *in toto* whereby Jesus identifies himself with *both* figures: the enthroned divine judge who gives authority and the human figure

---

LNTS 390 (London: T&T Clark, 2011), 159–77, here 167; also, Hurtado, *Lord Jesus Christ: Devotion to Jesus in Earliest Christianity* (Grand Rapids: Eerdmans, 2003), 290–306.

42. Certainly, the saints suffer in Daniel 7 (vv. 21, 25), but only by interpreting the one like a son of man as a corporate figure (= the saints)—an approach of which I would not approve—can a suffering son of man figure be found in Daniel 7.

43. This view, in the form earlier promoted by Geza Vermes, is critiqued by Adela Yarbro Collins, "The Influence of Daniel on the New Testament," in John J. Collins, *Daniel: A Commentary on the Book of Daniel*, Hermeneia (Minneapolis: Fortress, 1993), 90–123, here 94–95; see Vermes, *Jesus the Jew*, 163–68, 177–82.

44. Cf. Darrell L. Bock, "The Use of Daniel 7 in Jesus's Trial, with Implications for His Self-Understanding," in *"Who Is This Son of Man?"*, 78–100, here 89–93.

45. According to Benjamin E. Reynolds, *The Apocalyptic Son of Man in the Gospel of John*, WUNT 2/249 (Tübingen: Mohr Siebeck, 2008), 136: "'Son of Man' is continually found in the context of judgment in the Gospel of John." He points to John 3:16–21; 8:29; 9:34–41; 12:30–36.

46. Reynolds, *The Apocalyptic Son of Man*, 139–40.

47. Peter R. Carrell, *Jesus and the Angels: Angelology and the Christology of the Apocalypse of John*, SNTSMS 95 (Cambridge: Cambridge University Press, 1997), 148–74.

who receives it. There is no reason that Jesus cannot be represented by two figures in the one scene, for it is a *vision* (7:1) rather than a description of an actual event, whether in the past or in the future, a visionary scene that embodies and illustrates certain theological realities. A similar merging of the figures is the explanation behind Matthew 25:31 (cf. Matt. 19:28), where Jesus says that "[the son of man] will sit on his glorious throne" as universal judge.[48] In other words, the evangelist's use of son of man language originating in Daniel 7 feeds into and supports his high Christology.

Other than use of this key expression, there is no explicit link to Daniel 7, unlike in the Synoptics, but there are enough thematic features dependent on what is found in Daniel 7 to confirm the link to this Old Testament passage. There are twelve "Son of Man" sayings and thirteen instances of the use of the phrase in the Gospel (John 1:51; 3:13, 14; 5:27; 6:27, 53, 62; 8:28; 9:35; 12:23, 34 [2x]; 13:31), and these are connected to such key Johannine themes as heavenly descent and ascent, judgment, the giving of eternal life, and glorification, all of which are arguably derived from the theology of the book of Daniel.[49] For example, the one like a son of man is described in Daniel as coming "with the clouds of heaven" (Dan. 7:13), and he descends from the heavenly sphere to earth.[50] The goal of his descent is to receive a universal earthly kingdom from the hands of the one who was ancient of days, with the aim "that all peoples, nations, and languages should serve him" (7:14).[51] The theme of glory is not explicit in Daniel 7, but the theophanic depiction of the one who was ancient of days (7:9–12) is one of glory (cf. Matt. 16:27; 19:28; 24:30; 25:31),[52] and the use of glory in application to Jesus in the Gospel of John may be another example of the merging of the two figures of Daniel 7. The common suggestion is that the kingdom theme

---

48. For detailed argumentation, see Gregory Goswell, "Where Is David in the Book of Daniel?" *ResQ* 56 (2014): 209–21.

49. Other OT books also contain these themes, and I am not claiming that John is exclusively dependent on Daniel.

50. John E. Goldingay, *Daniel*, WBC 30 (Dallas: Word, 1989), 167; Ben Witherington III, *Jesus, Paul and the End of the World: A Comparative Study of New Testament Eschatology* (Downers Grove, IL: InterVarsity Press, 1992), 172.

51. Reynolds fails to connect the decent of the son of man in John (3:13) to what is found in Daniel 7, because, like many scholars, he views Daniel 7 as depicting the one like a son of man ascending to the throne of God (*The Apocalyptic Son of Man*, 106–7, 113); however, Daniel 7:9–12 depicts a judgment scene on earth wherein God judges earthly kingdoms (beasts).

52. Reynolds, *The Apocalyptic Son of Man*, 194–96, 211–12.

in the Synoptics has been transposed into the motif of "eternal life" in this Gospel.[53] This transposition (the term used by Köstenberger) could well derive from Daniel 12, where it is promised that some will awake to "everlasting life" (12:2 LXX ζωὴν αἰώνιον),[54] which is the only instance of the expression in the Old Testament, though other apocalyptic passages contain the same hope of the defeat of death (notably Isa. 25:7–8; 26:19). The predicted reign of the persecuted saints in Daniel requires that they be resurrected (7:22, 24, 27; 11:33, 35), and those raised are likened to "the stars," symbolizing their status as rulers in the future kingdom (12:3).[55] The rescue of the hero Daniel from certain death in the lions' den causes King Darius to acknowledge God's supreme kingship (6:26–27 [MT 27–28]).[56] In other words, God's kingdom and eternal life are linked themes in Daniel, and I am arguing that this connection was noted and developed by the evangelist, who, however, depicts judgment, the giving and receiving of eternal life, and glorification as present realities, without denying a future fulfillment as well.

3. THEMATIC CONVERGENCES WITH THE WRITINGS

The theology of the Fourth Gospel converges with certain theological concerns of the Psalter, Chronicles, and Ezra-Nehemiah, three of the larger books in the Writings. A certain type of Davidism is in view at the end of the Psalter, one in which David is a model of devotion to God and the temple.[57] The answer to the cry of the exiles in Psalm 137:4 ("How shall we sing the LORD's song in a foreign land?") is modeled by David in the mini-collection of Davidic psalms that follow (Pss. 138–145).[58]

---

53. See Andreas Köstenberger, "John's Transposition Theology: Retelling the Story of Jesus in a Different Key," in *Earliest Christian History: History, Literature, and Theology: Essays from the Tyndale Fellowship in Honor of Martin Hengel*, ed. Michael F. Bird and Jason Maston, WUNT 2/320 (Tübingen: Mohr Siebeck, 2012), 191–226, here 207–8; Köstenberger notes that in Matt. 19:16 and 24, gaining eternal life and entering the kingdom are equivalents (*John*, 122–23).

54. For the connections between Daniel 12:2 and the son of man's role in the double resurrection in John 5:28–29, see Köstenberger, "John," 442; Reynolds, *The Apocalyptic Son of Man*, 140–42.

55. N. T. Wright, *The Resurrection of the Son of God* (London: SPCK, 2003), 112.

56. For the rescues from the fiery furnace and the lions' den as quasi-resurrection stories, see Gregory Goswell, "Resurrection in the Book of Daniel," *ResQ* 55 (2013): 139–51.

57. For fuller argumentation, see Gregory Goswell, "The Non-Messianic Psalter of Gerald H. Wilson," *VT* 66 (2016): 524–41.

58. As noted, for example, by Harm Van Grol, "David and his *Chasidim*: Place and Function of Psalms 138–145," in *The Composition of the Book of Psalms*, ed. Erich Zenger, BETL 238 (Leuven: Peeters, 2010), 309–37.

In Book V of the Psalter, the model set by David is of one whose chief concern is to properly honor the divine King, whose rule over Israel is symbolized by the ark (his footstool), and so David seeks to ensure that the ark is properly housed (132:1–10). Similarly, in Psalm 145:21 ("My mouth will speak the praise of the LORD") David "announces and leads the praise of YHWH that takes place in the last five psalms of the Psalter."[59] This approach takes notice of what *kind* of future David is predicted in Book V, namely, one who takes a lead in the worship and service of the divine King.[60] The same kind of devotion to God is on display when the words of Psalm 69:9 (MT 10) are quoted and applied to Jesus in an early episode in the Gospel, as if they are the words of Jesus himself, "Zeal for your house will consume me" (John 2:17).[61]

A lot of attention is paid to David and Solomon in Chronicles, but the focus is on the role of the Davidic dynasty in relation to the temple, and the concluding chapter of the book gives little if any reason to assume the author looked forward to the reestablishment of the dynasty. We must reject the view that the Chronicler is "the guardian of the Messianic tradition";[62] rather, he writes to legitimate the cultic offices founded by David and to teach that loyalty to YHWH is shown by commitment to the Jerusalem temple. The focus on the temple, viewed as God's palace (לביה), supports a prevailing kingdom of God theology in Chronicles.[63] Support for the temple cultus emerges as the *raison d'être* of the Davidic dynasty and takes precedence over the existence of the monarchy as the main concern of the Chronicler (e.g., the repair of the temple by Joash [2 Chron. 24:4–14]; the great Passover under Hezekiah [30:1–27]).[64] The renewed hope for God's people made possible by the decree of Cyrus does not include the restoration of the Davidic house (2 Chron. 36:22–

---

59. Erich Zenger, "'Das alles Fleisch den Namen seiner Heiligung segne' (Ps 145, 21): Die Komposition Ps 145–150 als Anstoss zu einer christlich-jüdischen Psalmenhermeneutik," *BZ* 41 (1997): 1–27.
60. Cf. Georg P. Braulik, "Psalter and Messiah: Toward a Christological Understanding of the Psalms in the Old Testament and the Church Fathers," in *Psalms and Liturgy*, ed. Dirk J. Human and Cas J. A. Vos, JSOTSup 410 (London: T&T Clark, 2004), 15–40, here 23: "According to Psalm 101:1, it is the first task of David, as ruler, to sing praises to Yahweh."
61. Jobes, *John Through Old Testament Eyes*, 69–72.
62. Gerhard von Rad, *Old Testament Theology, Volume 1: The Theology of Israel's Historical Traditions* (Edinburgh: Oliver & Boyd, 1962), 351.
63. See Gregory Goswell, "Temple and Kingship in the Book of Chronicles," *ResQ* 62 (2020): 65–79.
64. Cf. J. L. Berquist, *Judaism in Persia's Shadow: A Social and Historical Approach* (Minneapolis: Fortress, 1995), 156: "Within this text's ideology, the true goal of history is the temple, and politicians are relevant only when needed to support the temple and its worship."

23). The concluding words of Chronicles, "let him go up [to rebuild the temple]," reiterate the prophetic hope of the return of God's people within the consummated kingdom of God, anticipated by the rebuilt temple (= God's palace), as the final goal of God's purposes in history.[65] If the return of the Davidic house is to be contemplated in the thought-world of the Chronicler—something not made explicit by the author—it would need to fit within this theological framework, namely the chief role of the future Davidic king would be to support the temple cultus.[66]

In the case of Ezra-Nehemiah, the figure of David is recalled a number of times in his role as organizer of cultic worship (Ezra 3:10; 8:20; Neh. 11:23; 12:24, 36, 45, 46) and his son Solomon once joins him in the same role (Neh. 12:45). Certain landmarks in Jerusalem act as memorials to David as a great figure of the past (Neh. 12:37 [2x]; cf. Neh. 3:16), but they do not imply that there is an important future for his descendants.[67] References to David as the patron of the liturgy (12:45–46) and the inventor of musical instruments used in worship (12:36) probably explain the prophetic status attributed to him ("the man of God") (Neh. 12:24, 36), for in Chronicles the performance of cultic musical duties is viewed as a type of prophesying (cf. 1 Chron. 25:1–3),[68] but none of the references to David in Ezra-Nehemiah have a futuristic orientation. If a royalist hope is to find a place in the theology of Ezra-Nehemiah, it must take the form of a future Davidic worship leader for a nation whose life is centered on the temple. More than one type of messianism is found in the Bible, and the portrait of David on display in the three books surveyed fosters the expectation of a future Davidic king (= Messiah) whose role is temple-centered and this anticipates the nuanced messianism in the Gospel of John. As well, the eschatology of these Old Testament books is

---

65. William Johnstone, "Hope of Jubilee: The Last Word in the Hebrew Bible," *EvQ* 72 (2000): 307–14.

66. Gerhard von Rad notes that if we wanted to develop a picture of what a future David might look like from what is said in Chronicles, he "would look on the care of the sanctuary and the ordering of sacral offices as the first of his main duties" (*Old Testament Theology*, 351).

67. Cf. Reiner Albertz, "The Thwarted Restoration," in *Yahwism after the Exile: Perspectives on Israelite Religion in the Persian Period*, ed. Reiner Albertz and Bob Becking, STR 5 (Winona Lake, IN: Eisenbrauns, 2004), 1–17, here 16: "The books of Ezra and Nehemiah . . . wrote a history of Persian Judah as if the monarchic restoration had never been at issue." The multiple mentions of David in Ezra-Nehemiah are not sufficient of themselves to require the detecting of a messianic hope in line with God's covenant with David (*pace* Dean R. Ulrich, "David in Ezra-Nehemiah," *WTJ* 78 [2016]: 49–64, here 57–61).

68. Kenneth E. Pomykala, "Images of David in Early Judaism," in *Of Scribes and Sages: Early Jewish Interpretation and Transmission of Scripture: Volume 1: Ancient Versions and Traditions*, ed. C. A. Evans, SSEJC 9 (London: T&T Clark, 2005), 33–46, here 40–42.

centered on the hope of the dawning of the kingdom of God, and this is picked up in the Gospel with its focus on Jesus as the divine King.

It is made clear in the Fourth Gospel that Jesus made multiple trips to Jerusalem, and the feasts mentioned include three Passovers (John 2:13, 23; 6:4; 11:55; 12:1; 13:1), as well as Tabernacles (Booths) (7:2) and Dedication (10:22). There is also the unspecified "feast of the Jews" in 5:1. Much that Jesus said and did, as recorded in John, is to be interpreted within the context of these feasts.[69] In all the varying sequences of books in the Writings, Psalms, Job, and Proverbs are always found together, followed by a group of five shorter works, *Megillot*, and finally Daniel, Ezra-Nehemiah, and Chronicles. In Hebrew Bibles, especially those used by Ashkenazic Jews, the order of the *Megillot* reflects the sequence of the annual cycle of the major Jewish festivals, the year starting with the month of Nisan: Song of Songs (Passover), Ruth (Weeks), Lamentations (Ninth of Ab), Ecclesiastes (Booths), and Esther (Purim),[70] but the link of these books with particular festivals and the reading of these books at the feasts is a development much later than New Testament times.[71] This is another conceptual link between the Writings (as presently arranged) and the Gospel,[72] though the connection is one of theological convergence in the one canon of Scripture rather than influence (either direct or indirect).

CONCLUSION

This investigation of the relationship between the Gospel of John and the Writings considered three main issues: the evangelist's use of the Psalter in the form of seven quotations; the influence of the book of Daniel by means of a series of texts about "the son of man"; and the convergence of some themes in the Gospel with certain theological concerns of the Psalter, Chronicles, and Ezra-Nehemiah. The use of the Psalms in applica-

---

69. For attempts to do so, see P. W. L. Walker, *Jesus and the Holy City: New Testament Perspectives on Jerusalem* (Grand Rapids: Eerdmans, 1996), 167–70; Gerry Wheaton, *The Role of Jewish Feasts in John's Gospel*, SNTSMS 162 (Cambridge: Cambridge University Press, 2015).

70. L. B. Wolfenson, "Implications of the Place of the Book of Ruth in Editions, Manuscripts, and Canon of the Old Testament," *HUCA* 1 (1924): 151–78, here 157.

71. Timothy H. Stone, *The Compilational History of the Megilloth: Canon, Contoured Intertextuality and Meaning in the Writings*, FAT 2/59 (Tübingen: Mohr Siebeck, 2013), 105–11.

72. Cf. Daly-Denton, *David in the Fourth Gospel*, 7: "This is a highly cultic gospel in which the narrative is entwined around the Jewish cycle of feasts and many of the discourses of Jesus are presented as having been uttered in the context of worship, that is, in the milieu of psalmody."

tion to Jesus assumes a typological relationship between Jesus and David, the chief psalmist, and this supports a messianic reading of his mission, especially his experience of rejection (John 2:17; 13:18; 15:25; 19:24), but it also testifies to his divine nature (6:31; 10:34; 12:13). The second aspect of the psalmic citations is more subtle but is evident. Jesus's self-identification as "the son of man" is more than just a way of referring to himself; the designation carries with it themes and motifs that find their source in Daniel 7. I argued that Jesus identifies himself with both figures in that vision, the one who was ancient of days and the one like a son of man. Lastly, theological convergences with the Writings include the focus on worship and feasts, such that the type of messianism found in the Psalter, Chronicles, and Ezra-Nehemiah in certain respects anticipates the presentation in the Gospel of John.

CHAPTER 8

JOHN AND THE SYNOPTICS

QUINN R. MOSIER

I first met Dr. Köstenberger at the Mathena Student Center on the campus of Midwestern Baptist Theological Seminary. I was a pesky new master's student, but he still graciously accepted my invite to coffee. To sweeten the pot, I promised I would not take up more than thirty minutes of his time *and* I would buy his coffee. However, as we got to talking, the thirty minutes soon turned into an hour and thirty minutes, and the hour and thirty minutes turned into years of friendship. What stretched the original conversation to over an hour? John's use of the Synoptics, which happens to be my focus in this essay.[1]

Over the years I have had the privilege of having Dr. Köstenberger as a mentor and boss, but more importantly as a trusted friend and brother in Christ. I will always be grateful not only for his encouragement in my studies, but for leaving me an example of what it means to be a loving father and husband, and for pointing me to Jesus Christ, whose glory and praise is the end of all things—even scholarship.

The perceptive reader will notice this essay is, perhaps controversially, placed under the section entitled, "John and the Canon." The other chapters include John's use of the Pentateuch, Prophets, and Writings. John is clearly saturated in Old Testament allusions, quotations, and motifs. However, is it clear he also knew of and used the Synoptic Gospels?

This essay aims to do two things: (i) explain the shortcomings of the Johannine independence view and (ii) show various ways John engages the Synoptic Gospels.

---

1. A portion of this essay comes from a paper I presented at the 2022 annual meeting of the Evangelical Theological Society called, "John and the Synoptics: Reassessing Past Methods and Assumptions."

1. THE RISE AND RETREAT OF JOHANNINE INDEPENDENCE

It is well known that discussions about John's relationship to the Synoptics are framed by categories of *independence* and *dependence* (or usually some hybrid position in between). In simple terms, independence is the idea that John did not know or use the Synoptics, but represents an independent stream of tradition. Dependence is the opposite idea that John knew, used, and presupposed one or more of the Synoptics as a source in the composition of his own Gospel. Yet, most proposals on John's relationship to the Synoptics are hybrids,[2] oscillating on the spectrum between the poles of independence and dependence. The reason for the many different complex theories[3] is because the question of Johannine-Synoptic relations does not stand alone, but is entangled in a web of critical issues, such as date, authorship, the development of Jesus traditions into written form, textual criticism, and more.[4] Where a scholar lands on these issues largely determines where they land on the spectrum between independence and dependence.

At the beginning of the twentieth century, it was "a foregone conclusion that John knew the Synoptics," as it had been for all of church history.[5] The question then was not "Did John know and use the Synoptics?" but rather "*In what way* did John know the Synoptics?" The landscape dramatically changed in 1938 with the publication of Percival Gardner-

---

2. Recently, William B. Bowes has given a useful taxonomy on the approaches that reflects the difficulty of mapping the variety of positions in between a hard independence and dependence view. They are: (1) Independent non-interaction, (2) Non-dependent interaction, (3) Dependent interaction in part, and (4) Dependent interaction in full. According to Bowes's criteria, this essay falls somewhere between Dependent interaction in part and Dependent interaction in full. See William B. Bowes, "The Relationship between John and the Synoptic Gospels Revisited," *JETS* 66, no. 1 (2023): 123–29.

3. As an example of how complex the theories can get, look no further than M.-É. Boismard and A. Lamouille, *L'Évangile de Jean*, vol. 3, Synopse des Quatre Évangiles en Français (Paris: Les Éditions du Cerf, 1977), and the subsequent critique of Frans Neirynck, Joël Delobel, Thierry Snoy, Gilbert Van Belle, and Frans Van Segbroeck, *Jean et Les Synoptiques: Examen critique de l'exégèse de M.-É Boismard*, BETL XLIX (Leuven: Leuven University Press, 1979).

4. To get a sense of the complexities involved in the Johannine-Synoptic problem, see D. Moody Smith, "John and the Synoptics: Some Dimensions of the Problem," *NTS* 26, no. 1 (1980): 425–44. He lists five dimensions to the problem, though there are doubtless many more, such as authorship: (1) textual criticism, (2) source and tradition criticism, (3) redaction criticism, (4) historical perspective, (5) and theological interests.

5. Hans Windisch, *Johannes und die Synoptiker* (Leipzig: J. C. Hinrichs'sche Buchhandlung, 1926), 43; cited in D. Moody Smith, *John among the Gospels*, 2nd ed. (Columbia: University of South Carolina Press, 2001), 14.

Smith's small book, *Saint John and the Synoptic Gospels*,[6] and the subsequent work of his colleague, C. H. Dodd.[7] Archibald M. Hunter said three decades later, "In 1938 Gardner-Smith was a lone voice protesting John's independence; in 1968 his view may almost be said to represent 'critical orthodoxy.'"[8] Almost every major twentieth-century Johannine commentator—with the notable exception of C. K. Barrett—agreed John wrote independently of the Synoptics, though expressing that independence in different ways.[9]

Yet, notwithstanding the rapid rise of the independence theory and the remarkable dominance it achieved in so little time, by the end of the twentieth century major proponents of the view expressed uncertainty that it would remain in the majority, due in large part to the work of the Louvain school led by Frans Neirynck.[10] D. Moody Smith wrote in 2001, "There is no question that the Gardner-Smith consensus is now significantly eroded."[11] Raymond Brown called scholars holding to independence "a very small majority by the end of the century."[12] Today the tides have shifted toward a position that looks more like traditional Johannine dependence, though it is not simply a return to the Johannine dependence of the early twentieth century.[13]

---

6. Percival Gardner-Smith, *Saint John and the Synoptic Gospels* (Cambridge: Cambridge University Press, 1938).

7. See C. H. Dodd, *Historical Tradition in the Fourth Gospel* (Cambridge: Cambridge University Press, 1965), 68, 172, 208; *The Interpretation of the Fourth Gospel* (Cambridge: Cambridge University Press, 1953), 449n2.

8. Archibald M. Hunter, *According to John: The New Look at the Fourth Gospel* (Philadelphia: Westminster, 1968), 14.

9. For an overview of multiple proposals, see D. Moody Smith, *John among the Gospels*. For a more recent overview, as well as a useful taxonomy of the various positions, see William B. Bowes, "The Relationship between John and the Synoptic Gospels Revisited," *JETS* 66, no. 1 (2023): 113–32.

10. See Raymond Brown, *An Introduction to the Gospel of John*, ed. Francis J. Moloney, The Anchor Bible Reference Library (New York: Doubleday, 2003), 98; D. Moody Smith, *John among the Gospels*, xiii.

11. Smith, *John among the Gospels*, 139.

12. Brown, *An Introduction to the Gospel of John*, 98.

13. Though it ought to be questioned whether *dependence* is the most accurate term to categorize certain authors, the following recent publications show a shift in thinking on John and the Synoptics away from independence: Wendy E. S. North, *What John Knew and What John Wrote: A Study in John and the Synoptics*, IJL (Lanham, MA: Lexington Books; Fortress Academic, 2020); Eve-Marie Becker, Helen K. Bond, and Catrin H. Williams, *John's Transformation of Mark* (New York: T&T Clark, 2021); Jörg Frey, "The Quest for the Jesus of History: Historical Tradition in the Fourth Gospel," in *Theology and History in the Fourth Gospel: Tradition and Narration*, 59–142 (Waco, TX: Baylor University Press, 2018); David F. Ford, "Reading Backwards, Reading Forwards, and Abiding: Reading John in the Spirit Now," *JTI* 11, no. 1 (2017): 69–84; William B. Bowes, "The Relationship between John and the Synoptic Gospels Revisited," *JETS* 66, no. 1 (2023): 113–32; Andreas Köstenberger, "John's Transposition Theology: Retelling the Story of Jesus in a Different Key," in *Earliest Christian History: History, Literature, and Theology. Essays from the*

The reasons the independence view has retreated in popularity can be attributed to a host of contextual factors within New Testament studies. However, there are three main reasons I see contributing to its decline: (i) an overreliance on outdated views of form criticism and oral tradition; (ii) an expectation for John to use his sources like the Synoptics appear to have used one another; (iii) overvaluing historical-grammatical data while undervaluing theological engagement as a legitimate means of detecting sources.

2. THREE SHORTCOMINGS OF THE JOHANNINE INDEPENDENCE VIEW

2.1 An Overreliance on Outdated Views of Form Criticism and Oral Tradition

The remarkable rise of Johannine independence did not happen in a vacuum. Instead, it was caught up in the exciting climate of Gospels scholarship at the time—form criticism, oral tradition, hypothetical written sources, community redaction of texts, and the resurgence of the quest for the historical Jesus. To rightly understand the shift from Johannine dependence to independence, the context of the wider changes taking place in twentieth-century New Testament scholarship must be considered.

The general concept of an isolated and independent John was appealing as part of a solution to a wide array of scholarly problems. For example, a historically reliable and independent Johannine tradition presented an alternate route back to the historical Jesus that much of the first quest dismissed,[14] appealed to conservative tendencies to defend John's historicity, and certainly contributed to the sprawling theories of a sectarian Johannine community that supposedly produced the Gospel as we know it.[15]

Tyndale Fellowship in Honor of Martin Hengel, ed. Michael F. Bird and Jason Maston, WUNT 2/320 (Tübingen: Mohr Siebeck, 2012), 191–226; Gary Greenberg, *Proving Jesus's Authority in Mark and John: Overlooked Evidence of a Synoptic Relationship* (Newcastle upon Tyne: Cambridge Scholars Publishing, 2018); Steven A. Hunt, *Rewriting the Feeding of Five Thousand: John 6.1–15 as a Test Case for Johannine Dependence on the Synoptic Gospels*, SBL 125 (New York: Peter Lang, 2011).

14. See Mark Goodacre, "Parallel Traditions or Parallel Gospels? John's Gospel as a Re-Imagining of Mark," in *John's Transformation of Mark*, 77.

15. See J. Louis Martyn, *History and Theology in the Fourth Gospel*, 3rd ed. (Louisville; London: Westminster John Knox, 2003); Raymond E. Brown, S.S., *The Community of the Beloved Disciple* (New York: Paulist

Due to this wider context, the foundations of Johannine independence are thoroughly form-critical. The theory of independence rests upon the assumption that we can isolate different Gospel traditions, identify their stages of development, and presumably go back to the earliest forms of the tradition; ultimately, to uncover the historical Jesus and the origins of the written Gospels. The vague use of traditions, then, becomes the one-size-fits-all answer to any similarities between John and the Synoptics and a kind of get-out-of-jail-free card to any problem that arises. As Mark Goodacre has poignantly observed, "Unseen sources provide untold explanatory power" and they have "the potential to explain every parallel between John and the Synoptics while at the same time guaranteeing some kind of historical pedigree."[16]

Any striking similarity in wording or pericope order can be explained away by cross-pollination between emerging "pre-Johannine" and "pre-Marcan" traditions. Take the following conclusion from Raymond Brown as an example of the great malleability and explanatory power of an appeal to oral traditions.

> The primitive Johannine tradition was closest to the pre-Marcan tradition but also contained elements found in the sources peculiar to Matthew (e.g., Petrine source) and to Luke. . . . During the oral formation of the Johannine stories and discourses (Stage 2), there very probably was some cross-influence from the emerging Lucan Gospel tradition.[17]

Consider the large leaps and assumptions one has to make in order to affirm Brown's conclusions. How can we know that sections of the "Johannine tradition" are more primitive than another? How certain are we that historical-grammatical data can reveal a reliable age of any given tradition? What does "pre-Marcan tradition" and "emerging Lucan Gospel tradition" mean? Surely, the appeal to Occam's Razor has driven many away from Johannine independence. For, which is more likely: an abstract entity of "emerging Lucan Gospel tradition"

Press, 1979). Brown writes, "I warn the reader that my reconstruction claims [are] at most probability; and if sixty percent of my detective work is accepted, I shall be happy indeed" (7).

16. Goodacre, "Parallel Traditions or Parallel Gospels?," 78.

17. Raymond E. Brown, *The Gospel According to John (I-XII)*, AB 29 (Garden City, NY: Doubleday & Company, Inc., 1966), xlvii.

somehow influenced the formation of Johannine stories and discourses, or that John the apostle, writing after the Synoptics, intentionally wrote to supplement the Synoptic accounts?[18] Of course, all answers on either side to the problem are educated guesswork, but the simpler explanation that John possessed Luke's final written form and used it seems more preferable than the explanation of abstract traditions mysteriously influencing one another.

Another blow to the form-critical foundations of Johannine independence is the development in our understanding of how ancient oral traditions worked. In his essay, "The Gospel of John and the Synoptic Problem," Richard Bauckham shows how arguments for Johannine independence typically depend on older models of oral tradition that err in significant ways. Their arguments assume too evolutionary and literary of a framework in the development of traditions. He argues that, unlike the editing process of a literary work, oral traditions do not develop in a straightforward, linear fashion. If the development of traditions is not linear, then we cannot expect to identify earlier and later forms of a tradition. If no basis for detecting development in a tradition can be identified, then the certainty of constructing tradition histories is futile and can provide no reliable answers to whether John knew and used the Synoptics.[19]

2.2 An Expectation for John to Use His Sources Like the Synoptics Appear to Have Used One Another

The second problem with Johannine independence is the unstated expectation that John used his sources in the same way the Synoptists appear to have used one another. This assumption is often explicitly denied, but still sneaks its way into much of the methodology and conclusions of those holding to independence.[20] The tools of doing Synoptics studies are

---

18. Richard Bauckham observes that given the interconnection and travel of the early Christian communities, it is probable to assume communities and persons exchanged gospel-like material often, especially through preaching. Thus, that "process of sharing was probably far too complicated for us to hope to reconstruct it" (Bauckham, "The Gospel of John and the Synoptic Problem," in *New Studies in the Synoptic Problem: Essays in Honour of Christopher M. Tuckett*, ed. P. Forster, A. Gregory, J. S. Kloppenborg, and J. Verheyden [Leuven; Paris; Walpole, MA: Peeters, 2011], 667).

19. This is not to suggest that oral traditions provide no value in Gospels study. Certainly, in its proper place they do. However, the return to literary dependence, in part, is the attractive simplicity of placing actual existing written Gospels in front of the scholar to examine similarities and differences.

20. Cf. D. A. Carson, *The Gospel According to John*, PNTC (Grand Rapids; Cambridge; Leicester: Eerdmans; Apollos, 1991), 49: "No-one argues that John used Mark in the way that Matthew used Mark (assuming

well-known: side-by-side comparative analysis of verbal similarity, word order, and pericope ordering. Yet, how useful are these tools when roughly eight percent[21] of John parallels the Synoptics and, on top of that, John writes in his own distinctive idiom? How useful are these granular tools in determining use or nonuse when John clearly has a natural tendency for allusion and subtlety?

John is John. His Gospel is clearly different from the other three and we must read with the grain and not against it. If we do not orient our methods and tools to fit around the special contours of his unique Gospel, we run the risk of making the Johannine-Synoptic question a subset of the Synoptic Problem and expecting the same tools used there to transfer over and yield the same kind of results. Moreover, forcing John to fit the Synoptic mold of verbatim reproduction of sources errs in two ways: (1) it misunderstands ancient compositional norms and (2) ignores John's known authorial tendencies. Let us consider these in order.

(1) *Misunderstands Ancient Compositional Norms.* One of the more impactful developments for the Johannine-Synoptic question in the last few decades has been a growing understanding of ancient compositional techniques. Richard Bauckham,[22] Craig S. Keener,[23] Thomas L. Brodie,[24] and others have demonstrated how the use of sources by ancient authors looks much more like John's free and creative paraphrase than the close micro-conflation of sources between the Synoptics. The emphasis in ancient compositional practices was not on originality, but imitation—the reworking of existing sources by swallowing them up into your own voice in order to use them for your own purposes.[25] We

---

the dependence of the first two Gospels ran that way)." Note that Carson does not hold to the independence or dependence view: "The thesis that John is *literarily* dependent on one or more of the Synoptic Gospels has not been demonstrated beyond reasonable doubt, but neither has the thesis that John is literarily *in*dependent of the Synoptics" (51, italics are original).

21. Köstenberger, "John's Transposition Theology," in *Earliest Christian History*, 194. Köstenberger is citing Gary M. Burge, *Interpreting the Gospel of John*, Guides to NT Exegesis (Grand Rapids: Baker, 1992), 23, who has references to Westcott.

22. Richard Bauckham, *Jesus and the Eyewitnesses: The Gospels as Eyewitness Testimony*, 2nd ed. (Grand Rapids: Eerdmans, 2008); "The Gospel of John and the Synoptic Problem," in *New Studies in the Synoptic Problem*.

23. Craig S. Keener, *Christobiography: Memory, History, and the Reliability of the Gospels* (Grand Rapids: Eerdmans, 2019).

24. Thomas L. Brodie, *The Quest for the Origin of John's Gospel: A Source-Oriented Approach* (New York; Oxford: Oxford University Press, 1993).

25. Brodie, *The Quest for the Origin of John's Gospel*, 42–43.

see this "reworking" in John when Synoptic sayings are transformed into his own idiom. For example,

> **Mark 8:35:** ὃς γὰρ ἐὰν θέλῃ τὴν ψυχὴν αὐτοῦ σῶσαι ἀπολέσει αὐτήν· ὃς δ' ἂν ἀπολέσει τὴν ψυχὴν αὐτοῦ ἕνεκεν ἐμοῦ καὶ τοῦ εὐαγγελίου σώσει αὐτήν.

> **John 12:25:** ὁ φιλῶν τὴν ψυχὴν αὐτοῦ ἀπολλύει αὐτήν, καὶ ὁ μισῶν τὴν ψυχὴν αὐτοῦ ἐν τῷ κόσμῳ τούτῳ εἰς ζωὴν αἰώνιον φυλάξει αὐτήν.[26]

As Brodie notes, this imitation was not "slavish," either in form or content. In fact, as Bauckham points out, the compositional habit of free paraphrase was expected and "inculcated by basic education in the Greco-Roman world."[27] And yet, as Catrin H. Williams points out, not only in the Greco-Roman compositional world is the transformation of sources practiced, but it is also widely attested to in the Jewish "rewriting" practices in the late Second Temple period. Jewish authors from this period would often adhere to the basic structure of a text while recasting themes and stories with striking literary and theological creativity, not unlike John.[28]

Besides Greco-Roman free paraphrase and Jewish "rewritten Scripture," there are even more factors at play, such as the use of scribal secretaries in writing,[29] the interplay of oral and written sources, and more. At the very least, when the problem of John and the Synoptics is seen against this backdrop, it should give us pause in how much verbatim reproduction we should expect to be necessary to "prove" dependence on a source. If anything, ancient compositional habits seem to suggest the bar is low, not high, for positing dependence, even when there is minimal verbal similarity or pericope ordering. This means that for those who argue for Johannine independence, the assumption that

---

26. References to the Greek text of the New Testament are based on the Nestle-Aland 28th edition. Aland et al., *Nestle-Aland – Novum Testamentum Graece*, 28th revised ed. (Stuttgart: Deutsche Bibelgesellschaft, 2012).

27. Bauckham, "The Gospel of John and the Synoptic Problem," 661.

28. See Catrin H. Williams, "John's 'Rewriting' of Mark: Some Insights from Ancient Jewish Analogues," in *John's Transformation of Mark*, esp. 57–59.

29. See E. Randolph Richards, *The Secretary in the Letters of Paul*, WUNT 2/42 (Tübingen: Mohr Siebeck, 1991), esp. 15–128.

a high volume of verbatim reproduction is necessary to establish dependence is historically and fundamentally flawed. As Bauckham points out, "It is not the differences between the Gospels [John and the Synoptics] that need explaining, but the high degree of verbatim agreement between the Synoptics."[30]

(2) *Ignores John's Known Authorial Tendencies.* Second, expecting John to use his source-material like the Synoptists ignores John's known authorial tendencies. A brief skim of his Gospel shows he is a highly allusive author, employing deep theological and literary creativity in order to serve his overall purpose of sparking belief in Jesus as the Messiah (John 20:31). His sensitivity to weaving together various themes, playing on the double meanings of words and events, and transforming various signs, events, and even whole Jewish festivals should dissuade us of any notions of him repeating sources in rote fashion.[31]

Going off hard data, John only explicitly cites the Old Testament approximately fourteen times compared to Matthew's fifty-five citations.[32] Yet, how we interpret the data and what conclusions we draw from it matters. Are we to say that because John contains forty-one fewer Old Testament citations than Matthew that he is any less concerned with the Old Testament? Certainly not! Explicit citation is only *one* way the Old Testament can be evoked.[33]

In John's Gospel, the Old Testament is suffused throughout every particle of his writing, from the Jewish festival cycles, to the midrash-like reflection on Genesis 1 in the Prologue, to the explicit appeal to Isaiah 6 to explain the unbelief of the Jewish people in John 12:36–43. He is so steeped in the Old Testament that it has become part of his authorial DNA and it creatively

---

30. Bauckham, "The Gospel of John and the Synoptic Problem," 661.

31. As an example of John's penchant for double meanings, see the section on Jesus's glory and the cross with reference to Isaiah 52:13–54:12 in Richard Bauckham, *Gospel of Glory: Major Themes in Johannine Theology* (Grand Rapids: Baker Academic, 2015), 72–74.

32. Data taken from Andreas J. Köstenberger, "John," in *Commentary on the New Testament Use of the Old Testament*, ed. G. K. Beale and D. A. Carson (Grand Rapids: Baker Academic; Downers Grove, IL: IVP Academic, 2007), 415; Craig L. Blomberg, "Matthew," in *Commentary on the New Testament Use of the Old Testament*, 1.

33. Although, Richard B. Hays is right to point out, "precisely because there are relatively few quotations, each citation that does appear in John's uncluttered narrative assumes proportionately greater gravity as a pointer to Jesus's identity" (Hays, *Echoes of Scripture in the Gospels* [Waco, TX: Baylor University Press, 2017], 78).

manifests itself in more ways than strict copy and paste.[34] The variegated nature of his use of the Old Testament makes for a tapestry of rich metaphors and transformation of themes and figures that potently express the embodiment of Israel's hopes and promises in the person of Jesus Christ.

Just as it would be a mistake to limit John's use of the Old Testament to where he directly cites them, it would also be a mistake to limit John's use of the Synoptics to only passages that express exact verbal parallel. If John used the Synoptics, we have little reason to doubt that he used them with a similar free style to that which he uses the Old Testament—through reworked, rephrased, and altered evocation of the base text by means of a vast array of creative literary techniques.[35]

Thus, these two errors—misunderstanding ancient compositional norms and ignoring John's known authorial tendencies—are present in the implicit assumption that John used his sources like the Synoptists. The consequence of this error leads, then, to my third and final critique.

2.3 Overvaluing Historical-Grammatical Data While Undervaluing Theological Engagement as a Legitimate Means of Detecting Sources

The third problem with Johannine independence is it overvalues historical-grammatical data while undervaluing, or even dismissing, theological engagement as a valid way of showing use and knowledge of the Synoptics. This undervaluing shows once more a lack of awareness of what was normal for first-century writing—particularly *gospel* writing.

In their recent book, *Gospel Reading and Reception in Early Christian Literature,* Madison Pierce, Andrew Byers, Simon Gathercole, and contributors argue how the evangelists were "engaged in a creative and dynamic act of theological reception. . . . The process of composition presupposes a creative and dynamic act of theological *reception*."[36] The

---

34. Andrew Montanaro, "The Use of Memory in the Old Testament Quotations in John's Gospel," *NovT* 59 (2017): 147–70, has recently proposed that John, writing in a predominantly oral culture, would have naturally had memory variants in his recall of the OT from memory. According to Montanaro, these memory variants explain why John does not quote from the source text verbatim, and may even provide reasons for some of the significant variance from the source text at certain places (see John 1:23; 7:38; 12:15, 40; 13:18; 19:36).

35. Along these lines, see David F. Ford, "Reading Backwards, Reading Forwards, and Abiding: Reading John in the Spirit Now," *JTI* 11, no. 1 (2017): 69–84. Ford says, "As all four Gospels. . .take up and transform Israel's Scriptures, so the Gospel of John can be read as taking up and transforming the Synoptic Gospels" (69).

36. Madison Pierce, Andrew Byers, and Simon Gathercole, eds., *Gospel Reading and Reception in Early Christian Literature* (Cambridge: Cambridge University Press, 2022), 3.

evangelists were not merely collecting all the Jesus traditions they could find and cobbling them together into a narrative. They were artistically weaving together their source materials—primarily Israel's Scriptures and other preexisting Jesus narratives—in order to present a compelling, polemical, *theological*, true, and even beautiful witness to the good news of Jesus Christ. Thus, since John is the most explicit theological writer of the four evangelists, the tools we use to determine his knowledge and use of the Synoptics must be able to account for the theological flexibility and subtlety of both the gospel genre and his known authorial tendencies.

For many in the Greek Orthodox tradition, if one only mentions "The Theologian," it is clear who is meant by the honorary title—St. John, the apostle. Without John our grasp of certain doctrines would be impacted for the worse—the Trinity, the divinity of Christ, the Holy Spirit's relationship to those abiding in Christ, God's providence, and much more. It is not a historical accident that time after time the great theologians of the church have turned to John's Gospel to defend and articulate the truths about God and his works in creation. The wealth of robust theology contained in the Johannine writings flows downstream from their author, John, who himself is immersed in the Godhead and all things in relation to him. He is the eagle soaring high above the biblical landscape, showing how all things participate and find their telos in the life and light of the *Logos*, who is one with the Father and the Spirit (1:4). If then, John the Theologian engages his subject matter (i.e., Jesus) from such a high theological starting point, would it not be reasonable to expect his engagement with the Synoptics to be primarily *theological* in nature, and not merely a historical and literary reduplication?

More than that, if we take the witness of the early church seriously that John wrote a spiritual Gospel to supplement and interpret the other three—and I do not see any compelling reason not to—then the complementary witness of the fourfold Gospel emerges as a convincing reason to think John was aware of and writing in consort with the written form of the Synoptic Gospels.[37] Both historically and theologically, John rounds out a fuller

---

37. I say "written form of the Gospels" for two reasons. First, because I take the historical tradition seriously that John had read the other Gospels and wrote to supplement them. For example, see Theodore of Mopsuestia, *Commentary on the Gospel of John*, trans. Marco Conti, ACT (Downers Grove, IL: IVP Academic, 2010), 3; Augustine seems to assume John's knowledge of the Synoptics, but does not state it explicitly, *Harmony of the Gospels* 4.10 (trans. Rev. S. D. F. Salmond, D.D., *NPNF* 1/6:231–36);

picture of who Jesus is that gives greater coherence to a reading of the other three Gospels. The shapes of the Synoptic stories are shaded in with more dogmatic depth and meaning when read against the backdrop of John.[38]

Arguably, the neglect of theological considerations as a valid way of showing knowledge and use of the Synoptics is one of the driving forces behind the recent shift toward dependence; it is also one of the main ways modern "dependence" differs from early twentieth-century dependence. Moreover, it seems that scholarship is realizing how much more there is to explore and marvel at when the fourfold Gospel is kept together rather than split apart. Exiling John to an island while the Synoptics are read only in light of each other limits the fourfold picture of Jesus the New Testament authors, and ultimately God, intended to give us.

And still, I recognize theological engagement as a way of proving knowledge of a source is not without legitimate critique. Can theological engagement be difficult to detect, somewhat speculative, and too dependent upon the tastes of the one interpreting? Perhaps. Is it definitive proof of John's literary use of the Synoptics? Not by itself. But when considered alongside the totality of the other historical and literary considerations, is theological engagement a significant and valid tool for detecting use? Yes.

The strength of the dependence view is not found in any one proof. Rather, it is found in the cumulative effect of many theological transformations, the supplementary nature of John's material, and the unbroken historical witness of the church. The move to dependence does not solve all the problems and tensions that accompany the thorny problem of Johannine-Synoptic relations. However, it gives us a set of problems and tensions that are easier to live with than those inherited by the independence view.

3. JOHN'S USE OF THE SYNOPTICS

Up until now, I have come at the Johannine-Synoptic question from the perspective of methodology and presuppositions that go into the

---

Eusebius of Caesarea, *The Ecclesiastical History* 3.24. Second, because I am not convinced that it was more likely for John to have only encountered Synoptic traditions through oral performances and not their written form, especially given the interconnectedness of the apostolic network in the earliest days of the church and the peculiar preference of Christians/Jews for the written word.

38.   Calvin likens John's Gospel as a key that opens the door to the other three Gospels: "for whoever shall understand the power of Christ, as it is here strikingly portrayed, will afterwards read with advantage what the others [the Synoptics] relate about the Redeemer who was manifested" (John Calvin, *Commentary on the Gospel According to John*, vol. 1, trans. Rev. William Pringle [Edinburgh: Calvin Translation Society, 1847], 22).

dependence and independence views. However, the question of *if* John knew and used the Synoptics is quite different from the question of *how* he did so. This portion of the essay will briefly explore a few of the ways John engages the Synoptics, though I admit the survey is necessarily limited in scope due to space. Think of this section as a metal detector scanning the ground that is only indicating to you where to dig later when you have your shovel.

3.1 Assumption

The first way John engages the Synoptics is through assumption. At times throughout John's narrative, he seems to assume his readers/hearers[39] already have knowledge about events he has not described. These remarks typically come in the form of a parenthesis. For example, in John 3:24 he writes that John the Baptist had not yet been put into prison, an event he does not expand on or describe in detail anywhere else in the Gospel. Richard Bauckham has carefully noted how the most logical reason John included this brief remark is to situate his Gospel in relation to the narrative sequence of Mark.[40] For readers of Mark (and Matthew), it would be expected after Jesus's baptism to read of the subsequent temptation and then the commencement of Jesus's Galilean ministry after John had been put into prison. But a first-time reader of John must have been puzzled to find so much material nestled in between Jesus's implied baptism in 1:29–34 and the commencement of the Galilean public ministry in 4:46.[41] John's parenthetical remark in 3:24, then, situates Jesus's ministry from 1:35–4:45 inside Mark 1:13 and 1:14.[42] Another example of John's assumption of Synoptic narrative can be found in John's description of Mary in John 11:2.[43]

---

39. I say readers/hearers because it is more likely that the first audiences of this Gospel encountered it initially through the ears rather than the eyes. However, for ease of reading I will use the word "reader" to encompass both readers and hearers.

40. Richard Bauckham, "John for Readers of Mark," in *The Gospels for All Christians: Rethinking the Gospel Audiences*, ed. Richard Bauckham (Grand Rapids: Eerdmans, 1998), 150–55.

41. While the miracle at Cana in 2:1–12 took place in Galilee, it was arguably not a public miracle given that only his mother, disciples, and the servants knew what took place. The cleansing of the temple, the signs he did in Jerusalem, and the teaching in Samaria, while public, did not take place in Galilee. Jesus's first public miracle in Galilee takes place in 4:46.

42. Bauckham, "John for Readers of Mark," 155.

43. For more on this parenthetical remark, see Bauckham, "John for Readers of Mark," 161.

3.2 Supplementation

The second way John engages the Synoptics is through supplementation. Given the sheer amount of unique material—whether events or teaching—it is clear John's purpose was not merely to copy the other three Gospels, but, as an eyewitness to the actual events himself, to provide new material that further rounded out the church's understanding of Jesus Christ and protected true believers from false doctrines regarding Christ's person.[44] The most striking way he does this is the explicit way he testifies to Jesus not only as Israel's Messiah and King (John 1:49; 4:26; 12:12–15; 18:33–38), but as the second person of the Trinity (1:1–5, 14, 18; 3:13, 31–36; 5:18–29; 15:26–27; 17; etc.).[45]

John supplements the other three Gospels in multiple ways. For example, whereas the relationship between the Father and Son in the Godhead is not touched upon in detail in the Synoptics, John moves it to center stage; whereas the Synoptics focus more on the miracles of Jesus's ministry, John focuses on the discourses that follow signs; whereas the Synoptics contain more of Jesus's public teaching, John's Gospel contains private interactions and instruction to various individuals, and even a private prayer to God the Father (Nicodemus, Samaritan woman, the Farewell Discourse, the high priestly prayer).

Leon Morris, who holds to Johannine independence, recognized this complementary nature and spoke of it as an *interlocking tradition*.[46] That is, there are many places where John and the Synoptics both mutually reinforce and explain one another, "without betraying overt literary dependence."[47] The strength of the interlocking tradition view is that it rightly points out many examples of where John and the Synoptics complement/supplement one another.[48] However, the weak-

---

44. See Theodore of Mopseustia, *Commentary*, 3.

45. Calvin captures this when he writes in his commentary on John, "And as all of them [the four Gospels] had the same object in view, to point out Christ, the three former exhibit his body, if we may be permitted to use the expression, but John exhibits his soul" (Calvin, *Commentary on the Gospel According to John*, 22).

46. The two well-known proponents of the interlocking traditions theory are D. A. Carson and Leon Morris. See D. A. Carson, *The Gospel According to John*, 51–55; Leon Morris, *Studies in the Fourth Gospel* (Grand Rapids: Eerdmans, 1969), 40–63.

47. Carson, *The Gospel According to John*, 52.

48. Leon Morris compiles an impressive list of seventeen specific ways John better enforces and explains the Synoptic accounts. However, it is puzzling that in light of these seventeen examples he still concludes Johannine independence. He lists the Judean ministry, the last journey to Jerusalem, the denial, "destroy this temple," the Roman trial, Jesus's enemies, the Sabbath, the healing miracles, the call to disciples, making Jesus king, prayer, the theological significance of synoptic incidents, living out synoptic precepts,

ness of the view, as Köstenberger puts it, is that it alleviates historical (and I would add theological) discrepancies between John and the Synoptics "on the premise that these are, at least in part, *undesigned coincidences*."[49] It seems more plausible that John, in accordance with the historical testimony of the early church, wrote to provide a fuller account of what he saw lacking in the other three rather than only "happening" to fill our gaps of knowledge by chance. Thus, as I see it, the interlocking tradition seems to tilt more in the direction of dependence than independence.

3.3 Theological Transformation

The third and most potent way John engages the Synoptics is through theological transformation. Old and new authors alike have observed the theological color John brings to the fourfold gospel witness.[50] In 2012 Andreas Köstenberger coined a term for this high-octane theological style of John—something he calls "theological transposition."[51]

Building on the work of Kevin Vanhoozer,[52] Köstenberger defines *theological transposition* as "the creative reworking of previous texts which realizes their hidden meaning potential and extends their message to a new distinctive context."[53] The taxonomy of transposition comes from the musical idea of taking a collection of notes and altering the pitches up and down (thus moving it to a new key) to alter the mood of a given piece of music. Thus, Köstenberger contends, "John did have their written material [Mark and possibly Luke-Acts] available to him and creatively reworked

---

the upper room, the palm Sunday enthusiasm, the greatness of John the Baptist, and a number of minor points (see Morris, *Studies in the Fourth Gospel*, 40–63). For Carson's own list, see Carson, *The Gospel According to John*, 52–54.

49. Köstenberger, "John's Transposition Theology," 220, emphasis mine. Like the apologetic argument of intelligent design, it appears the complementary nature of John's Gospel to the Synoptics is not mere happenstance, but by both divine and human design. The amount of times John explains something left unexplained in the other three is staggering. It is probable evidence of an author who is aware of the historical and theological lacunae in the Synoptic accounts and takes up his pen to fill them.

50. For example, C. H. Dodd, Edwyn Hoskyns, Richard Hays, C. K. Barrett, Leon Morris, Richard Bauckham, and many more.

51. David John Hawkin used the term "Johannine transposition" in his 1980 article, "The Johannine Transposition and Johannine Theology," *Laval théologique et philosophique* 36, no. 1 (1980): 89–98. However, Hawkin is using *transposition* to refer to the evangelist's transposing "into the narrative form their own confessional witness to Christ," which is a completely different way and category than how Köstenberger uses the term.

52. Kevin J. Vanhoozer, *The Drama of Doctrine: A Canonical Linguistic Approach to Christian Theology* (Louisville: Westminster John Knox, 2005).

53. Köstenberger, "John's Transposition Theology," 199.

various theological distinctives, literary patterns, and other features in keeping with his own theological purposes for writing."[54]

Köstenberger lists sixteen potential instances of transposition in Mark and four in Luke-Acts.

For Mark:

1. From miracles to signs.
2. From the temple cleansing to the raising of Lazarus.
3. From the Markan temple cleansing to the Johannine temple clearing.
4. From the Markan pivot at Caesarea Philippi to Peter's confession halfway through John's Book of Signs and/or to Martha's confession.
5. From the Markan Olivet Discourse to John's realized eschatology.
6. From Jesus's prediction of the destruction of the literal temple to Jesus's prediction of the destruction and raising of the spiritual temple, the body of Jesus.
7. From the kingdom of God to eternal life.
8. From Jesus's transfiguration to John's pervasive glory motif.
9. From the institution of the Lord's Supper to Jesus's teaching on eating his flesh and drinking his blood.
10. From the Markan parables to John's real-life "parables" and symbolic discourses.
11. From Jesus's demon exorcisms in Mark to Satan as the chief antagonist of Jesus in John.
12. From succinct pronouncement stories to selected extended discourses.
13. From the Markan reference to Jewish obduracy to John's strategic placement of the same reference.
14. From the Markan institution of the Lord's Supper to John's extensive Farewell Discourse.
15. From the cross as a place of shame and suffering in Mark to the cross as a place of glory and exaltation in John.
16. From Mark's presentation of Jesus's Jewish and Roman trials to the cosmic trial motif in John.

---

54. Köstenberger, "John's Transposition Theology," 199.

For Luke-Acts:

1. From the two volumes of Luke-Acts to John's one-volume work in two parts, the Book of Signs and the Book of Exaltation.
2. From the virgin birth to Jesus's eternal preexistence.
3. From the socioeconomic dimension of Jesus's ministry in Luke-Acts to John's singular focus on people's individual eternal destiny.
4. From the pattern of the early church's mission in the book of Acts to John's presentation of the pattern of Jesus's earthly mission.

In the spirit of Köstenberger's Johannine theological transposition, I will briefly present two ways John transposes the Synoptic narratives and sayings.

(1) *The first way John theologically transposes the Synoptics is by adding theological depth to historical incidents that the Synoptics do not.* For example, in Mark 14:10–11 and Matthew 26:14–16, the betrayal of Judas takes place in simply human terms. Judas, motivated by greed, goes to the officials. However, John explicitly paints the scene with more sinister forces at play. In the previous chapter, Jesus says his impending death is the "judgment of this world" where the "ruler of this world [will] be cast out" (John 12:31).[55] In a twist of irony, Satan, by the hand of Judas, hastens to set into motion the events that will further undo the power over his dominion (*i.e.*, the world). After Judas receives the morsel of bread, Satan enters into him (13:27).[56] John adds even more depth by playing on the double meaning of what it means for it to be "night" when Judas goes out to betray Jesus to the authorities (13:30; cf. 3:2). In typical and dense Johannine fashion this entire scene builds on the earlier testimony that Jesus is the light of the world (8:12) who enlightens every man (1:4) and cannot be overcome by darkness (1:5). Moreover, it fulfills the prophetic words of Jesus that night is coming when no man can work (9:4) and those who walk in darkness stumble (11:10). Thus, the example

---

55. Unless otherwise indicated, all Scripture quotations are from the ESV® Bible (The Holy Bible, English Standard Version®), © 2001 by Crossway, a publishing ministry of Good News Publishers. Used by permission. All rights reserved.

56. Luke mentions the entrance of Satan into Judas as well (Luke 22:3), but with a less dramatic flair and a less explicitly developed theology of Satan and his connection to the death and resurrection of Jesus.

of Judas's betrayal shows a typical way John shades in more theological irony and depth to historical incidents than the Synoptists.

(2) *The second way John theologically transposes the Synoptics is by expanding events or sayings to such a degree that it constitutes a central theme in John's presentation of who Jesus is.* I will give an example of how John does this through events and through sayings.

(a) *Expanding an event into a theme.* Given the prominence of the theme of light in John's Gospel, the explicit emphasis on Jesus's deity, and his presence on the mountain, it is rather baffling that John does not give an account of the transfiguration. Why would he not include a story that so neatly ties together major themes while also providing some of the clearest evidence of Jesus's divinity?

There are many reasons we could speculate about. It could be that: (1) John chose not to because it was already sufficiently covered in all three Synoptic Gospels (Matt. 17:1–8; Mark 9:2–8; Luke 9:28–36), though that does not stop his retelling of the feeding of the five thousand or walking on water (John 6:1–21); (2) John chose an alternative route that achieves the same effect—the identification of Jesus as Yahweh seated upon the throne in Isaiah 6 (John 12:41), and the transfiguration would detract from that example; (3) John wanted to show that Jesus's divine glory is manifested for his disciples to behold throughout the totality of his ministry ("Come and see" [1:39, 46]) and not just in a miraculous manifestation on the mountain; (4) for John, Jesus's suffering on the cross is the moment where his glory is most put on display (17:1), and the transfiguration would lessen the impact of his double meaning/inversion of suffering and glory on the cross.

Whatever John's reason for not including the transfiguration account, it appears he takes the core elements of the transfiguration narrative—the preexistence and deity of Christ, his shining glory/light, his coming crucifixion, his superiority to the Law and Prophets, the Father's affirmation of the Son and the command to listen to him, the beatific vision—and pulls out entire themes for his Gospel. For example, the glory theme: "We have seen his glory, glory as of the only Son from the Father" (1:14); the connection of Jesus's coming death with light themes in 8:21–29; the authority and honor of the Son from the Father to receive worship and to judge the earth in 5:19–29; his superiority over Moses and the Prophets (5:46; 8:56); seeing the face of God in Jesus (14:9; 20:28), and so on.

(b) *Expanding a saying into a theme.* There are times in John's Gospel where Jesus takes a saying found in the Synoptics and transforms it into an entire theme. Edwyn Hoskyns writes,

> These familiar Sayings [in the Synoptics] are not so much quoted [in John], or embedded in a discourse; rather, they constitute its theme. . . . They lie no longer on the periphery, as though they were just Sayings; rather they have moved into the centre and have taken control, not merely of single discourses, but of the whole presentation of what Jesus was and is.[57]

An example of this transformation can be seen in the saying of John the Baptist to the Pharisees and Sadducees: "You brood of vipers [γεννήματα ἐχιδνῶν]! Who warned you to flee from the wrath to come? Bear fruit in keeping with repentance. And do not presume to say to yourselves, 'We have Abraham as our father,' for I tell you, God is able from these stones to raise up children for Abraham" (Matt. 3:7–9). Jesus later picks up the same striking language "brood of vipers" to condemn the same groups in Matthew 12:34 and 23:33.

The idea of dividing humanity into two seeds, one descended from God and the other from Satan, cuts through the center of the Johannine landscape. In John 8, Jesus has his own encounter with the Pharisees and Sadducees that mirrors John the Baptist's episode in Matthew 3:7–9. When the discussion of Abraham as their father comes up, he instead tells them their father is the devil (John 8:44). Those who have the same faith as Abraham are rightly called his children (8:39).

John never uses the term γεννήματα ἐχιδνῶν (Matt. 3:7–9) to describe Jesus's opponents, but he gets very close. Not only in his Gospel, but more prominently in his epistles (esp. 1 John 3:10) does he gets closer to using the language of γεννήματα ἐχιδνῶν. Instead, he calls rebellious humanity τὰ τέκνα τοῦ διαβόλου. However, given that γεννήματα ἐχιδνῶν literally means "offspring of serpents" and the

---

57. Edwyn Clement Hoskyns, *The Fourth Gospel*, ed. F. N. Davey (London: Faber and Faber Unlimited, 1947), 73.

devil is identified as the serpent (John 8:44; Rev. 12:9), "children of the devil" and "offspring of serpents" functionally mean the same thing. So, for John, the division of humanity into two seeds is a foundational pillar to understanding his entire theology.

Another example of John taking a saying in the Synoptics and constituting a theme out of it for his Gospel would be the saying, "I will destroy this temple that is made with hands, and in three days I will build another, not made with hands" (Mark 14:58).[58] In John's Gospel, Jesus says this to defend his authority to cleanse the temple in 2:13–22. Whereas in the Synoptics this saying appears near the end of their Gospels and on the lips of Jesus's opponents, in John's Gospel it is found in the beginning and comes from Jesus's lips. Moreover, John shades in the prophetic utterance for the audience, saying, "But he was speaking about the temple of his body. When therefore he was raised from the dead, his disciples remembered that he had said this, and they believed the Scripture and the word that Jesus had spoken" (2:21–22). Thus, a somewhat peripheral saying in the Synoptics finds connection points to a number of interrelated themes within John—the temple, resurrection, and Jesus's identity as the Son of God who has life within himself.

CONCLUSION

This essay has explained why the Johannine independence view has recently faded in popularity and shown various ways John theologically engages the Synoptic Gospels. The Johannine independence view has retreated due to three main factors. First, Johannine independence depends too much on outdated models of form criticism and oral tradition. Second, Johannine independence assumes John to use his sources in the same way the Synoptists used one another, which in turn misunderstands ancient compositional norms and ignores John's known authorial tendencies. Third, Johannine independence undervalues theological engagement as a means of detecting sources.

In exploring how John theologically engages the Synoptic Gospels, we have seen how he does so through assuming knowledge about events he has not described, supplementing the Synoptic accounts through various discourses and events, and by theologically transforming Synoptic material.

---

58. I came upon this example in Hoskyns, *The Fourth Gospel*, 74.

Unless we have a time machine that travels back to Ephesus at the end of the first century, we will never know with certainty how John created his Gospel; I suspect the answer would surprise us all. Yet, a move toward Johannine dependence removes unnecessary roadblocks created by the speculations of the independence view, takes seriously the witness of the early church, and propels us forward to better understanding the witness of the one gospel of Jesus Christ expressed in the four canonical Gospels.

PART 3
JOHANNINE THEOLOGY AND SCHOLARSHIP

CHAPTER 9

THE CURRENT STATE OF JOHANNINE STUDIES

STANLEY E. PORTER

To understand the current state of Johannine studies, one must understand its past. Other contributions to this volume survey the patristic evidence regarding the Johannine writings, so I will not recount that evidence here. I merely wish to mention that John's Gospel—which I will concentrate upon in this essay[1]—was already described by the ancients regarding several key features. It was written by John the son of Zebedee (according to Irenaeus, *Haer.* 3.1.1), it was written last in relationship to the other Gospels, and, perhaps most importantly, it was regarded as a "spiritual Gospel" (πνευματικὸν . . . εὐαγγέλιον, cited in Eusebius, *Hist. eccl.* 6.14.7), by which phrase Clement of Alexandria was probably

---

1. A fuller exposition of some of these issues, upon which I rely at least in part, is found in Stanley E. Porter and Ron C. Fay, "Introduction to *The Gospel of John in Modern Interpretation*," in *The Gospel of John in Modern Interpretation*, ed. Stanley E. Porter and Ron C. Fay, Milestones in New Testament Scholarship (Grand Rapids: Kregel Academic, 2018), 15–43. Important surveys of scholarship include: Benjamin Wisner Bacon, *The Fourth Gospel in Research and Debate: A Series of Essays on Problems Concerning the Origin and Value of the Anonymous Writings Attributed to the Apostle John* (London: Fisher Unwin, 1910); Wilbert Francis Howard, *The Fourth Gospel in Recent Criticism and Interpretation*, rev. C. K. Barrett (London: Epworth, 1955 [1931]); Robert Kysar, *The Fourth Evangelist and His Gospel: An Examination of Contemporary Scholarship* (Minneapolis: Augsburg, 1975); Gerard S. Sloyan, *What Are They Saying about John?* (New York: Paulist, 1991); Raymond E. Brown, *An Introduction to the Gospel of John*, ed. Francis J. Moloney (New York: Doubleday, 2003); Klaus Scholtissek, "The Johannine Gospel in Recent Research," in *The Face of New Testament Studies: A Survey of Recent Research*, ed. Scot McKnight and Grant R. Osborne (Grand Rapids: Baker Academic, 2004), 444–72; Stanley E. Porter and Andrew K. Gabriel, *Johannine Writings and Apocalyptic: An Annotated Bibliography*, JOST 1 (Leiden: Brill, 2013); Porter, *John, His Gospel, and Jesus: In Pursuit of the Johannine Voice* (Grand Rapids: Eerdmans, 2015), at least on certain topics; and Alicia D. Myers, "The Gospel of John," in *The State of New Testament Studies: A Survey of Recent Research*, ed. Scot McKnight and Nijay K. Gupta (Grand Rapids: Baker Academic, 2019), 334–49.

asserting John's clear theological orientation, not necessarily denigrating its historicity.[2] Nevertheless, what we note from this early patristic discussion of John's Gospel is that many, if not most, of the major issues in subsequent discussion of it were raised early on.

In this essay, I will address the major trends and issues in current discussion of John's Gospel since most of the contemporary issues find precedent in previous discussion. Unlike some surveys of Johannine scholarship, I will only be able to focus upon a few scholars in an unfolding debate, recognizing that ideas are always embodied in those who hold them and advocate for them. While I organize the discussion by historical trajectory, I cannot hope to mention all the scholars involved or all the issues.

1. HISTORICAL CRITICISM AND ITS REACTIONS

The Enlightenment, which emerged in the seventeenth century and persisted into the late eighteenth century, brought fundamental shifts in understanding, so that rationalism, naturalism, and empiricism came to dominate human thought and exploration. Some of the intellectual products of the Enlightenment were the rise of deism with a personal God being displaced by natural causality and the emergence of theological liberalism looking to human achievement rather than divine intervention. As a result, there was a transformation in views of the Bible and the means of interpreting it. The Bible was no longer necessarily viewed as a sacred, inspired book but as the natural product of human achievement like any other book. Historical criticism of the Bible was a natural outgrowth of such a perspective, and it touched most areas of biblical studies, including textual criticism, interpretation and its methods, views of canon, and of course questions of date, authorship, and provenance, as the field of New Testament introduction came into its own. What used to be a relatively similar positive appreciation of John's Gospel before the early nineteenth century often became a critical skepticism regarding its apostolic origins and general reliability.

Two post-Enlightenment figures stand out in the reinterpretation of John's Gospel as a literary text to be understood on the same naturalistic

---

2. See Marianne Meye Thompson, "The 'Spiritual Gospel': How John the Theologian Writes History," in *John, Jesus, and History, Volume 1: Critical Appraisals of Critical Views*, ed. Paul N. Anderson, Felix Just, and Tom Thatcher (Atlanta: SBL Press, 2007), 103–8, esp. 103–4, although she does not refer to other statements in Eusebius that clarify Clement's statement.

and developmental terms as other ancient texts.[3] The history of subsequent Johannine research still responds to the critical views of these two major scholars. The first is David Friedrich Strauss (1808–1874) in his *The Life of Jesus Critically Examined* and his *A New Life of Jesus*.[4] Strauss places the composition of John's Gospel in the mid-second century, hence denying its apostolic authorship. Strauss sees relationships between John's Gospel and gnostic writings as well as other Hellenistic thought. As a result, he depicts John's Gospel as nonhistorical and instead mythical, a kind of "fiction." Strauss's views were so radical that they cost him an academic career. Nevertheless, they had a major influence on scholarship of the time. Second, Ferdinand Christian Baur (1792–1860) concluded similarly around the same time, but developed such skeptical views even more rigorously.[5] Baur argues that the layers of Johannine tradition indicate a date in the mid-second century, sometime around AD 160–170, explaining both the Gospel's developed theology and its independence of apostolic authority. Baur's influence led to other scholars arguing for dates sometime in the second century and this position becoming a mainstream view within at least German scholarship.

As one might imagine, not all scholars were convinced by the placement of John's Gospel in the second century and its implications, so some attempted to reaffirm views of authorship by John the son of Zebedee or someone closely associated with him, and thereby to reaffirm the essential historical reliability of John's Gospel, even if they also recognized differences from the Synoptic Gospels and its own theological emphases. This traditional reaction was found among contemporaries of Strauss and Baur, but also among scholars over the course of the rest of the nineteenth century and beyond. Many of these scholars argued for a date of around AD 80–100 for composition of John's Gospel, although a few even ventured to argue for a date of AD 70 or before. These scholars include

---

3. Even though Friedrich Schleiermacher (*The Life of Jesus*, ed. Jack C. Verheyden, trans. S. MacLean Gilmour [Philadelphia: Fortress, 1975]) believed that John's Gospel was more historically reliable than the Synoptics, he was still influenced by Enlightenment thought and skepticism.

4. David Friedrich Strauss, *The Life of Jesus Critically Examined*, trans. George Eliot, 4th German ed. (London: George Allen, 1848), 71–73, 365–86; Strauss, *A New Life of Jesus*, 2 vols. (London: Williams and Norgate, 1870), 1:33–36, 77–101.

5. F. C. Baur, *Kritische Untersuchungen über die kanonischen Evangelien, ihr Verhältnis zueinander, ihren Character und Ursprung* (Tübingen, 1847), cited in Werner Georg Kümmel, *The New Testament: The History of the Investigation of Its Problems*, trans. S. McLean Gilmour and Howard Clark Kee (Nashville: Abingdon, 1972), 137, 428; Baur, *The Church History of the First Three Centuries*, trans. Allan Menzies, 3rd ed., 2 vols. (London: Williams and Norgate, 1878–1897), 1:177–81.

German, French, and English representatives. For example, Constantine Tischendorf (1815–1874) wrote a popular booklet in 1865 in which he disputes the findings of Ernest Renan (who followed Baur's conclusions) and Strauss.[6] Tischendorf argues that the author was an eyewitness to the reported events, a close acquaintance of Jesus, and independent of the other Gospels.

Joseph Barber Lightfoot (1828–1889), in three lectures (and notes) from 1867 to 1872, published posthumously, argues for the "authenticity and genuineness" of John's Gospel.[7] His nearly two-hundred-page defense of Johannine authorship provides some of the most thorough arguments on the topic. His colleague, Brooke Foss Westcott (1825–1901), who began his commentary on John's Gospel in the 1850s, finally published his English-language commentary in 1880, with his Greek-language commentary appearing posthumously in 1908.[8] Like his colleague Lightfoot, Westcott provides another very thorough defense of authorship by a Jew from Palestine, an eyewitness, an apostle, and in fact John, the younger son of Zebedee. Westcott's introduction to his commentary is a direct response to the historical reconstruction of early Christianity promoted by Strauss and Baur in which Westcott posits a different construal of the evidence. Westcott also published a very important commentary on the Johannine letters, which he attributes to John as well.[9]

We see that, virtually from the outset of critical discussion, both critical skepticism and traditional beliefs regarding the Johannine literature have been maintained by renowned scholars.

2. HISTORY OF RELIGION AND RUDOLF BULTMANN

The survey above brings us to the twentieth century, which we might generally call *contemporary Johannine scholarship*. Although I have noted that Strauss and Baur had a major impact upon Johannine scholarship,

---

6. Stanley E. Porter, *Constantine Tischendorf: The Life and Work of a 19th Century Bible Hunter* (London: Bloomsbury, 2015), with Tischendorf's *When Were Our Gospels Written?* on 117–74. This booklet by Tischendorf aroused the ire of Eduard Zeller, one of Baur's followers (and his son-in-law).

7. J. B. Lightfoot, *Biblical Essays* (London: Macmillan, 1893), 1–193, with notes on 194–98.

8. Brooke Foss Westcott, *The Gospel According to St. John, The Authorized Version with Introduction and Notes* (London: John Murray, 1881), v–xxxii; Westcott, *The Gospel According to St. John*, 2 vols. (London: John Murray, 1908), 1:ix–cxcv. See Stanley E. Porter, "Brooke Foss Westcott: Johannine Scholar Extraordinaire," in *Gospel of John in Modern Interpretation*, 45–80.

9. Brooke Foss Westcott, *The Epistles of St John* (London: Macmillan, 1883).

the single most significant Johannine scholar, at least since Strauss and Baur, is the German Rudolf Bultmann (1884–1976).[10]

Although it is not always recognized or overtly acknowledged, Bultmann was a part of and was highly influenced by the history of religion movement.[11] This movement, which comprised a loose association of scholars from a variety of subject areas (Bible, classics, oriental religions), began in the late nineteenth century and was interested in the concept of religion and its development, with Christianity being one example among others. They were concerned to identify and trace the various religious traditions, especially as found in the world's religions, such as Greco-Roman religion and Egyptian religion, even if they also saw Christianity, a syncretistic religion, as attaining the heights of religious achievement. In many ways, the history of religion movement represented the culmination of Enlightenment thought and its rationalistic, naturalistic, and anti-supernatural presuppositions.

The Johannine writings were an object of interest to several scholars within the history of religion. Hermann Gunkel (1862–1932), the unofficial leader of the history of religion movement and originally a New Testament scholar, wrote his *Creation and Chaos*, in which, reflecting form-critical concerns, he argues that the Genesis 1 creation account is dependent upon ancient Babylonian creation myths and is the tradition responsible for Revelation 12.[12]

William Wrede (1859–1906), better known for his views on the Messianic Secret and Paul as the second founder of Christianity, contends that John's Gospel is widely misunderstood because it introduces a world foreign to the reader that is an apologetic attempt to defend Jesus's divine character.[13]

Johannes Weiss (1863–1914), who was on the edge of the history of religion movement, is known for his realized or thoroughgoing

---

10. See Bryan R. Dyer, "Rudolf Bultmann and the Johannine Literature," in *Gospel of John in Modern Interpretation*, 119–40, esp. 119–24.

11. On the history of religion as a movement in New Testament studies, see William Baird, *History of New Testament Research*, 3 vols. (Minneapolis: Fortress, 1992–2013), 2:222–53.

12. Hermann Gunkel, *Creation and Chaos in the Primeval Era and the Eschaton: A Religio-Historical Study of Genesis 1 and Revelation 12*, trans. K. William Whitney Jr. (repr., Grand Rapids: Eerdmans, 2006 [1895]).

13. William Wrede, *Charakter und Tendenz des Johannesevangeliums*, 2nd ed. (Tübingen: Mohr Siebeck, 1933 [1903]).

eschatology, which includes an apocalyptic view of Jesus.[14] Weiss also wrote a commentary on the book of Revelation in which he places it within its imperial context as a product of the history of religion.[15] Weiss is important in this regard not just for his ideas but for the fact that he was Bultmann's teacher at the University of Marburg.

Wilhelm Bousset (1865–1920), arguably the best-known member of the history of religion school, argues for a developmental view of Christianity as a form of Lord-cult.[16] What began in the complex religious environment of the first century developed into worship of Jesus as the Christ and then, under the influence of Greek thought in the Pauline churches, into the realized eschatology and deification of believers found in John's Gospel. Bousset also wrote a commentary on the book of Revelation.[17]

Bultmann, however, is by far the most significant of the Johannine scholars of the history of religion school. Whereas some have divided Bultmann's career into two halves, the first influenced by the history of religion and the second by the philosopher Martin Heidegger (1889–1976), Bultmann never fully escaped the history of religion perspective. This is seen in Bultmann's comparative study of traditions, such as Cynic and Stoic diatribe, the subject of his doctoral dissertation under Weiss; his use and development of form criticism following in the path of Gunkel; his entire post-Enlightenment worldview of the development of human religion, including his belief in a closed universe and the need for demythologization; and his view of the development of Christianity in relation to other religions, as seen in his 1949 *Primitive Christianity*.[18]

Bultmann's scholarship on John's Gospel extended over the course of much of his academic career. He published relatively early articles on the history of religion background of John's Prologue and on the significance

---

14. Johannes Weiss, *Jesus's Proclamation of the Kingdom of God*, trans. and ed. Richard Hyde Hiers and David Larrimore Holland (London: SCM, 1971 [1892]).

15. Johannes Weiss, *Die Offenbarung des Johannes: Ein Beitrag zur Literatur- und Religionsgeschichte* (Göttingen: Vandenhoeck & Ruprecht, 1904).

16. Wilhelm Bousset, *Kyrios Christos: A History of the Belief in Christ from the Beginnings of Christianity to Irenaeus*, trans. John E. Steely (Nashville: Abingdon, 1970; repr., Waco, TX: Baylor University Press, 2013 [1913]).

17. Wilhelm Bousset, *Die Offenbarung Johannis*, MeyerK (Göttingen: Vandenhoeck & Ruprecht, 1896).

18. For works that reflect his perspective, see Rudolf Bultmann, *Der Stil der paulinischen Predigt und die kynisch-stoische Diatribe* (Göttingen: Vandenhoeck & Ruprecht, 1910); Bultmann, *The History of the Synoptic Tradition*, trans. John Marsh (Oxford: Blackwell, 1963 [1921]); Bultmann, "New Testament Mythology," in *Kerygma and Myth: A Theological Debate*, ed. Hans Werner Bartsch, trans. Reginald H. Fuller (London: SPCK, 1953 [1941]), 1–44; and Bultmann, *Primitive Christianity in Its Contemporary Setting*, trans. Reginald H. Fuller (Philadelphia: Fortress, 1956 [1949]).

of Mandaean and Manichean sources on understanding John's Gospel.[19] Bultmann's major commentary on John's Gospel, written nearer the end of his career, reveals many elements of the history of religion.[20] These include the Gospel's dependence upon Mandaean Gnosticism, its mythological and eschatological or apocalyptic viewpoint, and the evidence of various forms of religious syncretism. However, Bultmann's influence upon Johannine studies extends much further than just the conclusion that John's Gospel was not apostolic and minimally historical (as he thought regarding all the Gospels).

Bultmann wrote his commentary without an introduction, but a short one was added later for the English translation by Walther Schmithals, one of Bultmann's students, summarizing what is indicated in the commentary but also probably providing a more systematized account of Bultmann's conclusions than one might gain simply from reading the commentary. Bultmann utilizes form criticism in varying ways in his commentary, both as a means of classifying various units of material (e.g., miracle story) and as part of his textual criticism in rearranging the Gospel. Bultmann believes that the Gospel itself was later compiled or redacted from the Gospel author's various writings, and so there were textual displacements that needed to be rectified, and Bultmann attempted to do so. Others had engaged in similar textual rearrangement, but Bultmann's were extensive throughout the entire Gospel. Although displacement theories are not as prevalent as they once were, they at one time were a major topic of discussion in Johannine studies.

Bultmann's approach also reflects a developmental hypothesis regarding the origin of the Gospel that has been more fully developed in research by later scholars. In this regard, Bultmann reflects both a naturalistic and a literary approach to the Gospel that epitomizes post-Enlightenment thought and the growth of literary studies. Bultmann also remains well known for his major source theories that continue to be debated, including the miracle source or sign-source that records the major miracles in Jesus's ministry (although Bultmann was not the first to propose this source, with its origins in the early twentieth century), a discourse or narrative

---

19. Rudolf Bultmann, "The History of Religions Background of the Prologue to the Gospel of John," in *The Interpretation of John*, ed. and trans. John Ashton, 2nd ed. (London: T&T Clark, 1997 [1923]), 27–40; and Bultmann, "Die Bedeutung der neuerschlossenen mandäischen und manichäischen Quellen für das Verständnis des Johnnesevangeliums," *ZNW* 14 (1925): 100–146.

20. Rudolf Bultmann, *The Gospel of John: A Commentary*, trans. G. R. Beasley-Murray (Oxford: Blackwell, 1971 [1941]).

source, a passion source, and miscellaneous other sources. However, the miracle source and the discourse source are Bultmann's major emphases in his commentary.

Bultmann's commentary on John's Gospel, which appeared in 1941, has cast a long shadow on Johannine studies, to the point where—despite the significant influence of Strauss and Baur—it can be said that much of Johannine studies is a continuing response to Bultmann and many of the issues that he raised, even if also proposed by Strauss and Baur before him.

3. SOURCES OF JOHN'S GOSPEL

The sources of John's Gospel, a topic already introduced by Bultmann and others, continues to be debated in Johannine studies in at least three very different, though related, venues, to the point that the notion of sources has taken a much more expanded role in current Johannine scholarship. The first concerns the relationship of John's Gospel to the Synoptic Gospels as possible sources, the second the sources within John's Gospel itself, and the third the use of the Old Testament in John as a major source.

Before source-critical theories regarding John's Gospel were fully developed, there already was discussion of the relationship of John's Gospel to the Synoptic Gospels (in fact, going back to the early church). This discussion is part of the larger debate during the nineteenth and early twentieth centuries regarding the historicity of John's Gospel, especially as determined by the historical reliability of its sources. The debate naturally turned to the relationship of John's Gospel to the Synoptics. This discussion has gone through several major phases.[21]

The first phase accepted that there was a relationship between John's Gospel and the Synoptics, especially Mark's Gospel but possibly other Gospels as well. This theory was widely held at the beginning of the last century by many major Johannine and Synoptic scholars, such as Benjamin Bacon (1860–1932), E. F. Scott (1868–1954), B. H. Streeter (1874–1937), W. F. Howard (1880–1952), and R. H. Lightfoot (1883–1953), among others.[22]

---

21. The phases are well summarized in more detail in D. Moody Smith, *John among the Gospels: The Relationship in Twentieth-Century Research* (Minneapolis: Fortress, 1992).

22. Bacon, *Fourth Gospel*, 356–84; E. F. Scott, *The Fourth Gospel: Its Purpose and Theology* (Edinburgh: T&T Clark, 1908), 29–43; B. H. Streeter, *The Four Gospels: A Study of Origins* (London: Macmillan, 1930), 393–420; Howard, *Fourth Gospel*, 128–43; and R. H. Lightfoot, *History and Interpretation in the Gospels* (London: Hodder & Stoughton, 1935), esp. 206–25.

The second phase in this discussion argued for independence of John's Gospel from the Synoptics. In a small book with much greater influence than one would imagine from its size, Percival Gardner-Smith examined several sections of John's Gospel chapter by chapter and concluded that the sections were not dependent upon the Synoptics but that both made use of a variety of oral and written historical sources that account for their similarities.[23] Gardner-Smith especially saw John's and Luke's Gospels sharing a common stream of tradition, a theory of semi-independence. This position has had a major abiding influence on Johannine studies to the present and is found in the works of such scholars as Barnabas Lindars (1923–1991), J. Louis Martyn (1925–2015), and Raymond Brown (1928–1998), among others (I will discuss Martyn and Brown further below).[24]

A variation on this theory has been adopted by some evangelical Johannine scholars, who argue for what has come to be called interlocking tradition, in which historically reliable oral and written traditions used by both John and the Synoptic Gospels interlock with each other, one helping to explain the other, to the point of relative dependence and independence. This view is most often attributed to Leon Morris and is followed by some other evangelicals (see below).[25] There were a number of scholars who were unwilling, however, to abandon completely the idea of John's dependence upon the Synoptic Gospels, even if they varied in their opinion regarding which Gospels and to what degree, a view represented by John Bailey and C. K. Barrett (1917–2011).[26]

However, in arguably a third phase, a number of Johannine scholars have gone further than Gardner-Smith and argued that the Johannine author used a variety of oral and written sources, but that these were not historical sources, nor were they shared by the authors of the Synoptic Gospels. The result is a theory of relatively complete independence of John and the Synoptics. This view has been promoted by such scholars as

---

23. Percival Gardner-Smith, *Saint John and the Synoptic Gospels* (Cambridge: Cambridge University Press, 1938). This position was followed by C. H. Dodd in his *The Interpretation of the Fourth Gospel* (Cambridge: Cambridge University Press, 1953) and Dodd, *Historical Tradition in the Fourth Gospel* (Cambridge: Cambridge University Press, 1963).

24. Besides Martyn and Brown (see below), see Barnabas Lindars, *The Gospel of John*, NCB (Grand Rapids: Eerdmans, 1972), 25–26, 46–54.

25. Leon L. Morris, *Studies in the Fourth Gospel* (Exeter: Paternoster, 1969), 15–63.

26. John A. Bailey, *The Tradition Common to the Gospels of Luke and John*, NovTSup 7 (Leiden: Brill, 1963); C. K. Barrett, *The Gospel According to St. John*, 2nd ed. (Philadelphia: Westminster, 1978 [1955]), 15–21.

Bultmann, Robert T. Fortna, D. Moody Smith (1931–2016), and Urban von Wahlde, among others.[27]

The fourth phase is a return to the first phase of Synoptic dependence of John. There are variations on this proposal, many of them involving high levels of complexity, but they all take the stance that there are strong indications that John relies upon the Synoptic Gospels, in particular Mark's Gospel, a proposal argued by Émile Boismard (1916–2004), Frans Neirynck, Richard Bauckham, Manfred Lang, Andrew Lincoln, and James Barker, among others.[28] It would appear that the question of John's relationship to outside sources will continue to be widely debated.

Once the question of the historical foundation of John's Gospel was disputed and even widely dismissed, it was natural that multiple internal source theories would be developed. Ever since Bultmann's commentary, there have been various suggestions regarding the sources of John's Gospel, although many of the proposals go back earlier even than the early twentieth century. The major debate has been over the sign-source, with many questioning or opposing it and others attempting to build upon it. The existence of the sign-source has been endorsed by a variety of interpreters, with the leading scholars being Howard Teeple (1911–1997), Robert T. Fortna, and William Nicol, as well as several commentary writers, such as Rudolf Schnackenburg (1914–2002) and Jürgen Becker.[29] Fortna has

---

27. Robert Fortna, *The Fourth Gospel and Its Predecessor: From Narrative Source to Present Gospel* (Philadelphia: Fortress, 1988); D. Moody Smith, *Johannine Christianity: Essays on Its Setting, Sources, and Theology* (Edinburgh: T&T Clark, 1984), 37–172; and Urban C. von Wahlde, *The Earliest Version of John's Gospel: Recovering the Gospel of Signs* (Wilmington, DE: Glazier, 1989).

28. É. Boismard and A. Lamouille, with G. Rochais, *L'Évangile de Jean: Commentaire*, vol. 3 of *Synopse des quatre Évangiles en Français* (Paris: Cerf, 1977); Frans Neirynck, "John 4.46–54: Signs Source and/or Synoptic Gospels," *Ephemerides Theologicae Lovanienses* 60 (1984): 367–75 (repr. in Neirynck, *Evangelica II, 1982–1991: Collected Essays*, ed. F. Van Segbroeck, BETL 99 [Leuven: Peeters/Leuven University Press, 1991], 679–88); Richard Bauckham, "John for Readers of Mark," in *The Gospels for All Christians: Rethinking the Gospel Audiences*, ed. Richard Bauckham (Grand Rapids: Eerdmans, 1998), 147–71; Manfred Lang, *Johannes und die Synoptiker* (Göttingen: Vandenhoeck & Ruprecht, 1999); Andrew T. Lincoln, *The Gospel According to Saint John*, BNTC (Peabody, MA: Hendrickson, 2005), 26–39; and James W. Barker, *John's Use of Matthew* (Minneapolis: Fortress, 2015). A minority position, noted above as held by Schleiermacher, is that John's Gospel reflects at least as early traditions as the Synoptics and therefore might take priority among the Gospels. This view is associated with John A. T. Robinson, *The Priority of John*, ed. J. F. Coakley (London: SCM, 1985). For a recent summary of various viewpoints, see Robert T. Fortna and Tom Thatcher, eds., *Jesus in Johannine Tradition* (Louisville: Westminster John Knox, 2001), esp. Thatcher, "Introduction," 1–9; and Kysar, *Fourth Evangelist*, 13–66.

29. Howard M. Teeple, *The Literary Origin of the Gospel of John* (Evanston, IL: Religion and Ethics Institute, 1974), 1–116; Robert Fortna, *The Gospel of Signs: A Reconstruction of the Narrative Source Underlying the Fourth Gospel*, SNTSMS 11 (Cambridge: Cambridge University Press, 1970), as well as his *Fourth Gospel*; William Nicol, *The Sēmeia in the Fourth Gospel: Tradition and Redaction*, NovTSup

probably been the most persistent in continuing to examine and support his source hypothesis.

The major works on the sources were published in the 1970s and into the 1980s, although debate over the signs and their being a source has continued to the present. The major issue around sources seems to involve the complexity of making source-critical judgments based upon differentiating various inconsistencies within John's Gospel that indicate the use of sources. As a result, other criteria are also sometimes introduced, but these, such as style or theology, appear to be equally problematic criteria for making judgments on sources. Arguments regarding displacements of sources, something Bultmann relies upon heavily in his analysis of John's Gospel, have probably proven the most problematic and been mostly abandoned in more recent source-critical work. For the most part, contemporary discussion of John's Gospel does not emphasize traditional source criticism. However, there is also the assumption that, even if John did not use an explicit source, he does make use of signs as a means of organizing or structuring his Gospel. In that regard, source criticism—or at least one of its results, even if used as a literary feature—has been integrated into current Johannine studies.

The third source hypothesis concerns the use of the Old Testament in John's Gospel. This source-critical theory does not usually have the same encompassing scope as do the previous two theories (although there are exceptions, such as in the work of Günter Reim and Thomas L. Brodie),[30] but they nevertheless emphasize how the use of the Old Testament provides important source material for John's Gospel. Although C. H. Dodd (1884–1973) is known for having worked in a variety of areas of New Testament study, he made a significant contribution to Johannine studies by using a similar perspective as Bultmann but arriving at very different conclusions (see also below). Whereas Bultmann tended to give radical and skeptical answers regarding the historical reliability of the

---

32 (Leiden: Brill, 1972); Rudolf Schnackenburg, *The Gospel According to St. John*, vol. 1, trans. Kevin Smyth (London: Burns & Oates, 1980 [1965]); and Jürgen Becker, *Das Evangelium nach Johannes*, 2 vols., Ökumenischer Taschenbuch-Kommentar 4/1, 2 (Würzburg: Echter-Verlag, 1979–1981). See Kysar, *Fourth Evangelist*, 16–24.

30. Günter Reim, *Studien zum alttestamentlichen Hintergrund des Johannesevangeliums*, SNTSMS 22 (Cambridge: Cambridge University Press, 1974); and Thomas L. Brodie, *The Quest for the Origin of John's Gospel: A Source-Oriented Approach* (New York: Oxford University Press, 1993). Reim attempts to bring source theories and use of the Old Testament together.

Gospels, Dodd believed that, using form criticism, one could get much closer to the historical Jesus even in John's Gospel. This is clear in Dodd's two major works on John's Gospel, *Interpretation of the Fourth Gospel* and *Historical Tradition in the Fourth Gospel.*

I include Dodd within discussion of source hypotheses because of his view of the Old Testament in John's Gospel. Dodd's view goes back to his belief in two major sources of the New Testament, the kerygma and the didache. The kerygma is the proclamation or message of the gospel that is being preached. Dodd proposed relatively early in his career that this kerygma had a form and structure to it, which is supported by Scripture.[31] In this regard, Dodd shows, as Beth Stovell has indicated, both how and why the Old Testament is used as it is in John's Gospel.[32] Since Dodd, there have been many different approaches to the use of the Old Testament in John's Gospel. They have been conveniently classified in some recent scholarship as indicating that the Old Testament is used either as a structuring device for the Gospel, following the earlier proposal of Dodd, or, as in most instances, in a variety of other ways that support various events, sayings, or topics within the Gospel.[33] Instances of the first include Michael Daise's examination of clusters of Isaianic passages,[34] and of the second most other studies, including those by Edwin Freed (1920–2014), Maarten Menken (1848–2016), Bruce Schuchard, and William Bynum, among others.[35]

---

31. C. H. Dodd, *The Apostolic Preaching and Its Developments* (London: Hodder & Stoughton, 1936). See also Dodd, *According to the Scriptures* (repr., London: Fontana, 1965 [1952]).

32. Beth M. Stovell, "C. H. Dodd and Johannine Scholarship," in *Gospel of John in Modern Interpretation*, 101–17, here 114.

33. Rekha M. Chennattu, "Scripture," in *How John Works: Storytelling in the Fourth Gospel*, ed. Douglas Estes and Ruth Sheridan (Atlanta: SBL Press, 2016), 171–86, esp. 171–81. Cf. also Thomas R. Hatina, ed., *Biblical Interpretation in Early Christian Gospels, Volume 4: The Gospel of John*, LNTS 613 (London: T&T Clark, 2020).

34. Michael A. Daise, *Quotations in John: Studies on Jewish Scripture in the Fourth Gospel*, LNTS 610 (London: T&T Clark, 2020); see also Ruth Sheridan, *Retelling Scripture: "The Jews" and the Scriptural Citations in John 1:19–12:15*, BibInt 110 (Leiden: Brill, 2012); and Andreas J. Köstenberger, "John's Appropriation of Isaiah's Signs Theology: Implications for the Structure of John's Gospel," *Them* 43.3 (2018): 376–86.

35. Edwin D. Freed, *Old Testament Quotations in the Gospel of John*, NovTSup 11 (Leiden: Brill, 1965); Maarten J. J. Menken, *Old Testament Quotations in the Fourth Gospel: Studies in Textual Form* (Kampen: Kok Pharos, 1996); Bruce G. Schuchard, *Scripture within Scripture: The Interrelationship of Form and Function in the Explicit Old Testament Citations in the Gospel of John*, SBLDS 133 (Atlanta: Scholars Press, 1992); and Wm. Randolph Bynum, *The Fourth Gospel and the Scriptures: Illuminating the Form and Meaning of Scriptural Citation in John 19:37*, NovTSup 144 (Leiden: Brill, 2012).

4. COMMUNITY HYPOTHESES AND THEIR RESPONSES

One of the most important discussions that continues to have major influence upon current Johannine studies revolves around the so-called community hypothesis. The community hypothesis grows out of the tension that has often been observed by scholars studying John's Gospel (and other works in the Johannine corpus according to some of the theories) between the story (text) about Jesus and the context in which the Gospel may have been written. These theories, while they introduce a wider range of issues, especially regarding the Johannine community, are types of source theories. It is hard to know who originated the community hypothesis in its recognized form, because two of the most important proponents, Brown and Martyn, seem to have been developing and publishing their theories at about the same time.

Brown, first writing in his commentary on John's Gospel and then in a full-length monograph,[36] argues for five stages or, later, four phases in the compositional process, moving from a core of historical material through its development into the Gospel and then being supplemented by the Johannine letters. Brown's theory is relatively comprehensive regarding the Johannine corpus (including views on Revelation). Martyn, using the analogy of a drama, originally posited two levels and then later three historical periods in the development of John's Gospel, extending his theory from his initial exploration of the exclusion from the synagogue of the healed blind man in John 9 as reflecting later synagogue regulations to other chapters such as John 5 and 7.[37] A third scholar to note here is Oscar Cullmann (1902–1999), who posits a Johannine "circle" formed around heterodox Jews who were at one time associated with John the Baptist, and whose tradition goes back as early as that of the Synoptic Gospels.[38] There have been many other theories of origin that posit various sources and/or levels

---

36. Raymond E. Brown, *The Gospel According to John 1-XII*, AB 29 (Garden City, NY: Doubleday, 1966), xxxiv–xl; and Brown, *The Community of the Beloved Disciple: The Life, Loves, and Hates of an Individual Church in New Testament Times* (New York: Paulist, 1979), now reprinted in 2024 with a new introduction by Paul N. Anderson (xi–xxiv). Moloney changes Brown's view of the compositional process from his earlier theory (found in the original commentary introduction of 1966) to his later theory in the revised *Introduction*, 62–85.

37. J. Louis Martyn, *History and Theology in the Fourth Gospel*, rev. and enlarged ed. (Nashville: Abingdon, 1979 [1968]); and Martyn, *The Gospel of John in Christian History: Essays for Interpreters* (New York: Paulist, 1978), esp. 90–121.

38. Oscar Cullmann, *The Johannine Circle: Its Place in Judaism, among the Disciples of Jesus and in Early Christianity. A Study in the Origin of the Gospel of John*, NTL (London: SCM, 1976).

of development and redaction, but these, especially those of Brown and Martyn, have had the most influence upon Johannine studies. Despite various responses (noted below), continue to set the agenda for how scholars think of and discuss Johannine origins, because the theories appear to retain some form of historical core to the Gospel but also accommodate ways of understanding apparent discrepancies or inconsistencies in the text.

There have, nevertheless, been various reactions—some of them very strong—to the community hypothesis. These responses have taken two primary forms: reassessment of the concept of community and, with it, audience, and redating John's Gospel or the tradition within it. The result is that current Johannine studies still reflect widespread acknowledgment of the community hypothesis, while also recognizing that there are other possible explanations of the origin of the Johannine writings. The history of discussion of what constitutes a Johannine community and its role in the development of the Gospel far predates this more recent discussion. However, as Edward Klink points out, the concept has always been problematic since the time of source, form, and redaction criticism, and even after the work of Martyn and Brown caused a major shift in Johannine scholarship.[39]

More recent discussion of the concept of community in Johannine studies includes the research of Martin Hengel (1926–2009) on the question of origins.[40] Hengel treats the Johannine author as a theologian grounded in early historical accounts. Hengel thus redefines community by dissolving much of the divide created by Martyn and further stratified by Brown. This view has been developed further by Jörg Frey.[41] Another attempt to redefine community is found in Bauckham's proposal that the Gospels were written for all Christians, rather than for those in a particular location.[42] This proposal sees a much broader conception of audience and minimizes the usual definition of community by creating broader contexts for the Gospels that resemble those of the epistles. Rather than

---

39. Edward W. Klink III, *The Sheep of the Fold: The Audience and Origin of the Gospel of John*, SNTSMS 141 (Cambridge: Cambridge University Press, 2007), 10–35, noting the work of R. Alan Culpepper, *The Johannine School: An Evaluation of the Johannine-School Hypothesis Based on an Investigation of the Nature of Ancient Schools*, SBLDS 26 (Missoula, MT: Scholars Press, 1975), among others (used in this discussion). For recent discussion, see Christopher Seglenieks and Christopher W. Skinner, eds., *The Johannine Community in Recent Debate* (Lanham, MD: Lexington/Fortress Academic, 2024).

40. Martin Hengel, *The Johannine Question*, trans. John Bowden (London: SCM, 1989).

41. Jörg Frey, *Theology and History in the Fourth Gospel: Tradition and Narration* (Waco, TX: Baylor University Press, 2018).

42. Bauckham, "For Whom Were Gospels Written?" in *Gospels for All Christians*, 9–48; cf. also Bauckham, "John for Readers of Mark."

taking what is sometimes referred to as an allegorical approach to reading the Gospels—such as Martyn takes—that limits references to a narrow conception of community, the Gospels, including John's Gospel, are part of a much larger context of shared texts. This revised view of community and audience is more rigorously presented in Klink's redefinition. He wishes to move away from what he terms "a territorial or ideological model of community," such as is found in Martyn and Brown, to instead endorse a relational model, in which the Gospels were written by Christians for Christians who may have been located in various areas throughout the Roman world of the time, all of them sharing in the same story about Jesus.[43]

The other response to the community hypothesis attempts to redefine community for John by arguing that John's Gospel, and not just its sources (although that is included), represents a tradition that should take priority and is as valuable as that of the Synoptic Gospels. The attempt to give John's Gospel priority, and usually with it to date John's Gospel relatively early, includes scholars reaching back to the nineteenth and early twentieth centuries. However, the major relatively recent proponent of such a view is John A. T. Robinson (1919–1983). He argues for a pre–AD 70 date for John's Gospel in his reconstruction of New Testament chronology, followed by his work specifically on John. In *The Priority of John*, Robinson argues that John's Gospel has priority in the sense that its traditions are at least as early as those of the Synoptic Gospels.[44] Robinson's general view of dating John's Gospel has been revived recently by Jonathan Bernier,[45] who has also argued from a historical standpoint that the rejection from the synagogue, emphasized by Martyn's view as justification for two levels, is plausible within the context of Jesus's ministry.[46]

5. LITERARY INTERPRETATION OF JOHN'S GOSPEL
The most active area within Johannine studies in recent years has probably been literary interpretation of John's Gospel. In an emerging climate of

---

43. Klink, *Sheep of the Fold*, 63.
44. John A. T. Robinson, *Redating the New Testament* (Philadelphia: Westminster, 1976), 254–311; Robinson, *Priority of John*, esp. 1–35. See Stanley E. Porter, "John A. T. Robinson: Provocateur and Profound Johannine Scholar," in *Gospel of John in Modern Interpretation*, 141–72.
45. Jonathan Bernier, *Rethinking the Dates of the New Testament: The Evidence for Early Composition* (Grand Rapids: Baker Academic, 2022), 87–111.
46. Jonathan Bernier, *Aposynagōgos and the Historical Jesus in John: Rethinking the Historicity of the Johannine Expulsion Passages*, BibInt 122 (Leiden: Brill, 2013).

literary interpretation of the New Testament—part of a general rethinking of critical methods beginning around 1980—R. Alan Culpepper published his *Anatomy of the Fourth Gospel* in 1983.[47] This work helped to set the agenda for literary interpretation, not just of John's Gospel but of the Synoptic Gospels and other books of the New Testament. Culpepper's book relies upon a combination of various literary critics, including the Russian Formalists, the Prague Linguistic Circle, narratology and structuralism, and the American New Criticism, among some others, to examine narratological questions related to point of view, time, plot, characters, implicit commentary, and the implied reader. Although there is not much that is methodologically new in Culpepper's work, he provides a compelling reading of John's Gospel using methods that were, at the time, relatively unknown within biblical studies. His work is now generally categorized as a form of narrative criticism of the New Testament, even though Culpepper's work is much broader than what has usually come to be called narrative criticism. The enduring significance of Culpepper's interpretation is evidenced by the fact that his work is still being discussed years later and by the existence of the literary interpretive movement that it helped to foster and encourage.[48]

Culpepper's work provided a model for most literary interpretation of John's Gospel as a mix of theories that often draw upon twentieth-century North American literary criticism and have come to be characterized as narrative criticism. Some of the most important publications in narrative criticism—and it is admittedly diverse as it draws in various ways upon secular literary theory—include the following selected representative works. Some early literary works emphasize narrative in relation to the response of the reader. Culpepper himself draws upon the reader-response perspective of Wolfgang Iser (1926–2007) in discussing the implied reader. Such reader-oriented studies are extended especially by Jeffrey Staley. Staley wrote several books that explore new approaches to literary interpretation of the New Testament. In his first book, *The Print's First Kiss*, he focuses upon the implied reader, and in his second, he examines various types of reader responses within John's

---

47. R. Alan Culpepper, *Anatomy of the Fourth Gospel: A Study in Literary Design*, Foundations and Facets: New Testament (Philadelphia: Fortress, 1983).

48. See Tom Thatcher and Stephen D. Moore, eds., *Anatomies of Narrative Criticism: The Past, Present, and Futures of the Fourth Gospel as Literature* (Atlanta: SBL Press, 2008).

Gospel.[49] Most literary interpretations, however, tend to draw upon a variety of literary theories to examine John's Gospel. Mark Stibbe wrote a major work of narrative criticism of John's Gospel, in which he draws upon practical criticism, proposed by the literary scholar I. A. Richards (1893–1979), genre criticism, socially situated analysis, and narrative-historical analysis.[50] Stibbe's volume remains an excellent introduction to these movements as they have been used in Johannine studies. One of the most adventuresome literary approaches is found in the work of Peter Phillips in what he calls a sequential reading of John's Prologue that draws together a variety of methods that may appear to be disharmonious.[51] I cannot neglect the work of the honoree of this volume, Andreas Köstenberger, who fashions his reading of John's Gospel, even within his theology, as a "close narrative reading."[52] Other literary treatments could easily be mentioned.

Around twenty or so years ago an emphasis upon the study of character in John's Gospel emerged. Comments on character have been made all along the way regarding John's Gospel, starting with Culpepper's formative work and including many of the works mentioned above. The literary categories of the novelist E. M. Forster (1879–1970), with his well-known terms of "flat" and "round" characters,[53] have tended to predominate in character studies, with some exceptions where other approaches have been utilized. Besides some of the works already mentioned above, some important works on character include David Beck's early monograph focusing upon readers and anonymous characters in John's Gospel.[54] Colleen Conway examines character from the standpoint of gender to determine if there are differences in presentation.[55]

---

49. Jeffrey Lloyd Staley, *The Print's First Kiss: A Rhetorical Investigation of the Implied Reader in the Fourth Gospel*, SBLDS 82 (Atlanta: Scholars Press, 1988); Staley, *Reading with a Passion: Rhetoric, Autobiography, and the American West in the Gospel of John* (London: Continuum, 1995).

50. Mark W. G. Stibbe, *John as Storyteller: Narrative Criticism and the Fourth Gospel*, SNTSMS 73 (Cambridge: Cambridge University Press, 1992). See also his commentary, Stibbe, *John*, Readings (Sheffield: Sheffield Academic, 1993).

51. Peter M. Phillips, *The Prologue of the Fourth Gospel: A Sequential Reading*, LNTS 294 (London: T&T Clark, 2006). See also Brian Larsen, *Archetypes and the Fourth Gospel: Literature and Theology in Conversation* (London: T&T Clark, 2018).

52. Andreas J. Köstenberger, *A Theology of John's Gospel and Letters* (Grand Rapids: Zondervan, 2009), 176.

53. E. M. Forster, *Aspects of the Novel* (repr., Harmondsworth: Penguin, 1962 [1927]), 73–89.

54. David R. Beck, *The Discipleship Paradigm: Readers and Anonymous Characters in the Fourth Gospel*, BibInt 27 (Leiden: Brill, 1997).

55. Colleen Conway, *Men and Women in the Fourth Gospel: Gender and Johannine Characterization* (Atlanta: Scholars Press, 1999).

Cornelis Bennema has probably written more extensively upon character within John's Gospel than any other.[56] His first major work focused upon individual characters in John's Gospel. He then took a step back and attempted to develop a theory of character that moved beyond what he considered earlier simplistic or reductionistic approaches to character that were too reliant upon theories from antiquity or earlier literary criticism. This led him to expand and refine his character studies in a second edition of his first book. Bennema's theoretical work appeared at about the same time as several edited volumes that contain a variety of Johannine character studies, from various methodological perspectives.[57] Nevertheless, most studies of character remain within literary and even structuralist theories, with very little recognition, for example, of cognitive character studies as a potential way forward.[58]

6. SOCIAL-SCIENTIFIC AND RELATED APPROACHES

Another relatively important recent development in Johannine studies is the acknowledgment of the social situatedness of a text, including the Johannine literature and in particular John's Gospel. Social-scientific criticism of the New Testament has developed in several different ways, and these ways are also reflected in Johannine studies. As a result, some studies are more descriptivist in nature while others are more social-scientifically theoretical. The recognition of the complexity of social situation has led to studies drawing upon various social-scientific approaches to John's Gospel.

One of the first works to approach John's Gospel in this way was an influential and often-cited article by Wayne Meeks (1932–2023) on the ascent/descent motif.[59] Jerome Neyrey's book, *An Ideology of Revolt*, is an early theoretical study that utilizes the concept of the sociology of knowledge and in particular the group and grid model of anthropologist Mary Douglas (1921–2007) to identify and describe the Johannine

---

56. Cornelis Bennema, *Encountering Jesus: Character Studies in the Gospel of John*, 2nd ed. (Minneapolis: Fortress, 2014 [2009]); and Bennema, *A Theory of Character in New Testament Narrative* (Minneapolis: Fortress, 2014).

57. See Steven A. Hunt, D. Francois Tolmie, and Ruben Zimmermann, eds., *Character Studies in the Fourth Gospel: Narrative Approaches to Seventy Figures in John* (repr., Grand Rapids: Eerdmans, 2013); and Christopher W. Skinner, ed., *Characters and Characterization in the Gospel of John*, LNTS 461 (London: Bloomsbury, 2013).

58. Cf. now, however, Tyler Smith, *The Fourth Gospel and the Manufacture of Minds in Ancient Historiography, Biography, Romance, and Drama*, BibInt 173 (Leiden: Brill, 2019).

59. Wayne A. Meeks, "The Man from Heaven in Johannine Sectarianism," *JBL* 91 (1972): 44–72.

community.[60] Norman Petersen draws upon the anthropological and linguistic work of Bruce Malina (1933–2017) to propose that the Johannine community creates an anti-language for its use.[61] More recent studies have raised questions about the relationship of John's Gospel to the Roman Empire and attempted to position the Gospel as a work that is formulated by and responds to Roman ideology.[62]

The most important area, however, where social-scientific and related issues have come to bear in Johannine studies concerns the question of how John's Gospel characterizes the Jews. The discussion of the Jews in John's Gospel has not always been treated by means of social-scientific theories, but the question is itself (at least) a social one, in that it deals with such categories as social identity, ethnicity, group membership, and categorization of self and others, among related topics. There has been long-standing debate about whether John's Gospel is anti-Semitic, or at least anti-Jewish, based upon how the Jews are depicted within the Gospel.

The topic was reopened in a major way by a conference held in Leuven in 2000, published as *Anti-Judaism and the Fourth Gospel*.[63] This volume contains a wide range of approaches to the question of Johannine anti-Judaism, categorized in different ways depending on their focus. This volume has set the agenda for a resurgence of interest in this topic and with it many new studies. This initial collection has, in some ways, been bookended by a similar study published in 2017 that treats the topic of John and Judaism as a "contested relationship in context," but again with a variety of approaches to the topic that attempt to determine the meaning of references to the Jews within the Gospel and its cultural context.[64]

---

60. Jerome Neyrey, *An Ideology of Revolt: John's Christology in Social-Science Perspective* (Minneapolis: Fortress, 1988). Cf. Mary Douglas, *Essays in the Sociology of Perception* (London: Routledge & Kegan Paul, 1982), 1–30.

61. Norman Petersen, *The Gospel of John and the Sociology of Light: Language and Characterization in the Fourth Gospel* (Valley Forge, PA: Trinity Press International, 1993), citing Bruce Malina, "The Gospel of John in Sociolinguistic Perspective," *Center for Hermeneutical Studies*, Colloquy 48 (Berkeley, CA: Center for Hermeneutical Studies, 1985), drawing upon the linguist Michael A. K. Halliday (1925–2018).

62. See, for example, Lance Byron Richey, *Roman Imperial Ideology and the Gospel of John*, CBQMS 43 (Washington, DC: Catholic Biblical Association of America, 2007); Warren Carter, *John and Empire: Initial Explorations* (London: T&T Clark, 2008); and Tom Thatcher, *Greater than Caesar: Christology and Empire in the Fourth Gospel* (Minneapolis: Fortress, 2009).

63. R. Bieringer, D. Pollefeyt, and F. Vandecasteele-Vanneuville, *Anti-Judaism and the Fourth Gospel: Papers of the Leuven Colloquium, 2000* (Assen: Royal Van Gorcum, 2001).

64. R. Alan Culpepper and Paul N. Anderson, eds., *John and Judaism: A Contested Relationship in Context* (Atlanta: SBL Press, 2017), including Reimund Bieringer, "Anti-Judaism and the Fourth Gospel Fifteen

In the earlier volume, Reimund Bieringer et al. outline five major proposals regarding the identification of the Jews in John's Gospel: (1) non-Johannine Jewish Christians, (2) Jewish leaders in Jerusalem, (3) Torah-observing Jews in Jerusalem, (4) residents of Judea or Judeans, or (5) Jews as heirs of the particular Jews who openly oppose Jesus,[65] to which may also be added several more recent proposals that attempt to refine questions of method. Two of the more recent attempts to deal with the topic of the Jews in John's Gospel have introduced more stringent linguistic criteria that have been lacking in previous study and have utilized to good effect social-scientific theories, such as social-identity theory and self-categorization theory.[66] The discussion of the Jews in John's Gospel reveals that such a topic is also clearly intertwined with examination of the Johannine community, the dating of John's Gospel, and Johannine theology.

7. JOHANNINE THEOLOGY

As noted at the outset, John's Gospel as the spiritual Gospel has meant that theological issues have always been at the forefront of discussion. Whereas many if not most topics within the scope of biblical theology have probably been addressed when discussing Johannine theology, there has been a greater emphasis upon Christology than any other, because of the persistent notion that John's Gospel reflects a "high" Christology, that is, a Christology that depicts Jesus as a divine figure from the outset (the Prologue) and throughout the Gospel, rather than as a man, even if elevated to divinity. Many of the major topics in Johannine studies mentioned above, even if they are focused upon historical issues, have often generated or reflected theological debate. These would include the theological implications of source hypotheses regarding Johannine Christology, such as whether John's Gospel is a much later theological interpretation of Jesus based upon or reflecting a later stage of discussion regarding Jesus than is found in the Synoptic Gospels; or the community hypothesis and its implications for who Jesus is in relationship to Judaism, in particular the synagogue. The study of Johannine theology has often been a continuation of debate over

---

Years after the Leuven Colloquium," 243–363. The volume includes more than just discussion of "the Jews."

65. Reimund Bieringer, Didier Pollefeyt, and Frederique Vandecasteele-Vanneuville, "Wrestling with Johannine Anti-Judaism: A Hermeneutical Framework for the Analysis of the Current Debate," in *Anti-Judaism and the Fourth Gospel*, 3–44.

66. Porter, *John, His Gospel, and Jesus*, 149–73, with examples of those holding the five positions listed above on p. 151; and Jonathan Numada, *John and Anti-Judaism: Reading the Gospel in Light of Greco-Roman Culture*, McMaster Biblical Studies Series (Eugene, OR: Pickwick, 2021).

the developmental hypotheses of Strauss and Baur mentioned above and then later seen in history of religion questions regarding the uniqueness of Christianity, and more particularly the uniqueness and possible divinity of Jesus in relation to other religions. Developmental hypotheses, especially concerning theology (such as is found in the history of religion movement), believe that more developed views of Jesus must indicate temporal subsequence (simpler becomes more complex), so that John's Christology must be later than that of the other Gospels, even significantly later. Despite the influences of such hypotheses, George Stevens (1854–1906) in his Johannine theology argued against the developmental hypothesis of Baur, although he claimed that his view of Johannine theology was not dependent upon theories of authorship.[67] This is perhaps because Stevens's theology is organized along the lines of a systematic theology and focused upon the major dogmas of Christian theology, an approach also followed in the surprisingly resilient Johannine theology of Howard.[68]

These works were both written before the most important works of Johannine theology of the modern era. More representative of critical scholarship would be the works of Bultmann and Dodd, even if they diverge in their findings. Bultmann is arguably the most important Johannine interpreter of the last century and he provides a synthesis of Johannine thought in the second volume of his New Testament theology.[69] Bultmann, reflecting the influence of Baur and of the history of religion, distances John's Gospel from the earliest proclamation of Jesus and New Testament writers such as Paul. Bultmann identifies a Johannine dualism that he attributes to Gnosticism and a Christology grounded in the gnostic Redeemer myth (but he sees this influencing Paul as well). By contrast, Dodd wishes to ground John's Gospel in early Christianity, although he also sees a complex set of influences including Hermeticism, Hellenistic Judaism, Rabbinic Judaism, Gnosticism, and Mandaism.[70] The influence of Bultmann and Dodd has been significant. Much of the difficulty regarding Johannine theology has arguably been compounded by a misplaced emphasis upon the supposedly

---

67. George B. Stevens, *Johannine Theology: A Study of the Doctrinal Contents of the Gospel and Epistles of the Apostle John* (London: Richard D. Dickinson, 1894).

68. W. F. Howard, *Christianity According to St. John*, Studies in Theology (London: Duckworth, 1943).

69. Rudolf Bultmann, *Theology of the New Testament*, 2 vols., trans. Kendrick Grobel (London: SCM, 1952–1955 [1948–1953]), 2:3–92. Bultmann wrote on this topic in other places, including his commentary on John's Gospel and other publications. John Ashton considers many of the Johannine theological issues in relation to Bultmann in *Understanding the Fourth Gospel* (Oxford: Clarendon, 1991; 2nd ed., 2007).

70. Dodd, *Interpretation of the Fourth Gospel*, esp. 3–130.

unique "high" Christology of the Gospel. Robinson rejects the developmental hypothesis and makes the trenchant point that the high Christology found in John's Gospel, in particular in the Prologue, is not significantly different from that found in Paul, in particular in Philippians 2:6–11 and Colossians 1:15–20. Even though Robinson believes that the Prologue (and John 21) was added later to the Gospel, he believes it was written by the original author and the entire document is to be dated to the late AD 60s before the fall of Jerusalem.[71] In other words, he sees no reason to question the high Christology of John's Gospel as indicating a later theological interpretation of Jesus than that found elsewhere in the New Testament, in particular in Paul.[72] Despite Robinson's insights, much scholarship has still followed the developmental hypothesis. The result is to see Johannine Christology as late and to find other major theological ideas to be dependent upon sources outside the environment of earliest Christianity.

Johannine theologies, as noted above, have tended to develop along several lines, from systematic theologies to biblical theologies, along with many studies of individual concepts. Dodd himself seems to have if not instigated at least encouraged this approach to Johannine theology by studying what he called the "leading ideas" in John's Gospel.[73] This approach has continued, with many volumes focusing upon individual topics. Over time, these ideas seem to have been narrowed down to a select few Johannine ideas. Five recent works illustrate the current state of Johannine theology. The first is a theology of John's Gospel by Craig Koester.[74] Koester is cautious regarding authorship, and treats many of the major ideas associated with John's Gospel: God, humanity, Jesus, crucifixion and resurrection, the Spirit, faith, and community. This is not a systematic or dogmatic approach to John's Gospel, but an approach that tries to define John's ideas

---

71. Robinson, *Redating the New Testament*, 283; cf. Robinson, *The Priority of John*, 379–94, with some modifications. This position is more fully explored in Stanley E. Porter, "Johannine and Pauline Christology," in *Johannine Christology*, ed. Stanley E. Porter and Andrew W. Pitts, JOST 3 (Leiden: Brill, 2020), 11–30. Robinson anticipated his views on John's Gospel in relation to the Synoptics as early as 1955 and in essays published over the course of his career. Many of these are found in Robinson, *Twelve New Testament Studies*, SBT 34 (London: SCM press, 1962), including his "The New Look on the Fourth Gospel" (1959).

72. Contra James D. G. Dunn, *Christology in the Making: A New Testament Inquiry into the Origins of the Doctrine of the Incarnation* (Philadelphia: Westminster, 1980; 2nd ed., Grand Rapids: Eerdmans, 1989), who sees John's "high" Christology as late, because he does not accept a high Christology in Paul, contrary to the vast majority of Pauline scholars.

73. Dodd, *Interpretation of the Fourth Gospel*, 133–285.

74. Craig R. Koester, *The Word of Life: A Theology of John's Gospel* (Grand Rapids: Eerdmans, 2008).

in distinctly Johannine ways. As noted above, Köstenberger takes a narrative approach to John's theology, reflecting some of the more recent literary discussion of John's Gospel, although his actual treatment of John's major themes is organized in a noncontinuous (and admittedly a bit confusing) fashion: after a prolegomena, he discusses the end of the Gospel with its thesis statement, then the beginning, and finally the middle.[75] Within this structure, the major ideas of the Gospel are discussed. The specific ideas discussed are similar to Koester's but with additional sections on Jesus as Messiah, the Word, John's love ethic, and some related topics. Although he claims that, to his knowledge, his is the "only English-language textbook on John's theology that aims to be both critical and comprehensive," Paul Rainbow's Johannine theology treats themes similar to those of Koester and Köstenberger, including the revelation of God, the world, Christ, the Spirit, faith, and community.[76] The fourth volume is a collection of essays specifically on Johannine Christology.[77] Narrower in scope than the previous three theology volumes but far from comprehensive, the content is organized around the formation of Johannine Christology, its Hellenistic and Jewish contexts, the literary character of the Johannine writings, and application to the Johannine audience, thereby attempting to introduce some new elements into the discussion. The final volume returns to some of the traditional topics within Johannine theology. Frey, in his *Theology and History in the Fourth Gospel*, treats Johannine Christology, historical tradition in John's Gospel, and John's as the spiritual Gospel, a work that is organized around several of the major themes of the history of Johannine research.[78]

8. TRADITIONAL RESPONSES TO THE JOHANNINE QUESTION

There have always been traditional advocates and responses to the more critical and deconstructive trends of some Johannine scholarship. By traditional, I do not necessarily mean theologically conservative (although some traditionalists definitely are) but viewpoints that have attempted to defend traditional views that often originated in the early church and

---

75. Köstenberger, *Theology of John's Gospel*, 273–546.

76. Paul A. Rainbow, *Johannine Theology: The Gospel, the Epistles and the Apocalypse* (Downers Grove, IL: InterVarsity Press, 2014), 9.

77. Stanley E. Porter and Andrew W. Pitts, eds., *Johannine Christology*, JOST 3 (Leiden: Brill, 2020).

78. Jörg Frey, *Theology and History in the Fourth Gospel: Tradition and Narration* (Waco, TX: Baylor University Press, 2018).

continue to be held, even if they are sometimes predominantly held outside of the lines of development of post-Enlightenment scholarship. Two noteworthy examples of such scholarship are found in the Johannine research of Adolf Schlatter (1852–1938) and Dodd.

Schlatter, a Tübingen scholar of a later generation, was clearly not of the same mind as his earlier Tübingen forebears. Schlatter wrote numerous works on the Johannine literature, including two commentaries on John's Gospel.[79] In his commentaries, he emphasizes the Jewish background of John's Gospel and refutes connections to Hellenistic literature, ostensibly because he believes that this background provides a more substantive support for the reliability of the Gospel and its depiction of Jesus. As already mentioned, Dodd wrote two major volumes on the Johannine writings, in which he deals extensively with the major themes and ideas, their interpretation, and the historical basis of this tradition. One can see in the work of Schlatter and Dodd many of the ideas that have been continued in other traditional Johannine scholarship.

More recently, several traditional (and usually theologically conservative) scholars have made significant and abiding contributions to contemporary Johannine studies. These include Leon Morris (1914–2006), D. A. Carson, Bauckham, Craig Blomberg, Craig S. Keener, and Köstenberger.[80] These authors have published a range of work that contributes to Johannine scholarship, including commentaries or commentary-like volumes on the Johannine literature, sometimes with apologetic overtones. Morris's commentary on John's Gospel marks a major contribution of traditional (and conservative) scholarship to Johannine studies. This commentary demonstrates a willingness by Morris (since followed by others, including some scholars mentioned immediately above) to enter

---

79. Adolf Schlatter, *Das Evangelium nach Johannes ausgelegt für Bibelleser* (Stuttgart: Calwer, 1928); and Schlatter, *Der Evangelist Johannes: Wie er spricht, denkt und glaubt. Ein Kommentar zum vierten Evangelium* (Stuttgart: Calwer, 1930), as well as in other works. See Robert Yarbrough, "Adolf Schlatter's Contribution to Interpretation of the Fourth Gospel," in *Gospel of John in Modern Interpretation*, 81–99.

80. Leon Morris, *The Gospel According to John*, NICNT (Grand Rapids: Eerdmans, 1971); D. A. Carson, *The Gospel According to John* (Grand Rapids: Eerdmans, 1991); Richard Bauckham, *The Testimony of the Beloved Disciple: Narrative, History, and Theology in the Gospel of John* (Grand Rapids: Eerdmans, 2007); Craig L. Blomberg, *The Historical Reliability of John's Gospel: Issues and Commentary* (Downers Grove, IL: InterVarsity Press, 2001); Craig S. Keener, *The Gospel of John: A Commentary*, 2 vols. (Peabody, MA: Hendrickson, 2003); and Köstenberger, *Theology of John's Gospel*. If I may be so bold as also to suggest, Porter, *John, His Gospel, and Jesus*, is another contributor to the discussion, although along slightly different lines. Barrett and Robinson might also be placed in this category because their views on John are generally traditional, but they have not come to be identified with this movement as have the others mentioned.

readily into the Johannine scholarly fray while arguing for unpopular views such as historical reliability.[81]

The most important recent, arguably traditional, turn in Johannine scholarship, however, belongs to the series of SBL sessions and resulting publications coordinated by Paul Anderson, Felix Just, and Tom Thatcher.[82] This series of seven planned volumes has already published four of the books, with the others in various stages of preparation. The papers within these volumes are not univocal in their approaches or their findings. What makes them noteworthy is the fact that they attempt to bring John's Gospel, and with it Jesus, into sustained historical discussion, in some ways fashioned after the kinds of discussions found in historical Jesus research of the Synoptic Gospels. Some have even gone so far as to call this a Fourth Quest, with this Fourth Quest integrating John's Gospel into the three previous quests for the historical Jesus heretofore reserved for the Synoptic Gospels. Calling this a Fourth Quest is not accurate, however, not least because one may easily dispute there being three previous quests in historical Jesus studies. This is a mischaracterization of historical Jesus scholarship based upon the influence of a select subgroup of German scholars particularly influenced by form criticism (including Bultmann, who has been highly influential in this discussion as well).[83] It is arguably better to call this latest effort in Johannine studies a legitimate attempt to reintegrate John's Gospel into the broad and enduring and even ancient stream of research and writing about the figure of Jesus, historical and otherwise, of which it was originally a part.

The four volumes in this series so far published form a developing argument regarding John's Gospel and its relationship to history and the Jesus of the Synoptic Gospels. In volume one, the major focus is on assessing how Johannine studies arrived at the place that it currently occupies in contemporary critical debate.[84] This means that the authors address the questions of why John's Gospel came to be emphasized as the spiritual Gospel rather than a historical Gospel, and also the relationship of John's Gospel to

---

81. See Andreas J. Köstenberger, "Leon Morris on John's Gospel: An Assessment and Critical Reflection on His Scholarship," in *Gospel of John in Modern Interpretation*, 197–209.

82. See Paul N. Anderson, *The Fourth Gospel and the Quest for Jesus: Modern Foundations Reconsidered* (London: T&T Clark, 2006).

83. See Stanley E. Porter, *The Criteria for Authenticity in Historical-Jesus Research: Previous Discussion and New Proposals*, JSNTSup 191 (Sheffield: Sheffield Academic, 2000), 28–62.

84. Paul N. Anderson, Felix Just, and Tom Thatcher, eds., *John, Jesus, and History, Volume 1: Critical Appraisals of Critical Views* (Atlanta: SBL Press, 2007).

history, especially regarding Jesus. Even though these remain major questions within current Johannine scholarship, as we have seen in this survey of Johannine studies, these questions go back much earlier, at least to Strauss and Baur and even before them to questions of the early church regarding John's Gospel. With the earlier ground appropriately cleared for new proposals, volume two addresses in more detail the question of historicity.[85] The volume is divided into three parts, each of which focuses upon a section of John's Gospel (chs. 1–4, 5–12, and 13–21), with each part treating what is characterized as "aspects of historicity" in those groups of chapters. The third volume offers what are called "glimpses" of the Johannine Jesus in the passion, works, and teachings of Jesus in comparison with the Synoptic Gospels, with an emphasis on finding historical material within the Johannine account, even if it differs from the Synoptics.[86] The fourth volume, the largest to date, focuses upon memory of Jesus in the Johannine contexts. These contexts, labeled as "situations," include early, middle, and late periods and extend into the development of pluriform early Christianity.[87] The three remaining volumes in this series promise to bring further insights into this approach and the relationship of John's Gospel to the Synoptic Gospels.

CONCLUSION

The final chapter regarding the history of Johannine scholarship is far from being written. In this chapter, I have concentrated on John's Gospel, recognizing that I have had to forgo comments about the Epistles and Revelation at many turns. Nevertheless, John's Gospel provides more than sufficient material to examine the contours of its scholarship. On the one hand, we see that the major issues regarding John's Gospel were broached by the early church and certainly made clear in the emergence of post-Enlightenment scholarship as historical criticism gained a foothold in biblical interpretation and then became the platform for much subsequent scholarship. Although there have always been dissenting voices that have argued for more traditional conclusions, the Enlightenment agenda has in many ways continued to drive the interests of contemporary scholarship. On the other hand, we

---

85. Paul N. Anderson, Felix Just, and Tom Thatcher, eds., *John, Jesus, and History, Volume 2: Aspects of Historicity in the Fourth Gospel* (Atlanta: SBL Press, 2009).

86. Paul N. Anderson, Felix Just, and Tom Thatcher, eds., *John, Jesus, and History, Volume 3: Glimpses of Jesus through the Johannine Lens* (Atlanta: SBL Press, 2016).

87. Paul N. Anderson, Felix Just, and Tom Thatcher, eds., *John, Jesus, and History, Volume 4: Jesus Remembered in the Johannine Situation* (Atlanta: SBL Press, 2024)

see that Johannine scholarship, especially as it focuses on John's Gospel, has proven to be a fecund area of intellectual exploration. At virtually every stage of Johannine studies new theories and ideas have been developed that address the traditional questions regarding John's Gospel, often by suggesting new and challenging ways of addressing such questions. This has led to a variety of responses and continuing debate over these topics. If the past is any indication of what we might expect in the future, we may look forward to much more challenging and interesting Johannine scholarship.

CHAPTER 10

JOHN IN THEOLOGIES OF THE NEW TESTAMENT SINCE GABLER: CRITICAL AND CANONICAL

ROBERT W. YARBROUGH

One factor contributing to the value of Andreas J. Köstenberger's body of scholarship on matters Johannine has been his grasp of the history of interpretation. Another has been his willingness to lean against certain historical trends that have resulted in negative verdicts on Johannine authorship of the writings historically attributed to him in the canon, to say nothing of the rejection of the veracity of the claims John makes regarding Jesus's divinity (along with his humanity—in other words, what theologians call the hypostatic union), the new birth, Jesus's atoning death, the miracles John reports including Jesus's resurrection from the dead, and other central features or claims of the Fourth Gospel.

The conflict of visions between two views of John—which we will here call the *critical* and the *canonical*—is a tacit theme informing all of Andreas J. Köstenberger's Johannine study. In this essay I wish to illustrate the conflict over recent centuries by looking at three pairs of New Testament theologies. While "New Testament theology" has various definitions, here we refer to a well-known genre of study like Rudolf Bultmann's or I. Howard Marshall's,[1] the broad aim of which is to present the totality of the New Testament contents (however conceived) in some organized and synthetic form.

---

1. See Rudolf Bultmann, *Theology of the New Testament*, trans. Kendrick Grobel, 2 vols. (New York: Scribner, 1951–55); I. Howard Marshall, *New Testament Theology: Many Witnesses, One Gospel* (Downers Grove, IL: InterVarsity Press, 2004).

New Testament theology as an academic discipline, or "biblical theology"[2] of the New Testament if one prefers, is traditionally traced back to J. P. Gabler (1753–1826) and a lecture he gave in 1787.[3] It has resulted in a steady stream of studies, often taking on markedly different forms, since that time. We will restrict ourselves primarily to a pair of such studies in each of the three centuries since Gabler: the nineteenth, the twentieth, and the twenty-first. We will see that the Johannine legacy, however it be assessed, is a central component in the long-standing contrast between the critical and the canonical readings, respectively. While the critical approach pronounced canonical outlooks as exemplified below untenable centuries ago, the resilience of New Testament theologies reflecting canonical assessments of John bears notice, not least in recognition of Andreas Köstenberger's important contribution to this minority-status outlook.

1. JOHN IN 19TH-CENTURY NT THEOLOGIES: F. C. BAUR AND J. J. VAN OOSTERZEE

The critical-canonical divide is clearly illustrated in the respective New Testament theologies of the German F. C. Baur (1792–1860) and the Dutch J. J. Van Oosterzee (1817–1882).

1.1 *Baur's* Lectures on New Testament Theology

Baur is a familiar name in New Testament scholarship in connection with the Protestant Tübingen school. The rise and contribution of this movement have been recounted elsewhere.[4] What concerns us here is his lectures on New Testament theology, *Vorlesungen über neutestamentliche Theologie* (1864), edited and published posthumously by his son. A

---

2. For Köstenberger's most comprehensive contribution to the genre, see the New Testament portion of Andreas J. Köstenberger and Gregory Goswell, *Biblical Theology: A Canonical, Thematic, and Ethical Approach* (Wheaton, IL: Crossway, 2023). For a recent New Testament theology with "biblical theology" in the title, see Peter Stuhlmacher, *Biblical Theology of the New Testament*, trans. Daniel P. Bailey (Grand Rapids: Eerdmans, 2018).

3. John Sandys-Wunsch and Laurence Eldredge, "J. P. Gabler and the Distinction between Biblical and Dogmatic Theology: Translation, Commentary, and Discussion of His Originality," *SJT* 33 (1980):133–58.

4. See Horton Harris, *The Tübingen School* (Grand Rapids: Baker, 1990); Martin Bauspiess, Christof Landmesser, and David Lincicum, eds., *Ferdinand Christian Baur und die Geschichte des frühen Christentums*, WUNT 333 (Tübingen: Mohr Siebeck, 2014).

measure of the respect still accorded Baur is the translation and commendation of this work in 2016.[5]

Baur held John's Gospel to be "not a historical gospel like the others," meaning the Synoptic Gospels. It is rather a spiritualization of ideas. So it is understandable that in Baur's New Testament theology, John's Gospel plays no role in Part One, which covers Jesus's teaching as Baur derives it from the Synoptics (94–148). A Johannine hand first comes into view in Part Two, "The Teaching of the Apostles," which covers Paul based solely on the four epistles Baur regards as genuine (Romans, 1–2 Corinthians, Galatians; 153–215) and then more briefly the Book of Revelation (215–33). Baur thinks Revelation was written prior to AD 70, since the fall of Jerusalem is not mentioned, and that it could have been written by the apostle John.

Crucial to grasping Baur's account of Paul, Revelation, and subsequent New Testament documents is his view of Jesus's resurrection (152–53; quotes in this paragraph are found on these two pages). According to Baur, there was no "actual, physical miracle." Resurrection reports in the New Testament all flow from a "spiritual process that ensued in the minds of the disciples after Jesus's death." They believed in Jesus so deeply and absolutely that despite his death and demise, they were able to use fragmentary recollections and Old Testament passages to construct a plausible framework for presenting him as yet alive. Due to "a very ecstatic kind of consciousness" that prevailed in "that original period of Christianity," ideas established themselves "in the disciples' minds in such a vital way" that they took "the shape of visions counting for them as appearances of the resurrected one." He did not rise bodily but merely psychologically and "spiritually in the faith of the disciples."

In the Book of Revelation John presents a kingdom concept that is antithetical to that found in Jesus's teachings. There is "no consummation in heaven" (218). All that Revelation envisions "can only take place on the material soil of the finite, albeit transfigured, earth" (218). Unlike Paul who has a universal conception of Jesus's reign, John "never distinguishes himself from his Old Testament particularism" (218). Revelation is confusing because it narrates "the absoluteness of the idea" that grips John "disintegrating into inadequate and self-contradictory representations" (218).

---

5.   Ferdinand Christian Baur, *Lectures on New Testament Theology*, ed. Peter C. Hodgson, trans. Robert F. Brown (Oxford: Oxford University Press, 2016). Parenthetical page numbers in this section will refer to this English translation.

Much in Revelation contradicts historic Christian teaching. Paul was not an apostle (221). The Messiah in Revelation is not a divine figure (223). The Word of God in Revelation 19 is not the λόγος of John 1 (223); he is actually a created being (224). Relationship with God in Revelation is depicted as solely about fear and works (228–29). "Faith" in Revelation is one of many works required; "one must struggle and conquer as Christ did" (229). "The inner aspect of the Christian life on the whole very much takes a back seat to the outer aspect" (230). Quite bluntly, Revelation reflects "a worldview analogous to Manichaean dualism," and its symbolic character of the whole book "often makes it impossible to derive a more specific dogmatic conception from the way it represents things" (233).

John's letters play no role in Baur's New Testament theology.[6] John's Gospel, however, dominates the final division, entitled "Third Period: The Theological Frameworks of the Pastoral Epistles and the Johannine Writings." Baur states that "New Testament theology attains its highest level and its most complete form in the Johannine theological framework" found in John's Gospel (331). This is not because it is a reliable historical source for recovering the teaching or history of Jesus—it is not. It is rather because John presents an "idealism in which, in the self-certainty of its own inner intuition or point of view, even the historical reality is ultimately just an external form that mediates for consciousness what is true for itself" (376). Those words conclude Baur's *Vorlesungen über neutestamentliche Theologie*.

What does this mean? It means that John's Gospel, far from being the witness to discourses and events it reports, is "obviously the product of a very rich theological imagination, which clothes itself in the form of a gospel, a story about Jesus, but which ultimately puts historical mediation aside" (59). The "eternal life" for which John's Gospel is renowned is likewise not about the concrete temporal future; "eternal life is now indeed the immanent content of Christian consciousness" (373). Salvation itself is about alteration of human consciousness, "letting the full impression of [Jesus's] personhood operate on ourselves," "by surrendering to it and

---

6.   See Robert F. Brown's editorial observation in *Lectures on New Testament Theology*, 331n11: Baur makes no mention of John's letters "presumably because they contain nothing noteworthy for theology as distinct from other religious concerns."

letting it determine us in practice," so that "we take part in the salvation in which humanity has come to share because of Jesus" (371).

There is scarcely a vestige, in Baur's theological construal, of the preexistent Son of God whom John's Gospel arguably presents, who took on flesh, lived a sinless life, died as a propitiation for sin, bodily rose and ascended to the Father, and calls for a new birth in every human soul so that "whoever believes in him should not perish but have eternal life" (John 3:16 ESV).

1.2 Van Oosterzee's The Theology of the New Testament

Unlike Baur, Jan Jacob (or Johannes Jacobus) van Oosterzee (1817–1882) is not well known among New Testament scholars. Admittedly, Otto Merk lists him among over a dozen New Testament theologians (all German or Swiss except for Oosterzee) who viewed their work in line with Gabler's program[7] and contributed to that vision in significant ways: E. Reuss, B. Weiss, W. Beyschlag, A. Immer, H. Holtzmann, and others.[8] But Merk favors Baur's "historical-critical" hermeneutic and dismisses Oosterzee in a one-sentence paragraph for having the same conservative tendencies as his contemporary B. Weiss. The miscue Merk singles out is that Oosterzee finds "a higher unity" in the contrasting voices of the Synoptics and the Fourth Gospel; to find such unity is, in Merk's view, to give up "historical" interpretation as he (here following F. C. Baur's lead) conceives it.[9]

Oosterzee's university studies were at the University of Utrecht (1835–1839). He pastored churches in Holland from 1841 to 1862, most of that time in his native Rotterdam. In 1863 he was appointed to a professorate at his alma mater in Utrecht. For the rest of his life he was active lecturing and publishing both popular and scholarly works, many of them translated into English, including commentaries on Mark, John, Paul's Pastoral Letters and Philemon, and James. He also wrote a Christian dogmatics and a practical theology. But it is with his New Testament theology that we will concern ourselves now.[10]

---

7. For Gabler's program see note 3 above. For Oosterzee's acknowledgment of it see Otto Merk, *Biblische Theologie des Neuen Testaments in ihrer Anfangszeit*, MThSt 9 (Marburg: N. G. Elwert, 1972), 1n2.

8. Merk, *Biblische Theologie des Neuen Testaments*, 236–52.

9. Merk, *Biblische Theologie des Neuen Testaments*, 240.

10. J. J. van Oosterzee, *The Theology of the New Testament: A Handbook for Students*, trans. Maurice J. Evans (New York: Dodd, Mead & Company, 1871). Parenthetical page numbers in this section refer to this volume.

Oosterzee locates his New Testament theology carefully with reference to the history of biblical (or New Testament) theology preceding him. After discussing its definition (1–8), he treats its history, finding precursors in the patristic period (10) but the first true flowering of biblical theological impulses in Reformation and post-Reformation times (11–12). Gabler affirms from "the rationalistic side" that "the Biblical theology of the New Testament must be treated as an independent part of historic science" (12). This impulse develops not only in "the wholly or half rationalistic school of theology" (Oosterzee surveys works by G. L. Bauer, C. F. Ammon, G. P. C. Kayser, W. M. L. de Wette, and others) but also "on the supernaturalistic side" where Oosterzee places himself (12). He mentions Old Testament scholars including Gustav Oehler (14–15) and New Testament scholars like August Neander, C. F. Schmid, and others (15–16).

Oosterzee recognizes, then, the "critical" and "canonical" divide explored in this essay, just under different labels (rationalistic, supernaturalistic). In the latter vein he notes the influence of D. F. Strauss (F. C. Baur's student) and the Tübingen school that Baur is credited with founding (16). Noting how philosophy can influence the putatively "historical" work of biblical theology, Oosterzee traces the influence of "Hegelian philosophy" in the biblical-theological work of J. K. Vatke, Bruno Bauer, E. Reuss, and finally F. C. Baur himself with "the well-known bright and dark sides" of his so-called school (16–17). Noting how Baur isolates the New Testament's Johannine material as "by far the latest in the whole canon," Oosterzee summarizes Baur's approach as follows: "Thus the whole conception and method rests upon a system of isagogics[11] and criticism, to which no one will give the name of impartial" (18).

All of this is to say that Oosterzee is not ignorant or simply dismissive of Baur's critical hypotheses and results; he is simply unconvinced by Baur's synthesis and believes that his canonical account is more plausible hermeneutically and historically. He is aware that with the rise of "critical" investigation of Scripture, "never was the genuineness and credibility of this Gospel [i.e., John] so bitterly assailed as now" (130). But while acknowledging at length the contrasts between John and the Synoptics (129–34), he

---

11. This is an older term for what today is called "introduction" or in German *Einleitung*. See works like D. A. Carson and Douglas Moo, *An Introduction to the New Testament*, or Udo Schnelle, *Einleitung in das Neue Testament*.

regards it as "entirely inconceivable" that the author of the Fourth Gospel (who, in contrast to Baur, he believes is John the son of Zebedee) placed words on Jesus's lips that he never spoke (132). The Johannine-Synoptic contrast is accounted for, among other factors, by the fact that the Synoptics focus on "what the Lord proclaims concerning His kingdom in general, concerning the Father, or mankind," while John's Gospel highlights "what He teaches concerning Himself, in relation to all these" (134).

Consequently, unlike Baur, Oosterzee treats John's Gospel as a credible witness to "The Theology of Jesus Christ" (61–189) parallel to, though separate from, the Synoptic Gospels. The chapter titles in the respective divisions are:

Table 10.1 Chapter Titles in the Respective Divisions	
Synoptics (68–128)	**Gospel of John (129–74)**
The Kingdom of God	The Son of God in the Flesh
The Founder	The Son of God in His Relation to the Father
The King of Kings	The Son of God in His Relation to the World
The Subjects	The Son of God in Relation to His Disciples
Salvation	The Son of God in Relation to His Future
The Way of Salvation	
The Completion	

Oosterzee caps his treatment of Jesus Christ's theology as presented in the four Gospels with two chapters under the heading "Higher Unity." In the first chapter ("Diversity and Unity"), he quotes his contemporary French colleague, F. Godet: "As far as the religious side of the contrast [between the Synoptics and John] is concerned, it is remarkable that the conscience of the Church has never been perplexed by it, and that it is exclusively the learned who pronounce it insoluble" (176). In the second ("Result") he prepares to move from Christ's person and theology as a fulfillment of Old Testament promises (186–87; cf. "Old Testament Basis," 28–60) to "The Theology of the Apostles" found subsequent to the Gospels in the New Testament canon (190–415).

In this longest of the four divisions of his New Testament theology, Oosterzee's contrast to his near contemporary Baur continues to be striking. In "The Johannine Theology" (372–405), he integrates (principally as to their shared Christology) John's Gospel, three epistles, and Revelation (agreeing with Baur on the primitive nature of the Apocalypse, 374). In response to a "critical" reader like Baur, Oosterzee articulates a canonical verdict:

> He who regards it as absolutely impossible that one and the same John should have written the Gospel and the Apocalypse, has not duly considered either the wealth of the individuality, or the considerable period of time which had elapsed between the composition of the one writing and that of the other, or the great difference of their contents, aim, and character. (378)

Oosterzee concludes: "Only an Evangelist like this could have written the Apocalypse, and only an Apocalyptist like this could have written the Gospel" (378). In a concluding major section on the "Higher Unity" of the New Testament writings and the theology they contain in fulfillment of Old Testament writings and history, and in adumbration of things to come as affirmed on Johannine eschatology, Oosterzee delivers a subtle but telling verdict on the "critical" historiography of Baur and the Tübingen school: "The whole conception of the Apostolic Epistles, as written for a certain bias (*Tendenzschriften*)—for the combating or reconciliation of adverse schools—belongs not to the domain of history, but of romance" (426).

2. JOHN IN TWENTIETH-CENTURY NEW TESTAMENT THEOLOGIES: RUDOLF BULTMANN (1884–1976) AND ADOLF SCHLATTER (1852–1938)

In hindsight, the "critical" trajectory in New Testament theology in the nineteenth century peaked not in F. C. Baur's in many ways pioneering effort but in the New Testament theology of H. J. Holtzmann (1832–1910). Holtzmann's two-volume *Lehrbuch der neutestamentlichen Theology* (1897) reflected the methods and findings nurtured by the arc of liberal theology stretching from F. D. E. Schleiermacher (1768–1834) to Albrecht Ritschl (1822–1889) and finally in classic form in Adolf von Harnack (1851–1930).

Liberal theology of this era fell from favor in German theology, the source of most New Testament theologies at that time, due in part to its association with support for the German ruling establishment, which plunged Europe into the cataclysmic Great War (later called World War

I). In its wake arose what was called "crisis" or "neo-orthodox" theology. The New Testament theology that emerged from the neo-orthodox decades (1920s–ca. 1950s) associated most of all with Karl Barth was written by New Testament scholar Rudolf Bultmann. In international academia it is regarded as the most influential New Testament theology of the twentieth century, as Bultmann is commonly viewed as that century's most significant New Testament scholar.

2.1 *Bultmann's* Theology of the New Testament

How does John (whether his Gospel, epistles, or Revelation) fare in Bultmann's famous *Theology of the New Testament*?[12] Bultmann covers John and John's letters in about ninety pages (2:3–92) out of the six hundred that he devotes to the New Testament overall. Michael Waldstein has investigated Bultmann's interpretation of John as a whole, as well as a wide swath of scholarship analyzing how Bultmann understood the Johannine corpus. Waldstein makes the important point that Bultmann's reading of John reflected "the concerns of late Nineteenth and early Twentieth century German culture rather than those of the Gospel of John."[13] Specifically, Waldstein shows that Bultmann's "ontology is closer to Gnosticism than it is to the biblical tradition."[14] He also "does not sufficiently respect the historical meaning of the biblical texts as normative" for the theological synthesis he derives from them.[15] Waldstein plausibly argues that Bultmann does not practice critical exegesis; rather, his program of "demythologizing is not a hermeneutical procedure, but the expression of a disagreement with the text. In its de-objectifying aspect, it replaces the text's theology with an opposed theology."[16] Another way of putting this is that in Bultmann Johannine interpretation (and this would extend to his handling of Paul too), Bultmann's "dialectic doctrine of knowledge determines what can, and what cannot, be Word of God. [T]his determination gives too normative a role to philosophy; it separates the Word of God too much from the historically concrete meaning of Scripture."[17]

---

12. Rudolf Bultmann, *Theology of the New Testament* (see note 1 above). Parenthetical page numbers refer to the respective two volumes of this English translation.
13. Michael Waldstein, "The Evolution of Bultmann's Interpretation of John and Gnosticism," *Lateranum* 70 (2004): 313–52 (here 313).
14. Waldstein, "The Evolution of Bultmann's Interpretation," 350.
15. Waldstein, "The Evolution of Bultmann's Interpretation," 350.
16. Waldstein, "The Evolution of Bultmann's Interpretation," 351.
17. Waldstein, "The Evolution of Bultmann's Interpretation," 351.

I have arrived at similar findings in a thorough analysis of Bultmann's *Theology of the New Testament* and related writings.[18] A wide range of scholars and scholarship concurs that despite his creativity and influence, Bultmann does not really interpret the historical documents of the New Testament era in their chronological setting, John's writings among them, but rather strains them through a grid of existentialist understanding. As Andreas Köstenberger notes, Bultmann viewed the Fourth Gospel as myth.[19] He did not think that either John or the other Gospels reported things that happened in history; they were rather composed of cult legends.[20] Bultmann wrongly argued that John's Jesus reveals nothing but the Revealer and collapses theology into Christology.[21] He was mistaken in arguing that the Beloved Disciple was not a disciple of Jesus or an actual person at all but an ideal figure.[22] Like many critics, Köstenberger faults Bultmann for arguing that Gnosticism is the source of much of the language and thought of the New Testament writers.[23] Nor is Bultmann correct to argue that John denies that Jesus's death was an atonement for sin;[24] quite the opposite is true.

These deficiencies did not lead Köstenberger to ignore Bultmann's interpretation of John, either in Bultmann's commentary on John's Gospel (1941) or in his *Theology of the New Testament*. In fact, Köstenberger cites him as "an inspiration" in discerning John's theological themes.[25] Bultmann was right to insist that John's narrative summons the reader to a decision.[26] He was correct about the importance of judgment as a Johannine theme.[27]

Nevertheless, the shortcomings of Bultmann's "critical" handling of John are part of the reason why his *Theology of the New Testament*, for all the acclaim it received in its day, served for many to demonstrate its dubious value as a historically plausible reconstruction of apostolic and subapostolic testimony and thought. John Ashton, while giving Bultmann credit

---

18. Robert W. Yarbrough, *The Salvation Historical Fallacy? Reassessing the History of New Testament Theology* (Leiden: Deo, 2004), especially chapter 6.
19. Andreas J. Köstenberger, *A Theology of John's Gospel and Letters*, BTNT (Grand Rapids: Zondervan, 2009), 54.
20. Köstenberger, *A Theology of John's Gospel and Letters*, 40 n9.
21. Köstenberger, *A Theology of John's Gospel and Letters*, 361.
22. Köstenberger, *A Theology of John's Gospel and Letters*, 493.
23. Köstenberger, *A Theology of John's Gospel and Letters*, 529.
24. Köstenberger, *A Theology of John's Gospel and Letters*, 534; see also 177 with n7.
25. Köstenberger, *A Theology of John's Gospel and Letters*, 47 n35.
26. Köstenberger, *A Theology of John's Gospel and Letters*, 183.
27. Köstenberger, *A Theology of John's Gospel and Letters*, 486.

for greatness in Johannine interpretation, asserts that "in spite of his preeminence, every answer Bultmann gives to the really important questions he raises—is wrong."[28] This limitation justifies a look at the two-volume "canonical" New Testament theology that Bultmann critiqued and that he regarded his *Theology of the New Testament* as superseding.

2.2 Adolf Schlatter's The History of the Christ[29] and The Theology of the Apostles[30]

Schlatter was born a generation before Bultmann, but his major publications appeared during the first third of the twentieth century, overlapping Bultmann's publishing years over some three decades. The contemporaneity of these two doyens is reflected in the fact that when Bultmann summarizes the history of New Testament theology, while he touches on Gabler, F. C. Baur, and H. J. Holtzmann,[31] he interacts most directly with Schlatter's two-volume work.[32] The contrast between each scholar's regard for John in their respective New Testament theologies is seen first in how they handle the history of Jesus's life. For Bultmann, Jesus's earthly history and message are "a presupposition for the theology of the New Testament" to which he devotes less than thirty pages.[33] Nowhere in those pages does Bultmann cite John's Gospel as a source of information.

For Schlatter, the Gospels, including John, are true-to-fact narratives of Jesus's life and teachings (which he viewed as an inseparable unity, in contrast to Bultmann's highlighting of selected Jesus sayings and exclusion, for example, of his miracles as real events). He warns against limiting reconstruction of Jesus's message "solely to the Synoptics."[34] He also calls opting for Marcan priority "seriously ill-advised" if it crowds out the full input of the other Gospels.[35] This proved to be prophetic, in that Bultmann affirmed the priority of an earlier version of Mark than we now possess and valued Matthew and Luke primarily as repositories of Q, which

---

28. John Ashton, *Understanding the Fourth Gospel* (Oxford: Clarendon, 1993), 45.
29. Adolf Schlatter, *The History of the Christ*, trans. Andreas J. Köstenberger (Grand Rapids: Baker, 1997). The first edition of this work appeared in 1909 and a second in 1923.
30. Adolf Schlatter, *The Theology of the Apostles*, trans. Andreas J. Köstenberger (Grand Rapids: Baker, 1999). The first edition of this work appeared in 1910 and a second in 1922.
31. Bultmann, *Theology of the New Testament*, 2:242, 244–45.
32. Bultmann, *Theology of the New Testament*, 2:246, 248–50.
33. Bultmann, *Theology of the New Testament*, 1:3–32.
34. Schlatter, *The History of the Christ*, 20.
35. Schlatter, *The History of the Christ*, 20.

he placed parallel to a now-lost proto-Mark.[36] In Bultmann, Schlatter's projection came to pass: "The fewer the statements that are acknowledged by the witnesses are admitted, the more wide-ranging and daring will be the conjectures, and the imagination of historians will supplement the silence of witnesses."[37] Schlatter regarded the Gospels, including John, as containing eyewitness reminiscence of the teachings and actions of Jesus that they reported. This helps explain the vast difference between Bultmann's sparse "critical" reconstruction of Jesus and Schlatter's full canonically derived account running to nearly four hundred pages in translation. As Schlatter puts it, "In the evaluation of the sources I agree with the judgment of those who produced the canon of the four Gospels at the transition from the first to the second century."[38] In the same passage he justifies his approach over approaches like Bultmann's.

Because of Schlatter's regard for the Gospels as historical sources, Bultmann criticized Schlatter for his emphasis on the Old Testament and Jewish background (an indisputable feature of the Gospels) for his interpretation of Jesus.[39] Schlatter failed "to recognize the importance of Hellenistic syncretism."[40] But for Schlatter, the Gospels represent Jesus as the fulfillment of Old Testament prophecies and God's saving purposes in the world because he *was* that fulfillment, the awaited messianic king, not because of Hellenistic (or Gnostic[41]) myths projected back onto legendary accounts. Accordingly, Schlatter begins his New Testament theology with "The Expectation of the Anointed One."[42] He finds it significant that "the Christ's office is . . . described by the angel entirely from the standpoint of

---

36. Bultmann, *Theology of the New Testament*, 1:3.

37. Schlatter, *The History of the Christ*, 20.

38. Schlatter, *The History of the Christ*, 24.

39. Another Johannine titan, C. H. Dodd, also emphasized the Old Testament and Jewish background for understanding John's Gospel. Schlatter likely had an indirect influence on Dodd, as he influenced scholars like C. F. Burney, Edwyn Hoskyns, and Francis Noel Davey, who helped steer English New Testament scholarship in Dodd's era to reaffirming the importance of the Old Testament and Jewish backgrounds for understanding the Gospels. See Stephen Neill and Tom Wright, *The Interpretation of the New Testament 1861–1986*, 2nd ed. (Oxford: Oxford University Press, 1988), 339–40 (Burney and Schlatter), 345 (Hoskyns), 228–37 (Hoskyns and Davey), 346–47 (Dodd).

40. Bultmann, *Theology of the New Testament*, 2:250.

41. For an example of Schlatter's refutation of "gnostic speculation" as the source of New Testament accounts of Jesus, see Schlatter, *The History of the Christ*, 136 n. 18. See also 384 n. 5. Pushback against Gnosticism as a source of New Testament belief (as in Bultmann) is frequent in his New Testament theology. On the other hand, Schlatter's chapter on Jude in *The Theology of the Apostles* (103–8) is entitled "The Refutation of Gnosticism by Jude."

42. Schlatter, *The History of the Christ*, chapter 1.

Old Testament expectation," referring to Luke's account of Jesus's birth.[43] For Bultmann, angels are mythology, not possible historical actors. Schlatter connects Psalm 2 to John 1:49 as evidence for the correlation between God's anointed one and his kingship: "Nathanael answered him, 'Rabbi, you are the Son of God! You are the King of Israel!'"[44] Bultmann denied the phenomenon of fulfilled biblical prophecy.

Bultmann denied Jesus's bodily resurrection from the dead; for Schlatter the resurrection did happen, and he devotes a meaty and profound section to showing its historical plausibility in the face of all theories like Bultmann's "using the concept of vision or illusion to interpret the Easter story."[45] Not only does Schlatter treat the event; he ponders its details and implications in "The Content of the Easter Report,"[46] in which among much else Schlatter connects Jesus's resurrection with his creation of "the Trinitarian concept of God":

> How profoundly the events of Easter touched the disciples' entire relationship with God and renewed their concept of God is evident in the fact that the Trinitarian name of God is tied to the events of Easter. John provides a parallel to the baptism in the name of the Father and of the Son and of the Holy Spirit by noting that the disciples' faith in the presence of the Risen One is completed by the adoration of him as their Lord and God (Matt. 28:19; John 20:28). Jesus became the creator of the Trinitarian concept of God placing his office into the eternal and complete revelation of divine grace, setting the sending of the Spirit beside himself as a second testimony to God. Thereby it became the religion of the community that it possessed its communion with God in fellowship with the Christ and with the Spirit.[47]

A "critical" account like Bultmann's regards the Easter event and the Trinity in a quite different light. For Bultmann, Jesus's "*resurrection* cannot be an event of special significance"; like other "'facts of salvation' in the traditional sense," the resurrection (which Bultmann denies actually occurred)

---

43. Schlatter, *The History of the Christ*, 29.
44. Schlatter, *The History of the Christ*, 26 with n4.
45. Schlatter, *The History of the Christ*, 382; for the whole discussion see 375–83.
46. Schlatter, *The History of the Christ*, 383–89.
47. Schlatter, *The History of the Christ*, 388.

plays "no important role in John."[48] Jesus's exchange with Thomas (John 20:29) is for Bultmann "a warning against taking the Easter-stories for more than they are able to be."[49]

In volume two of Schlatter's New Testament theology, John figures substantially into the opening synthesis: "The Disciples' Vantage Point at the Beginning of Their Work."[50] John's distinctive contribution is noted in a lengthy section entitled "John's Message to the Greeks According to John."[51] This includes a section on Revelation (written by John, in Schlatter's view) entitled "The Prophet and the Evangelist."[52] Schlatter also offers chapters on "John and Matthew," "John and Paul," and "John and Jesus."[53] John's contribution to a theology of the New Testament can also be profitably explored in a book, called "a New Testament theology *in nuce*" by Bultmann,[54] that was recently translated into English.[55] Sections on John's view of faith (and related matters) are found in chapters five, six, and elsewhere. "The nerve of faith" lies in Jesus's claim that it is God who sent him, and saving reception of that claim is "a miracle of knowledge" worked by God.[56] These are canonical not critical depictions of New Testament theology. "John," his message, and the person and work of Christ are quite different entities in the two academic trajectories.

3. JOHN IN TWENTY-FIRST-CENTURY NEW TESTAMENT THEOLOGIES: UDO SCHNELLE AND ECKHARD SCHNABEL

In the generations since Bultmann's heyday, both critical and canonical New Testament theologies have appeared. No single towering figure like Bultmann has dominated New Testament studies like he once did, and New Testament theology as a discipline has taken a back seat in many circles to, for example, Life of Jesus studies in connection with the Third Quest and the Jesus Seminar, and Pauline studies due to the vitality and controversy surrounding the New Perspective on Paul. Moreover, much

---

48. Bultmann, *Theology of the New Testament*, 2:56, 58.
49. Bultmann, *Theology of the New Testament*, 2:57.
50. Schlatter, *The Theology of the Apostles*, 27–50.
51. Schlatter, *The Theology of the Apostles*, 108–85.
52. Schlatter, *The Theology of the Apostles*, 150–66.
53. Schlatter, *The Theology of the Apostles*, 175–85.
54. Bultmann, *Theology of the New Testament*, 2:248.
55. Adolf Schlatter, *Faith in the New Testament*, trans. Joseph Longarino (Bellingham, WA: Lexham, 2022).
56. Schlatter, *Faith in the New Testament*, 136–37.

current scholarly interaction with the New Testament is a-theological in orientation, focusing rather on cultural, anthropological, social-scientific, hermeneutical, linguistic, political, gender, racial, and other issues. Yet, a steady succession of New Testament theologies attests to the continuing importance of the enterprise. As has been the case for two centuries, some are critical and some canonical.

3.1 *Udo Schnelle's* Theology of the New Testament[57]

Udo Schnelle frequently takes issue with Bultmann's views, including those expressed in his *Theology of the New Testament* (discussed above). He disagrees with "the real foundation of Bultmann's theses": "A deep historical and theological chasm between a purportedly unmessianic self-understanding of Jesus and the christologically packed kerygma never existed" (44 with note 8). This is in direct contradiction to Bultmann. He rejects Bultmann's contention that there is no real unity to be found in the New Testament documents in the sense of a unity that transcends the diversity of the various writings (49), pointing out that Bultmann actually smuggles a unity back in "by the dominant place he gives Paul and John as the center of his *Theology*" (50 n. 23). He disagrees with Bultmann's devaluing of the cross as having "no preeminent importance for salvation" (695 with note 101). He differs from Bultmann on the identity of the Paraclete (707 with note 135). He rejects Bultmann's view that faith produced John's miracles claims: "For the evangelist John the miracle effects faith" (718). "It is thus not the case that faith has only the 'that' of the revelatory event as its content" (718 with note 160). Schnelle contradicts Bultmann's view that "sin" in John's view should be seen as "localized historically and applied only to the Ἰουδαῖοι" (725 with note 174). He rejects Bultmann's conclusion that John's Gospel is bereft of ecclesiology or even ecclesiological interest, commenting sagely: "The lack of the word ἐκκλησία ('church') in the Gospel of John says nothing at all about the subject matter itself, for this word is also missing in Mark, but no one can deny a concept of the church to him!" (734 n. 194).

If Schnelle is accurate in these (and other) corrections of Bultmann, it points to a hazard in the "critical" outlook: its instability and volatility. Its verdict on the meaning of the *word of God* (if that term be admitted in

---

57. Udo Schnelle, *Theology of the New Testament*, trans. M. Eugene Boring (Grand Rapids: Baker Academic, 2009). Parenthetical page numbers in this section refer to this work unless otherwise noted.

connection with the Bible and its message) is as permanent as the current academic hegemony. The word of God in the next generation may have the opposite meaning even on as fundamental a question as whether, for example, the cross, or faith in Jesus including the miracles he performed, are central features of John's view of salvation. For the many who did (and still do) follow Bultmann's guidance, they are not. Which gospel message should pastors and churches affirm, as these are mutually exclusive understandings?

That aside, Schnelle commendably makes numerous corrections to former errors (he argues) of guild exegesis and interpretation. But at two major points there is no break with the critical trajectory.

First, with respect to introductory issues involving the Johannine writings, Schnelle refers the reader to his *The History and Theology of the New Testament Writings*.[58] There we learn that John's writings come not from anyone who heard or did what Jesus said or did but from "the Johannine school."[59] In the case of John's Gospel, on the basis of how Schnelle reads it, "John was *a theologian of the later period* who, on the basis of comprehensive traditions, rethought the meaning of Jesus's life, and interpreted and presented it in his own way" (474, Schnelle's italics). Among other reasons given is "the thought world explicitly oriented to the post-Easter perspective," showing that "the Fourth Gospel was not composed by an eyewitness of the life of Jesus" (474). This is no different from Bultmann's view, and like Bultmann depends on the method of *Sachkritik* (eliminating what the Gospel says about its eyewitness grounding [see, e.g., John 19:35; 21:34] based on what the interpreter thinks the writer actually meant). The author of 2 John is an elder in the Johannine school, not John the son of Zebedee (440–42). Schnelle does not account for Peter calling himself a "fellow elder" (συμπρεσβύτερος, 1 Peter 5:1), an indicator that an apostle known also as an "elder" was not unknown in the apostolic era.[60]

Third John also comes from this Johannine school elder (447). First John, however, was from a different author (455). Likewise, "the world of theological concepts presupposed, and the different situation point to

---

58. Trans. M. Eugene Boring (Minneapolis: Fortress, 1998). Parenthetical page numbers in this and the following paragraph refer to this work.

59. Schnelle's entire handling of John's works. Udo Schnelle, *The History and Theology of the New Testament Writings*. "The Writings of the Johannine School" (434–538).

60. This is on the assumption that Peter authored 1 Peter. Schnelle holds, however, that it is "a pseudepigraphical writing, permeated and shaped by early Christian traditions that were attributed to Peter and Silvanus by the circle of early Christian tradents in which they were handed on" (401).

the conclusion that 1 John and the Gospel are *by different authors*" (456, Schnelle's italics). When it comes to Revelation, while the early church affirmed its authorship by Jesus's disciple John, Schnelle thinks that "the testimony of the book itself does not support the dominant tradition of the ancient church" (520). He holds that "the author of Revelation is a Jewish-Christian *wandering prophet* who has worked for a long time in the area of Paul's previous mission in Asia Minor, who now attempts to give them a new orientation in view of the mass or troubles he sees approaching" (523, Schnelle's italics). In a word, in Schnelle's assessment of the origin of the documents, he differs little from Baur and Bultmann in denying the general consensus of Christians prior to the Enlightenment that the apostle John is the author of the canonical documents associated with his name.

A second and fundamental indicator of Schnelle's location as a "critical" interpreter is the firewall he places between the Johannine writings as he views them and those same writings as holy Scripture in the sense that Schnabel (see below) or Schlatter and Oosterzee (above) affirms. Schnelle concedes, regarding Revelation: "According to its own claim, the Apocalypse derives from Jesus Christ, and through him its ultimate author is God (Rev. 1:1a; cf. 22:16)."[61] The God-given nature of the Old Testament is axiomatic for Jesus (according to the Gospels) and New Testament writers, and a similar status was accorded New Testament writings from a very early date (2 Peter 3:16: Paul's writings; 1 Tim. 5:18: Gospel of Luke).[62] But as we have seen, Schnelle derives Revelation from a hypothetical wandering Jewish prophet, not from God. John's writings, and all New Testament writings, are rather the result of "the process of the formation of theology as creative meaning-formation" (659; this and subsequent page numbers in this section refer to Schnelle, *Theology of the New Testament*).

Schnelle's *Theology of the New Testament* opens with an erudite defense of an understanding of history and historical knowledge (25–40) in which he concludes: "We have no records that come directly from Jesus or from his immediate associates but only testimony from a somewhat later time" (39). He claims that "this is in no way a lack" (39). But the denial of eyewitness connection between the New Testament writings and what they report stands in tension with, for example, Luke 1:1–4 regarding

---

61. *The History and Theology of the New Testament Writings*, 518.
62. See more fully L. T. Swinson, *What Is Scripture? Paul's Use of* Graphe *in the Letters to Timothy* (Eugene, OR: Wipf & Stock, 2014).

eyewitnesses, with the explicit testimony of 1 John 1:1–3 (about which Schnelle says nothing with respect to its eyewitness claims in either his *Theology* or his *History and Theology of the New Testament Writings*), with the church's historic understanding of apostles (who wrote or contributed to the writing of much of the New Testament) as witnesses to Jesus from his baptism to his ascension (Acts 1:22), and with the doctrine of Scripture's divine inspiration found within Scripture itself.[63] It also conflicts with scholarship like that of Richard Bauckham.[64]

In the end, to a considerable degree Schnelle adopts a view of the New Testament reminiscent of F. C. Baur (and echoed in Bultmann), who regarded it as solely human-generated dogmatic formation,[65] not divinely conditioned revelation upon which subsequent Christian confession, worship, living, and mission should be based. While "the task of a theology of the New Testament is to apprehend" the "achievements of meaning-formation" that the New Testament sources testify to, and "the aim is to facilitate authentic representation of the New Testament's meaning-formation in the present" (40), in Schnelle's view the New Testament interpreter (like the writers he or she interprets) is walled off from direct access to Jesus and those he schooled—the disciples and apostles found in and responsible for the Gospels we possess. The results of their meaning-formation are not necessarily better informed, and certainly no more binding, than our own.

3.2 *Eckhard Schnabel's* New Testament Theology (NTT)[66]

Schnabel's *New Testament Theology* takes explicit issue with the inadequacy of "critical" readings like Schnelle's, which he points out are as tied to dogmatic loyalties as his own canonical approach.[67] While Schnelle

---

63. For articulations of this conviction from the Reformation to the present, among a sizable literature, see Peter A. Lillback and Richard B. Gaffin, Jr., *Thy Word Is Still Truth* (Phillipsburg, NJ: P&R Publishing, 2013).

64. Richard Bauckham, *Jesus and the Eyewitnesses: The Gospels as Eyewitness Testimony*, 2nd ed. (Grand Rapids: Eerdmans, 2017).

65. See Ferdinand Christian Baur, *History of Christian Dogma*, ed. Peter C. Hodgson, trans. Robert F. Brown and Peter C. Hodgson (Oxford: Oxford University Press, 2014), 50. Here he makes clear that New Testament or biblical theology (Baur uses both terms) is not the foundation for Christian theology, just distant attestations of first stages in the historical expression of "the teaching of Jesus" defined as "the universal and essential form of Christian consciousness" (51 n. 5). The substance of that consciousness is determined by the interpreter, not the sources.

66. Eckhard Schnabel, New Testament Theology (Grand Rapids: Baker Academic, 2023). Parenthetical citations in this section beginning with *NTT* refer to this work.

67. Schnabel defends his methodological premise of the general historical reliability of the New Testament sources, which he calls "advance confidence," observing: "Advance confidence means not simply a

interacts little or not at all with scholarship that does not share his critical premises, Schnabel interacts with critical scholarship in a thoroughgoing manner. He points out that a truly critical discipline must be willing to allow its assumptions to be challenged by examination of the data (in this case the New Testament writings) from a vantage point outside its own hegemony.[68] "If we allow the hypotheses of some scholars who analyze the Gospels and Acts as a matter of principle with skepticism regarding their historical reliability, then intellectual integrity demands that other scholars be permitted to explore these same sources with advance confidence that they convey reliable information."[69]

Schnabel's *NTT* treatment of John's canonical writings builds on the formidable bedrock of his 1,200-page two-volume *Early Christian Mission*. John the son of Zebedee and his writings feature substantially in both volumes. The cultural and social world of Jesus and John takes on tangible shape as Schnabel analyzes not primarily a conceptual world construed from the New Testament writings viewed skeptically as to their link with Jesus and actual witnesses (cf. Schnelle), but the fuller world surrounding Jesus's time in terms of Judaism and its history and informing texts, geography, cities and towns, the economic and social situation, religious and political developments, communication structures, and much more. Growing out of this wide-ranging attention to the world around the New Testament and the concrete life setting of those allegedly described in the New Testament writings, Schnabel admits: "My analysis of the authorship of the New Testament texts took the external evidence of attestation more seriously than is often the case" (*NTT*, 37). He continues: "The readers of the Gospels around AD 100 would have thought that Matthew, Mark, Luke and John wrote the Gospels attributed to them. . . . As I analyze the theology of the New Testament texts, not the theology of reconstructed texts and traditions [cf. Schnelle], I will do the same" (*NTT*, 37).

---

confidence resulting from dogmatic loyalties (as if traditional historical-critical skepticism is not tied to dogmatic conditions!) but one grounded in the experience that the data that the Gospels and Acts recount can be explained adequately and perhaps even better without some other hypothesis" (Schnabel, *Early Christian Mission*, 2 vols. [Downers Grove, IL: InterVarsity Press, 2004], 1:21–22). By "some other hypothesis" Schnabel refers to variations of "critical" views that the best way to explain the New Testament data is to make skepticism of the writings' surface claims to be describing real events and discourses the leading premise.

68. Schnabel, *Early Christian Mission*, 1:13, drawing on Dieter Sänger.
69. Schnabel, *Early Christian Mission*, 1:21.

Schnabel's *NTT* is marked by two notable distinctives. One is the missionary focus of the New Testament writings, their authors, and the communities of faith within which the writings arose and to which the writings were addressed. "It should be possible to integrate the New Testament texts into the historical context of the early Christian mission" (*NTT*, 12). Schnabel explains:

> The Gospels and the letters that constitute the canon of the New Testament literature were not written by academics, professionals of the spoken and written word. . . . They were written by theologians who had missionary experience, who had led people to faith in Jesus, who had planted new churches, and who taught both new and mature believers in Jesus. (*NTT*, 12)

There has perhaps been no other New Testament theology written from this particular (and plausible) missiologically charged conceptualization of the canonical writers.

A second distinctive is in Schnabel's determination to produce a New Testament theology that is not novel, as if the goal were to produce the latest and greatest work of this genre. "My goal is not innovation, but faithfulness to the sources that the church has regarded as the authoritative scriptural revelation of God, who procured salvation for sinners through the death and resurrection of Jesus Messiah" (*NTT*, 17). Just as his *Early Christian Mission* begins with the words, "In the beginning was Jesus,"[70] Schnabel deems "that the foundation and heart of the New Testament texts, the basic conviction that unites all its authors, is not a particular theme but a person: Jesus of Nazareth, acknowledged and worshiped as Israel's Messiah and Savior of sinners" (*NTT*, 58). The stress on the real personhood of Jesus, and not concepts about him or teachings ascribed to him apart from that personhood, is a notable feature of Schnabel's entire *NTT*.

A final contrast, already hinted at, between Schnabel's canonical *NTT* and the critical theologies touched on above, lies in his assessment of the authorship of the Johannine writings. He argues that John the son of Zebedee wrote all five (*NTT*, 27–31). In *Early Christian Mission* (1:242–47), this hypothesis, with the help of communication theory, enables

---

70. Schnabel, *Early Christian Mission*, 1:3.

Schnabel to shed fresh and extended light on the conversation between Jesus and the Samaritan woman. He comments, "Scholars who think it impossible that Jesus could have had a conversation such as John narrates in Jn 4 have to postulate an anonymous missionary at the end of the first century who was capable of brilliant, rhetorically flexible and theologically creative conversations with believers."[71]

The account of Jesus and the Samaritan woman finds its way into *NTT* (759–61), helping to anchor a chapter called "The Theological Convictions of John" (*NTT*, 710–62). This rich précis of Johannine belief highlights main themes (like dualisms and dualities, Old Testament fulfillment and Jesus's mission, eternal life, love, faith, and truth) but zeroes in as well on "The Life, Death, Resurrection, Exaltation, and Return of Jesus Messiah" (729–50). There is an equally full account of "The Community of Believers in Jesus," on the basis of Schnabel's conviction that "John's five texts [i.e. Gospel, epistles, Revelation] provide a rich tapestry of the reality of the congregations of Jesus Messiah" (750).

Space precludes detailing Schnabel's reference to John's "five texts" in connection with his *NTT*'s summative section on "The Message of the New Testament" treating the New Testament's variety yet unity, the fundamental reality of God, revelation that is incarnational, a salvation that is personal, a transformation that is continuing, and an expectation (of Jesus's return and eternal life) that is joyful (789–961). Full utilization of all of John's writings as Schnabel expounds them stands in notable contrast to use made of them in the critical trajectory traced above. It results in a very different picture of what life in Christ meant in apostolic times and should mean currently at the personal, ecclesial, and missional levels.

CONCLUSION

International scholarship on the New Testament reflects myriad perspectives and historiographical convictions. But as Nicholas Hardy has shown, going back into at least the seventeenth century, what eventually came to be known as historical criticism was itself fueled by confessional convictions, however covert or obscure today due to the passage of time.[72] It is Hardy's service to have dispelled some of the obscurity. "Critical" reading of the New

---

71. Schnabel, *Early Christian Mission*, 1:243.
72. Nicholas Hardy, *Criticism and Confession: The Bible in the Seventeenth Century Republic of Letters*, Oxford-Warburg Studies (Oxford: Oxford University Press, 2017).

Testament was as confessionally committed as the orthodox figures and works it opposed—the new criticism's theology[73] just took on contrasting forms.

This bifurcation of approaches to the New Testament persists, as is perhaps inevitable. In Jesus's own day, by the testimony of the Gospels (much of which is admittedly spurious by critical measures), there were two very different readings of the Scriptures of Israel: that of various Jewish sects and leaders, and that affirmed by the messianic claimant Jesus from Nazareth. He claimed that in fundamental ways those Scriptures pointed to him; he was in fact fulfilling them and would do so to the end of the age and beyond. This claim was adjudged to be blasphemous and was instrumental in his conviction and death. Non-messianic interpretation of Jesus in both Old and New Testaments, meaning rejection or radical reinterpretation of Christ as confessed in the church's historic creeds, remains de rigueur, not just in Judaism but among critical New Testament scholars, who reject out of hand the kinds of canonical readings of John found in New Testament theologies outlined above.

It is the service of scholars pursuing a canonical view of John's historicity and theological plausibility to have provided a scholarly alternative to the readings of John typically favored in the critical tradition. Andreas Köstenberger's place among canonical interpreters is acknowledged when, for example, Jörg Frey groups him with Theodor Zahn, Leon Morris, D. A. Carson, Craig Blomberg, and Ben Witherington, all of whom Frey dismisses for their "historicizing approach" in which Jesus's earthly life and work are the focus. From Frey's critical vantage point, as for Baur-Bultmann-Schnelle above, this approach's viability terminated at the Enlightenment when the dichotomy between history and theology was affirmed, when eyewitness authorship of the Fourth Gospel was rejected, and when John's Gospel came to be understood as a mythical or poetic or allegorical (cf. "spiritual") presentation.[74]

For those inclined to extend more trust to John's writings than to critical assessment of them, the extensive canonical work of Andreas Köstenberger on the Johannine corpus merits attention and our thanks.

---

73. On the transition from the era Hardy (previous note) treats and the emergence of critical theology finding expression in biblical theology after Gabler (see n. 3 above), see the useful survey and summation "Neologian Theology," in Constance M. Furey et al., eds., *Encyclopedia of the Bible and Its Reception*, vol. 21: *Negative Theology–Offspring* (Berlin/Boston: De Gruyter, 2023), cols. 106–9.

74. Jörg Frey, *Die Herrlichkeit des Gekreuzigten. Studien zu den Johanneischen Schriften I*, ed. Juliane Schlegel, WUNT 307 (Tübingen: Mohr Siebeck, 2013), 5–6.

CHAPTER 11

THE RECEPTION OF JOHN'S GOSPEL IN THE EARLY CHURCH

MICHAEL J. KRUGER

In the modern church, there's little doubt that the Gospel of John is one of the most beloved Gospels—if not *the* most. If forced to pick just one Gospel, many would prefer the Gospel of John. On the rare occasion when a singular gospel is published as a stand-alone book (or booklet), it is almost always John. And the reasons for its popularity are not hard to find. Along with an accessible and flowing style, John contains some of the most memorable descriptions and teachings of Jesus: the poetic Prologue (1:1–18), the changing of water to wine (2:1–12), the conversation with Nicodemus (3:1–21), the healing of the man born blind (9:1–41), the raising of Lazarus from the dead (11:17–44), the High Priestly Prayer (17:1–26), and more.

Curiously, the situation was very much the same in the early Christian movement. While most scholars would agree that John was the last published among the canonical four—probably sometime in the 90s—it quickly became one of the most influential and beloved Gospels.[1] If extant manuscripts are a reliable indication of usage,[2] then John was certainly one of the most commonly read (and copied) with nineteen manuscripts

---

1. C. S. Keener, *The Gospel of John* (Peabody, MA: Hendrickson, 2003), 1:140–42. For general discussions of John's date (not all of which place John in the 90s), see R. E. Brown, *The Gospel According to John* (New York: Doubleday, 1966), lxxx–lxxxvi; Leon Morris, *Studies in the Fourth Gospel* (Grand Rapids: Eerdmans, 1969), 215–92; S. Smalley, *John: Evangelist and Interpreter* (London: Paternoster Press, 1978), 75–93; D.A. Carson, *The Gospel According to John*, PNTC (Grand Rapids: Eerdmans, 1991), 82–87.
2. L. W. Hurtado, *The Earliest Christian Artifacts: Manuscripts and Christian Origins* (Grand Rapids: Eerdmans, 2006), 26–27.

from the second and third centuries, more than any other Gospel.[3] Moreover, John proved to be enormously influential on early Christian theology, particularly Christology.[4] In short, the Gospel of John appears to have been one of the most popular Gospels in early Christianity.

But not all agree. Some scholars would acknowledge that John found a quick and ready reception in these early centuries, but just not among the mainstream "orthodox" church.[5] Rather, it was the heterodox groups—Gnostics or Valentinians in particular—who seemed to have an early affinity for John.[6] The fact that John was favored by these aberrant groups, it has been argued, led to a widespread hesitancy toward John within the broader Christian movement.[7] It took a while to overcome that hesitancy, requiring the help of heavyweights like Irenaeus and others to turn the tide in John's favor. Thus, according to this narrative, it was only later—primarily in the third century and beyond—that the "orthodox" church warmed up to John and received it as genuine.

The purpose of this chapter is to revisit the reception of John's Gospel, particularly in the debated and shadowy time of the second century, in

---

3. Manuscripts of John possibly from the second/third centuries: P5 (P.Oxy. 208); P22 (P.Oxy. 1228); P28 (P.Oxy. 1596); P39 (P.Oxy. 1780); P45 (P.Chest.Beatty I); P52 (P.Ryl. 457); P66 (P.Bod. II); P75 (P.Bod. XIV–XV); P80 (P.Barc. 83); P90 (P.Oxy. 3523); P95 (P.Laur.inv. II/31); P106 (P.Oxy. 4445); P107 (P.Oxy. 4446); P108 (P.Oxy. 4447); P109 (P.Oxy. 4448); P119 (P.Oxy. 4803); P121 (P.Oxy. 4805); P134 (Willoughby Papyrus); GA 0162 (P.Oxy. 847). For more on John's early textual history, see Lonnie D. Bell, *The Early Textual Transmission of John: Stability and Fluidity in Its Second and Third Century Greek Manuscripts* (Leiden: Brill, 2018); and Juan Chapa, "The Early Text of the Gospel of John," in *The Early Text of the New Testament*, ed. C. E. Hill and M. J. Kruger (Oxford: Oxford University Press, 2011), 140–56.

4. J. N. Sanders, *The Fourth Gospel in the Early Church: Its Origin and Influence on Christian Theology up to Irenaeus* (Cambridge: Cambridge University Press, 1943); T. E. Pollard, *Johannine Christology and the Early Church* (Cambridge: Cambridge University Press, 1970). For a more recent survey of John's theology, see Andreas J. Köstenberger, *A Theology of John's Gospel and Letters*, BTNT (Grand Rapids: Zondervan, 2009).

5. Ever since the publication of Walter Bauer, *Orthodoxy and Heresy in Earliest Christianity*, ed. R. Kraft and G. Krodel (Philadelphia: Fortress, 1971), terms like "orthodoxy" and "heresy" have been regarded as anachronistic and prejudicial. There is not space to address this debate here, but I will keep the terms in quotation marks as an acknowledgment of their limitations. For more on the Bauer thesis, see A. J. Köstenberger and M. J. Kruger, *The Heresy of Orthodoxy: How Modern Culture's Fascination with Diversity Has Reshaped Our Understanding of Early Christianity* (Wheaton: Crossway, 2010); and Michael J. Kruger, *Christianity at the Crossroads: How the Second Century Shaped the Future of the Church* (Downers Grove, IL: IVP Academic, 2018), 108–66.

6. Bauer was a foundational influence on the idea that John's Gospel was a favorite among the heretics (*Orthodoxy and Heresy*, 206–12). See also Sanders, *Fourth Gospel in the Early Church*, 86; C. K. Barrett, *The Gospel According to John* (London: SPCK, 1978), 109–15; R. Schnackenburg, *The Gospel According to St. John* (London: Burns and Oates, 1982), 192–202. For more, see discussion in C. E. Hill, *The Johannine Corpus in the Early Church* (Oxford: Oxford University Press, 2004), 11–55.

7. Hill refers to this paradigm as "orthodox Johannophobia" (*Johannine Corpus*, 11–55).

hopes of showing that this traditional scholarly narrative is problematic and that John was more widely received by the "orthodox" church than critics have typically acknowledged.

I trust this chapter will be a fitting tribute to my friend Andreas Köstenberger, as he is honored with this Festschrift. Over the years, we have worked together in a number of ways, particularly responding to the scholarly paradigm known as the Bauer thesis—a theme that has particular relevance for this article. I am thankful for Andreas's solid and even-handed scholarship, which has enriched me and many others in the world of biblical studies.

1. DEFINING OUR TERMS

In order to proceed with our exploration of the reception of John's Gospel in the early church, we need to begin by defining the term "reception." What must be true for a book to be regarded as received by the church? Lack of clarity over terminology is not a new issue in the study of the New Testament canon. Brevard Childs once observed, "Much of the present confusion of the problem of canon turns on the failure to reach an agreement regarding terminology."[8] Indeed, there has been a long-standing scholarly debate—spanning more than a century—over what conditions have to be in place for a book to be regarded as accepted into the canon.[9] Zahn, for example, understood a book to be received when it was cited by early Christian writers, while Harnack, in contrast, insisted that the mere usage of a book is not the same as reception of that book as canonical.[10] Instead, Harnack argued that a book is only received when it is cited *as Scripture*—a status typically designated by γραφὴ or γέγραπται. Other scholars have gone even further, arguing that a book is not received until it finds a place on a fixed, final, closed list of books.[11] This debate does not appear to have an end in sight, and it is not our purpose here to resolve

---

8. Brevard Childs, *Introduction to the Old Testament as Scripture* (Philadelphia: Fortress, 1979), 51.

9. For more on the different definitions for the term "canon," and an overview of the debate, see Michael J. Kruger, "The Definition of the Term 'Canon': Exclusive or Multi-Dimensional?," *TynBul* 63 (2012): 1–20.

10. T. Zahn, *Geschichte des neutestamentlichen Kanons* (Erlangen: A. Deichert, 1888); A. von Harnack, *Origin of the New Testament and the Most Important Consequences of a New Creation* (London: Williams & Northgate, 1925). A fuller assessment of the Zahn-Harnack debate can be found in J. Barton, *The Spirit and the Letter: Studies in the Biblical Canon* (London: SPCK, 1997), 1–34.

11. A. C. Sundberg, "Towards a Revised History of the New Testament Canon," *Studia Evangelica* 4 (1968): 452–61; Sundberg, "The Making of the New Testament Canon," in *The Interpreter's One-Volume Commentary on the Bible*, ed. C. M. Layman (Nashville: Abingdon, 1971), 1216–24.

it. In the meantime, we shall follow Harnack's approach and consider a book (in this case, John) as "received" once it is regarded as, or functions as, Scripture in the early Christian movement.

A second (and related) issue that must be addressed is whether we must determine the authorship of John's Gospel before we can assess its reception. In John 21:24 we learn that it is the beloved disciple "who testifies [μαρτυρῶν] to these things and who wrote [γράψας] them down."[12] The identity of this mysterious individual has been a point of significant disagreement.[13] While arguably the dominant position of the early church was that the author was John the son of Zebedee,[14] a number of modern scholars have argued that the "beloved disciple" was in fact the enigmatic John the Elder.[15] Regardless of which view one takes, it will not need to be resolved before we assess the reception of John's Gospel in the second century. When we examine any ancient author's view of John, we are not obligated to determine *which* John that author thinks wrote the Gospel before we can determine whether he received it as authoritative.

2. THE CASE AGAINST JOHN

As we turn to the reception of John's Gospel, we begin by observing the case against its early acceptance by the "orthodox" church is built on two claims: (a) John was particularly favored among the "heretics"; and (b)

---

12. There is a long-standing debate about whether John 21:24 is referring to the author of John or merely the "source" of John; e.g., J. H. Bernard, *A Critical and Exegetical Commentary on the Gospel According to St. John* (Edinburgh: T&T Clark, 1928). Richard Bauckham, *Jesus and the Eyewitnesses: The Gospels as Eyewitness Testimony* (Grand Rapids: Eerdmans, 2006), 358–62, argues that 21:24 is referring to authorship.

13. J. H. Charlesworth has cataloged twenty-three different positions on the authorship of John: *The Beloved Disciple: Whose Witness Validates the Gospel of John?* (Valley Forge, PA: Trinity Press International, 1995), 225–437. In recent years, a number of scholars have suggested the "beloved disciple" is a literary device of a pseudonymous author: M. David Litwa, "Literary Eyewitnesses: The Appeal to an Eyewitness in John and Contemporaneous Literature," *NTS* 64 (2018): 343–61; Hugo Méndez, "Did the Johannine Community Exist?," *JSNT* 42 (2020): 350–74.

14. E.g., Irenaeus, *Haer.* 2.22.5; 3.3.4; 3.11; Eusebius, *Hist. eccl.* 3.23.3–4; 4.14.3–8; 5.8.4; Muratorian Fragment (see section on John). The traditional view that the beloved disciple was John the apostle, son of Zebedee, is still held by a number of scholars: Keener, *Gospel of John*, 1:83–104; Leon Morris, *The Gospel According to John* (Grand Rapids: Eerdmans, 1995), 775–77; Carson, *Gospel According to John*, 682–85; and C. Blomberg, *The Historical Reliability of John's Gospel: Issues and Commentary* (Downers Grove, IL: InterVarsity Press, 2001), 22–41.

15. The most developed version of this approach can be found in Martin Hengel, *Die Johanneische Frage* (Tübingen: Mohr Siebeck, 1993); idem, *The Johannine Question* (London: SCM, 1989). Following Hengel is Richard Bauckham, *The Testimony of the Beloved Disciple: Narrative, History, and Theology in the Gospel of John* (Grand Rapids: Baker Academic, 2007); idem, *Jesus and the Eyewitnesses*, 358–437; and John Behr, *John the Theologian and His Paschal Gospel: A Prologue to Theology* (Oxford: Oxford University Press, 2021).

this favored status led some "orthodox" writers to oppose the Gospel. Let's consider each of these claims in turn.

2.1 John Among the "Heretics"

It should be acknowledged from the outset that John does appear to have been used in the second century by some so-called "heretical" groups, though there is not space for a detailed survey here.[16] Most commonly mentioned is the fact that the Valentinian Heracleon wrote a commentary on John.[17] However, Heracleon's commentary does not seem to have made much of an impact. Irenaeus never mentions it, nor does Clement of Alexandria, even though both were aware of Heracleon.[18] In fact, we only know about Heracleon's commentary because Origen critiques it extensively in his own later commentary on John. Scholars have also appealed to Ptolemy the Valentinian who references the Prologue of John (1:3) in his *Letter to Flora*.[19] But, Ptolemy also cites from the Synoptic Gospels extensively—Matthew in particular—and even seems to know of some of Paul's letters. Thus, there is no reason to think John is particularly favored by him. In the case of both Heracleon and Ptolemy, we should not forget that "heretics" often utilized canonical books—attaching their own interpretation to them—but this does not mean those books were therefore viewed negatively by the "orthodox."[20] Indeed, elsewhere Irenaeus points out how all four Gospels were used by heretics from time to time.[21] Instead of causing Irenaeus to doubt these Gospels, it causes him to defend them against misuse and misunderstanding.

In addition to specific citations of John by heterodox authors, scholars have also observed that a number of so-called gnostic Gospels seem to show dependence on (or at least awareness of) Johannine

---

16. A more thorough overview can be found in Hill, *Johannine Corpus*, 205–93; and R. A. Culpepper, *John, the Son of Zebedee: The Life of a Legend* (Columbia: University of South Carolina Press, 1994), 107–38.

17. There are doubts about whether Heracleon was even a Valentinian: Michael Kaler, "Was Heracleon a Valentinian? A New Look at Old Sources," *HTR* 99 (2006): 275–89.

18. *Haer.* 2.4; Clement of Alexandria, *Strom.* 4.71.

19. Epiphanius, *Pan.* 33.3–7. It is also possible that Irenaeus had Ptolemy in mind when he mentions a Valentinian exegesis of John's Prologue (*Haer.* 1.8), but we cannot be sure. For an overview of this letter, see Christoph Markschies, "New Research on Ptolemaeus Gnosticus," *ZAC* 4 (2000): 225–54.

20. It is worth noting that Irenaeus's complaints against the heretics were not just about them having different books, but rather that the heretics used orthodox books but corrupted and twisted their meaning (*Haer.* 1.8.1). See further discussion in John Behr, *Formation of Christian Theology, Vol. 1: The Way to Nicea* (Crestwood, NY: St. Vladimir's Seminary Press, 2001), 30–32.

21. *Haer.* 3.11.7.

material.[22] The Nag Hammadi texts in particular have been linked to John, such as the *Tripartite Tractate*, the *Thunder, Perfect Mind*, the *Gospel of Truth*, the *Gospel of Phillip*, the *Apocryphon of James*, and others.[23] Needless to say, there is not space to evaluate each of these texts here. But there are reasons to doubt whether they demonstrate a distinctive proclivity among Gnostics for the Gospel of John—at least the kind which could have caused the "orthodox" church to balk at its acceptance. After all, some of these texts are probably too late to have caused anyone to hesitate over the Gospel of John because the Gospel of John was largely accepted by the time they were written and disseminated.[24] Others of these texts may share ideas or concepts in common with John, but that is entirely different from showing dependence.[25] The authors of these other Gospels could have acquired Johannine tradition in a number of different ways beyond actually knowing and using John's Gospel. It should also be observed that the most famous text discovered at Nag Hammadi, the *Gospel of Thomas*, actually shows significant affinities not with John but with the Synoptics.[26] But no scholars would suggest, on this basis, that Gnostics had a distinctive affinity for the Synoptic Gospels.[27]

2.2 Orthodox Opposition to John

In addition to the argument that John was favored by the Gnostics—which, as just noted, has rather thin evidence in its support—scholars have also claimed that some "orthodox" individuals were also opposed to John's Gospel (presumably because of its connection to these "heretical" groups). The most mentioned individual in this regard is Gaius of Rome.

---

22. There are significant doubts about how to define "Gnosticism" and whether it is even a legitimate category: M. A. Williams, *Rethinking "Gnosticism": An Argument for Dismantling a Dubious Category* (Princeton, NJ: Princeton University Press, 1996); Karen L. King, *What Is Gnosticism?* (Cambridge, MA: Harvard University Press, 2003).

23. For an overview and translation of these texts, see J. M. Robinson, *The Nag Hammadi Library in English* (Leiden: Brill, 1988).

24. Hill, *Johannine Corpus*, 236–38.

25. For generations, scholars have explored the complexity of demonstrating literary dependency on a written source as opposed to just dependency on ideas/concepts that were circulating at the time. For the Synoptics, this was most notably done by H. Köster, *Synoptische Überlieferung bei den apostolischen Vätern* (Berlin: Akademie-Verlag, 1957). For John, see Melvyn R. Hillmer, "The Gospel of John in the Second Century" (ThD dissertation, Harvard University, 1966).

26. Simon Gathercole, *The Composition of the Gospel of Thomas: Original Language and Influences* (Cambridge: Cambridge University Press, 2012); M. S. Goodacre, *Thomas and the Gospels: The Case for Thomas's Familiarity with the Synoptics* (Grand Rapids: Eerdmans, 2012).

27. Of course, doubts have been raised about whether the *Gospel of Thomas* is even Gnostic: W. K. Grobel, "How Gnostic Is the Gospel of Thomas?," *NTS* 8 (1962): 367–73.

Eusebius describes Gaius as a "very learned person" and an "ecclesiastical man" who lived in Rome toward the end of the second century and wrote an anti-Montanist treatise entitled *Dialogue with Proclus*.[28] Curiously, however, Eusebius never mentions anything about Gaius objecting to the Gospel of John.[29] Moreover, when Epiphanius discusses the *Alogoi*—a group that he claims rejected both the Gospel of John and the book of Revelation—he also never mentions Gaius.[30] And when Gaius is mentioned later by Photius of Constantinople, again no mention is made of Gaius's supposed objection to John's Gospel.[31]

In fact, the first mention of Gaius being opposed to the Gospel of John comes from a twelfth-century Syriac commentary on Revelation by Dionysius bar Salibi.[32] There, bar Salibi purports to preserve excerpts from a lost work of Hippolytus, possibly *Heads Against Gaius*, where Gaius is said to have regarded the Gospel of John and Revelation as forgeries of Cerinthus.[33] But the authenticity of these excerpts has been seriously challenged, with some scholars arguing that they are merely another example of Hippolytan pseudepigrapha that was common during the medieval time period.[34]

So, we are left with substantial doubt about whether we have any named "orthodox" individual from the second century that opposed John's Gospel, and even less reason to think that opposition was in any way connected to the use of John by gnostic heretics. All we are left with is a singular group, namely the mysterious and anonymous *Alogoi* mentioned by Epiphanius. But, as others have argued, it is possible that

---

28. *Hist. eccl.* 6.20.3. English translations of Eusebius, unless otherwise noted, are taken from Kirsopp Lake, *Eusebius: Ecclesiastical History: Books I-V*, Loeb Classical Library (Cambridge, MA: Harvard University Press, 2001); and J. E. L. Oulton, *Eusebius: Ecclesiastical History: Books VI-X*, Loeb Classical Library (Cambridge, MA: Harvard University Press, 2000). Although Gaius is often referred to as the "bishop" of Rome, this was not a title give to him by Eusebius. The first time such a title is given is by Photius of Constantinople in the ninth century, which is itself in doubt (Hill, *Johannine Corpus*, 196–97).

29. It is possible (though not altogether clear) that Gaius may have been critical of the book of Revelation. For more, see Michael J. Kruger, "The Reception of the Book of Revelation in the Early Church," in *Book of Seven Seals: The Peculiarity of Revelation, Its Manuscripts, Attestation, and Transmission*, ed. Thomas J. Kraus and Michael Sommer (Tübingen: Mohr Siebeck, 2016), 159–74.

30. Epiphanius, *Pan.* 51.3.1–6.

31. *Bibl.* 48.

32. T. H. Robinson, "The Authorship of the Muratorian Canon," *The Expositor* 7 (1906): 481–95; John Gwynn, "Hippolytus and His 'Heads against Caius,'" *Hermathena* 6 (1888): 397–418.

33. The title *Heads Against Gaius* is not mentioned by bar Salibi but comes from a fourteenth-century catalog of Hippolytan works compiled by Ebed-Jesus (Hill, *Johannine Corpus*, 180).

34. Allen Brent, *Hippolytus and the Roman Church in the Third Century: Communities in Tension before the Emergence of the Monarch-Bishop* (Leiden: Brill, 1995), 144–84.

the *Alogoi* were not an actual historical group but rather a catchall term used by Epiphanius to refer to anyone opposed to Johannine literature— an amalgamation, of sorts.[35] Even if the *Alogoi* were an actual group, Schnackenburg observes that "they were a restricted group without any great influence."[36] So, while Epiphanius does indicate that some opposition to John existed at some point, the idea that such opposition was widespread—or primarily from "orthodox" figures—seems in need of serious modification.

3. THE RECEPTION OF JOHN IN THE SECOND CENTURY

If our analysis above proves correct, then we have little reason to think "orthodox" Christians would have had a predetermined negative assessment of John due to its connections to heterodox groups. This clears the deck for a fresh look at John's reception in the second century. No longer are we obligated to assume that any "silence" shown by a patristic author must entail an unspoken, negative assessment of John. And, as shall be seen below, our patristic sources are not nearly so silent about John as many have supposed.

Due to space constraints, the survey below is just that, a survey, and must inevitably be selective. But it should still provide an overall impression of the status of the Fourth Gospel in this critical time period. We shall begin at the end of the second century and work backward toward the beginning.

3.1 End of the Second Century

By the end of the second century, the Gospel of John appears to be widely received within the early Christian movement. Whatever earlier doubts might have existed, they seemed to have dissipated rather quickly. Tertullian, writing at the tail end of the century (and beginning of the third), clearly affirms all four Gospels as part of the "evangelical testament," and notes that Matthew and John are penned by "apostles" while Mark and Luke are regarded as "apostolic men."[37] At one point he refers to John

---

35. T. Scott Manor, "Epiphanius' Account of the Alogi: Historical Fact or Heretical Fiction," *Studia Patristica* 52 (2012): 161–70.

36. Schnackenburg, *Gospel According to St. John*, 201.

37. *Marc.* 4.2. All English translations from the Ante-Nicene fathers, unless otherwise noted, are taken from A. Roberts and J. Donaldson, eds., *The Ante-Nicene Fathers* (Peabody, MA: Hendrickson, 1885).

as "the Lord's Gospel,"[38] quotes from it extensively,[39] affirms that it is authored by the apostle himself (the son of Zebedee),[40] and does not indicate any notable controversy or doubts about the authenticity of the Gospel, even as he battles various "heretical" groups.[41] Writing around the same time frame, Clement of Alexandria appears to have the same views as Tertullian. He, too, affirms four (and only four) Gospels, obviously including the Gospel of John,[42] citing it as Scripture,[43] and attributing it to John the apostle.[44] While Clement is well known for drawing upon extracanonical writings—even apocryphal Gospels from time to time—he is clear that their authority is not the same as the canonical four.[45] As Martin Hengel observes, "Clement's relative generosity towards 'apocryphal' texts and traditions, which is connected with the unique spiritual milieu in Alexandria and his constant controversies with many kinds of discussion partners . . . should not obscure the fact that even for him the apostolic origin and special church authority of the four gospels was already unassailable."[46]

One of the most influential figures at the end of the second century is undoubtedly Irenaeus, bishop of Lyons.[47] Writing circa 180, he makes one of the boldest (and most well-known) claims about the origins of the four Gospels: "It is not possible that the gospels can be either more or fewer than the number they are. For, since there are four zones of the world in which we live and four principle wind s. . . [and] the cherubim, too, were four-faced."[48] While some scholars have insisted Irenaeus's unusual argument implies his views are an "innovation,"[49] there are good reasons to think this connection between the four Gospels and the four creatures

---

38. *Bapt.* 15.1.
39. See overview in Hill, *Johannine Corpus*, 139–46.
40. *Praescr.* 22.1–9.
41. In particular, see his treatises *Against Marcion* and *Prescription against Heretics*.
42. *Hist. eccl.* 6.14.5–7.
43. *Paed.* 1.7.
44. *Strom.* 6.15; *Quis div.* 8.
45. *Strom.* 3.13.
46. M. Hengel, *The Four Gospels and the One Gospel of Jesus Christ* (Harrisburg, PA: Trinity Press International, 2000), 18–19.
47. For general introductions to Irenaeus, see Robert M. Grant, *Irenaeus of Lyons* (London: Routledge, 1997); and Eric Osborn, *Irenaeus of Lyons* (Cambridge: Cambridge University Press, 2001).
48. *Haer.* 3.11.8.
49. G. M. Hahneman, *The Muratorian Fragment and the Development of the Canon* (Oxford: Clarendon, 1992), 101.

around the throne is drawn from a much older tradition.[50] As for John in particular, Irenaeus calls this Gospel "Scripture,"[51] attributes it to an "apostle,"[52] and regards the author as John "the disciple of the Lord."[53] Irenaeus does indicate that the Valentinians used (and abused) the Gospel of John,[54] but he also acknowledges that Matthew, Mark, and Luke are also used by varying "heretical" groups.[55] Moreover, John was certainly not the only (canonical) Gospel used by the Valentinians, nor is there any indication that its use by the Valentinians hampered its acceptance (any more than Synoptic Gospels were tainted by heretics utilizing them).

Particularly noteworthy is that Irenaeus, at several points, mentions earlier generations that knew the apostle John personally, including Polycarp,[56] Papias,[57] and a number of unnamed "presbyters."[58] Such historical connections are suggestive that these individuals would have been familiar with (and presumably favorable toward) the Johannine writings long before the time of Irenaeus.[59]

We also see a well-established, closed gospel canon in the Muratorian fragment, our earliest canonical list (c. 180). While some have argued for a fourth-century date for the list, the second-century date has been reaffirmed and upheld.[60] The fragment affirms that John's content, like the Synoptics, is from "one sovereign Spirit," and that the Gospel is authored by John, "one of the disciples" and "an eyewitness and hearer."[61] Most

---

50. T. C. Skeat, "Irenaeus and the Four-Gospel Canon," *Novum Testamentum* 34 (1992): 194–99.
51. *Haer.* 1.8.2.
52. *Haer.* 3.21.3.
53. *Haer.* 3.1.1; 3.16.2.
54. *Haer.* 1.8.5; 3.11.7; 3.11.9. The latter reference has been taken by some as a reference to an "orthodox" group that was opposed to John (e.g., Bauer, *Heresy and Orthodoxy*, 141), but that is not at all clear in the original context of Irenaeus's remarks.
55. *Haer.* 3.11.7. Irenaeus indicates Matthew was used by the Ebionites, Luke by the Marcionites, and Mark by the docetists.
56. *Haer.* 3.3.4.
57. *Haer.* 5.33.4.
58. *Haer.* 5.30.1.
59. At one point, these earlier presbyters appear to cite John 14:2 (*Haer.* 5.34.2).
60. P. Henne, "La Datation du canon de Muratori," *RB* 100 (1993): 54–75; Charles E. Hill, "The Debate over the Muratorian Fragment and the Development of the Canon," *WTJ* 57 (1995): 437–52; Everett Ferguson, "Review of Geoffrey Mark Hahneman, *The Muratorian Fragment and the Development of the Canon*," *JTS* 44 (1993): 691–97; T. K. Heckel, *Vom Evangelium des Markus zum viergestaltigen Evangelium* (Tübingen: J.C.B. Mohr, 1999), 339–54; and J. Verheyden, "The Canon Muratori: A Matter of Dispute," in *The Biblical Canons*, ed. J. M. Auwers and H. J. de Jonge (Leuven: Leuven University Press, 2003), 487–556.
61. English translation from B. M. Metzger, *The Canon of the New Testament: Its Origin, Development, and Significance* (Oxford: Clarendon, 1987), 305–7.

notably, there is no mention here of any doubts about John or connections to gnostic or Valentinian groups.[62]

3.2 Middle of the Second Century

As we move further back into the second century, we come to the philosopher Tatian, one of Justin Martyr's most famous students. He was most well-known for his harmony of the four Gospels known as the *Diatesseron* (c. 170)—meaning "through four"—which quickly became very popular.[63] As the title indicates, Tatian wove all our four Gospels together, showing that "all four Gospels were regarded as authoritative, otherwise it is unlikely that Tatian would have dared to combine them into one gospel account."[64] Moreover, John's Gospel finds pride of place in the *Diatesseron* since all the material from the Synoptics is woven around John's timeline.[65] Tatian's high opinion of John is also demonstrated by his significant interaction with the text of John in his earlier work, *Oration to the Greeks* (c. 165).[66]

If Tatian had a high view of John, we should not be surprised if his mentor, Justin Martyr, did as well.[67] Writing in Rome circa 150–160, Justin claims to know plural "gospels,"[68] which he calls "memoirs of the apostles,"[69] and describes as "drawn up by His apostles and those who followed them"[70]—language which naturally lends itself to a fourfold collection.[71] It is commonly accepted that three of these Gospels are clearly the Synoptics,[72] and there are good reasons to think that John

---

62. Although the fragment acknowledges that the four Gospels have been critiqued for having "various elements" that are different from one another, these sorts of complaints were standard fare given that there were four separate accounts that could be compared to one another.

63. W. L. Petersen, *Tatian's Diatesseron: Its Creation, Dissemination, Significance, and History in Scholarship* (Leiden: Brill, 1994).

64. Metzger, *Canon of the New Testament*, 115.

65. It seems that John's Gospel was widely regarded as the Gospel that was written "in order" (Muratorian Fragment 33), while Papias notes that Mark (and presumably Matthew too) was not written in order (*Hist. eccl.* 3.39.15–16).

66. Robert M. Grant, *Greek Apologists of the Second Century* (London: SCM, 1988), 128.

67. For an overview of Justin, see Sara Parvis and Paul Foster, eds., *Justin Martyr and His Worlds* (Minneapolis: Fortress, 2007).

68. *1 Apol.* 66.3.

69. *1 Apol.* 67.3.

70. *Dial.* 103.

71. G. Stanton, "The Fourfold Gospel," *NTS* 43 (1997): 317–46; O. Skarsaune, "Justin and His Bible," in *Justin Martyr and His Worlds*, ed. Sara Parvis and Paul Foster (Minneapolis: Fortress, 2007), 53–76.

72. E.g., *Dial* 100.1; 103.8; 106.3–4. H. Koester, *Ancient Christian Gospels: Their History and Development* (London: SCM, 1990), declares that the citations in Justin "derive from written gospels, usually from Matthew and Luke, in one instance from Mark" (38).

is the fourth.[73] Justin shows extensive familiarity with the text of John's Gospel,[74] including "logos" language,[75] distinctive Johannine themes,[76] and likely cites John directly, "For Christ also said, 'Except ye be born again, ye shall not enter into the kingdom of heaven'" (cf. John 3:3).[77] The likelihood that Justin knew John is strengthened by the fact that he received the book of Revelation,[78] attributed it to John the apostle,[79] and regarded it as one of "our writings," a nod to an emerging canonical collection distinctive from the Old Testament books.[80]

As for the authority attributed to these "memoirs of the apostles," which we have argued would have included John, Justin often cites them using the standard formula for introducing Scripture, "it is written,"[81] and even describes how they are read in public worship services alongside the Old Testament Scriptures.[82] In regard to Justin's description of how the Gospels were used in worship, Hengel comments, "It is striking that the reading of the Gospels is mentioned before the prophets; to some extent it has taken over the significance of the Jewish reading of the Torah."[83]

3.3 Early Second Century

It should be no surprise that as we go further back into the second century our historical data becomes increasingly murky. This is particularly true for the writings known as the Apostolic Fathers, which are limited in scope and tend to paraphrase their sources.[84] Indeed, some scholars have

---

73. C. E. Hill, "Was John's Gospel among Justin's Apostolic Memoirs?" in *Justin Martyr and His Worlds*, ed. Sara Parvis and Paul Foster (Minneapolis: Fortress, 2007), 88–94. Some scholars concede that Justin knew John but did not regard it as authoritative; e.g., J. W. Pryor, "Justin Martyr and the Fourth Gospel," *SecCent* 9 (1992): 153–67; and L. W. Barnard, *Justin Martyr* (Cambridge: Cambridge University Press, 1967), 63.

74. Hill, *Johannine Corpus*, 316–37.

75. *1 Apol.* 46.2; cf. *Dial.* 88.7. K. L. Carroll, "The Creation of the Fourfold Gospel," *BJRL* 37 (1955): 68–77, argues that "logos" language can be explained in other ways, such as access to the teachings of Philo (70).

76. E.g., Jesus as μονογενὴς (Dial. 105.1; cf. John 1:18; 3:16); piercing Jesus's hands and feet with nails (*1 Apol.* 35.7; cf. John 20:25, 27).

77. *1 Apol.* 61.4.

78. Eric Francis Osborn, *Justin Martyr* (Tübingen: Mohr Siebeck, 1973), 135.

79. *Dial.* 81.4.

80. *1 Apol.* 28.1.

81. *Dial* 100.1; 103.6–8; 104.1; 105.6; 106.3–4; and 107.1.

82. *1 Apol.* 67.3.

83. Martin Hengel, "The Titles of the Gospels and the Gospel of Mark," in *Studies in the Gospel of Mark* (London: SCM, 1985), 76.

84. More up-to-date discussions about identifying New Testament texts in the Apostolic Fathers can be found in: Andrew Gregory and Christopher Tuckett, eds., *The Reception of the New Testament in the*

adopted such a strict methodology for proving an ancient writer knew/ used a source that they do not acknowledge that *any* written Gospel—not just John—was utilized during this time period.[85] Even so, there are a number of hints that the Gospel of John still found a place among some of these earliest Christian writers.

Papias, bishop of Hierapolis, is one of the key figures during this time frame because, as a hearer of John and a friend of Polycarp, he is well-positioned to know about the origins of the Gospels.[86] In addition, Papias's information about the Gospels relies on an earlier source, "the Elder,"[87] whom Papias identifies elsewhere as a disciple of Jesus and eyewitness,[88] and likely takes us back to the end of the first century.[89] When Papias relays what this "Elder" told him about the Gospels, he mentions two Gospels that contained eyewitness testimony, namely that of Mark—which effectively contained Peter's own eyewitness recollections—and that of Matthew, an apostle and eyewitness himself.[90]

While Papias does not mention the Gospel of John by name, there are good reasons to think it was still part of his gospel collection: (a) When Papias lists the disciples of Jesus, they are in an order that seems clearly dependent on the Gospel of John (1:35–51; 21:2).[91] (b) Irenaeus mentions that certain "elders" from a prior generation knew and used the Gospel of John[92]—material almost certainly drawn from the writings of Papias himself.[93] (c) Papias indicates that Mark was not written "in

---

Apostolic Fathers (Oxford: Oxford University Press, 2005); Andrew Gregory and Christopher Tuckett, eds., *Trajectories through the New Testament and the Apostolic Fathers* (Oxford: Oxford University Press, 2005); and Michael J. Kruger, "The New Testament in the Apostolic Fathers," in *Ancient Literature for New Testament Studies, Vol. 4: The Apostolic Fathers*, ed. Paul Foster (Grand Rapids: Zondervan, forthcoming).

85. Particularly strict in methodology is Stephen E. Young, *Jesus Tradition in the Apostolic Fathers* (Tübingen: Mohr Siebeck, 2011).

86. For recent overviews of Papias as a source, see Stephen C. Carlson, *Papias of Hierapolis Exposition of Dominical Oracles: The Fragments, Testimonia, and Reception of a Second-Century Commentator* (Oxford: Oxford University Press, 2021); and Monte Shanks, *Papias and the New Testament* (Eugene, OR: Wipf & Stock, 2013).

87. *Hist. eccl.* 3.39.15–16. English translations of the Apostolic Fathers, unless otherwise noted, are taken from B. D. Ehrman, *The Apostolic Fathers*, 2 vols., *Loeb Classical Library* (Cambridge, MA: Harvard University Press, 2003).

88. *Hist. eccl.* 3.39.3–4.

89. Bauckham, *Jesus and the Eyewitnesses*, 202–39.

90. *Hist. eccl.* 3.39.15–16.

91. *Hist. eccl.* 3.39.4. For a more detailed argument, see Hengel, *Johannine Question*, 16–23.

92. *Haer.* 5.36.1–2. These "presbyters" cite from John 14:2.

93. J. B. Lightfoot, *Essays on the Work Entitled Supernatural Religion* (London: MacMillan & Co., 1889), 195–98; Bauckham, *Testimony of the Beloved Disciple*, 51.

The Reception of John's Gospel in the Early Church

order," and implies that Matthew also had his own chronological issues (due to Papias's belief that Matthew's *logia* were originally in Hebrew and the readers "interpreted them" the best they could).[94] This has led some scholars to conclude that Papias must be contrasting Mark and Matthew's chronology with *another* Gospel whose chronology was well-established, namely the Gospel of John.[95] (d) Hill has made a substantial argument that a section of Eusebius about the Gospels of John and Luke actually derives from Papias[96]—even though Eusebius never mentioned his source.[97] This section of Eusebius therefore forms a natural parallel with the portion discussing Mark and Matthew, showing Papias likely had a fourfold Gospel. (e) Papias also knew 1 John[98] and Revelation,[99] suggesting he was familiar with a corpus of Johannine writings, and making his knowledge of John's Gospel all the more likely. All these factors can be summed up by Bauckham: "There should be no doubt that Papias knew the Fourth Gospel."[100]

Ignatius, bishop of Antioch, wrote numerous epistles at the turn of the century en route to his martyrdom in Rome (c. AD 110).[101] At numerous places he shows familiarity with the text of John's Gospel, which cannot be reviewed in detail here.[102] As one example, Ignatius declares, "The Spirit . . . knows where it comes from and where it is going"—a near direct quote from John 3:8.[103] So substantive are these links that even Inge's very minimalist 1905 study concluded that it was "highly probable" that Ignatius used the Gospel of John.[104] If so, then Ignatius's very high view

---

94. *Hist. eccl.* 3.39.15–16.
95. Bauckham, *Testimony of the Beloved Disciple*, 55.
96. *Hist. eccl.* 3.24.5–13.
97. C. E. Hill, "What Papias Said About John (and Luke): A New Papias Fragment," *JTS* 49 (1998): 582–629.
98. *Hist eccl.* 3.39.17.
99. Andrew of Caesarea, *On the Apocalypse* 34.12.
100. Bauckham, *Testimony of the Beloved Disciple*, 51.
101. For introductions to Ignatius and his writings, see Paul Foster, *The Writings of the Apostolic Fathers* (London: T&T Clark, 2007), 81–107; W. R. Schoedel, *Ignatius of Antioch* (Philadelphia: Fortress, 1985); and Thomas A. Robinson, *Ignatius of Antioch and the Parting of the Ways: Early Jewish-Christian Relations* (Grand Rapids: Baker Academic, 2009).
102. E.g., *Magn.* 8.2 (John 1:14; 17:16); *Magn.* 7.1 (John 5:19; 8:28); *Phld.* 7.1 (John 3:8); *Phld.* 9.1–2 (John 10:7, 9, 14; 17:20–23).
103. W. R. Schoedel, *Ignatius of Antioch* (Philadelphia: Fortress, 1985), refers to this passage as the "strongest possibility" that John is being used, but still remains uncertain (206).
104. W. Inge, "Ignatius," in *The New Testament and the Apostolic Fathers*, ed. A Committee of the Oxford Society of Historical Theology (Oxford: Clarendon, 1905), 61–83, at 83.

of the apostles and their writings suggests he would have regarded John as an authoritative source for the life of Jesus.[105]

Polycarp, bishop of Smyrna, also provides some links to Johannine writings—something that would not be surprising given Polycarp's personal knowledge of John himself.[106] Polycarp shows awareness of 1 John 3:8; 4:2–3; and 2 John 7, suggesting he was aware of some corpus of Johannine literature.[107] While there is no explicit use of the Gospel of John, we should remember that we have only a singular letter from Polycarp which, by virtue of its genre, would not be likely to draw upon a document that largely consists of historical narrative.

CONCLUSION

It has been our purpose here to review the early reception of John's Gospel, with a special focus on the second century. The impetus for this survey is the oft-repeated claim that John's Gospel was a favorite of "heretical" groups like the Gnostics and Valentinians, and that such associations caused a widespread hesitancy about John's Gospel among the "ortho-dox" communities. But neither of these claims can be substantiated by the historical evidence. As we observed above, there is surprisingly little evidence that John was a favorite of these "heretical" groups—indeed, all four Gospels were utilized by fringe groups from time to time. Even more notably, we see little indication that these purported associations affected John's reception.

On the contrary, by the end of the second century, and even by the middle, John's Gospel seems well-established and widely used, with no indication that there were serious doubts over its status. As for the early second century, the evidence is much more limited due to the paucity of the sources. But, even there, we see a number of notable echoes of John, suggesting it was being utilized by the likes of Papias and Ignatius, and possibly Polycarp.

---

105. C. E. Hill, "Ignatius and the Apostolate," in *Studia Patristica*, ed. M. F. Wiles and E. J. Yarnold (Leuven: Peeters, 2001), 226–48.

106. *Haer.* 3.3.4.

107. *Phil.* 7.1. Hill, *Johannine Corpus*, 419–20, argues there may also be links to John 3:8; 8:44; 19:34–35. For arguments that Polycarp did not know John, see Paul Hartog, *Polycarp and the New Testament: The Occasion, Rhetoric, Theme, and Unity of the Epistle to the Philippians and Its Allusions to New Testament Literature* (Tübingen: J.C.B. Mohr Siebeck [P. Siebeck], 2001); M. W. Holmes, "Polycarp of Smyrna, Epistle to the Philippians," in *The Writings of the Apostolic Fathers*, ed. Paul Foster (London: T&T Clark, 2007), 108–25.

So, we conclude where we began. It seems that John's Gospel may be one of the most popular Gospels today precisely because it was one of the most popular Gospels from the very start.

CHAPTER 12

THE ETERNAL PROCESSION OF THE HOLY SPIRIT IN THE GOSPEL ACCORDING TO JOHN

GREGG R. ALLISON

Andreas Köstenberger is a good friend and I trust he will be honored by this contribution to his well-deserved Festschrift. Andreas and I worked on our PhD at the same time at Trinity Evangelical Divinity School. When he became the general editor of the *Journal of the Evangelical Theological Society*, he asked me to become a book review editor for the disciplines of systematic theology, church history and historical theology, philosophy and philosophical theology, and the like. This long collaboration reached its high point with the coauthorship of a scholarly volume—*The Holy Spirit*—that brought together a biblical theologian and a systematic theologian on the topic of pneumatology.[1]

My essay develops one of the topics I treated in our book: the eternal procession of the Holy Spirit, with particular attention to the Gospel of John's contribution—and Thomas Aquinas's commentary on key passages of the Gospel—to that long-held doctrine. In terms of procedure, I discuss Trinitarian theology under two headings: first, the two eternal processions of the Son from the Father and the Holy Spirit from the Father and the Son, and, second, the two temporal missions of the Son and the Spirit that flow from and fittingly express the two eternal processions. As a note to my readers, I affirm with the tradition of the Western churches—the Roman Catholic Church and Protestant churches—the double procession of the Spirit

---

1. Gregg R. Allison and Andreas J. Köstenberger, *The Holy Spirit*, Theology for the People of God (Nashville: B&H Academic, 2020).

from the Father and the Son. I do not follow the Eastern churches and their traditional doctrine of the single procession of the Spirit from the Father (and not the Son).[2] Third, I present the relationship of the two processions and the two missions, concluding with several reasons why the eternal procession of the Holy Spirit is an important doctrine. Fourth, I offer biblical support for this doctrine from four key passages in the Gospel of John (14:15–17; 14:26; 15:26; 16:7, 13–15), joined with commentary on those Johannine passages from Thomas Aquinas, a major contributor to the doctrine.[3]

1. TRINITARIAN THEOLOGY: TWO PROCESSIONS

The church has historically affirmed two eternal processions of the triune God. By *procession* is meant a coming or going forth: thing A proceeds from thing B in terms of A coming forth from B. To speak of *trinitarian processions* requires an important qualifier and an explanation: the two are *eternal processions*, and they *constitute the three distinct Persons* of the Trinity. The first eternal trinitarian procession is called the *eternal generation* of the Son from the Father.[4] The first Person eternally generates the second Person such that the Son eternally comes forth from the Father. Biblical support includes John 5:26 (ESV): "For as the Father has life in himself, so he has granted the Son also to have life in himself." The Father eternally grants the Son his divine Person-of-the-Son.[5] The second eternal trinitar-

---

2. The doctrine of double procession found early articulation by Leo I (the Great) in his *Letter* 15 to Turribius in AD 447. He referred to the Holy Spirit as "the Other who proceeds from both [the Father and the Son]." The Athanasian Creed added its support: "The Holy Spirit is from the Father and the Son, neither made, nor created, nor begotten, but proceeding." The Third Council of Toledo (Spain) in 589 officially sanctioned this doctrine by modifying the Nicene-Constantinopolitan Creed by the addition of one word: *filioque* ("and the Son"). Thus, the Creed reads: "I believe in the Holy Spirit, the Lord and giver of life, who proceeds from the Father and the Son." I affirm this creed and the eternal procession of the Holy Spirit from the Father and the Son.

3. Thomas Aquinas, *Commentary on the Gospel of John: Chapters 13–21*, trans. Fabian Larcher and James A. Weisheipl (Washington, DC: Catholic University of America Press, 2010).

4. Though the theological term *begotten* may be used in these trinitarian discussions, such that "the Son is eternally *generated*" and "the Son is eternally *begotten*" are two interchangeable phrases, for simplicity's sake I will only use the term *generation*.

5. As to the definition of *procession*, debate continues over whether it is the divine nature or the divine Person that is eternally communicated. Even in the first case, the communication of the divine nature does not mean that the Son, the recipient of the first procession, comes into existence in the sense that he is divine in a way he previously was not, and that the Holy Spirit, the recipient of the second procession, comes into existence in the sense that he is divine in a way he previously was not. In other words, procession is not about lending, bestowing, borrowing, or deriving deity. As John Calvin affirmed, the three divine Persons are *autotheos*; the Father is God of himself, the Son is God of himself, and the Holy Spirit is God of himself. John Calvin, *Institutes of the Christian Religion*, 1.13.25, Library of Christian Classics (Philadelphia: Westminster, 1960), 21:153–54.

ian procession is called the *eternal procession* of the Holy Spirit from the Father and the Son. The first Person and second Person eternally separate the third Person such that the Spirit eternally comes forth from the Father and the Son.[6] With biblical support to follow, eternal procession means that the Father and the Son eternally grant the Holy Spirit his divine Person-of-the-Spirit. By these two processions, the three Persons of the Godhead are distinguishable from one another. Stephen Holmes presents this eternal action that God is as "the single, simple, unrepeatable, eternal generation-of-the-Son-and-procession-of-the Spirit."[7]

Three specifications are needed: First, this eternal divine operation of two processions is *the divine life* and not something distinguishable from it.[8] God simply is these two relations of the Father with the Son, and the Father and Son with the Holy Spirit. Second, these two processions are *necessary*: God eternally exists as Father, Son, and Holy Spirit related according to these two processions, and God could not be any other way. Third, these two processions are *incommunicable*. To the Father alone belongs eternal paternity; he is not generated, nor does he proceed.[9] To the Son alone belongs eternal sonship; he is eternally generated from the Father. To the Holy Spirit alone belongs eternal procession; he eternally proceeds from the Father and the Son.

2. TRINITARIAN THEOLOGY: TWO MISSIONS

From these two eternal processions flow two missions.[10] By *mission* is meant a sending: thing A engages on a mission as sent from thing B in terms of A embarking upon and accomplishing a specific operation on behalf of B. To speak of *trinitarian missions* requires an important qualifier and an explanation: the two are *temporal missions*, and they *establish a new relationship with created beings* to whom and on behalf of whom the missions are directed. The first temporal mission is the Father's sending of the Son that can be

---

6. The expression *eternal spiration* refers to the eternal action of the Father and the Son with respect to the Holy Spirit, with the corollary of the *eternal procession* of the Holy Spirit with respect to the Father and the Son.
7. Stephen R. Holmes, "Trinitarian Action and Inseparable Operations," in *Advancing Trinitarian Theology: Explorations in Constructive Dogmatics*, ed. Oliver D. Crisp and Fred Sanders (Grand Rapids: Zondervan, 2014), 71.
8. Holmes, "Trinitarian Action and Inseparable Operations," 71.
9. Processions are true only of the Son and the Holy Spirit because the Father is the source of the two and thus does not proceed.
10. For further discussion see Adonis Vidu, *The Divine Missions: An Introduction* (Eugene, OR: Cascade Books, 2022).

briefly described as the Son's incarnation and accomplishment of salvation on behalf of sinful human beings.[11] The second temporal mission is the Father and the Son's sending of the Holy Spirit that can be summarized as the Spirit's outpouring on the day of Pentecost and ongoing work of the application of salvation on behalf of sinful human beings.[12]

Three specifications arise and serve as contrasts with the two processions: First, these two missions *do not constitute the divine life* but are something distinguishable from it. God would still be God apart from them, that is, if the missions had never occurred. Second, these two missions are *contingent*: while God necessarily exists as the Father, the Son, and the Holy Spirit related according to the two processions, the triune God did not have to create, sovereignly rule, providentially provide, save human beings, and engage in other *ad extra* works, but was free to engage or not engage in the two missions. They are dependent on the divine will to send the Son and the Holy Spirit on mission. Third, though we distinguish the two missions in terms of both missional agent and missional purpose—the first is the Son's mission of incarnation and accomplishment of salvation, the second is the Spirit's mission of outpouring and application of salvation—they are *inextricably linked* according to the doctrine of the inseparable operations of the trinitarian Persons in their *ad extra* works.[13] "Indeed, the mission of the Holy Spirit is coextensive with the mission of the Word (the Lord Jesus Christ)."[14]

---

11. As is true of the next point, the mission of the Son and the mission of the Holy Spirit refer to their works in relation to the new covenant and should not be misunderstood as denying their divine operations previous to the Son's incarnation and the Spirit's outpouring. For further discussion of the Son's and Spirit's operations during the old covenant, see Allison and Köstenberger, *The Holy Spirit*, 347–50.

12. So as to avoid misunderstanding, the temporal sending of the Son does not mean that the second Person, who is eternal and omnipresent, came into existence at the moment of his incarnation. Similarly, the temporal sending of the Spirit does not mean that the third Person, who is eternal and omnipresent, came into existence at the moment he was poured out on the day of Pentecost. Thomas Aquinas explains that such movement "has no place in the mission of a divine person; for the divine person sent neither begins to exist where he did not previously exist, nor ceases to exist where he was [with the Father]." *Summa Theologica*, pt. 1, q. 43, art. 1, ad. 2. Matthew Levering adds, "Instead, the change described by a divine 'mission' consists in a creature gaining a new real relation to the Son or Holy Spirit, a relation of intimacy that elevates the creature into a participation in the trinitarian communion." Matthew Levering, *Engaging the Doctrine of the Holy Spirit: Love and Gift in the Trinity and the Church* (Grand Rapids: Baker Academic, 2016), 189.

13. For further discussion of inseparable operations, see Adonis Vidu, *The Same God Who Works All Things: An Exposition and Defense of the Doctrine of Inseparable Operations* (Grand Rapids: Eerdmans, 2020).

14. Christopher R. J. Holmes, *The Holy Spirit*, New Studies in Dogmatics (Grand Rapids: Zondervan Academic, 2015), 21; cf. 26–28.

3. THE RELATIONSHIP OF TRINITARIAN PROCESSIONS AND TRINITARIAN MISSIONS

"If we conceptualize (1) the trinitarian processions as the inner life and eternal relations of the Father, the Son, and the Holy Spirit, and (2) the trinitarian missions as the external activity and temporal works of the triune God, then we can consider (3) the trinitarian missions to be the trinitarian processions turned outside and in time."[15] The two eternal processions appropriately express themselves as the two temporal missions. As for the first eternal procession with the first temporal mission, the Son eternally proceeds, that is, is eternally generated, from the Father, who accordingly sent the Son on his temporal mission to become incarnate and accomplish the work of salvation on behalf of fallen human beings. As for the second eternal procession with the second temporal mission, the Holy Spirit eternally proceeds from the Father and the Son, who accordingly sent the Spirit on his temporal mission by pouring him out on the day of Pentecost for his work of applying salvation to the lives of fallen human beings. Diagrammatically:[16]

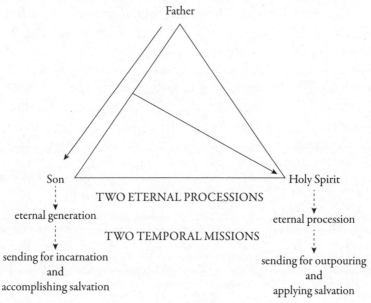

Figure 12.1 The relationship of Trinitarian processions and Trinitarian missions

---

15. Allison and Köstenberger, *The Holy Spirit*, 275–76. Thomas Aquinas addressed the relationship between the processions and the missions in *Summa Theologica*, pt. 1, q. 43, art. 2, ad. 3.
16. This diagram has been modified from Allison and Köstenberger, *The Holy Spirit*, 263, 276.

Using the traditional model of an equilateral triangle to symbolize the Trinity, this diagram represents that the two eternal processions—the eternal generation of the Son and the eternal procession of the Holy Spirit—express themselves as the two temporal missions of the Son and the Holy Spirit; the latter reflect the former: "There is an appropriateness to the incarnation and salvation as the particular mission of the Son as eternally generated by the Father. And there is an appropriateness to the outpouring and indwelling as the particular mission of the Holy Spirit as eternally proceeding from the Father and the Son."[17]

This discussion of eternal processions and temporal missions highlights the importance of our specific focus, the eternal procession of the Holy Spirit from the Father and the Son. To summarize, this eternal procession constitutes the third Person and distinguishes him from the other two Persons of the Trinity. This procession is (together with the eternal generation of the Son, one aspect of) the divine life and not something distinguishable from it. Indeed, this procession is both necessary and incommunicable, so when we think of who God is, we must also think of the eternal procession of the Spirit. Moreover, from this procession flows the logic of the temporal mission of the Holy Spirit. As appropriate to his procession from the first Person and the second Person, the Spirit was poured out on the day of Pentecost by the Father and the Son, sent for this work of applying the salvation accomplished by the incarnate Son (in accordance with his temporal mission) on behalf of sinful human beings. Thus, this relationship of procession and mission theologically grounds the work of the Holy Spirit, which is extensive and intensive and engages every aspect of redemption.[18]

Still, the question arises: Is the eternal procession of the Holy Spirit from the Father and the Son biblically warranted?[19]

---

17. Allison and Köstenberger, *The Holy Spirit*, 276–77.
18. For further discussion see Allison and Köstenberger, *The Holy Spirit*, 367–414.
19. A number of recent theologians (exemplified by John Feinberg, *No One Like Him: The Doctrine of God* [Wheaton, IL: Crossway, 2001]) deny this doctrine and present several reasons for their rejection of it: (1) Feinberg does not find an adequate biblical basis, averring that "biblical support seems limited primarily (if not exclusively) to John 15:26," particularly the phrase in reference to the Spirit as he "who proceeds from the Father" (491). (2) He does not make a connection between the sending/mission of the Holy Spirit and his eternal procession (491). (3) He lacks exegetical discussion of biblical passages used in support of the doctrine. For example, Feinberg does not address the difference in verb tenses between Jesus's promise that he "will send" (future tense) the Spirit (John 15:26; 16:7; cf. Jesus's promise that the Father "will give/send" the Spirit; 14:16, 26) and Jesus's statement (present tense) that the Spirit proceeds from the Father (491–92). (4) Feinberg objects that to interpret John 15:26 as referring to the eternal

4. THE ETERNAL PROCESSION OF THE HOLY SPIRIT ACCORDING TO THE GOSPEL OF JOHN

In his Upper Room Discourse (John 14–16), Jesus pledged a future coming of the Holy Spirit. It is particularly in this section of the Gospel of John that the church has historically grounded its doctrine of the eternal procession of the Spirit. These words of promise, together with commentary from Thomas Aquinas, are concentrated in four passages: John 14:15–17; 14:26; 15:26; and 16:7, 13–15. Before examining this biblical basis, a word about Aquinas's exegesis is in order, especially for those who are unfamiliar with this interpretive approach to Scripture.

Three points of explanation: First, Aquinas puts on display Augustine's hermeneutical principle that, according to Matthew Levering, "the Triune God wills to teach us about himself through Scripture, so that we might come to know and to love the living God. The faith-based expectation that God in Scripture is teaching us about his triunity leads Augustine to be alert for clues to the identity of the Holy Spirit."[20] As will become evident, interpreting the four passages in John's Gospel within a trinitarian framework that includes the eternal procession of the Holy Spirit from the Father and the Son, Aquinas understands these passages as affirming this double procession. One might say that Aquinas exemplifies what is currently referred to as theological interpretation of Scripture, prompting him to interpret these passages in a way conducive to supporting double procession.

Second, some may find Aquinas's exegesis perplexing at times, even outside of the traditional grammatical-historical-typological exegesis familiar to and employed by many evangelicals. For example, as we will see immediately below, Aquinas interprets Jesus's identification of the third Person as "the Spirit of truth" (John 14:16–17) as an affirmation that the third Person is "the Spirit of the Son" because Jesus is "the way, and the *truth*, and the life" (John 14:6 ESV, emphasis added). Though an interesting move, some will find it questionable at best. Nonetheless, we should not immediately dismiss such an interpretation as necessarily wrong. Quite the contrary: Paul affirms that the third Person is both "the

---

procession of the Spirit "means that we think the apostle John intended to make this subtle metaphysical point about the internal relations of the members of the Godhead," a metaphysical point that would not be made for several centuries until the early church councils—Nicaea and Constantinople—and the *filioque* controversy (492).

20. Levering, *Engaging the Doctrine of the Holy Spirit*, 54.

Spirit of God," that is, the Father, and "the Spirit of Christ," that is, the Son (Rom. 8:9). This may be a case of the right doctrine from the wrong biblical passage. All this to say that, though we may find it strange, we should be cautious in dismissing Aquinas's exegesis out of hand.

Third, some may be unfamiliar with Aquinas's metaphysical emphasis involving nature, characteristics, relations of origin, and the like. This dearth may be due to various factors and cannot be addressed in this short chapter. Thankfully, in recent years evangelical theology has experienced a revival of interest in metaphysics, so this lacuna may find resources to be filled in.[21]

John 14:15–17

To his commandment-keeping disciples (v. 15), Jesus promises (vv. 16–17), "I will ask the Father, and he will give you another Helper, to be with you forever, even the Spirit of truth, whom the world cannot receive, because it neither sees him nor knows him. You know him, for he dwells with you and will be in you" (ESV). Aquinas explains the promise: "the Father, *although not without the Son*, will give the Holy Spirit,"[22] a clear affirmation of the double sending of the Spirit on Pentecost, which elsewhere, as we will see, Aquinas traces to the double procession of the third Person. More specifically, Aquinas unpacks Jesus's descriptor of the Helper as "the Spirit of truth": "Jesus adds 'of truth' because *this Spirit proceeds from the Truth* and speaks the truth. . . . The Holy Spirit leads to the knowledge of the truth because *he proceeds from the Truth*, who says, 'I am the way, and the truth, and the life' (14:6)."[23] Simply put, the Spirit proceeds from the Son. Aquinas uses an analogy between human love and truth, and divine Love (the Holy Spirit) and Truth (the Son): "In us, love of the truth arises when we have conceived and considered truth. So also in God, Love proceeds from conceived Truth, which is the Son."[24] Thus, Jesus promises the sending of the Spirit from the Father and himself (the Son) on Pentecost because the Spirit proceeds from the Son and (clearly understood though not mentioned) the Father. Aquinas affirms double procession.

---

21. These resources include Oliver D. Crisp and Fred Sanders, eds., *The Third Person of the Trinity*, Explorations in Constructive Dogmatics (Grand Rapids: Zondervan Academic, 2020); Fred Sanders, *The Holy Spirit: An Introduction*, Short Studies in Systematic Theology (Wheaton, IL: Crossway, 2023); Holmes, *The Holy Spirit*.
22. Aquinas, *Commentary on the Gospel of John*, 1911.
23. Aquinas, *Commentary on the Gospel of John*, 1916.
24. Aquinas, *Commentary on the Gospel of John*, 1916.

John 14:26

Jesus continues with another specific promise of the sending of the Spirit: "The Helper, the Holy Spirit, whom the Father will send in my name, he will teach you all things and bring to your remembrance all that I have said to you."[25] Aquinas explains this "sending" in terms of "mission," which entails a new effect on creatures: "When Jesus says, 'whom the Father will send in my name,' he refers to the mission of the Spirit. We should not think the Spirit comes by a local motion, but rather by being in them [human beings] in a new way in which he was not before: 'When you send forth your Spirit, they are created,' that is, with a spiritual existence (Ps. 103:30)."[26] Aquinas again emphasizes the double sending and its substantial biblical basis in this section of John's Gospel:

> Notice that the Holy Spirit is sent by the Father and the Son. To show this Christ sometimes says that the Father sends him, as he does here [14:26]; and he sometimes says that he himself sends him, "I will send him to you" (16:7). Yet Christ never says that the Spirit is sent by the Father without mentioning himself. So, he says here, "whom the Father will send in my name." Nor does Christ say that the Spirit is sent by himself, the Son, without mentioning the Father: "the Paraclete, whom I shall send to you from the Father" (15:26).[27]

From the Father and the Son, the Holy Spirit would embark on his mission on the day of Pentecost.

Aquinas underscores an important detail in this verse: Jesus affirmed that "the Father will send [the Spirit] in my [i.e., the Son's] name. "Why does he say, 'in my name'?" wonders Aquinas.[28] He draws a parallel: "just as the Son comes in the name of the Father—'I have come in my Father's name' [John 5:43]—so the Holy Spirit comes in the name of the Son. Now the Son comes in the name of the Father not because he is the Father, but because he is the Son of the Father. In a similar way, the Holy Spirit comes in the name of the Son not because he was to be called the Son, but because he is the Spirit of the Son" (with appeal to Rom. 8:9, 29;

---

25. All Scripture references in this chapter will be taken from the ESV translation unless otherwise noted.
26. Aquinas, *Commentary on the Gospel of John*, 1956.
27. Aquinas, *Commentary on the Gospel of John*, 1956.
28. Aquinas, *Commentary on the Gospel of John*, 1957.

Gal. 4:6).[29] Importantly, Aquinas concludes his explanation with a nod to ontology: "The basis for this is the consubstantiality of the Son with the Father and of the Holy Spirit with the Son."[30] Behind the common nature of the three eternal Persons lurks the two processions, including the eternal procession of the Holy Spirit.

John 15:26

In his most extensive commentary on the procession of the Spirit,[31] Aquinas explains Jesus's words: "When the Counselor comes, *the one I will send to you from the Father*—the Spirit of truth *who proceeds from the Father*—he will testify about me." Aquinas notes Jesus's treatment of "the twofold procession of the Holy Spirit" under the headings of the *temporal procession* (mission) of the Spirit and the *eternal procession* of the Spirit:[32] As for the former, Jesus "mentions the temporal procession when he says, 'whom I shall send to you from the Father.'"[33] As before, Aquinas clarifies that such sending of the Spirit should not be understood as a change of location, for the Spirit is omnipresent, but to refer to the new effect in creatures: as the result of the Spirit being sent, he graciously indwells Jesus's disciples (1 Cor. 3:16) as never before. Importantly for our purpose, Aquinas affirms that the Spirit "is said to be sent to indicate his procession from another," that is, the Son, from whom the Spirit "sanctifies the rational creature by indwelling . . . , from whom he has it that he is, just as it is from another that the Son has whatever he does."[34] In other words, as the Son has from the Father everything that the Son does, so too the Spirit has from the Son everything that the Spirit does. Still, the Son alone does not send the Spirit, as Aquinas offers two points.

First, Aquinas underscores Jesus's teaching on the double sending of the Spirit on his *temporal mission*: "The Holy Spirit is sent by the Father and the Son together; and this is indicated in 'He showed me the river of the water of life,' that is, the Holy Spirit, 'flowing from the throne of God and of the Lamb,' that is, of Christ (Rev. 22:1). Therefore, when speaking of the sending of the Holy Spirit, he [Jesus] mentions the Father and

---

29. Aquinas, *Commentary on the Gospel of John*, 1957.
30. Aquinas, *Commentary on the Gospel of John*, 1957.
31. Aquinas, *Commentary on the Gospel of John*, 2061–65.
32. Aquinas, *Commentary on the Gospel of John*, 2061.
33. Aquinas, *Commentary on the Gospel of John*, 1957.
34. Aquinas, *Commentary on the Gospel of John*, 2061.

the Son, who send the Spirit by the same and equal power."[35] As before, Aquinas provides biblical warrant for this double sending: John 14:26 for the Father's sending ("but not without the Son"), and the current passage (15:26) for the Son's sending ("but not without the Father").[36] Aquinas concludes this explanation with a return to his earlier axiom: "whatever the Son does [sending the Holy Spirit] he has from the Father: 'The Son cannot do anything of himself' (5:19)."[37]

Second, Aquinas treats Jesus's teaching on the *eternal procession* of the Holy Spirit—"the Spirit of truth who proceeds from the Father"—affirming double eternal procession: the Holy Spirit proceeds from the Father and the Son. For Aquinas, and as we have seen earlier, Jesus "shows the Spirit as related to the Son when he says, 'the Spirit of truth,' for the Son is the Truth: 'I am the way, and the truth, and the life' (14:6)."[38] Moreover, Jesus shows the Spirit as related to the Father when he says, 'who proceeds from the Father.' So, to say that the Holy Spirit is the Spirit of truth, is the same as saying the Holy Spirit is the Spirit of the Son" (with appeal to Gal. 4:6).[39] Thus, as the Spirit of Truth and the Spirit of the Son, and as producing an effect in creatures in keeping with his source (i.e., the Son), the Holy Spirit "makes those to whom he is sent like the one [the Son] whose Spirit he is," in two ways: as the Spirit of Truth, he teaches the truth (John 16:13) and grants understanding (Job 32:8), and "because he is the Spirit of the Son, he produces sons" (Rom. 8:15).[40]

This affirmation of double procession immediately demands that the controversy between churches of the West and the East be addressed. Aquinas first underscores the obvious biblical problem that the Western churches' double procession encounters: Jesus affirms that the Holy Spirit "proceeds from the Father" without the *filioque* "and the Son." Accordingly, the Eastern churches "say that the Holy Spirit does not proceed from the Son but only from the Father."[41] Aquinas objects: "But this absolutely cannot be. For the Holy Spirit could not be distinguished from the Son unless he either proceeds from the Son, or on the other hand, the

---

35. Aquinas, *Commentary on the Gospel of John*, 2061.
36. Aquinas, *Commentary on the Gospel of John*, 2061.
37. Aquinas, *Commentary on the Gospel of John*, 2061.
38. Aquinas, *Commentary on the Gospel of John*, 2062.
39. Aquinas, *Commentary on the Gospel of John*, 2062.
40. Aquinas, *Commentary on the Gospel of John*, 2062.
41. Aquinas, *Commentary on the Gospel of John*, 2063.

Son proceeds from him (and no one claims this)."[42] As I've diagrammed elsewhere:[43]

the Son and the Holy Spirit must be related to each other by opposed relations; either:

Holy Spirit ⟶ Son
in relation to
(the Son is from the Holy Spirit, which nobody says)

or

Son ⟶ Holy Spirit
in relation to
(the Holy Spirit is from the Son, which we say)

By process of elimination, we arrive at the affirmation that the Holy Spirit proceeds from the Son.

Aquinas emphasizes that the distinction between the trinitarian Persons cannot be qualitative (i.e., pertaining to the divine attributes such as omnipotence, goodness, and holiness), as they share in the one divine essence. Rather, the only possible way to distinguish the Persons is by their opposed relations (i.e., different or distinct relations): "If, then, the Son and the Holy Spirit are distinct persons proceeding from the Father, they have to be distinguished by some properties [relations] that are opposed [different or distinct]. . . . So, in order for the Holy Spirit to be distinguished from the Son, they must have relations that are opposed, by which they will be opposed to each other."[44] Aquinas further explains that such opposed relations can only be "relations of origin, insofar as one person is from the other. Thus, it is impossible, granting the Trinity of persons, that the Holy Spirit not be from the Son."[45]

---

42. Aquinas, *Commentary on the Gospel of John*, 2063. For further discussion see Aquinas, ST I, q. 28, a. 3: "The very nature of relative opposition includes distinction. Hence, there must be real distinction in God, not, indeed, according to that which is absolute—namely, essence, wherein there is supreme unity and simplicity—but according to that which is relative." Cf. ST I, q. 36, a. 3.

43. Allison and Köstenberger, *The Holy Spirit*, 262 (with some modification).

44. Aquinas, *Commentary on the Gospel of John*, 2063.

45. Aquinas, *Commentary on the Gospel of John*, 2063. For further discussion see ST I, q. 36, a. 3.2.

Aquinas next addresses another proposal for distinguishing the Son and the Spirit, one that differs from his discussion of relations of origin: "Some say that the Holy Spirit and the Son are distinguished by the different ways they proceed, insofar as the Son is from the Father by being born [i.e., eternal generation] and the Holy Spirit by proceeding [i.e., eternal procession]."[46] Once again, Aquinas finds this proposal problematic, for it does not, indeed cannot, distinguish between what is received by the Son in being eternally generated from the Father and what is received by the Spirit as eternally proceeding from the Father: "For the very same nature is received by the Son by being born [generated] from the Father and by the Holy Spirit by proceeding."[47] That is, this proposal of different ways of proceeding fails because it envisions that what is communicated by both eternal generation and eternal procession is the same divine nature that is received by both the Son and the Spirit, which does not distinguish the two as distinct trinitarian persons. Aquinas concludes by returning to relations of origin: the Holy Spirit proceeds from the Father and the Son "insofar as the birth [i.e., eternal generation] of the Son is a principle[48] of the procession of the Holy Spirit."[49]

In so stating, Aquinas expresses Augustine's position that in generating (Augustine prefers the language of "begetting") the Son, the Father made it such that the Spirit would proceed from both of them:

> It is not to no purpose that in this Trinity, the Son and none other is called the Word of God, and the Holy Spirit and none other is called the Gift of God, and God the Father alone is he from whom the Word is born [i.e., eternal generation/begottenness], and from whom the Holy Spirit principally proceeds [i.e., eternal procession]. And, therefore, I have added the word *principally*, because we find that the Holy Spirit proceeds from the Son also. But the Father gave him [the Son] this too, not as to one already existing, and not yet having it; but whatever he gave to the only-begotten Word, he gave by begetting [generating] him. Therefore, he so

---

46. Aquinas, *Commentary on the Gospel of John*, 2064.
47. Aquinas, *Commentary on the Gospel of John*, 2064. For further discussion see ST I, q. 35, a. 2.
48. Here and elsewhere, a "principle" is "that from which something flows in any way whatsoever." Romanus Cessario, *The Seven Sacraments of the Catholic Church* (Grand Rapids: Baker Academic, 2022), 36.
49. Aquinas, *Commentary on the Gospel of John*, 2064.

begat [generated] him as that the common Gift should proceed from him also, and the Holy Spirit should be the Spirit of both.[50]

As Aquinas expresses it, "if the Holy Spirit were not from the Son, the Spirit would not be distinguished from the Son and procession would not be distinguished from birth [eternal generation]."[51]

From this point, Aquinas acknowledges that "even the Greeks [i.e., the Eastern churches] admit some order between the Son and the Holy Spirit. For they say that the Holy Spirit is of the Son, and that the Son acts through the Holy Spirit, but not conversely. And some even admit that the Holy Spirit is from the Son, but they will not concede that the Holy Spirit proceeds from the Son."[52] Aquinas rebukes the Eastern view for its "imprudence," highlighting the propriety of "the word 'procession' in all cases in which one thing is from another in any way. And so, this word, because it is so general, has been adapted to indicate the existence of the Holy Spirit as from the Son."[53] We may link Aquinas's point to our earlier discussion of the two eternal processions in God, with "processions" being applied, as just noted, "in all cases in which one thing is from another in any way." Thus, the first eternal procession—"which give(s) us the special term of 'generation'"—is that of the Son from the Father; and the second eternal procession is that of the Holy Spirit from (the Father and) the Son.[54]

Aquinas confronts a final objection to the double procession of the Spirit: "Nevertheless, some of the Greeks [i.e., the Eastern churches] assert that one should not say that the Holy Spirit proceeds *from* the Son because for them the preposition 'from' indicates a principle which is not from a principle, and this is so only of the Father."[55] Echoing Augustine's affirmation (cited above), Aquinas assesses the objection to be "not compelling because the Son with the Father is one principle of the Holy Spirit."[56] Specifically, Aquinas affirms that "the Son has it from the Father that the Son is a principle of the Holy Spirit"; accordingly, "it can be said that the

---

50. Augustine, *On the Trinity*, 15.17/29; NPNF, ed. Alexander Roberts, James Donaldson, Philip Schaff, and Henry Wace, 1st ser., 14 vols. (Peabody, MA: Hendrickson, 1994), 3:216.
51. Aquinas, *Commentary on the Gospel of John*, 2064.
52. Aquinas, *Commentary on the Gospel of John*, 2064.
53. Aquinas, *Commentary on the Gospel of John*, 2064.
54. Aquinas, *Commentary on the Gospel of John*, 2064.
55. Aquinas, *Commentary on the Gospel of John*, 2065.
56. Aquinas, *Commentary on the Gospel of John*, 2065.

Holy Spirit proceeds from the Son."[57] Still, Jesus's teaching is that the Holy Spirit "proceeds from the Father" (John 15:26), seemingly an affirmation of a single procession of the Spirit. Aquinas counters: "Nor does it make any difference that we read here, 'who proceeds from the Father' instead of 'from the Father and the Son.'"[58] He returns to his earlier biblical evidence from John's Gospel concerning the (temporal) sending of the Spirit: Jesus promises that he will send the Spirit and that the Father will send the Spirit (John 14:26; 15:26). This temporal sending of the Spirit from the Father and the Son supports the eternal procession of the Spirit from the Father and the Son. Additionally, Aquinas returns to his earlier evidence from the Spirit's identification as "the Spirit of truth"—in other words, for Aquinas, "the Spirit of the Son"—as support for his contention that "the Spirit proceeds from the Son. For . . . when the procession of the Holy Spirit is mentioned, the Son is always joined to the Father, and the Father to the Son; and, so, these different ways of expression indicate a distinction of persons."[59] Though the Father and the Son are two distinct Persons, they are the one principle from whom the Holy Spirit eternally proceeds.

John 16:7, 13–15

As he nears the end of his Upper Room Discourse, Jesus once again offers comfort to his disciples as he rehearses his forthcoming departure from them. In what was certainly another shocking revelation, Jesus promises that his departure will be advantageous for his disciples: "It is for your benefit that I go away, because if I don't go away the Counselor will not come to you. If I go, *I will send him to you*" (emphasis added). Though he does not again treat Jesus's affirmation that he (Jesus) would send the Spirit, Aquinas assumes that this sending confirms the double procession of the Spirit; that is, because the Spirit is temporally sent by the Son (and, by implication, by the Father) on Pentecost, such double sending supports the eternal procession of the Spirit by the Father and the Son.

After detailing the benefit to the world of the Spirit's coming (conviction of sin, righteousness, and judgment; vv. 8–11), Jesus notes both the limitation placed on his own current teaching of his disciples—at this stage in redemptive history, they were incapable of bearing it (v. 12)—and, by contrast, the

---

57. Aquinas, *Commentary on the Gospel of John*, 2065. For further discussion see Aquinas, ST I, q. 33, a. 1; I, q. 36, a. 4.
58. Aquinas, *Commentary on the Gospel of John*, 2065.
59. Aquinas, *Commentary on the Gospel of John*, 2065.

unlimited future teaching to be communicated by the sent Spirit: "When the Spirit of truth comes, he will guide you into all the truth, for he will not speak on his own authority, but whatever he hears he will speak, and he will declare to you the things that are to come. He will glorify me, for he will take what is mine and declare it to you. All that the Father has is mine; therefore I said that he will take what is mine and declare it to you" (vv. 13–15).

Aquinas capitalizes yet again to underscore the Spirit's procession from the Son: "since the Holy Spirit is from the Truth, it is appropriate that the Spirit teach the truth, and make those he teaches like the one who sent him."[60] As noted before, Aquinas identifies the Spirit of Truth as the Spirit of the Son, who is the Truth; thus, there is both "from-ness"—the Spirit is eternally *from* the Truth/the Son—and "sent-ness"—the Spirit is temporally *sent* by the Son.

As to the Spirit's teaching of the truth to the disciples, Aquinas explains that Jesus "excludes a difficulty which could have arisen. If the Holy Spirit will teach them, it seems that he is greater than Christ."[61] Aquinas summarizes Jesus's earlier affirmations of trinitarian revelation: the Father speaks and the Son hears and teaches that revelation (John 8:28; 12:49–50; 14:10); the Son speaks and the Holy Spirit hears and teaches that revelation (16:12–15); the Holy Spirit speaks and the disciples hear and teach that revelation (16:12–15; cf. 1 Cor. 2:10–13).[62] Because this trinitarian structure of divine revelation is true, the possible objection that the Spirit's teaching would make him superior to Christ is (in Aquinas's words, summarizing Jesus's explanation) "not true, because the Spirit will teach them by the power of the Father and the Son, for he will not speak from himself, but from me [Christ], because he will be *from* me."[63] Again, Aquinas capitalizes on this notion of "from-ness" to affirm the double procession of the Spirit: "Just as the Son does not act from himself but from the Father, so the Holy Spirit, because *he is from another, that is, from the Father and the Son*, will not speak from himself, but whatever he will hear by receiving knowledge as well as his essence from eternity, he will speak."[64]

---

60. Aquinas, *Commentary on the Gospel of John*, 2102.
61. Aquinas, *Commentary on the Gospel of John*, 2103.
62. For further discussion see Gregg R. Allison, "The Word of God and the People of God: The Mutual Relationship between Scripture and the Church," in *Scripture and the People of God: Essays in Honor of Wayne Grudem*, ed. John DelHousaye, John J. Hughes, and Jeff T. Purswell (Wheaton, IL: Crossway, 2018), 27–46.
63. Aquinas, *Commentary on the Gospel of John*, 2103.
64. Aquinas, *Commentary on the Gospel of John*, 2103.

Indeed, one aspect of the Spirit's forthcoming ministry—and thus another reason for the advantage of the Son's departure and the Spirit's coming in his place—is the Spirit's glorification of Christ (vv. 14–15). Aquinas underscores that this future pneumatological work further justifies the double procession of the Spirit:

> Now we see the reason why the Holy Spirit will glorify Christ: it is because the Son is the principle of the Holy Spirit. For everything which is from another manifests [glorifies] that from which it is. Thus, the Son manifests [glorifies] the Father because he is from the Father. And, so, because *the Holy Spirit is from the Son*, it is appropriate that the Spirit glorify the Son. He says, he will glorify me, for he will receive from me [ESV: take what is mine].[65]

As discussed earlier, the Son is the principle of the Holy Spirit, as is the Father; thus, Aquinas affirms the double procession of the Holy Spirit from the one (Father-Son) principle.

Aquinas understands Jesus's words "the Spirit will receive from me" to be a metaphysical affirmation, expanding it to include (1) the taxis in the relations of origin and (2) consubstantiality. First, in receiving from the Son (in terms of eternal procession), "the Holy Spirit receives his entire substance" from the Son, as the Son (in terms of eternal generation) receives his entire substance from the Father.[66] Furthermore, because this is an eternal receiving (eternal procession), it is not a reception of something that was lacking previously in the Spirit. Appealing to the parallel case of eternal generation, Aquinas explains "what the Son receives from the Father, the Son has from eternity"; correspondingly, "what the Holy Spirit receives from the Father and the Son, the Spirit has from eternity. Accordingly, the Holy Spirit receives from the Son like the Son receives from the Father. . . . Thus, when the expression 'to receive' is used of the divinity, it indicates an order in origin."[67] Once again, Aquinas affirms double procession.

Second, Aquinas explains that the notion of "receiving from" indicates consubstantiality of the three Persons. Interestingly, Aquinas underscores

---

65. Aquinas, *Commentary on the Gospel of John*, 2107. For further discussion see Aquinas, ST I, q. 36, a. 4.
66. Aquinas, *Commentary on the Gospel of John*, 2107.
67. Aquinas, *Commentary on the Gospel of John*, 2107.

the fact that because the Spirit receives "the whole substance of the Son," who is "the Word of God," the Spirit's future ministry will be that of declaring the Word of God to Jesus's disciples.[68]

Aquinas expands on the idea of consubstantiality, starting with the Father and Son.[69] Jesus affirmed that "all that the Father has is mine," a reference to the divine nature that is shared equally between the two Persons but that does not include the paternity of the Father (the first Person's unique eternal characteristic) or the filiation of the Son (the second Person's unique eternal characteristic). Moreover, Aquinas highlights the taxis of the first Person and the second Person:

> We have conceded that whatever the Father has the Son has, but not that the Son has it in the same order as the Father. For the Son has as receiving from another; while the Father has as giving to another. Thus, the distinction is not in what is had, but in the order of having. Now relations of this kind, that is, of fatherhood and sonship, signify a distinction of order: for fatherhood signifies a giving to another and sonship a receiving from another.[70]

He summarizes: "if fatherhood is compared to the essence of the Father, all that the Father has the Son has, because fatherhood is not other than the essence of the Father; but the Son does not have it in the same order."[71]

As for the Father and Son with the Holy Spirit, Aquinas returns to Jesus's affirmation that the Holy Spirit receives from the Son (v. 14): "If all things which the Father has are the Son's, and the Son is consubstantial to the Father, it is necessary that the Holy Spirit proceed from the Son as

---

68. Aquinas, *Commentary on the Gospel of John*, 2108.
69. Aquinas, *Commentary on the Gospel of John*, 2110–11.
70. Aquinas, *Commentary on the Gospel of John*, 2112. Aquinas offers a profound summary of relations of origin (2113): "One might ask whether a relation is something real in the divinity. It seems that it is: for if not, then since the divine persons are distinguished by relations, the distinction of the persons would not be real. The answer to this is that in the divinity a relation is considered in two ways. In one way, a relation is considered in comparison to the essence or person of the Father. And in this way the relation of Father is not other than the essence or person of the Father. In the other way, a relation can be considered in comparison to the opposite relation, for example, to sonship. In this way fatherhood is a real relation, because it signifies an order of the nature which the Father gives the Son by an eternal generation. And this order is really in God. Therefore, if fatherhood is compared to the essence of the Father, all that the Father has the Son has, because fatherhood is not other than the essence of the Father, but the Son does not have it in the same order, as was said."
71. Aquinas, *Commentary on the Gospel of John*, 2113.

he proceeds from the Father, as Hilary[72] and Didymus[73] argue."[74] Aquinas adds the missing apodosis; thus, we have this reconstructed argument:[75]

protasis:
if all that the Father has, he gives to the Son [except his paternity];
and if the Son is consubstantial with the Father;
apodosis:
then the Father gives his nature to the Son
implication (Aquinas's affirmation of double procession):
it is necessary that the Holy Spirit proceed from the Father and the Son

Specifically, Aquinas explains that the Holy Spirit receives the substance of the Father and the Son or, conversely, the Father and the Son give the divine substance to the Spirit:

> Thus, what is communicated to the Holy Spirit is what is common to the Father and the Son. Now in the divinity the principle of communication must be the same as what is communicated. And, so, if what is communicated to the Holy Spirit is as essence, that which communicates must be this essence. This essence, however, is common to the Father and the Son. So, if the Father gives his essence to the Holy Spirit, the Son must also do so. For this reason Jesus says, all that the Father has is mine. And if the Holy Spirit receives from the Father, he will also receive from the Son.[76]

Aquinas again champions the double procession of the Holy Spirit from the Father and the Son.

CONCLUSION

In his Upper Room Discourse (John 14–16), Jesus affirms several truths about the Holy Spirit:

---

72. Hilary of Poitiers, *On the Trinity*, 8.20; PL 10, col. 250–51; https://www.newadvent.org/fathers/330208.htm.
73. Didymus the Blind, *On the Holy Spirit*, 38; PL 23, col. 136A.
74. Aquinas, *Commentary on the Gospel of John*, 2114.
75. Aquinas, *Commentary on the Gospel of John*, 2115.
76. Aquinas, *Commentary on the Gospel of John*, 2115.

- "I will ask *the Father*, and he *will give you another Helper*, to be with you forever, even the Spirit of truth" (14:16–17, emphasis added).
- "The Helper, the Holy Spirit, whom *the Father will send in my name*" (14:26, emphasis added).
- "When the Counselor comes, *the one I will send to you from the Father*—the Spirit of truth *who proceeds from the Father*—he will testify about me" (15:26 CSB, emphasis added).
- "If I don't go away the Counselor will not come to you. If I go, *I will send him to you*" (16:7 CSB, emphasis added).

Jesus's words of promise express a tandem sending (the italicized sections) of the Holy Spirit: the Father, from whom the Spirit proceeds, will send the Holy Spirit (in Jesus's name), and Jesus himself will send the Holy Spirit (from the Father). This promise of sending pointed forward to the day of Pentecost, when the promise was fulfilled. This understanding is confirmed by Peter's words as he preached the gospel on that day: "Being therefore exalted at the right hand of God, and having received from the Father the promise of the Holy Spirit, he [Jesus] has poured out this that you yourselves are seeing and hearing" (Acts 2:33).

The question arises: Why did the Father and the Son (get to) send the Holy Spirit on Pentecost? The church's historical answer is the eternal procession of the Spirit from the Father and the Son. The Spirit's mission of being outpoured for the ongoing work of applying salvation to the lives of sinful human beings mirrors fittingly his eternal procession: he was sent by the first Person and the second Person because he eternally proceeds from the Father and the Son. Accordingly, to rightly think of God entails such an affirmation. Additionally, the mission upon which the Holy Spirit was sent by the Father and the Son produces the gracious effect on sinful human beings of applying the salvation accomplished by the incarnate Son as sent on his mission by the Father.

My friend Andreas Köstenberger has dedicated his life and ministry to making this gospel known. I dedicate this chapter to him.

CHAPTER 13

"BORN AGAIN" IN JOHANNINE THOUGHT

THOMAS R. SCHREINER

It is my pleasure to contribute to this volume celebrating the scholarship of Andreas Köstenberger. Andreas and I met in the early 1990s, collaborating on a book on 1 Timothy 2:9–15.[1] In God's providence this book has gone through three editions and has stood the test of time. Of course, Andreas has written voluminously on many other subjects, and I am thankful for his faithful and wise scholarship that has left a legacy for succeeding generations. I dedicate this brief essay on John's theology of regeneration to him.

1. SOME OLD TESTAMENT ANTECEDENTS

The verb *gennaō* in the Old Testament typically refers, as we would expect, to natural birth, to physical birth, to mothers giving birth to children. Still, we have a few interesting examples in the Old Testament where the verb is used metaphorically. We read in Deuteronomy 32:18 that "You ignored the Rock who gave you birth (γεννήσαντα, *gennēsanta*); you forgot the God who gave birth to you" (CSB).[2] The verse probably refers to the birth of Israel at the exodus, signaling its inauguration as a nation. Bratcher and Hatton rightly remark, "Some suggest that the writer deliberately used a male figure and a female figure; but it seems more reasonable to suppose that the two parallel lines have the same meaning, in both of them God

---

1. See *Women in the Church: An Interpretation and Application of 1 Timothy 2:9–15*, ed. Andreas Köstenberger and Thomas R. Schreiner, 3rd ed. (Wheaton, IL: Crossway, 2016).
2. Unless indicated otherwise, all translations are my own.

being compared to a mother."[3] Israel's beginning as a nation is traced to God giving birth to them as a mother gives birth to a child. The metaphor of the Lord birthing the nation points to his grace and power so that the nation is brought to life through divine action.

Another fascinating use of the metaphor of being born again, or of begetting, surfaces in Psalm 2:7, where the Lord says to the Davidic king, "You are my Son; today I have become your Father [γεγέννηκα, *gegennēka*]" (CSB). Traditionally the phrase in question is rendered, "today I have begotten you" (ESV). In the historical context of the psalm, the begetting of the Davidic king represents the day of his enthronement, the day he is installed and celebrated as king. New Testament writers apply this to Jesus's resurrection and ascension (Acts 13:33; Heb. 1:5), to his being exalted to God's right hand as Lord and Christ over all (cf. Acts 2:36). The metaphor signifies the close relationship between the Lord and the Davidic king, a familial relationship that is, of course, true in the deepest sense of the relationship of the eternal Son and the everlasting Father.

The last example from the Old Testament hails from Proverbs 8:25. "Before the mountains were established, prior to the hills, I was given birth [γεννᾷ, *genna*]." The reference here is to wisdom, and the author emphasizes in these famous verses that the created world was formed and shaped in the wisdom of God (Prov. 8:22–31). Obviously, the birth of wisdom is metaphorical, and we have a poetic reflection on the wisdom and artistry and beauty that informed the world as it was created by God.

2. "BORN AGAIN" IN OTHER NEW TESTAMENT WRITERS

2.1 Matthew

We have several other instances in the New Testament, apart from the Johannine corpus, where the authors speak of new birth or being born again. Jesus, in Matthew 19:28, envisions the renewal or regeneration (παλιγγενεσία, *palingenesia*) when the Son of Man will be enthroned and the apostles will rule over the twelve tribes of Israel. Here regeneration

---

3.   R. G. Bratcher and H. A. Hatton, *A Handbook on Deuteronomy* (New York: United Bible Societies, 2000), 546. But see M. J. J. Menken ("'Born of God' or 'Begotten by God'? A Translation Problem in the Johannine Writings?" *NovT* 51 [2009]: 352–68) who argues that the term means "begotten" and not "born" in the Johannine writings. Even if this is correct, it doesn't change the theological point, as he admits, and it is the theology of the text that I am pursuing in this essay.

isn't applied to new life but to the new creation, the new world that is coming. Trummer says that the term "designates faith in a new creative act of God and the 'hope of eternal life' (Titus 3:9)."[4] The term has a Stoic background but accords in Matthew with the new creation that is predicted in the Old Testament (Isa. 65:17; 66:22).[5]

2.2 Paul

Paul uses the language of giving birth on several occasions. In 1 Corinthians 4:15 he affirms that he gave birth (ἐγέννησα, *egennēsa*) to the Corinthians through the gospel, and it is clear that he means that the Corinthians were converted through his ministry. The same conception is present in Philemon 10 where Paul informs Philemon that he "gave birth" (ἐγέννησα, *egennēsa*) to Philemon's slave Onesimus when Onesimus visited him in prison. One of the reasons that Philemon should welcome back Onesimus with warmth and cordiality is that the latter was converted under Paul's ministry and is now "a dearly loved brother" (Philem. 16).

Metaphorical uses of the word "born" also surface in Paul's famous allegory in Galatians 4:21–31. Ishmael is described as the child "born [γεγέννηται, *gegennētai*] according to the flesh" (Gal. 4:23), and his birth accords with the Sinai covenant, and the children of that covenant (Gal. 4:24) "are borne [γεννῶσα, *gennōsa*] to slavery." In Galatians 4:29 Paul contrasts the child "born [γεννηθείς] according to the flesh," with the one born according to the Spirit. Some are born with a reliance on the human potential and human strength, but believers are born supernaturally and by the Spirit, and in this latter case the Pauline understanding matches in significant ways what we find in John.

Titus 3:5 is quite similar in this regard. The notion that works of the human being—that is, the righteousness of a human being—can be the root and origin of our new life is rejected. Instead, salvation is ascribed to the mercy of God, "to the washing that comes from the regeneration and renewal that stems from the Holy Spirit" (λουτροῦ παλιγγενεσίας καὶ ἀνακαινώσεως πνεύματος ἁγίου, *loutrou palingenesias kai anakainōseōs*

---

4.   P. Trummer, "παλιγγενεσία," *in Exegetical Dictionary of the New Testament*, ed. H. Balz and G. Schneider (Grand Rapids: Eerdmans, 93), 3:9.

5.   See John Nolland, *The Gospel of Matthew: A Commentary on the Greek Text*, NIGTC (Grand Rapids: Eerdmans, 2005), 798–99.

pneumatos hagiou).[6] The words "regeneration" (παλινγενεσίας) and "renewal" (ἀνακαινώσεως) should be understood as overlapping synonyms here, describing the new life of believers. As in Galatians 4:29, new life, regeneration, and being born anew comes from the Spirit and does not find its origin in human goodness or human choices.

2.3 Peter

The references to being born again in Peter accord with what we find in Paul, in the sense that new life comes from God. Believers are "born again" (ἀναγεννήσας, *anagennēsas*) because of God's abundant mercy (1 Peter 1:3), and thus praise belongs to the Lord for the new life believers enjoy. Leonard Goppelt remarks that the new life of Christians is not based on human choice or keeping a command, but finds its roots in the mercy of God.[7] The means by which believers are born anew is articulated in 1 Peter 1:23 in that we are "born again" (ἀναγεγεννημένοι, *anagegennēmenoi*) by means of God's living and enduring word. The miraculous nature of God's saving work continues to be underscored, though here the means God uses to produce new life is explicated.

3. "BORN AGAIN" IN JOHN

In approaching John's understanding of being born again we recognize that the metaphor is not limited to his writings. In the past scholars found roots for the concept of being born again in mystery writings, but such a notion has been rejected by most scholars today.

> Because some kind of spiritual transformation was taught by the mystery religions of the Roman world, scholars in the *religionsge-schichtliche Schule* at the end of the 19th cent. assumed that the NT writers had borrowed the concept of rebirth from their pagan environment. In fact, however, the vb. ἀναγεννάω is extremely rare outside Christian writers (the only comparable use is by the 4th-cent.-AD philosopher Sallustius, who speaks of initiates as ὥσπερ ἀναγεννωμένων [*De deis et mundo* 4]). . . . More impor-

---

6. "In the NT regeneration is not understood in a materialistic or magical fashion as in the mystery cults, as if it could be effected by lustrations and blood ceremonies. In short, baptism does not effect regeneration by its mere performance. Yet the least we must acknowledge is that baptism represents, witnesses to, and publicly validates the spiritual washing that is the work of the Spirit" (NIDNTTE 1.574).

7. Leonard Goppelt, *A Commentary on I Peter* (Grand Rapids: Eerdmans, 1993), 81.

tant, it is clear that the fundamental concerns of early Christianity, within the context of its Jewish background, are sufficient to account for the NT emphasis on new birth.[8]

John 1:13

The first reference to God giving birth to his children appears in John 1:13, where John says that those who are God's children "were born [ἐγεννήθησαν, *egennēthēsan*] not from blood, nor from the will of the flesh, nor from the will of the husband but from God." It is significant that being born of God surfaces in the Prologue (John 1:1–18) since the Prologue sets the stage for the entire Gospel. Borchert claims that the three phrases designate ways human beings attempt to gain favor with God.[9] It is more likely, however, that John contrasts human birth with God's work in regeneration so that blood refers to the mixing of bloods that takes place in birth, which is reflected in some English translations "not of natural descent" (CSB, NIV).

In the next two phrases John clarifies that new life does not come from the desire of the flesh, "flesh" standing for human desire or the human will. The last phrase probably points to the desire or will of a husband,[10] and is reflected in some translations (e.g., CSB, NET, NIV). We learn from this that receiving Christ, i.e., believing in his name (John 1:12), is not a natural event. The birth in view here is supernatural, a birth that stems from God himself. We should notice that the will of human beings is not absent since those who "become the children of God" do so by accepting, receiving, and believing, which represent human choices. This raises the question about the logical and temporal relationship between human beings receiving and believing and being born of God. Does one come before the other? Barrett says that the "birth is conditional upon receiving Christ and believing on his name."[11] Are they both present in equal proportions—a sort of fifty-fifty proposition? Perhaps the text is

---

8. NIDNTTE, 1.563. See also the studies of G. Wagner, *Pauline Baptism and the Pagan Mysteries: The Problem of the Pauline Doctrine of Baptism in Romans VI.1–11, in the Light of Its Religio-Historical "Parallels,"* trans. J. P. Smith (Edinburgh: Oliver & Boyd, 1967); A. J. M. Wedderburn, *Resurrection: Studies in Pauline Theology against Its Graeco-Roman Background*, WUNT 44 (Tübingen: Mohr Siebeck, 1987). They show that Christian baptism cannot be traced to the mystery religions.

9. Gerald L. Borchert, *John 1–11*, NAC (Nashville: Broadman & Holman, 1996), 118.

10. D. A. Carson, *The Gospel According to John*, PNTC (Grand Rapids: Eerdmans, 1991), 126; Colin G. Kruse, *John: An Introduction and Commentary*, TNTC (Downers Grove, IL: InterVarsity Press, 2003), 68.

11. C. K. Barrett, *The Gospel According to St. John*, 2nd ed. (Philadelphia: Westminster, 1978), 164.

indistinct so that we cannot draw any firm conclusions.[12] It is fair to say that John 1:12–13 on its own does not resolve the matter definitively. And yet, ruling out the human will as the source of the new birth in verse 13 (even if it is the will of the husband) suggests that being born of God precedes human receiving and believing.

John 3:1–8

The most famous text about being born in John's corpus is without doubt Jesus's conversation with Nicodemus in John 3. Many fascinating questions emerge in this text, but we will restrict ourselves to what we learn about regeneration. Nicodemus begins the conversation by commending Jesus as a teacher whose authority is supported by his miracles (John 3:1–2). Jesus ignores the compliment and takes the conversation in a startling direction (John 3:3), asserting that no one can see God's kingdom unless he or she is "born from above" (γεννηθῇ ἄνωθεν, *gennēthē anōthen*). The word ἄνωθεν clearly means above, and this is evident in John 3:31, and in other texts as well (Gen. 49:25; Josh. 3:16; James 3:15). At the same time the word can also mean "again" (see Gal. 4:9). It is doubtful we have to choose between these options since John is famous for double meanings, and thus Jesus emphasizes that one must be born above and again.[13] Being born above shows that new life is supernatural, a transcendent work of God, while being born again shows that physical birth is not sufficient.

Nicodemus is nonplussed and astonished, wondering what to make of what Jesus has just said. It seems senseless since we cannot enter into the wombs of our mothers and be born a second time. One of John's key themes emerges here in which those engaged with Jesus misunderstand what he says.[14] Often the misunderstanding occurs when people take what Jesus says literally, as in the case of the Samaritan woman who thinks that Jesus is offering her drinking water drawn from a well (John 4:11–12). Similarly, when Jesus said one must eat his flesh in order to believe, some were scandalized by the thought of consuming his physical flesh and drinking his blood (John 6:52). Nicodemus falls prey to a similar literal misunderstanding, and thus Jesus clarifies that entrance into

---

12. Carson, *Gospel According to John*, 126.
13. Cf. Barrett, *The Gospel According to St. John*, 205.
14. See D. A. Carson, "Understanding Misunderstandings in the Fourth Gospel," *TynBul* 33 (1982): 59–91.

God's kingdom belongs to those "born of water and Spirit" (γεννηθῇ ἐξ ὕδατος καὶ πνεύματος, *gennēthē ex hydatos kai pneumatos*, John 3:5).

Some have taken "water and Spirit" to refer to physical birth where water refers to the breaking of water before birth so that Jesus teaches that one must be born both physically and spiritually. This reading is not convincing for at least two reasons. First, both "water" and "Spirit" are preceded by one preposition (ἐξ), suggesting they should be read together as describing the same reality. The physical breaking of water, on the other hand, is contrary to new life from the Spirit. Second, a reference to physical birth should be rejected since such requirement is prosaic and obvious. Speaking of physical birth represents the errant construal of Nicodemus, and it is not picked up by Jesus.

A better solution is that we have a reference to John's baptism and regeneration by the Spirit,[15] but this fails as well since it also divides the two terms (water and Spirit) that are preceded by the same preposition (ἐξ). John's baptism was part of the old era, while the regenerating work of the Spirit cannot occur until Jesus is exalted (John 7:39). An even better solution is to see a reference to Christian baptism and the work of the Spirit, for this fits with the reference to water and to the new life that is attested by baptism. The problem with this reading is that Nicodemus, if we take the text seriously as a historical event and as an accurate representation of what was said to Nicodemus, would have no understanding of Christian baptism, though that doesn't entirely remove a reference to baptism, as we shall see. In any case, Linda Belleville rightly argues for an allusion to Ezekiel 36:25–27.[16] The Lord declares, "I will sprinkle you with pure water, and you will be clean from all your impurities. I will purify you from all your idols" (Ezek. 36:25 NET). Then in verse 27 he promises to give them the Spirit so that they will obey his instructions. The reference to Ezekiel explains why Jesus says to Nicodemus that he should understand, as a teacher in Israel, the Old Testament promise of being born again (John 3:9–10). At the same time, when the Gospel was completed, it is probably also the case that readers would see a reference to Christian baptism, which symbolizes the cleansing believers receive with water (cf. Eph. 5:26; Titus 3:5; 1 Peter 3:21). In any case, what

---

15. C. K. Barrett, *The Gospel According to St. John*, 203, though he sees a reference to Christian baptism as well (209).

16. Linda L. Belleville, "'Born of Water and Spirit': John 3:5," *TJ* 1 (1980): 125–41.

stands out is that being born again is a divine work, a work of the Spirit, a work where God cleanses and animates.

In verse 6 Jesus explains further that flesh begets flesh and Spirit begets spirit. The flesh cannot give birth to the spirit, which means that the flesh (standing for human capacity, potential, and energy) cannot produce new life. Only the Spirit can breathe life so that a new nature, a new being, becomes a reality. Thus, Nicodemus should not be astonished (θαυμάσῃς, *thaumasēs*) that it is necessary to be born from above/again (γεννηθῆναι ἄνωθεν, *gennēthēnai anōthen*). Nicodemus should be well aware (John 3:9–10) that life can only come from God, that only the Spirit of God can produce life where there is death. Nicodemus should know this because this is the message of the Scriptures. The dry bones in Ezekiel 37, symbolizing the spiritual and physical death of both Israel and Judah, will only come to life when the Spirit of God breathes on them, which is rendered as the "Spirit of life" (πνεῦμα ζωῆς, *pneuma zōēs*) in Ezekiel 37:5. We have a play of words on the word "breath" (πνεῦμα) here so that it can stand for both God's breath or the Spirit (see Ezek. 37:9–10). In Ezekiel 37:14 the Lord promises that he will give of his Spirit (πνεῦμα) and as a result people will live (ζήσεσθε, *zēsesthe*). Jesus almost certainly alludes to Ezekiel 37 along with Ezekiel 36 (as we have seen), and thus Nicodemus should have understood what Jesus taught.

Finally, an analogy between wind and the Spirit is drawn in John 3:8. The analogy makes sense since the word for wind and Spirit is the same in Greek (πνεῦμα). The wind is outside the control of human beings, blowing here and there apart from our constraint. We only hear its sound and see its effects, and we do not realize where it comes from and where it is going. What is true of the wind is also the case with "everyone being born from the Spirit" (πᾶς ὁ γεγεννημένος ἐκ τοῦ πνεύματος, *pas ho gegennēmenos ek tou pneumatos*). Being born of the Spirit, then, depends on God's sovereign will and does not stem from the will and direction of human beings. Jesus is informing Nicodemus that regeneration from the Spirit is a miracle, that only God can fit us to enter God's kingdom.

4. REGENERATION IN 1 JOHN

The verb for giving birth (γεννάω, *gennaō*) is quite prominent in 1 John with nine instances in this relatively short letter. John particularly ties regeneration to the moral life of believers, seeing the former as foundation and basis for the latter. In doing so, the grace of God functions as the foundation and basis for all good in the lives of those who belong to God.

1 John 2:29

The first usage of γεννάω is in 1 John 2:29 where John affirms, "If you know that he is righteous, you may be sure that everyone who practices righteousness has been born of him" (πᾶς ὁ ποιῶν τὴν δικαιοσύνην ἐξ αὐτοῦ γεγέννηται, *pas ho poiōn tēn dikaiosynēn ex autou gegennētai*). The "he" that is righteous is clearly Jesus as verse 28 verifies, and believers are to be like Jesus in that they practice righteousness, but it is probably the case, as Marshall argues, that the "him" in the phrase "of him" is a reference to God since he is the one who gives birth to believers.[17]

Arguments rage nowadays about the significance of the tenses in terms of verbal aspect with respect to New Testament Greek,[18] but I will argue that the use of the perfect tense with the verb γεννάω is exegetically significant. We see in 1 John 2:29 that the participle in the phrase "practices righteousness" (ὁ ποιῶν τὴν δικαιοσύνην) is in the present tense, while the verb "has been born" (γεγέννηται) is in the perfect tense. Jobes remarks that "the perfect tense [denotes] that the new birth precedes the ability to live righteously."[19] Certainly John is not saying that *first* we practice righteousness and as a result we are born from Christ. No, it is quite clear that first we are born and granted new life and the consequence and result is that believers practice righteousness (1 John 4:19).[20] The righteousness we do, therefore, is a result of God's grace.

1 John 3:9 and 5:18

The notion of being born of God surfaces again in 1 John 3:9. Here we are told that "everyone who has been born of God does not practice sin [Πᾶς ὁ γεγεννημένος ἐκ τοῦ θεοῦ ἁμαρτίαν οὐ ποιεῖ, *pas ho gegennēmenos ek tou theou hamartian ou poiei*], because his seed remains in him, and he is not able to sin because he has been born of God [ὅτι ἐκ τοῦ θεοῦ γεγέννηται, *hoti ek tou theou gegennētai*]." It is not my intention to resolve every question in this verse, especially the vexed issue of what is meant by

---

17. I. Howard Marshall, *The Epistles of John*, NICNT (Grand Rapids: Eerdmans, 1978), 168n13.
18. See, e.g., Robert E. Picirilli, "The Meaning of Tenses in New Testament Greek: Where Are We?" *JETS* 48 (2005): 533–55.
19. Karen H. Jobes, *1, 2, & 3 John*, ZECNT (Grand Rapids: Zondervan Academic, 2014), 140.
20. Rightly Marshall, *The Epistles of John*, 169.

God's seed since resolving that matter is not necessary for the purposes of this article.

It is instructive that not practicing sin is in the present tense in both the first instance (ἁμαρτίαν οὐ ποιεῖ) and the second instance (καὶ οὐ δύναται ἁμαρτάνειν, *kai ou dynatai hamartanein*) in which it is mentioned. Once again this stands in contrast to the word *born* so that both the participle "the one who has been born" (ὁ γεγεννημένος) and the indicative "he has been born" (γεγέννηται) are in the perfect tense. Just as we saw in 1 John 2:29, the present and perfect tense seem in this instance to be distinguished from one another.[21] John communicates that being born of God is the basis for believers not practicing sin.[22] The perfect tense precedes the present tense so that first one is born of God and the result is that one does not practice sin.

When John says that one is not able to sin, he does not mean that one is sinless, which would contradict both 1 John 1:8 and 10 where those who claim to be without sin are designated as liars and as those who are separated from the truth of the gospel. Certainly, John is not saying that not practicing sin precedes being born of God. On the contrary, the power over sin hails from new life that comes from God himself so that regeneration is the basis for the new life believers live.

We find a similar theme at the conclusion of the letter (5:18) where John declares, "We know that everyone who has been born of God does not sin, but the one who has been born of God keeps him, and the evil one doesn't touch him" (Οἴδαμεν ὅτι πᾶς ὁ γεγεννημένος ἐκ τοῦ θεοῦ οὐχ ἁμαρτάνει, ἀλλ' ὁ γεννηθεὶς ἐκ τοῦ θεοῦ τηρεῖ αὐτόν, καὶ ὁ πονηρὸς οὐχ ἅπτεται αὐτοῦ, *oidamen hoti pas ho gegennēmenos ek tou theou ouch hamartanei, all ho gennētheis ek tou theou tērei auto, kai ho ponēros ouch haptetai autou*). The pattern is the same in that the one born (ὁ γεγεννημένος) of God is a perfect participle, while not sinning (ἁμαρτάνει) is present tense. Kruse remarks, "By the use of a present tense form of the verb 'to sin', the author portrays the sinning here (as also in 3:9) as an ongoing process."[23] And "the perfect tense participle suggests the abiding results of regeneration."[24] The logic is clear, signaling as in 1 John 3:9 that being

---

21. I am not claiming that this distinction works everywhere in Greek literature or in the New Testament generally.
22. See here Robert W. Yarbrough, *1–3 John*, BECNT (Grand Rapids: Baker Academic, 2008), 195.
23. Colin G. Kruse, *The Letters of John*, PNTC (Grand Rapids: Eerdmans, 2000), 195.
24. Stephen S. Smalley, *1, 2, 3 John*, WBC (Nashville: Thomas Nelson, 2007), 289.

born of God frees believers from a pattern of sin. The second use of born (ὁ γεννηθεὶς) of God in the verse could refer to believers,[25] but it makes more sense to see here a reference to Jesus himself.[26] Every time we have a reference to believers John uses the perfect tense, but here he uses the aorist (γεννηθεὶς), and we see elsewhere in John's writings (John 17:12) that Jesus keeps believers.

1 John 4:7

One of the important themes in 1 John is the call to love one another, and in 1 John 4:7 the call to love one another is rooted in God's love. John goes on to say in the verse that "everyone who loves has been born of God and knows God" (πᾶς ὁ ἀγαπῶν ἐκ τοῦ θεοῦ γεγέννηται καὶ γινώσκει τὸν θεόν, *pas ho agapōn ek tou theou gegennētai kai ginōskei ton theon*). The tenses are again important as the participle describing love (ὁ ἀγαπῶν) is present tense as is the statement that those who love know (γινώσκει) God. Once again, however, the verb for born (γεγέννηται) is in the perfect tense. Loving one another in the present tense describes the characteristic action of believers and the present tense of the verb "know" signifies the present state of believers.

The pattern we have observed thus far emerges again. The perfect tense verb clarifies the relationship between love and being born of God. It is not the case that first we love and then as a result we are born of God; it is precisely the opposite. Those who have been born of God love one another as a consequence and fruit of being born of God.[27] In addition, those who have been born of God can be described as those who know God. The priority of grace is preserved in that regeneration produces love; new life from God leads to a transformation of one's actions and affections.

1 John 5:1, 4–5

We put together here 1 John 5:1, 4–5 since they both speak of being born of God and of faith. Verse 1 reads, "Everyone who believes that Jesus is the Christ has been born of God, and everyone who loves the begetter loves also the one born from him" (Πᾶς ὁ πιστεύων ὅτι Ἰησοῦς ἐστὶν ὁ χριστὸς, ἐκ τοῦ θεοῦ γεγέννηται, καὶ πᾶς ὁ ἀγαπῶν τὸν γεννήσαντα

---

25. Raymond E. Brown, *The Epistles of John*, AB (Garden City, NY: Doubleday, 1982), 620–22.
26. See Marshall, *The Epistles of John*, 252; Smalley, *1, 2, 3 John*, 289; Daniel L. Akin, *1, 2, 3 John*, NAC (Nashville: Broadman & Holman, 2001), 212; Yarbrough, *1–3 John*, 316.
27. Rightly Smalley, *1, 2, 3 John*, 227.

ἀγαπᾷ καὶ τὸν γεγεννημένον ἐξ αὐτοῦ, *pas ho pisteuōn hoti Iēsous estin ho christos, ek tou theou gegennētai, kai pas ho agapōn ton gennēsanta agapa ton gegennēmenon ex autou*). The pattern observed in 1 John 2:29; 3:9; 4:7; and 5:18 is present here as well. Believing (πιστεύων) and loving (*agapōn*) are characteristic acts of Christians and are in the present tense.

In the first instance we observe that those who believe Jesus is the Messiah have been born (γεγέννηται) of God, and the verb is in the perfect tense. We have noticed earlier that practicing righteousness, a pattern of victory over sin, and love for brothers and sisters are the consequence of being born of God. Since John follows the same grammatical pattern, it is fair to conclude that believing that Jesus is the Messiah is the consequence and result of being born of God.[28] To put it another way: regeneration precedes faith.

As Yarbrough says, "Spiritual rebirth seems to precede and ultimately create faith: those who believe do so not so much as the result of human volition as of prior divine intention."[29] The belief of Christians stems from the supernatural and miraculous work of God. Smalley misses the mark in saying, "The regenerate Christian (past) must constantly live out (present) his faith in Jesus as Messiah, and also give his sustained allegiance to the love command."[30] What Smalley says is true to the New Testament, but he strays from the meaning of this verse. Here, John is not exhorting believers but stating facts: the one who believes in Christ is born of God, and the one who loves God as the begetter also loves his children.

One more comment should be added to the claim that regeneration precedes faith. I was told on occasion that the first act of belief precedes regeneration, but the pattern of believing after the first act is the product of regeneration. But this is clearly mistaken, for no one would say on the basis of 1 John 2:29; 3:9; 4:7; and 5:18 that the first act of true righteousness, or the first occasion of true victory over sin, or the first time we genuinely loved brothers and sisters was something believers did before regeneration. Clearly, all true righteousness, love, and belief are a result of God's powerful grace.

John also speaks of God as the begetter (γεννήσαντα) here, as the one who produces new life in his children. Those who love God as the beget-

---

28. Rightly Yarbrough, *1–3 John*, 269. Brown (*The Epistles of John*, 535) thinks it is simultaneous.
29. Yarbrough, *1–3 John*, 270.
30. Smalley, *1, 2, 3 John*, 266–67.

ter also express love to the one begotten by him (τὸν γεγεννημένον ἐξ αὐτοῦ). The one begotten by him could refer to Jesus himself, but in no other case does the perfect tense of the verb γεννάω refer to Jesus, but in every other case refers to believers. Thus, John is almost certainly referring to believers here instead of to Jesus and affirming that those who love God also love fellow believers.

The last use of the phrase "born of God" is in 1 John 5:4–5, "Because everything being born of God overcomes [πᾶν τὸ γεγεννημένον ἐκ τοῦ θεοῦ νικᾷ, *pan to gegennēmenon ek tou theou nika*] the world; and this is the victory that overcomes the world, our faith. Who is the one who overcomes the world except the one who believes that Jesus is the Son of God." Our pattern stays consistent as the word for "born" (τὸ γεγεννημένον) is perfect tense, and the verb for "overcome" (νικᾷ) is present tense. The neuter refers here to persons, not things.[31] Thus, only those who have been born again overcome, showing again that life from God provides the resources to conquer. John goes on to say that overcoming can be traced to faith, to the one who believes that Jesus is the Christ. We saw in 1 John 5:1 that believing Jesus is the Messiah is not autonomous, certifying that all faith and obedience are rooted in God's astonishing grace.

CONCLUSION

John uses the verb γεννάω (give birth to) to designate God's supernatural and sovereign work in the lives of believers. We saw in John 3 that being born again can be traced to the prophecies in Ezekiel 36–37 that promise the transforming work of the Spirit in the lives of God's people. We also saw in 1 John that righteous living, victory over sin, a life of love, and belief in Jesus are the result of being born of God. Righteousness, triumph over sin, loving brothers and sisters, and faith are all marks of new life; they are not the means of regeneration but the product of it.

---

31. Rightly Yarbrough, *1–3 John*, 275.

CHAPTER 14

GOD'S PRESENCE AND THE ABSENCE OF TEARS (REV. 7:17; 21:4)

ECKHARD J. SCHNABEL

The description of the redeemed who have faithfully followed the Lamb and who stand before the throne of God (Rev. 7:15–17; 21:1–4) employs allusions to several prophetic passages. God will shelter them with his presence (Ezek. 37:27); they will never again hunger or thirst or suffer from the sun or heat because the Lamb, who is their shepherd, will lead them to springs of living water (Isa. 49:10); and God "will wipe away every tear from their eyes" (Rev. 7:17; 21:4; cf. Isa. 25:8).[1] The description of the new heaven and the new earth, which is the new Jerusalem, assures the redeemed that God will be present among his people and that he "will wipe every tear from their eyes" and that there will be no more death, mourning, crying, or pain (Rev. 21:4).

John Climacus, a seventh-century monk at the monastery of Mount Sinai, distinguished three levels of tears: contra-natural tears, which are triggered when the human will is thwarted (e.g., tears of anger, of jealousy, of frustration); natural tears caused by emotional and physical suffering, experienced by the person who weeps for another person for whom one feels sympathy (e.g., tears of grief, pain, compassion), which are tears

---

1. Unless otherwise noted, translations are taken from the NIV. Andreas Köstenberger has served the church with distinction for a long time, assisting pastors, students, and indeed all Jesus followers to have a proper understanding of Scripture and of their missionary and pastoral task. It is an honor to contribute to this Festschrift.

God's Presence and the Absence of Tears (Rev. 7:17; 21:4)

that contribute to our healing; supra-natural tears experienced by mystics (who call them "the gift of tears").[2]

The Dutch theologian Gisbertus Voetius developed a classification of tears in the seventeenth century in which he distinguished between a single specific state of mind and a complex, more general state of mind.[3] Remorse, suffering, and pity cause shame, anger, and sadness, which are negative emotions. Grace and honor as well as commitment to God and neighbors cause the positive emotions of desire, love, and joy, which also characterize devotion.

A recent model conceptualizes "a complex interaction of psychobiological, cognitive, and social processes" on the assumption that "emotions result from an individual's appraisal of memories and events in his or her environment."[4] When an individual (re-)appraises an objective situation via an internal representation and association (loss/separation, rejection, personal inadequacy, criticism/rebuke, positive appraisals), an emotional state ensues, which causes crying.[5]

Obviously, nobody who sheds tears follows consciously a particular model, presumably not even the most determined Stoic or modern academic. Before we analyze the tears in Revelation 7:17; 21:4, we will survey linguistic matters, the shedding of tears in Greco-Roman traditions, in Israel's traditions, and in other New Testament passages.

1. LINGUISTIC MATTERS

The reference to tears is one of many examples of the limited vocabulary used by the authors of the New Testament texts, who would have heard and used a wider range of words in their everyday encounters with Jesus

---

2. John Climacus, *The Ladder of Divine Ascent*, trans. C. Luibheid and N. Russell (Mahwah, NJ: Paulist, 1982); from Ad J. J. M. Vingerhoets, *Why Only Humans Weep: Unravelling the Mysteries of Tears* (Oxford: Oxford University Press, 2013), 444.

3. Gisbertus Voetius, "De tranen en huntegendeel, het lachen (1664)," in *De Praktijk der Godzaligheit*, ed. C. A. de Niet (Utrecht: Banier, 1996) taken from Vingerhoets, *Tears*, 245.

4. Ad J. J. M. Vingerhoets, Lauren M. Bylsma, and Jonathan Rottenberg, "Crying: A Biopychosocial Phenomenon," in *Tears in the Graeco-Roman World*, ed. T. Fögen (Berlin: De Gruyter, 2009),439–75, 452; their chart (453) has been published in Ad J. J. M. Vingerhoets et al., "Adult Crying: A Model and Review of the Literature," *Review of General Psychology*9 (2000):68–74; Vingerhoets, *Tears*, 6.

5. This process is influenced by instrumental, cognitive, and emotional support and by moderating factors such as demographic and personality, biological factors such as one's physical state or hormonal levels, and by situational factors such as social norms, location, and the presence of others.

followers and unbelievers. A search of BDAG yields two entries with the word "tear" indicated as part of the semantic range of the word:[6]

δακρύω: shed tears, *weep*[7]
δάκρυον: fluid that drops from the eye, *tear*[8]

In addition, we find seven entries that refer to phrases with a reference to tears:

κλαίω: weep, cry[9]
ἄνεσις: relief, rest, relaxation[10]
βρέχω: cause something to become wet[11]
διαλιμπάνω: stop, cease[12]
ἐπιβάλλω: put on; set to[13]
διὰ πολλῶν δακρύων: with many tears[14]
μετὰ δακρύων: in tears[15]

A consultation of LSJ yields a much richer semantic range of terms.[16] A total of one-hundred and ten Greek entries (verbs, adjectives and adverbs, and nouns, and assorted phrases) refer to tears. It seems impossible to convey the scope of the Greek vocabulary of tears without listing all

---

6. Walter Bauer, Frederick W. Danker, William F. Arndt, F. Wilbur Ginrich, *A Greek-English Lexikon of the New Testament and Other Early Christian Literature* (Chicago: University of Chicago Press, 2000). The definitions and glosses are taken from BDAG. The main terms δακρύω, δάκρυον, and κλαίω are mentioned first.

7. Attested in the NT once in the phrase ἐδάκρυσεν ὁ Ἰησοῦς, "Jesus wept," in John 11:35. The LXX has eight occurrences: Job 3:24; Ezek. 27:35; Mic. 2:6; 2 Macc. 4:37; 3 Macc. 4:4; 6:23; 4 Macc. 15:20; Sir. 12:16.

8. Attested in Luke 7:38, 44; Acts 20:19, 31; 2 Cor. 2:4; 2 Tim. 1:4; Heb. 5:7; 12:17; Rev. 7:17; 21:4.

9. Note the reference to Phil. 3:18: κλαίων λέγω ("I say with tears"). The NT has 40 references to κλαίειν, the LXX has 137 references (the first reference, in Gen. 21:16, refers to Hagar weeping about Ishmael).

10. *Acts of Paul* 6:5–6: εἰς [ἄ]νεσι[ν] τὸ λοιπὸν τὰ δάκρυα αὐτοῦ γενέ[σ]θαι ("so that his tears finally brought relief").

11. Luke 7:38: τοῖς δάκρυσιν ἤρξατο βρέχειν τοὺς πόδας αὐτοῦ ("she began to wet his feet with her tears"); 7:44: αὕτη δὲ τοῖς δάκρυσιν ἔβρεξέν μου τοὺς πόδας ("she wet my feet with her tears").

12. Acts 8:24 in Codex D: ὃς πολλὰ κλαίων οὐ διελίμπανεν ("who could not cease shedding many tears").

13. In the discussion of the phrase ἐπιβαλὼν ἔκλαιεν in Mark 14:72, suggesting that "both REB ('he burst into tears') and NRSVUE ('he broke down and wept') capture the sense" (BDAG s.v. ἐπιβάλλω 2b). CSB, NIV, RSV translate ἐπιβαλών "he broke down and wept."

14. 2 Cor. 2:4.

15. Heb. 5:7; 12:17.

16. Henry George Liddell, Robert Scott, and Henry Stuart Jones, *A Greek-English Lexicon*, new ninth edition revised and augmented throughout by Henry Stuart Jones, with the assistance of Roderick McKenzie, completed 1940, with revised supplement edited by Peter G. W. Glare (Oxford: Clarendon, 1996).

relevant terms. The evidence is as follows.[17] Fifty-five distinct terms refer to and describe the shedding of tears (eleven verbs, ten nouns, and thirty-four adjectives and adverbs).

δακρύω: weep, shed tears
δακυρροέω: melt into tears, shed tears
δακρυπλώω: swim with tears, of drunken men
δακρυχοέω: shed tears
ἀποδακρύω: weep much for, lament loudly; be melted to tears
ἐκδακρύω: burst into tears, weep aloud[18]
καταδακρύω: bewail; make weep, move to tears
δάκρυον: tear
δακρυογόνος: author of tears
δακρυόεις: tearful persons; things causing tears
δάκρυμα: that which is wept for, a subject for tears
δακρυοπετής: one making tears fall
δακρυοποιός: one inducing tears
δακρύρροια: shedding of tears
δακρυσταγή: one marked by flowing tears
ἀποδάκρυσις: flow of tears
δακρυότιμος: honored with tears
δακρύρροος: flowing with tears
δακρυσίστακτος: in floods of tears
δακρυτός: wept over, tearful
δακρυχαρής: delighting in tears
ἄδακρυς: tearless; costing no tears
ἄδακρυτος: without tears
αἰολόδακρυς: with glistening tears
ἀκριτόδακρυς: shedding floods of tears
ἀμφιδάκρυτος: all-tearful
ἀναγκόδακρυς: shedding forced tears
ἀξιοδάκρυτος: worthy of tears
ἀπειρόδακρυς: ignorant of tears
ἀποδακρυτικός: calling forth tears

---

17. The main terms δακρύω, δάκρυον, and κλαίω, and their compounds, are mentioned first. References to specific occurrences can be found in the LSJ entries.
18. Note the phrase ἐνδακρύω ὄμμασι: suffuse them with tears.

ἀρίδακρυς: very tearful
γλυκύδακρυς: shedding sweet tears
ἔνδακρυς: in tears
ἐπίδακρυς: tearful
ἑτοιμόδακρυς: easily moved to tears
εὐδάκρυτος: tearful
ἱερόδακρυς: with hallowed tears
πανδάκρυτος: all-tearful
περίδακρυς: tearful[19]
ποικιλόδακρυς: shedding many tears
πολύδακρυς: of or with many tears; hence: much-wept, lamented;
   tearful
πολυδάκρυτος: much-wept for; lamentable, tearful
πολυδάκρυτως: with many tears
ταχύδακρυς: soon moved to tears
φιλόδακρυς: loving tears, given to weeping
κλαΐω: cry, wail, lament; weep for, lament; bewail oneself, weep
   aloud[20]
ἀνακλαίω: weep aloud, burst into tears
ἐπικλαίω: weep in response to
ὑποκλαίω: shed secret tears
κλαιωμιλία: fellowship in tears
κλαυσίγελως: smiles mingled with tears
ἄκλαυτος: without funeral lamentation
ἐπίκλαυτος: tearful
παγκλαυστος: all-tearful
πολυκλαύστος: much lamented[21]

Many terms focus on the intensity of emotion that triggers a flood of tears, such as δακρύρροος (flowing with tears) and δακρυσίστακτος (in floods of tears). Noteworthy are characterizations of tears as "sweet tears" (γλυκύδακρυς), hallowed tears (ἱερόδακρυς), and smiles mingled with tears (κλαυσίγελως), and of persons who are honored with tears (δακρυότιμος), who delight in tears (δακρυχαρής), who are worthy of tears

---

19. Gloss on ἀμφιδάκρυτος.
20. Note the perfect participle passive κεκλαυμένος ("bathed in tears"). Note the phrase κλαίοντα καθιστάναι τινά ("*bring* one to tears").
21. Note the phrase πολυκλαυστος ποταμός ("swollen with tears").

(ἀξιοδάκρυτος), or who belong to a "fellowship in tears" (κλαιωμιλία). In addition to the distinct terms listed above, fifty-six entries in LSJ have phrases referring to tears:

δάκρυα δυσδάκρυτος: tears of anguish
δάκρυα νικηφορέω: to win naught but tears
δάκρυά τ' ὠμόργνυντο: they were drying their tears
δακρυσίστακτον ῥέος: stream of tears
δακρύων λιβάδες: streams of tears
δακρύων πένθιμον αἰδῶ: tears of grief and shame
δακρύων χάριν: if tears would serve[22]
ἀθρόος δάκρυ: one flood of tears
διάβροχος δάκουσι: tearful
διέξοδος: passage, of tears[23]
ἐλεεινός δάκρυον: a tear of pity
θαλερός κατὰ δάκρυ χέουσα: shedding big tears
Μεγαρέων δάκρυα: crocodile's tears[24]
μείζω ἢ κατὰ δάκρυα: too great for tears
πηγαὶ κλαυνάτων, δακρύων: streams of tears
ποθεινὴ δακρύοισι συμφορά: desired by tears, i.e., desiring, calling for tears
ποθεινός δάκρυα: tears of regret
πολιὸς δάκρυον ἐκβάλλων: shedding an old man's tear
τὰ σὰ δάκρυα μᾶλα ῥέοντι: your tears run like apples, i.e., big round tears[25]
τἀπ' ἐμοῦ σοφά, δάκρυα: my tears, all the resources that I have
ὑπὸ δακρύων βασανίζεσθαι: to be convicted of being painted by tears (washing off the cosmetic)
χλωρὸς δάκρυ: fresh, bursting tear
ᾀών: metaphorical, of the lower part of the face (over which the tears flow)
ἐκμάσσω: wipe off, wipe away; wipe away one's tears
ἐξ ὀμμάτων δὲ δίψιοι πίπτουσι σταγόνες: tears checked in their flow

---

22. LSJ s.v. χάρις: VI. special usages (1b).
23. Ps. 119:136 (LXX 118:136).
24. LSJ comments: "because of the quantity of onions grown near Megara."
25. From μῆλον ("apple").

ἐπιφορά: persistent flow of tears, as a disease; also of morbid humors

ἕρπω: of a tear stealing from the eye

ἵμερος . . . γόου ἵμερον ὦρσε: roused (in them) a yearning after tears[26]

καταλειβομένης ἄλγεσι πολλοῖς: melt away in tears[27]

καταρρήγνυμι: fall, rush down, of tears

κατασπένδω: honor with offerings of tears; lament with tears

λείβω: pour forth; let flow, shed; of tears: to be shed, pour forth[28]

λίβος: in tears

λιπαίνω: of the eyes: glistening with tears

λίπασυα ὀφθαλμῶν: a glistening of the eyes, i.e., a tear

μέζω κακὰ ἢ ὥστε ἀνακλαίειν: woes too great for tears

μύρω: flow, trickle[29]

νοτίζω: moisten, water[30]

ὀλοφύρομαι: beg with tears and lamentations

ὀμματοσταγεῖς πηγαί: founts of welling tears

πίμπλημι: fill[31]

πομφολύζω: bubble, boil up[32]

προσμύρομαι: make tearful lament in answer to

ῥήγνυμι: break asunder, rend; later: rend garments, in sign of grief[33]

σταγόνες . . . δυσχίμου πλημυρίδος: flood, deluge of tears

σταγών: drop; δίψιοι σ; of tears

στάζω: drop, let fall; especially of tears

ταρβαλέος: afflicted[34]

τέγγω: wet, moisten, frequently of tears[35]

τέρσομαι: to be or become dry[36]

τήκω: melt, to be moved, of being moved to tears[37]

ὑποπίμπλημι: fill[38]

---

26. LSJ: a desire of the soul to disburden itself in grief.

27. The verb ἀλγέω denotes feeling bodily pain, suffering, being ill; the verb καταλείβω means "pour down."

28. Note the phrase λείβομαι δάκρυσιν κόρας ("I have my eyes running with tears").

29. Note the phrases δάκρυσι μύρον ("they trickled with tears [of poisoned arrows]"); πολέες δ᾽ ἀμφ᾽ αὐτὸν ἑταῖροι μύρονθ᾽ ("melt into tears, shed tears").

30. Note the phrase νενοτισμένα χεῖτε δάκρυα ("wet tears").

31. Note the phrase δακρύων ἔπλησεν ἐμέ ("they filled me full of tears").

32. Note the phrase πομφόλυξαν δάκρυα ("tears gushed forth").

33. Also note the phrase δακρύων ῥήξασα . . . νάματα ("having let loose, having burst into floods of tears").

34. Note the expression ταρβαλέος δάκρυα ("tears of distress").

35. Note the phrase δάκρυσι κόλπους τέγγουσι ("wetting with tear-floods their bosoms").

36. Note the phrase ὄσσε δακρυόφιν τέρσοντο ("his eyes become dry from tears").

37. Note the phrase Ὀδυσσεὺς τήκετο ("Odysseus was moved to tears;" Homer, Od. 8.522).

38. Note the phrase ὑποπίμπλαμαι τοὺς ὀφθαλμοὺς δακρύων ("have my eyes *filling* with tears").

ὑποτρέχω: run in under[39]
φύρω: mix[40]
φύω: bring forth, produce[41]
χέω: pour, pour out[42]

Four verbs, for which compound forms exist, denote groaning, weeping, wailing, shrieking, and lamenting. Since the LSJ entries do not refer to tears, these verbs have not been included in the above statistics.

γοᾶν: groan, weep[43]
κωκύειν: shriek, wail
οἰμώζειν: wail aloud, lament
στενάχειν: groan, sigh, wail

2. TEARS IN THE GRECO-ROMAN WORLD

Hesiod writes of hateful Strife (Eris) which bore "painful Toil, and Forgetfulness, Famine, and tearful Pains (Ἄλγεα δακρυοέντα), Fights, Battles, Murders and Manslaughters, Quarrels, Lying Words, and Disputations, Lawlessness and Delusion."[44] In Homer's epic poems, crying was an essential element of the behavioral repertoire of the heroes: Odysseus and Achilles, Agamemnon and Antilochus, Patroclus and Telemachus, Priam and Hecabe, Helen and Penelope, cry often and with great emotion. The reasons for weeping and tears are, above all, rage, despair, personal loss, fear in battle and in hopeless situations, joy about a homecoming or an unexpected return, yearning for spouses or one's native land, and defeat in a sporting event.[45]

Hellenistic historiography exemplified by Herodotus, Thucydides, Xenophon, Timaeus, Polybius, Plutarch, and others, describe three prin-

---

39. Note the phrase ὡς τὸ δάκρυον συμπεπηγὸς ὑποτρέχειν ποιέῃς ("so as to make the coagulated tears run off").
40. Note the phrase δάκρυσιν εἵματ' ἔφυρον ("they wetted, sullied, their garments with tears").
41. Note the phrase γυνὴ . . . ἐπὶ δακρύοις ἔφυ ("the woman is by nature prone to tears").
42. Note the phrase χέω δάκρυα ("shed tears").
43. The term is used, together with δάκρυα χέειν and κλαίειν, for the ritual lamentation of the dead; cf. Dominique Arnould, *Le rire et les larmes dans la littérature grecque d'Homère à Platon*, Études anciennes 138 (Paris: Les Belles Lettres, 1990), 144–52.
44. Hesiod, *Theog.* 226–30. Cf. Glenn W. Most, *Hesiod. Theogony, Works and Days, Testimonia*, Hesiod I, LCL (Cambridge: Harvard University Press, 2006).
45. Sabine Föllinger, "Tears and Crying in Archaic Poetry (especially Homer)," in *Tears in the Graeco-Roman World*, ed. T. Fögen (Berlin: De Gruyter, 2009),17–36.

cipal categories: tears of despair that regulate distance from others; tears of supplication pleading for meeting one's need; and tears of joy that celebrate an event.[46] Tears for a fallen enemy and tears for human ephemerality[47] are rooted in Achilles's sympathies for Priam mourning his son Hector.[48]

As regards the Roman historians, Livy hardly ever questions the sincerity of people who shed tears. He seems to convey the notion that "true Romans do not cry false tears."[49] Shedding tears usually proves successful, as people who witness the weeping of a person may respond with empathetic tears and grant *misericordia*, the pity, mercy, and forgiveness that is being sought. Besides appealing tears, Livy describes inappropriate shedding of tears that evoke anger or disdain, tears of grief, tears of joy, and tears of distress. In Tacitus, wailing and shedding of tears is reported in all imaginable locations and among all groups of people, among friends and enemies, relatives and strangers, men and women, husbands and wives.

A survey of the literature points to the fact that situations that made Greeks and Romans cry are often remarkably similar to situations in which modern men and women cry.[50] Given the human condition in a world of life and death, love and war, friendship and enmity, this is not surprising.

Plato, who is not a typical representative on the matter of shedding tears, held that the gods never wept and that crying should be left to women and lower-class men while men and women of repute control their emotions.[51] Philodemus of Gadara, who had studied with Zeno of Sidon, the head of the Epicurean school in Athens, and who was the protégé of L. Calpurnius Piso Caesoninus, the father-in-law of Julius Caesar and consul in 58 BC, writes in his treatise *De morte* that death leaves behind "parents or children or a wife or certain others of those close to us" who will be "in dire straits on account of our death or even lack necessities"; this means that death has "of course a natural sting, and this alone, or more than anything else, stirs

---

46. Donald Lateiner, "Tears and Crying in Hellenic Historiography: Dacryology from Herodotus to Polybius," in *Tears in the Graeco-Roman World*, ed. T. Fögen (Berlin: De Gruyter, 2009),105–34, 107.
47. Xerxes, in Herodotus 7.45–52.
48. Homer, *Il.* 24.507–551; cf. Lateiner, "Tears," 121.
49. Loretana de Libero, "*Precibus ac lacrimis*: Tears in Roman Historiographers," in *Tears in the Graeco-Roman World*, ed. T. Fögen (Berlin: De Gruyter, 2009), 209–34, 215; for the following see Libero, 216–22.
50. Cf. Vingerhoets, *Tears*, 240.
51. Vingerhoets, *Tears*, 241.

up emotions of tears in the sensible man" (δ]α[κ]ρύων προέσεις ἐγείρει τῶι νοῦν ἔχοντ[ι] μόνον ἢ μάλιστα).[52]

Seneca takes a "disciplined Stoic line" in his last of five extant consolations, written to Marullus who has lost a young son and who bears the loss with less self-command than one can expect of a man of estimable character.[53] He admonishes him to mourn without grief since the death of a child does not deprive a parent of any positive good, the reason being that the child's character has not been fully formed. While a "bite" of mental pain is understandable, he should accept the loss with equanimity.[54] Attending the funeral of a member of the family without any outward display of grief or pain would be inhuman. While tears are not objectionable as such, virtue requires that Marullus relinquishes the error of thinking that death is inherently evil as well as the effort to conform to the expectations of others about how one should be grieving: "bursts of sobbing, beating oneself on the head, rolling off the couch, praying aloud for death" are conventional forms of grieving that are additions to the natural response to death performed in the presence of others.[55] Wise persons sheds tears when they weep involuntarily, tears flowing "of their own accord," and when they consciously "indulge" in tears as an expression of a positive response to the "element of sweetness" triggered by "the memory of the enjoyable conversations, the cheerful presence, and loving services of the departed."[56]

Plutarch, committed to the Stoic ideal of the "iron will" and the "self-disciplined guard to weep," reports weeping for secondary figures rather than for his "heroes."[57] In his *Parallel Lives*, "It is an almost typical test of a person's character whether or not he gives free rein to his tears on such occasions," a test which only "people possessed of particular

---

52. *P.Herc.* 807 col. 25, lines 2–10. W. Benjamin Henry, *Philodemus, On Death*, Writings from the Greco-Roman World 29 (Atlanta: Society of Biblical Literature, 2009), 56–57.

53. Margaret Graver, "The Weeping Wise: Stoic and Epicurean Consolations in Seneca's 99th Epistle," in *Tears in the Graeco-Roman World*, ed. T. Fögen (Berlin: De Gruyter, 2009),235–52, 236.

54. Seneca, *Ep.* 99.3, 14.

55. Graver, "Consolations," 239; Seneca, *Ep.* 99.12, 15, 16.

56. Graver, "Consolations," 240; Seneca, *Ep.* 99.28–19. For involuntary tears cf. Galen, *De placitis Hippocratis et Platonis* 4.7.16–17 (citing Chrysippus); Plutarch, *Virt. mor.* 449a; Cicero, *Tusc.* 3.82–83; also Philo, *QG* 2.57; 4.73 (Graver, "Consolations," 241–43; who points out that it is along these lines that Origen explains Jesus's weeping at Gethsemane in Matt 26:38–39, cf. *PG* 12.1741–1742). For eupathic tears, tears of "good emotion" or "proper feeling" (εὐπάθεια), cf. Cicero, *Tusc.* 4.12–15; Diogenes Laertius 7.115; Plutarch, *Virt. mor.* 449a.

57. Lateiner, "Tears," 129, 130; cf. his survey ibid., 128–32.

greatness of the soul" meet when they suffer the death of a loved one.[58] In the consolation written for his wife Timoxena on the occasion of the loss of a child, Plutarch argues that a self-controlled person displays continence in both joy and sorrow, which the masses who have an insatiable greed for lamentation mistake for an indication of a lack of parental love.[59] Zeus allowed Penthos, grief personified, to receive honors, but only "from humans who chose to give them freely."[60] Plutarch seems to have believed that crying immediately, after losing a loved one through death, and in the company of relatives, has a calming effect that hastens the end of grief.[61]

In Roman society, tears highlighted the importance of the family and of social virtues such as piety, faithfulness, mercy, and *civilitas*, while not weeping conveyed virtue, gravitas, and dignity; in courts of law, orators shed tears in order to elicit mercy and invoke clemency, and magistrates, senators, generals, and sometimes emperors wept when their authority was questioned or rejected, the tears aimed at establishing consensus and *fides* between groups of people of different social status.[62]

Tears are mentioned in papyri letters and in inscriptions on funerary epitaphs.[63] In a petition for protection from an unidentified official, the petitioner writes "with tears" (μετὰ δακρύων).[64] A hexameter text from the late Hellenistic or early imperial period refers to shedding many tears.[65] An unnamed author of a letter written circa 14–13 BC in Alexandria complains about having been slandered in the garden and house of a certain Terentius by a fellow slave and a fellow freedman in the presence

---

58. Stefan Schorn, "Tears of the Bereaved: Plutarch's *Consolatio ad uxorem*," in *Tears in the Graeco-Roman World*, ed. T. Fögen (Berlin: De Gruyter, 2009),335–65, 351, 356.
59. Plutarch, *Cons. Ux.* 4 (609a–b); Schorn, "Tears," 347–48.
60. Schorn, "Tears," 349; cf. Plutarch, *Cons. Ux.* 6 (609f).
61. Plutarch, *Cohib. Ira* 5 (455c); *Quast. Conv.* 3.8.2 (657a); Schorn, "Tears," 356–57.
62. Johan Vekselius, *Weeping for the res publica: Tears in Roman Political Culture* (Lund: Media-Tryck, Lund University, 2018); see ibid., 73–105 on the political use of tears of mourning; ibid., 107–86 on tears in Roman courts of law and on tears and authority. Cf. also Judith Hagen, *Die Tränen der Mächtigen und die Macht der Tränen. Eine emotionsgeschichtliche Untersuchung des Weinens in der kaiserzeitlichen Historiographie* (Stuttgart: Steiner, 2017).
63. Some papyri mentioning tears preserve fragments of Aeschylus (*P.Oxy.* XVIII 2162), Demosthenes (*P.Lond.* V 1814; *P.Oxy.* LXVII 4578), Euripides (*P.Oxy.* LIII 3716; LXVII 4457; 4558; 4559), Herodotus (*P.Oxy.* XLVIII 3381), Homer (*P.Oxy.* III 446; *PSI* XIII 1299; XVI 1580).
64. *P.Petr.* II 1, line 4.
65. *P.Oxy.* LXIX 4714, Frag. 1, lines 5, 17 (πολύδακρυ, δακυόεντος).

God's Presence and the Absence of Tears (Rev. 7:17; 21:4)

of Piramos, Philoxenos, and Hilaros, asserting that if it were possible he would be "writing tears, writing with tears."[66]

Numerous epitaphs mention tears.[67] The honorific herm set up for Aurelius Apphianus, a young man who was accidentally killed during a religious festival, contains the phrase "but about my fate the whole host shed tears," which is interpreted as "a common expression to create an emotional community."[68] A funerary epitaph from Miletus speaks of Lethe, the goddess of oblivion who represented one of the rivers of the Hades, who cast a dark shadow in which Polydamantis has died, so that only "tearful pains" (ἄλγεα δακρυοέντα) remain.[69] Another funerary epitaph from Miletus, set up for Demetria, the daughter of Antipatros and Philistias, mentions the shedding of tears (γενέταις δάκρυα) triggered by the reality that she was not born as immortal and that her life has not been free of the eternal rule of the daughter of Zeus, the goddess of Kythera, and the Moirai.[70] Lack of immortality explains why her mother now has to mourn for her, as she already had to mourn for Dionysos, Demetria's first husband, who died at sea and with whom she had a child.[71] An epitaph for Acilius Theodoros, a physician in Claudiopolis, Bithynia, mentions that his son Theodoros and his relative also named Theodoros buried him "while shedding tears" (ἐπιλελίβων δάκρυ).[72] An epitaph for Marcellus, a seven-year-old child who had died, mentions "wreaths, libations, tears (δακρύοις), and songs" with which people honored the tomb.[73]

---

66. *BGU* IV 1141, lines 27–28: δάκρυα σοὶ γράφειν γεγραφήκειν ἂν ἀπὸ τῶν δακρύων; for a German translation cf. Peter Arzt-Grabner, *2. Korinther*, Papyrologische Kommentare zum Neuen Testament 4 (Göttingen: Vandenhoeck & Ruprecht, 2014), 64–65.

67. *ISmyrna* 523; 531; 534; 543; 544; 549; 551; *IMiletos* 747; 2104; *IGLSyr* III.1 944 (Antioch); *SEG* XXXIX 1574 (Apameia); *IG* XIV 2437 (Massalia). The database of the Packard Humanities Institute (PHI) returns for the search δακρ 447 matches in 398 texts, most of which are funerary texts.

68. *IG* II² 3765, lines 12–13: ἀμφὶ δ' ἐμῆς μοίρης πᾶς ἐδάκρυσε λεώς (date: 226–234 BC). Cf. Christopher de Lisle, *Attic Inscriptions in UK Collections: Ashmolean Museum Oxford*, Attic Inscriptions in UK Collections 11 (Oxford: https://www.atticinscriptions.com/papers/aiuk-11/, 2020), 123–28 (no. 16), quotation ibid., 126. Cf. Angelos Chaniotis, "Displaying Emotional Community: The Epigraphic Evidence," in *Emotion and Persuasion in Classical Antiquity*, ed. E. Sanders and M. Johncock (Stuttgart: Steiner, 2016), 93–112, 106, who points to *IG* II² 7447 and other inscriptions.

69. *IMiletos* 746 (III BC). Cf. Werner Peek, "Milesische Versinschriften," *ZPE*7 (1971):193–226, 216–17 (no. 13).

70. *IMiletos* 738 (date: II BC). Aphrodite, the goddess of Kytheras, was sometimes regarded as the oldest of the Fates; cf. Pausanias 10.24.4.

71. Cf. Peter Herrmann, "Grabepigramme von der milesischen Halbinsel," *Hermes* 86 (1958):117–21; Peter Herrmann, *Inschriften von Milet II*, Milet VI.ii (Berlin: De Gruyter, 1998), 70–71 (no. 738).

72. Reinhold Merkelbach and Josef Stauber, *Steinepigramme aus dem griechischen Osten* (Stuttgart/München: Teubner/Saur, 1998–2004), 2:239 (date: I/II AD).

73. *IEphesos* 2103 (date: AD 150–200).

3. TEARS IN ISRAEL'S TRADITIONS

The Hebrew noun meaning "tears" (דִּמְעָה) occurs twenty-four times in the Old Testament,[74] the verb דמע only in Jeremiah 13:17.[75] The LXX translates invariably with δάκρυον and δακρύειν.[76] The references to weeping are more extensive: בכה ("to weep") occurs 113 times;[77] translated in LXX with κλάιειν and ἀποκλαίειν,[78] the noun בְּכִי ("weeping") occurs thirty times.[79]

The most memorable passages mentioning tears are found in psalms of lament. David expresses anguish during a sickness, which brings him close to death, with the words, "all night long I flood my bed with weeping and drench my couch with tears" (Ps. 6:6). Exhaustion triggered tears so profuse that they cause his bed to be flooded, the insomnia triggered by the pain of the illness and also by "the spiritual anguish and sense of separation from God."[80] In another psalm in which David writes of oppression, with lament and confidence alternating, he asks God to "record my misery" followed by the line, "put thou my tears in thy bottle" (Ps. 56:8, RSV; cf. CSB, ESV, NASB, NRSVUE).[81] The metaphor of keeping tears in a "skin bottle" or flask conveys the idea that the "tears of lament be preserved with care similar to that given to water, wine, or milk," which is "especially meaningful in dry climates where fluids must be treated with great care lest they be lost and unavailable when needed."[82] There

---

74. 2 Kings 20:5; Pss. 6:7; 39:13; 42:4; 56:9; 80:6[bis]; 116:8; 126:5; Eccl. 4:1; Isa. 16:9; 25:8; 38:5; Jer. 8:23; 9:17; 13:17; 14:17; 31:16; Lam. 1:2; 2:11, 18; Ezek. 24:16; Mal. 2:13.

75. Cf. Isa. 15:9 (conj.); also Sir. 12:16.

76. For the verb see also Micah 2:6 where LXX has μὴ κλαίετε δάκρυσιν, μηδὲ δακρυέτωσαν ἐπὶ τούτοις ("stop weeping with tears, nor let them shed tears over these matters"; NETS), for MT אַל־תַּטִּפוּ יַטִּיפוּן ("'do not preach—thus they preach—one should not preach of such things"; NRSVUE); also Ezekiel 27:35 where the kings of the islands "cried tears" (ἐδάκρυσε τὸ πρόσωπον αὐτῶν; MT reads רָעֲמוּ פָּנִים, "their faces are convulsed"; NRSVUE).

77. V. Hamp, *TDOT* 2:116–20; for the Qumran literature cf. F. Zanella, *TWQ* 1:446–49.

78. E.g., Gen. 21:16; 28:38; 29:11; Ps. 137:1 (LXX 136:1); Eccl. 3:4; for ἀποκλαίειν cf. Prov. 26:24; Jer. 31:32; 38:15.

79. E.g., Gen. 45:2; Deut. 34:8; 2 Sam. 13:36; 2 Kings 20:3; Pss. 30:6; 102:10; Job 16:16; Isa. 15:3–4; Jer. 3:21; Mal. 2:13.

80. Peter C. Craigie, *Psalms 1–50*, WBC 19 (Dallas: Word, 1983), 93.

81. Marvin E. Tate, *Psalms 51–100*, WBC 20 (Dallas: Word, 1990), 67, accepts the conventional translation, but comments, "The word refers to a skin bottle used for water, milk, or wine (Josh. 9:4, 13; Judg. 4:19; also Job 14:17; Hos. 13:12)"; thus NET ("put my tears in your leather container").

82. Tate, *Psalms 51–100*, 70–71. Cf. NIV ("record my misery; list my tears on your scroll"). Despite the fact that one can buy "tear bottles" on Amazon, the claim of the online "tear catcher shop" that the use of small containers made of glass, stone, or ceramic, usually shaped like a teardrop for collecting the tears of mourners, can be traced back to ancient Greece and Rome, is a myth. The only "authority" for the suggestion of "tear bottles" is Psalm 56:8. The unguentaria (sometimes called *lacrimarii*, or "tears vessels") found in graves probably stored oils or perfumes; cf. Catriona Hodge, "A Container of Grief? The Myth of

is no evidence that people collected their tears in Old Testament times. The psalmist uses "a metaphor for keeping the tears so as to keep them in mind."[83] The sons of Korah invite the people to formulate their suffering with the words, "My tears have been my food day and night, while people say to me all day long, 'Where is your God?'" (Ps. 42:3). Despair amid personal trouble, whether it be sickness or other calamities, triggers a sense of having been deserted by God: instead of being sustained by a sense of the presence of God, the sufferer feeds on tears instead of being refreshed by God's presence. God assures King Hezekiah that he has heard his prayers and seen his tears and that he will heal him from his serious illness (2 Kings 20:5).

The divine lament over Israel's sin is expressed in the contrary-to-fact wish, "O that my head were a spring of water, and my eyes a fountain of tears, so that I might weep day and night for the slain of my poor people!" (Jer. 9:1 NRSVUE).[84] Ezekiel and Malachi speak of people "weeping for Tammuz" (Ezek. 8:14) and covering the altar with tears because God "no longer regards the offering or accepts it with favor" (Mal. 2:13 NRSVUE); the latter is also "an attack on foreign cultic weeping in Jerusalem by which the temple was being profaned."[85] The lament over Jerusalem's devastation in 587–586 BC uses the metaphor of the grieving widow who "weeps bitterly in the night, with tears on her cheeks" because she has no one to comfort her (Lam. 1:2 NRSVUE). The prophet's eyes "are spent with weeping" (Lam. 2:11 NRSVUE; translated in LXX with the phrase ἐξέλιπον ἐν δάκρυσιν οἱ ὀφθαλμοί μου, "my eyes failed in tears," NETS). He asks God's people to "let tears stream down like a torrent day and night" (Lam. 2:18 NRSVUE), an image which stresses "urgency and power."[86]

When Ptolemy IV, Philopator of Egypt, attempted to enter the temple in Jerusalem, despite being informed that this was not possible,

---

the Tear Bottle," *ethnographica.net* 9/18 (2017); Virginia R. Anderson-Stojanović, "The Chronology and Function of Ceramic Unguentaria," *AJA* 91 (1987):105–22; Susan I. Rotroff, "Fusiform Unguentaria," in *Hellenistic Pottery: The Plain Wares*, The Athenian Agora XXXIII, ed. S. I. Rotroff (Princeton: The American School of Classical Studies at Athens, 2006),137–60; Vingerhoets, *Tears*, 240.

83. John Goldingay, *Psalms*, Baker Commentary on the Old Testament Wisdom and Psalms (Grand Rapids: Baker Academic, 2006–8), 2:187.

84. Page Kelley, in Peter C. Craigie, Page H. Kelley, and Joel F. Drinkard, *Jeremiah 1–25*, WBC 26 (Dallas: Word, 1991), 144.

85. Ralph L. Smith, *Micah-Malachi*, WBC 32 (Dallas: Word, 1984), 322, quoting Flemming F. Hvidberg, *Weeping and Laughter in the Old Testament*, trans. N. Hauslund (Leiden: Brill, 1962), 120.

86. Paul R. House, *Lamentations*, WBC 23B (Dallas: Word, 2004), 392.

the priests "prostrated themselves and entreated the supreme God to aid in the present situation and to avert the violence of this evil design, and they filled the temple with cries and tears" (κραυγῆς τε μετὰ δακρύων; 3 Macc. 1:16). When Jews were deported to Alexandria, some of their enemies had pity and "reflected on the uncertainty of life and shed tears at the most miserable expulsion of these people" (3 Macc. 4:4). When Maccabaeus and his men heard that Lysias, the general of Antiochus IV, besieged their fortresses, "they and all the people, with lamentations and tears [μετὰ ὀδυρμῶν καὶ δακρύων], prayed the Lord to send a good angel to save Israel" (2 Macc. 11:6).

The difference between "tears" (הָעֶמְךָ; δάκρυα) and "weeping" (עמד; κλαίειν) can be assigned to the origin of the physical expression of emotion: the former comes from the eyes, the latter from the mouth and voice, though the two expressions are often connected.[87] Weeping occurs in connection with the joy of meeting a person one has not heard from or seen for a long time,[88] anger and anxiety,[89] emotional grief,[90] mourning for the dead,[91] lament over individual distress,[92] collective lament,[93] acts of repentance,[94] awe in view of one's consciousness of the almighty God,[95] and the promise that God will wipe away tears from all faces.[96] Indeed, there is "a time to weep and a time to laugh" (Eccl. 3:4), although at times weeping is predominant: "By the rivers of Babylon, there we sat down and there we wept when we remembered Zion" (Ps. 137:1 NRSVUE).

4. TEARS IN THE NEW TESTAMENT

On the occasion of a banquet given by a Pharisee named Simon, an unnamed woman who had brought an alabaster flask of ointment stood at Jesus's feet, weeping, and "began to wet his feet with her tears" (τοῖς

---

87. Cf. V. Hamp, *TDOT* 2:117, with reference to Terence Collins, "The Physiology of Tears in the OT," *CBQ*33 (1971):18–38, 185–97. For the connection between the two terms cf. Isa. 16:9; Jer. 8:23[9:1]; 13:17; 31:16; Ezek. 24:16; Mal. 2:12; Ps. 126:5–6; Lam. 1:2, 16. For the following cf. Hamp, *TDOT* 2:117–20.

88. Cf. Gen. 29:11; 33:4; 42:24; 43:30; cf. 4Q197 Frag. 4 III, 8; 4Q538 Frag. 1–2, 6.

89. Judg. 14:16–17; Jer. 31:9; 50:4.

90. Ruth 1:9, 14; 1 Sam. 1:7, 8, 10; 11:4; 2 Sam. 15:23, 30; 2 Kings 8:11–12; Ps. 137:1; Isa. 15:3, 5; Jer. 8:23[9:1]; cf. 4Q179 II, 9; 4Q383 I, 2.

91. 2 Sam. 1:11–12, 24; 3:32–34; Eccl. 12:5; Isa. 15:2–6; Amos 5:16–17.

92. Deut. 1:45; 2 Kings 20:3; Ps. 6:7–9; Isa. 30:19.

93. Judg. 20:23, 26; 21:2; Jer. 3:21; Lam. 2:18; Zech. 7:3; Mal. 2:13.

94. Ezra 10:1; Neh. 1:4; Joel 2:12–17.

95. Neh. 8:9; Hos. 12:5; also Ps. 95:6 (LXX 64:6).

96. Isa. 25:8; cf. 65:19.

δάκρυσιν; Luke 7:38; her tears are mentioned by Jesus when he defends her action).[97] Her tears seem to have been tears of joy on account of her experience of the forgiveness of her sins by Jesus, although they also express repentance.

In Paul's review of his missionary ministry in Ephesus, he states that he "served the Lord with great humility and with tears" (μετὰ πάσης ταπεινοφροσύνης καὶ δακρύων; Acts 20:19). The following reference to "the trials that came to me through the plots of the Jews" suggests that Paul's tears were caused by his anguish and sorrow due to the unbelief of Jews in Ephesus who continued to devise plots meant to harm him.[98] When he reminds the Ephesian elders that "for three years I never stopped warning each of you night and day with tears [μετὰ δακρύων]" (Acts 20:31), he highlights his intense personal involvement. Paul clarifies that when he wrote the severe letter to the congregation in Corinth, he wrote "out of great distress and anguish of heart and with many tears [διὰ πολλῶν δακρύων], not to grieve you but to let you know the depth of my love for you" (2 Cor. 2:4). The great distress triggered by the difficult situation in the congregation that he had planted several years earlier, and which caused him anguish and grief (2:5), caused tears to flow. The reference to his deep love for the believers in Corinth indicates that the tears were probably caused by mixed emotions: anger triggered by the behavior of some of the believers; sadness on account of the fact that the problems in the congregation persisted despite several attempts to resolve the issues; longing for the absent beloved; intense affection for his "children" in Corinth (cf. 1 Cor. 4:14–15; 2 Cor. 6:13; 12:14–15). In Paul's second letter to Timothy, he recalls Timothy's tears (μεμνημένος σου τῶν δακρύων) when he expresses his longing to see him again (2 Tim. 1:4). The parting that caused Timothy to shed tears is an event not reported by Paul (or Luke).[99]

---

97. Cf I. Howard Marshall, *The Gospel of Luke*, NIGTC (Grand Rapids: Eerdmans, 1978), 306, for the argument that this is not an adapted version of the narrative in Mark 14:3–9//Matt. 26:6–13//John 12:1–8, in which Mary anoints Jesus (tears are not mentioned).

98. Eckhard J. Schnabel, *Acts*, ZECNT 5 (Grand Rapids: Zondervan Academic, 2012), 839. Less likely is the suggestion that Paul's tears may have served a rhetorical function intended to demonstrate sincerity, an essential component of persuasive rhetoric (Craig S. Keener, *Acts: An Exegetical Commentary* [Grand Rapids: Baker Academic, 2012–15], 3:3008–9), given Paul's rejection of rhetorical performance in the proclamation of the gospel of a crucified Messiah (1 Cor. 1:18–2:5).

99. I. Howard Marshall, *The Pastoral Epistles*, in collaboration with Philip H. Towner, ICC (Edinburgh: T&T Clark, 1999), 693; William D. Mounce, *Pastoral Epistles*, WBC 46 (Nashville: Nelson, 2000), 470.

The preacher who wrote what we call the epistle to the Hebrews reminds his readers of "the days of Jesus' life on earth" when he "offered up prayers and petitions with fervent cries and tears [μετὰ κραυγῆς ἰσχυρᾶς καὶ δακρύων] to the one who could save him from death, and he was heard because of his reverent submission" (Heb. 5:7). The context of Jesus's "prayers and petitions" is the prospect of suffering and death,[100] and the reference to "a loud cry and tears" suggests that the preacher refers to a specific event during the last days of Jesus's earthly life. Most probably the reference is not the loud cry at the cross[101] but to where Jesus "began to be grieved and agitated" (ἤρξατο λυπεῖσθαι καὶ ἀδημονεῖν, Matt. 26:37 NRSVUE; Mark 14:33: ἤρξατο ἐκθαμβεῖσθαι καὶ ἀδημονεῖν).[102] Since the Gospels do not mention tears in Gethsemane, the preacher may access a tradition that described the "prayers and supplications" of Jesus to be saved from death with the language of the psalms of lament, especially the wording of Psalm 116 (LXX Ps 114/115).[103]

The context indicates that Jesus did not utter cries and shed tears to be spared from the experience of death. Jesus came into the world to share "flesh and blood" with the specific purpose that "by his death he might break the power of him who holds the power of death—that is, the devil" (Heb. 2:14; cf. 9:15). He prays that God would deliver him from the state or realm of death.[104] Jesus prays with intense, audible, and visible emotion that he will have the strength to remain "without sin" (χωρὶς ἁμαρτίας; Heb. 4:15) in submission to the will of God (Heb. 5:7; ἀπὸ τῆς εὐλαβείας, "because of his reverent submission").[105] The preacher asserts that Jesus's prayer was heard: God answered his prayer, which explains why he was able to suffer the death on the cross as the once-for-all sacrifice. Jesus's prayers and petitions accompanied by fervent cries and tears

---

100. Cf. Paul Ellingworth, *The Epistle to the Hebrews. A Commentary on the Greek Text*, NIGTC (Grand Rapids: Eerdmans, 1993), 288: the reference to tears clarifies that the "cry" is one of suffering.

101. Matt. 27:46: ἀνεβόησεν ὁ Ἰησοῦς φωνῇ μεγάλῃ; Mark 15:34: ἐβόησεν ὁ Ἰησοῦς φωνῇ μεγάλῃ.

102. The verb ἐκθαμβεῖν denotes "to be moved to a relatively intense emotional state because of something causing great surprise of perplexity," in Mark 14:33 with the meaning "be distressed" (BDAG). Some link the statement in Hebrews 5:7 to the totality of Jesus's ministry rather than to particular moments in his life, e.g., William L. Lane, *Hebrews*, WBC 47 (Dallas: Word, 1991), 1:119.

103. Hans-Friedrich Weiß, *Der Brief an die Hebräer*, KEK 13 (Göttingen: Vandenhoeck & Ruprecht, 1991), 312.

104. Peter T. O'Brien, *The Letter to the Hebrews*, The Pillar New Testament Commentary (Grand Rapids: Eerdmans, 2010), 199; cf. Craig R. Koester, *Hebrews*, AB 36 (New York: Doubleday, 2001), 288: "God did not deliver Jesus from crucifixion, but he did deliver him from death by raising him to life again."

105. Erich Gräßer, *An die Hebräer*, EKKNT 17 (Zürich/Neukirchen-Vluyn: Benziger/Neukirchener Verlag, 1990–97), 1:300, 301.

were offered up (προσενέγκας) as the offering of the high priest who is the Son of God who "learned obedience from what he suffered" (5:8).[106] On the contrary, the tears of Esau who sought his father's blessing are tears of contrition and remorse, which "could not change what he had done" (12:17).

As regards weeping (κλαίειν), New Testament texts mention a wide range of people who are weeping. The widow in Nain who walks behind the coffin of her son weeps (Luke 7:13). The woman who pours perfume on Jesus's feet weeps and wets his feet with her tears (Luke 7:38). The family and friends of Jairus, the synagogue president, respond to the death of the girl with weeping (Mark 5:38, 39; Luke 8:52). Jesus declares people blessed "who weep now" (μακάριοι οἱ πεινῶντες νῦν; Luke 6:21; cf. Matt. 5:4: "blessed are those who mourn"), describing the response to "the suffering of painful injustice in a world where God's people are pressured, persecuted, and exiled, just as the prophets were."[107]

In his parable of the children who invite other children to play "wedding" or "funeral" in the market square, Jesus connects singing a dirge with weeping (Luke 7:32). The villagers of Bethany think that when Mary leaves the house, she would go to the tomb in which Lazarus has been buried in order to weep there (John 11:31). Instead, she goes to meet Jesus, and weeps as she speaks to him, as do the people who have accompanied her (11:33). Jesus is "deeply moved in spirit and troubled" (ἐνεβριμήσατο τῷ πνεύματι καὶ ἐτάραξεν ἑαυτόν) and when they show him the tomb, he also weeps (11:35: ἐδάκρυσεν ὁ Ἰησοῦς).

When Jesus approaches Jerusalem in his triumphal entry, he weeps over the city (Luke 19:41), the emotion triggered by his "foreknowledge of the city's impending destruction because of her refusal to accept him and because they will choose the way of the sword."[108] Jesus predicts that his disciples will weep and mourn (κλαύσετε καὶ θρηνήσετε) as a reaction to his death but that their grief will turn to joy (John 16:20) after he has risen from the dead.[109] Peter, after he had denied Jesus for the third time, "broke down and wept" (ἐπιβαλὼν ἔκλαιεν, Mark

---

106. Gräßer, *Hebräer*, 1:305.

107. Darrell L. Bock, *Luke*, BECNT (Grand Rapids: Baker Academic, 1995–96), 1:577, with reference to Psalms 126:5–6; 137:1; Isaiah 40:1–2.

108. David E. Garland, *Luke*, ZECNT (Grand Rapids: Zondervan Academic, 2011), 773; cf. Nicholas Perrin, *Luke*, TNTC (Downers Grove, IL: IVP Academic, 2022), 379.

109. Andreas J. Köstenberger, *John*, BECNT (Grand Rapids: Baker Academic, 2004), 475.

14:72; Matt. 26:75; Luke 22:62: ἔκλαυσεν πικρῶς, he "wept bitterly"). When Jesus is taken to Golgotha, Jesus tells the women of Jerusalem who mourn and wail for him (ἐκόπτοντο καὶ ἐθρήνουν αὐτόν; Luke 23:27) not to weep for him on account of his impending crucifixion but to weep for themselves and for their children (Luke 23:28) on account of the difficult times ahead for the city. On the day of Jesus's resurrection, Mary of Magdala stands outside the tomb weeping (κλαίουσα . . . ἔκλαιεν . . . κλαίεις . . . κλαίεις; John 20:11, 13, 15), as a response to Jesus's death.

The widows in Joppa respond to Tabitha's death with weeping (Acts 9:39). The believers in Caesarea and Paul's coworkers weep when they hear the prophet Agabus predicting that Paul would be arrested in Jerusalem (Acts 21:13). Paul's dictum, "Rejoice with those who rejoice; weep with those who weep" (Rom. 12:15 NRSVUE), challenges believers whose normal emotional state is joy to allow themselves to be shaken by new circumstances that trigger in fellow believers deep agitation, pain, or sorrow, which cause tears and weeping.[110] Similarly, he describes weeping and rejoicing as two states of emotion (1 Cor. 7:30) that belong to the "world in its present form," which will pass away (7:31). Paul reminds the believers in Philippi, weeping as he tells them (κλαίων λέγω), that there are some believers who are enemies of the cross because their way of life ignores the implications of Jesus's death for everyday behavior (Phil. 3:18).[111] The weeping, perhaps accompanied by tears,[112] is triggered by Paul's intense anger caused by these people and empathy for the fate of these enemies of the cross in God's judgment.[113]

As James warns his readers about accommodation to the values and behavior of the world, he calls believers to repentance with the words "lament and mourn and weep" (ταλαιπωρήσατε καὶ πενθήσατε καὶ κλαύσατε; James 4:9 NRSVUE), terms used by Israel's prophets to describe the reactions of people who suffer God's judgment and to

---

110. Eckhard J. Schnabel, *Der Brief des Paulus an die Römer*, Historisch-theologische Auslegung (Witten: SCM R. Brockhaus, 2015–16), 2:633–34.

111. Peter T. O'Brien, *The Epistle to the Philippians*, NIGTC (Grand Rapids: Eerdmans, 1991), 451–53.

112. Many English versions translate κλαίων "with tears" (CSB, ESV, GNB, NET, NIV, NRSVUE; NLT even has "with tears in my eyes"); differently NASB.

113. Angela Standhartinger, *Der Philipperbrief*, HNT 11/1 (Tübingen: Mohr Siebeck, 2021), 251–52, who points to tears accompanying prayer for the prevention of disaster (1 Macc. 7:36; *4 Bar.* 2:1, 5, 10; 3:14; 4:6).

call the people to repentance.[114] The challenge James extends to the rich who misuse their wealth, calling them to "weep and wail {κλαύσατε ὀλολύζοντες] because of the misery that is coming on you" (James 5:1), similarly warns of condemnation in God's judgment.

In Revelation, John weeps profusely (ἔκλαιον πολύ) when no one is found who is worthy to open the scroll that God holds in his right hand and break its seals (Rev. 5:4–5). He weeps as he realizes that no human being nor any transcendent creature can read and put into action God's purposes for the world.[115] He weeps on account of the universal inability to see (βλέπειν) the heavenly document of God's rule as one perceives the earthly realities.[116] John's weeping ends when his gaze is directed to "the Lion of the tribe of Judah, the Root of David" who "has conquered, so that he can open the scroll and its seven seals" (5:5 NRSVUE). Israel's Messiah has triumphed as the slaughtered and risen Lamb of God (5:6), whose sacrificial death ransomed people "from every tribe and language and people and nation" and who has thus received "power and wealth and wisdom and might and honor and glory and blessing" (5:9, 12 NRSVUE).

The kings of the earth, the ruling class who had accommodated and supported the political, economic, and religious system (Babylon), "weep and wail" (κλαύσουσιν καὶ κόψονται; Rev. 18:9)[117] when they see its judgment, as do the merchants of the earth who will "weep and mourn" (κλαίουσιν καὶ πενθοῦσιν; 18:11; cf. v. 15: κλαίοντες καὶ πενθοῦντες), as well as the sea captains, the sailors, and all who benefit from the sea trade who cry out "with weeping and mourning" (κλαίοντες καὶ πενθοῦντες; 18:19). Their weeping is triggered by the perception of loss: loss of political control and influence, loss of economic prosperity, loss of personal safety. They weep because they realize that they had made a terrible

---

114. Douglas J. Moo, *The Letter of James*, PNTC (Grand Rapids: Eerdmans, 2000), 195, with reference to Isa. 15:2; Jer. 4:13; Hos. 10:5; Joel 1:9–10; Mic. 2:4; and Hos. 2:12. Cf. Wiard Popkes, *Der Brief des Jakobus*, THKNT 14 (Leipzig: Evangelische Verlagsanstalt, 2001), 276, who emphasizes the call to lament and weeping as a present event in terms of an indication of internal commotion and of the willingness to repent.

115. David E. Aune, *Revelation*, WBC 52 (Dallas: Word, 1997–98), 1:349; Gregory K. Beale, *The Book of Revelation: A Commentary on the Greek Text*, NIGTC (Grand Rapids: Eerdmans, 1999), 348.

116. Martin Karrer, *Johannesoffenbarung*, EKKNT 24 (Ostfildern/Göttingen: Patmos/Vandenhoeck & Ruprecht, 2017), 1:449.

117. Here κόπτειν denotes beating one's breast as an act of mourning.

mistake of trusting a seemingly invincible political, economic, and religious system.[118]

5. THE END OF ALL TEARS

The history of the world is a history of tears. The account of the sin of Adam and Eve and its consequences in Genesis 3 does not mention weeping or tears, but it predicates death: human life outside God's garden is a life of hard work amid thorns and thistles, giving birth in pain, and a life that ends when they return to the ground, dust returning to dust (Gen. 3:16–19). Death is the universal and most fundamental trigger for tears, as is mourning, crying, and pain, which cause tears to be shed, whether involuntarily or voluntarily.

John sees in his vision of the great multitude of the redeemed who stand before the throne of God the new reality of life in the presence of God when God will wipe away "every tear from their eyes" (Rev. 7:17; cf. Isa. 25:8). In the vision of the new heaven and the new earth, which is the new Jerusalem, the redeemed are assured that God's dwelling place is now among his people and that God "will wipe every tear from their eyes" (Rev. 21:4) as there will be no more death, mourning, crying, or pain. Both references to God wiping away tears allude to Isaiah 25:8:[119]

Rev. 7:17	ἐξαλείψει ὁ θεὸς	πᾶν δάκρυον ἐκ τῶν ὀφθαλμῶν αὐτῶν
Rev. 21:4	ἐξαλείψει	πᾶν δάκρυον ἐκ τῶν ὀφθαλμῶν αὐτῶν
Isa. 25:8 LXX	πάλιν ἀφεῖλεν ὁ θεὸς	πᾶν δάκρυον ἀπὸ παντὸς προσώπου
Isa. 25:8 MT	וּמָחָה אֲדֹנָי יְהוִה דִּמְעָה מֵעַל כָּל־פָּנִים

John's vision of God wiping away every tear from the eyes of his people represents the fulfillment of his assurance that one day the faithful in Israel who endured suffering and captivity will experience the joy of salvation in the presence of God when God will have swallowed up death forever (Isa. 25:8–9). However, the ubiquitous shedding of tears in every human being's experience, reflected in history, in literature, and in documentary texts, suggests that John's vision is intended to do much more than point

---

118. Craig R. Koester, *Revelation*, AB 38A (New Haven, CT: Yale University Press, 2014), 717.

119. The varied diction of the allusion appears to rely on a precursor-version to Symmachus; cf. Juan Hernández, "Recensional Activity and the Transmission of the Septuagint in John's Apocalypse," in *Die Johannesoffenbarung. Ihr Text und ihre Auslegung*, ed. M. Labahn and M. Karrer, ABG 38 (Leipzig: Evangelische Verlagsanstalt, 2012), 83–98, here 89–90.

God's Presence and the Absence of Tears (Rev. 7:17; 21:4)

his readers to the fulfillment of "the OT hope of Israel's joyous restoration . . . in the salvation of Christian multitudes who have so faithfully suffered for Christ" and continuing "the line of thought that the bliss of the eternal state is a fulfillment of prophecy."[120] John's focus is not on an Old Testament text and its fulfillment. He does not write a midrash on the Old Testament. He writes on the reality of life in the new creation (Rev. 21:4): There will be no more death (θάνατος), hence there will be no more tears; there will be no more mourning (πένθος) over loss, hence there will be no more tears; there will be no more crying (κραυγή) on account of suffering, hence there will be no more tears; there will be no more emotional or physical pain (πόνος), hence there will be no more tears.

In the context of Revelation 21:4, the tears that God wipes away are visible expressions of the reality of death, mourning, crying, and pain. Standing in the immediate, unmediated presence of God as his people with royal and priestly status rules out "contra-natural" tears of anger, jealousy, frustration, rage, and rhetorical play-acting. The tears of the redeemed who stand before God are certainly not triggered by a yearning for their native lands: as much as they were one's "home" they were located in the old creation of sin and death, which has been replaced by the new creation of God's presence and eternal life. And their tears are not tears of fear and tears of facing a hopeless situation, since the presence of Jesus who has atoned for their sins has driven away fears about their past behavior; there is no longer a present predicament that causes fear and thus tears. The shedding of tears ends not because the redeemed recall their virtue, dignity, and honor; they end because God dries their tears, and because their dignity and honor have been granted them by virtue of the atoning death and the resurrection of Jesus Messiah. Our tears come to an end not because of the iron will of our self-discipline, but because God comforts and grants unmitigated joy *extra nos*, having become our Father who loves his children (Rev. 21:7).

The tears could be tears of sympathy for loved ones who rejected a commitment to the one true God and to Jesus Messiah. They could be tears of joy about the homecoming into the promised new creation of eternal light with access to the Tree of Life, about finally seeing God face-to-face.

---

120. Beale, *Revelation*, 443, 1049. The image of "a father gently wiping away his children's tears" is not part of Isaiah's metaphor in Isaiah 25:8: Isaiah refers to הוִהְי יָנֹדֲא, Israel's "Sovereign Lord" (NIV); *pace* Beale, *Revelation*, 443, on Rev. 7:17. God is called "our Father" only later in Isa. 63:16; 64:8; the "Everlasting Father" of Isaiah 9:6 is the child who is to be born.

The tears could represent the "gift of tears" of the mystic who experience the presence of God. The almighty, holy, and merciful God will bring to an end tears of sympathy, and even tears of joy. The joy of the new creation is so complete and pure that this is perfect joy without tears. There is no longer a time to weep (Eccl. 3:4). The new time of the new creation, which is no longer measured by sun and moon (Rev. 21:23), is a time of eternal joy that will never become "old" since the redeemed are nourished by the water of life, received as a gift from the spring of the water of life (21:6), and by the Tree of Life with its twelve kinds of fruit (22:2).

CONCLUSION

The elimination of the realities of death, mourning, crying, and pain, which characterized after the fall the old creation, is exemplified in the assurance that when the new creation becomes a reality, God will wipe every tear from the eyes of his people. When the redeemed meet up with God in his new creation in which there is no longer any curse (Rev. 22:3), they will see his face (ὄψονται τὸ πρόσωπον αὐτοῦ; 22:4). What has been impossible after Adam and Eve's fall[121] is now possible because the barrier of sin has been removed. As the redeemed see God's face, they apparently do not fall down before him, as the twenty-four elders had fallen down before God on his throne.[122] The bride and her husband (21:2) look at each other as they embrace. The God who dwells with his people is present with his people (21:3).[123] The "old order of things has passed away" (21:4: τὰ πρῶτα ἀπῆλθαν). God's people have stopped being embarrassed of their sins or being scared of God, because God has made "everything new" (21:5: καινὰ ποιῶ πάντα), which includes a new existence without sin. God's people stand before the holy and almighty God, and they remain standing because the curse has been eliminated, their sins have been atoned by the death of Jesus Messiah, and death is no longer a reality. God touches their faces as they see his face. God wipes away the tears from their eyes as he looks into their eyes, the one who is the Alpha and the Omega.

---

121. Cf. Gen. 3:8; Exod. 33:20; John 1:18; 1 John 4:12. Passages such as Gen. 32:30 (Jacob at Peniel); Exod. 24:11 (the leaders of Israel on Mt. Sinai); 33:11 (Moses on Mt. Sinai; cf. Num. 12:8); Judg. 13:22 (Manoah at Zorah), speak of people seeing God, but an unmediated seeing God face-to-face was an eschatological hope: Matt. 5:8; 1 Cor. 13:12; Heb. 12:14; 1 John 3:2. Cf. Koester, *Revelation*, 824.

122. Rev. 4:10: πεσοῦνται . . . ἐνώπιον τοῦ καθημένου ἐπὶ τοῦ θρόνου; 7:11: ἔπεσαν ἐνώπιον τοῦ θρόνου ἐπὶ τὰ πρόσωπα αὐτῶν; 11:16: ἔπεσαν ἐπὶ τὰ πρόσωπα; 19:4: ἔπεσαν; in 5:8 they fall down before the Lamb; in 5:14 they fall down before God and the Lamb.

123. Rev. 21:3: σκηνώσει μετ' αὐτῶν . . . αὐτὸς ὁ θεὸς μετ' αὐτῶν ἔσται.

BIBLIOGRAPHY OF THE WRITINGS OF ANDREAS J. KÖSTENBERGER

The listing of books authored, coauthored, edited, or coedited by Andreas Köstenberger below is exhaustive until January 2024. The bibliography is continually being updated at Köstenberger's website, https://biblicalfoundations.org/andreas-kostenbergers-publications.

BOOKS

2023

Biblical Theology: A Canonical, Thematic, and Ethical Approach. Coauthored with Gregory Goswell. Wheaton, IL: Crossway.

Nancy S. Dawson. *All the Genealogies of the Bible: Visual Charts and Exegetical Commentary*. With Eugene H. Merrill and Andreas J. Köstenberger. Grand Rapids: Zondervan Academic.

2022

John. The Gospel Coalition Bible Commentary. Available for free download at The Gospel Coalition website.

2021

Signs of the Messiah: An Introduction to John's Gospel. Bellingham, WA: Lexham.

Invitation to Biblical Interpretation. Invitation to Theological Studies. 2nd edition. With Richard D. Patterson. Grand Rapids: Kregel Academic.

Invitation to Biblical Interpretation Study Guide. Grand Rapids: Kregel Academic.

1–2 Timothy and Titus. Evangelical Biblical Theology Commentary. Bellingham, WA: Lexham.

279

2020

Going Deeper with New Testament Greek: An Intermediate Study of the Grammar and Syntax of the New Testament. 2nd edition. With Benjamin L. Merkle and Robert L. Plummer. Nashville: B&H Academic.

Salvation to the Ends of the Earth: A Biblical Theology of Mission. With T. D. Alexander. New Studies in Biblical Theology 53. 2nd edition. Downers Grove, IL: IVP Academic.

Handbook on Hebrews through Revelation. Edited by Benjamin Gladd. Handbooks on the New Testament. Grand Rapids: Baker Academic.

Parenting Essentials: Equipping Your Children for Life. Coauthored with Margaret Köstenberger. Fearn, Ross-shire: Christian Focus.

The Holy Spirit. Coauthored with Gregg R. Allison. Theology for the People of God. Edited by David Dockery, Christopher Morgan, and Nathan Finn. Nashville: B&H Academic.

The Jesus of the Gospels: An Introduction. Grand Rapids: Kregel Academic.

2018

Equipping for Life: A Guide for New, Aspiring, and Struggling Parents. Coauthored with Margaret E. Köstenberger. Fern, Ross-shire: Christian Focus.

2017

Commentary on 1-2 Timothy and Titus, vol. 35 in Biblical Theology for Christian Proclamation Commentary series. Edited by T. D. Alexander, Thomas R. Schreiner, and Andreas J. Köstenberger. Nashville: B&H Academic.

Jesus and the Future: Understanding What He Taught about the End Times. Coauthored with Alexander Stewart and Makara Apollo. Wooster, OH: Weaver Book Company; Bellingham, WA: Lexham.

2016

Going Deeper with New Testament Greek. Coauthored with Benjamin L. Merkle and Robert L. Plummer. Nashville: B&H Academic.

Intermediate Greek Charts. Coauthored with Benjamin L. Merkle and Robert L. Plummer. Nashville: B&H Academic.

Inductive Bible Study: Observation, Interpretation, & Application through the Lenses of History, Literature & Theology. Coauthored with R. Alan Fuhr. Nashville: B&H Academic.

The Cradle, the Cross, and the Crown: An Introduction to the New Testament. 2nd edition. Coauthored with L. Scott Kellum and Charles L. Quarles. Nashville: B&H Academic.
Women in the Church: An Interpretation and Application of 1 Timothy 2:9–15. 3rd edition. Coedited with Thomas R. Schreiner. Wheaton, IL: Crossway.

2015

The First Days of Jesus: The Story of the Incarnation. Coauthored with Alexander Stewart. Wheaton, IL: Crossway.
For the Love of God's Word: An Introduction to Biblical Interpretation. Coauthored with Richard D. Patterson. Grand Rapids: Kregel Academic.

2014

The Final Days of Jesus: The Most Important Week of the Most Important Person Who Ever Lived. Coauthored with Justin Taylor. Wheaton, IL: Crossway.
Truth Matters: Confident Faith in a Confusing World. Coauthored with Darrell Bock and Josh Chatraw. Nashville: B&H Academic.
God's Design for Man and Woman: A Biblical-Theological Survey. Coauthored with Margaret E. Köstenberger. Wheaton, IL: Crossway.
Truth in a Culture of Doubt: Engaging Popular Distortions of the Bible. Coauthored with Darrell Bock and Josh Chatraw. Nashville: B&H Academic.

2013

"John." Pages 499–634 in *The Holman Apologetics Commentary on the Bible: The Gospels and Acts.* Edited by Jeremy Royal Howard. Nashville: Holman Reference.
Encountering John: The Gospel in Historical, Literary, and Theological Perspective. 2nd edition. Encountering Biblical Studies. Grand Rapids: Baker Academic.

2012

Marriage and the Family: Biblical Essentials. Wheaton, IL: Crossway.
The Lion and the Lamb: New Testament Essentials from The Cradle, the Cross, and the Crown. Coauthored with L. Scott Kellum and Charles L. Quarles. Nashville: B&H Academic.
Which Bible Translation Should I Use? Leading Experts Discuss 4 Major Versions. Coedited with David Croteau. Nashville: B&H Academic.

2011

Understanding the Times: New Testament Studies in the 21st Century: Essays in Honor of D. A. Carson on the Occasion of His 65th Birthday. Coedited with Robert W. Yarbrough. Wheaton, IL: Crossway.

Invitation to Biblical Interpretation. Invitation to Theological Studies. Coauthored with Richard D. Patterson. Grand Rapids: Kregel Academic.

Excellence: The Character of God and the Pursuit of Scholarly Virtue. Wheaton, IL: Crossway.

2010

God, Marriage, and Family. 2nd edition. With David W. Jones. Wheaton, IL: Crossway.

The Heresy of Orthodoxy: How Contemporary Culture's Fascination with Diversity Has Reshaped Our Understanding of Early Christianity. Coauthored with Michael J. Kruger. Wheaton, IL: Crossway.

Entrusted with the Gospel: Paul's Theology in the Pastoral Epistles. NAC Monograph Series. Coedited with Terry Wilder. Nashville: B&H Academic.

2009

The Cradle, the Cross, and the Crown: An Introduction to the New Testament. Coauthored with L. Scott Kellum and Charles L. Quarles. Nashville: B&H Academic.

The Theology of John's Gospel and Letters: The Word, the Christ, the Son of God. Biblical Theology of the New Testament. Grand Rapids: Zondervan Academic.

2008

Father, Son, and Spirit: The Trinity and John's Gospel. New Studies in Biblical Theology. Coauthored with Scott Swain. Downers Grove, IL: IVP Academic.

2007

Quo Vadis, Evangelicalism? Perspectives from the Past, Direction for the Future: Select Presidential Addresses from the First Fifty Years of the Journal of the Evangelical Theological Society. Edited by Andreas J. Köstenberger. Wheaton, IL: Crossway.

"John." Pages 415–512 in *Commentary on the New Testament Use of the Old Testament*. Edited by G. K. Beale and D. A. Carson. Grand Rapids: Baker Academic.

2006

"1–2 Timothy, Titus." Pages 488–625 in *Expositor's Bible Commentary*. Vol. 12. Revised edition. Edited by Tremper Longman and David Garland. Grand Rapids: Zondervan.

2005

Women in the Church: A Fresh Analysis of 1 Timothy 2:9–15. 2nd edition. Coedited with Thomas R. Schreiner. Grand Rapids: Baker Academic.

Do We Know Jesus? by Adolf Schlatter. Translated by Andreas J. Köstenberger and Robert W. Yarbrough. Grand Rapids: Kregel Academic.

Whatever Happened to Truth? Edited by Andreas J. Köstenberger. Wheaton, IL: Crossway.

2004

John. Baker Exegetical Commentary of the New Testament. Grand Rapids: Baker Academic. *Note:* The book has been withdrawn by the publisher. A new commentary on John is forthcoming in Lexham's Evangelical Exegetical Commentary (EEC) series.

God, Marriage, and Family: Restoring the Biblical Foundation. With David W. Jones. Wheaton, IL: Crossway.

2003

The Book Study Concordance. Coauthored with Raymond Bouchoc. Nashville: Broadman & Holman.

2002

"John." Pages 1–216 in *Zondervan Illustrated Bible Backgrounds Commentary*. Edited by Clinton E. Arnold. Grand Rapids: Zondervan. Released as a separate volume in paperback as *Zondervan Illustrated Bible Backgrounds Commentary: John*. Grand Rapids: Zondervan, 2007. *Note:* This work has been withdrawn by the publisher. But see now "John." Pages 953–1001 in *Baker Illustrated Bible Background Commentary*. Edited by J. Scott Duvall and J. Danny Hays; Grand Rapids: Baker Books, 2021.

2001

Salvation to the Ends of the Earth: A Biblical Theology of Mission. Coauthored with Peter T. O'Brien. New Studies in Biblical Theology 11. Downers Grove, IL: IVP Academic. *Note:* This book has been withdrawn by the publisher. A second edition was published in 2021 (see above).

Studies in John and Gender: A Decade of Scholarship. Studies in Biblical Literature 38. New York: Peter Lang.

1999

The Theology of the Apostles: The Development of New Testament Theology by Adolf Schlatter. Translated by Andreas J. Köstenberger. Grand Rapids: Baker Academic.

Encountering John: The Gospel in Historical, Literary, and Theological Perspective. Encountering Biblical Studies. Grand Rapids: Baker Academic.

1998

The Missions of Jesus and the Disciples in the Fourth Gospel: With Implications for the Fourth Gospel's Purpose and the Mission of the Contemporary Church. Grand Rapids: Eerdmans.

1997

The History of the Christ: The Foundation of New Testament Theology by Adolf Schlatter. Translated by Andreas J. Köstenberger. Grand Rapids: Baker Academic.

1995

Women in the Church: A Fresh Analysis of 1 Timothy 2:9–15. Coedited with Thomas R. Schreiner and H. Scott Baldwin. Grand Rapids: Baker.

ARTICLES, ESSAYS, AND DICTIONARY ENTRIES

2024

"The Doctrine of Angels and a Pastor's Ministry." In *The Focused Pastor* (January 1, 2024).

2023

"Geerhardus Vos: His Biblical-Theological Method and a Biblical Theology of Gender." *Themelios* 48/3 (2023): 505–23.

"John," "Mission." Pages 393–400 and 546–50 in *Dictionary of the New Testament Use of the Old Testament*. Edited by G. K. Beale, D. A. Carson, Benjamin L. Gladd, and Andrew David Naselli. Grand Rapids: Baker Academic.

"The Doctrine of the Bible and a Pastor's Ministry." *The Focused Pastor* (December 17, 2023).

"The Doctrine of Sin and a Pastor's Ministry." *The Focused Pastor* (October 26, 2023).

"The Doctrine of the Church and a Pastor's Ministry." *The Focused Pastor* (September 30, 2023).

"The Doctrine of Humanity and a Pastor's Ministry." *The Focused Pastor* (September 4, 2023).

"The Doctrine of the Holy Spirit and a Pastor's Ministry." *The Focused Pastor* (July 31, 2023).

"7 Truths the Church Needs to Know about Jesus." *The Focused Pastor* (July 2, 2023).

"The Character of Kingdom Citizens (Matthew 5:1–16)." *TableTalk Magazine* 47, no. 3 (March 2023): 4–9.

"Paul's Teaching on Male Elders in 1 Timothy 2–3." *Christ over All* (March 2023).

"Day of No Hope: The Saturday between Good Friday and Easter Sunday." *The Focused Pastor* (April 8, 2023).

"The Role of Pastors in Fostering a Healthy, Biblical Self-Image." *The Focused Pastor* (May 18, 2023), coauthored with Margaret Köstenberger.

"The Doctrine of God and a Pastor's Ministry." *The Focused Pastor* (May 31, 2023).

2022

"Jewish Messianic Hope." *TableTalk Magazine* 46, no. 2 (February 2022): 24–26.

"Exodus in John." *Exodus in the New Testament*. Pages 88–108. LNTS 663. Edited by Seth M. Ehorn. London: T&T Clark.

2021

"Grounded in Allegiance to Christ and Affection for God: Worship in John's Letters." Pages 469–80 in *Biblical Worship: Theology for God's Glory*. Edited by Benjamin K. Forrest, Walter C. Kaiser Jr., and Vernon M. Whaley. Grand Rapids: Kregel Academic.

"1–2 Timothy, Titus." Pages 1675–96 in *Grace and Truth Study Bible*. Edited by R. Albert Mohler. Grand Rapids: Zondervan.

"The Use of the Old Testament in the Gospel of John and the Johannine Epistles." *Southwestern Journal of Theology* 64, no. 1 (Fall 2021): 41–55.

2020

"The Family of Jesus, Jewish Festivals, Pharisees and Sadducees, Pontius Pilate, The Sabbath, Samaritans, John (Commentary)." Pages 735, 747–48, 765–66, 767–68, 778–79, 780–81, 953–1001 in *Baker Illustrated Bible Background Commentary*. Edited by J. Scott Duvall and J. Daniel Hays; Grand Rapids: Baker Books.

"The Cosmic Drama and the Seed of the Serpent: An Exploration of the Connection between Gen 3:15 and Johannine Theology." Pages 265–85 in *The Seed of Promise: The Sufferings and Glory of the Messiah: Essays in Honor of T. Desmond Alexander*. Edited by Paul Williamson and Rita Cefalu. Wilmore, KY: GlossaHouse.

"Reconceiving a Biblical Theology of Mission: *Salvation to the Ends of the Earth* Revisited," *Themelios* 45, no. 3 (December 2020): 528–36.

With Margaret Köstenberger. "Equipping for Life: Excellence in Parenting," *Midwestern Journal of Theology* 19, no. 1 (2020): 30–44.

With Margaret Köstenberger. "Preparing Our Children for Their Mission in Life." *Poimenas* (September 22, 2020).

With Margaret Köstenberger. "Preparing Our Children for Marriage." *Poimenas* (November 24, 2020).

"The Context of Jesus's Prayer." *TableTalk Magazine* 44, no. 12 (December 2020): 4–11.

"Presenting Jesus at the Temple." *Biblical Illustrator* (December 2020).

With David W. Chapman. "Jewish Intertestamental and Early Rabbinic Literature: An Annotated Bibliographic Resource Updated Again (Part 1)." *Journal of the Evangelical Theological Society* 63, no. 3 (September 2020): 559–609.

With David W. Chapman. "Jewish Intertestamental and Early Rabbinic Literature: An Annotated Bibliographic Resource Updated Again (Part 2)." *Journal of the Evangelical Theological Society* 63, no. 4 (December 2020): 789–843.

2019

"Faithful Stewardship in God's Household: Discipleship in the Letters to Timothy and Titus." Pages 193–212 in *Following Jesus Christ: The New Testament Message of Discipleship for Today.* Edited by John K. Goodrich. Grand Rapids: Kregel Academic.

"An Investigation of the Mission Motif in the Letters to Timothy and Titus with Implications for the Pauline Authorship of the Pastoral Epistles." *Bulletin of Biblical Research* 29, no. 1 (2019): 49–64.

With Peter R. Schemm Jr. "The Gospel as Interpretive Key to 1 Corinthians 10:31–11:16: On Christian Worship, Head Coverings, and the Trinity." *Themelios* 44, no. 2 (2019): 249–57.

"'I Am' Statements," "Trials and Crucifixion," "Jesus as Rabbi," and "The Jewish Disciples in the Gospels." Pages 159–64, 164–70, 178–84, 203–6 in *A Handbook on the Jewish Roots of the Christian Faith.* Edited by Craig A. Evans and David Mishkin. Peabody, MA: Hendrickson.

With Margaret Köstenberger. "5 Myths about Complementarianism." https://www.crossway.org/articles/5-myths-about-complementarianism/ (January 15, 2019).

With Margaret Köstenberger. "How to Pray when Preparing for Family Vacation." https://www.crossway.org/articles/how-to-pray-when-preparing-for-family-vacation/ (June 21, 2019).

2018

"John's Appropriation of Isaiah's Signs Theology: Implications for the Structure of John's Gospel." *Themelios* 43, no. 3 (2018): 376–86.

With Jimmy Roh. "Where Was Jesus Born? 5 Things to Know about Bethlehem." *Crosswalk.com* (October 4, 2018).

"Leon Morris's Scholarship on John's Gospel: An Assessment and Critical Reflection on His Scholarship." Pages 197–209 in *The Gospel of John in Modern Interpretation.* Milestones in New Testament Scholarship. Edited by Stanley E. Porter and Ron C. Fay. Grand Rapids: Kregel Academic.

"The Sizemore Lectures 2018: The Promise of Biblical Theology: What Biblical Theology Is and What It Isn't." *Midwestern Journal of Theology* 17, no. 1 (Spring 2018): 1–13.

"The Sizemore Lectures 2018: The Practice of Biblical Theology: How Is Biblical Theology Done?" *Midwestern Journal of Theology* 17, no. 1 (Spring 2018): 14–27.

"5 Reasons Why You Should Reflect on the Final Days of Jesus." *Credo Magazine* (March 26, 2018).

With Margaret Köstenberger. "Presence: The Essence of Parenting." *Credo Magazine* (June 6, 2018).

With Margaret Köstenberger. "The Missing Ingredient in Our Parenting." *The Gospel Coalition* (June 14, 2018).

2017

With David Crowther. "Leading with Love: Leadership in the Johannine Epistles." Pages 475–92 in *Biblical Leadership: Theology for the Everyday Leader*, Biblical Theology for the Church. Edited by Benjamin K. Forrest and Chet Roden. Grand Rapids: Kregel Academic.

"Last Words of Jesus: Reception in Europe and America." Pages 859–61 in *The Encyclopedia of the Bible and Its Reception*, volume 15. Edited by Gary S. Helft. Berlin: Walter de Gruyter.

2016

"Who Were the First Disciples of Jesus? An Assessment of the Historicity of the Johannine Call Narrative (John 1:35–51)." Pages 189–99 in *John, Jesus, and History*, Volume 3: Glimpses of Jesus through the Johannine Lens: Early Christianity and Its Literature 18. Edited by Paul N. Anderson, Felix Just, and Tom Thatcher. Atlanta: Society of Biblical Literature; Leiden: E. J. Brill.

"Theodor Zahn, Adolf Harnack, and Adolf Schlatter." Pages 163–88 in *Pillars in the History of Biblical Interpretation*, vol. 1: *Prevailing Methods before 1980*. McMaster Biblical Studies 2. Edited by Stanley E. Porter and Sean A. Adams. Eugene, OR: Wipf & Stock.

"Humility (New Testament)." Pages 544–46 in *The Encyclopedia of the Bible and Its Reception*, volume 12. Edited by Stefan Selbmann. Berlin: Walter de Gruyter.

"Jesus and the Love of God." Pages 51–73 in *The Love of God*. Theology in Community 7. Edited by Christopher Morgan. Wheaton, IL: Crossway.

"Christmas Is Too Big for One Day: Why We Celebrate Advent." https://www.desiringgod.org/articles/christmas-is-too-big-for-one-day (November 28, 2016).

2015

With Margaret Köstenberger. "A Match Made in Heaven." *Answers Magazine* (July–September 2015): 52–55.

"Mission." Pages 2691–92 in *The NIV Zondervan Study Bible*. Edited by D. A. Carson. Grand Rapids: Zondervan.

"Mission in the Gospels." Pages 53–67 in *Missiology*. 2nd edition. Edited by Mark Terry. Nashville: B&H Academic.

With Alexander Stewart. "Five Errors to Drop from Your Christmas Sermon." *Christianity Today* (December 18, 2015).

"I and the Father Are One (John 10:30)." *TableTalk Magazine* 39, no. 10 (October 2015): 15–16.

2014

"Shepherds and Shepherding in the Gospels." Pages 35–62 in *Shepherding God's Flock: Biblical Leadership in the New Testament and Beyond*. Edited by Benjamin L. Merkle and Thomas R. Schreiner; Grand Rapids: Kregel Ministry.

"Mission and Ethics in John's Gospel and Epistles: Sensitivity to Outsiders in John's Gospel and Letters and Its Implication for the Understanding of Early Christian Mission." Pages 171–86 in *Sensitivity towards Outsiders: Exploring the Dynamic Relationship between Mission and Ethics*. Edited by Jacobus Kok, Tobias Nicklas, Dieter T. Roth, and Christopher M. Hays. WUNT 2/364. Tübingen: Mohr Siebeck.

"The Cosmic Trial Motif in John's Letters." Pages 157–78 in *Communities in Dispute: Current Scholarship on the Johannine Epistles*. Early Christianity and Its Literature 13. Edited by R. Alan Culpepper and Paul N. Anderson. Atlanta: Society of Biblical Literature.

"Heaven in John's Gospel and Revelation." Pages 139–57 in *Heaven*. Theology in Community 6. Edited by Christopher W. Morgan and Robert A. Peterson. Wheaton, IL: Crossway.

"Placing the Cross in History." *Answers Magazine* 9, no. 2 (2014): 38–39.

"April 3, A.D. 33: Why We Believe We Can Know the Exact Date Jesus Died." *First Things* (April 3, 2014).

With Justin Taylor. "Five Errors to Drop from Your Easter Sermon." *Christianity Today* (April 15, 2014).

With Justin Taylor. "No Turning Back: Monday of Holy Week," and "Escalating Conflict: Tuesday of Holy Week." https://www.desiringgod.org /articles/no-turning-back (April 14, 2014).

With Benjamin L. Merkle and Robert L. Plummer. "'Scholarship that helps men to preach': The Pastoral Legacy of A. T. Robertson." *Towers* 13, no. 2 (September 2014): 12–13.

"Logical Fallacies." *TableTalk Magazine* (January 2014): 22–25.

2013

"The Church in the Gospels." Pages 35–63 in *The Community of Jesus: A Theology of the Church*. Edited by Kendell H. Easley and Christopher W. Morgan. Nashville: B&H Academic.

"Abide," "New Birth," "Wine," and "Witness." Pages 1–2, 625–28, 993–95, 1000–1004 in *Dictionary of Jesus and the Gospels*. 2nd edition. Edited by Joel B. Green, Jeannine K. Brown, and Nicholas Perrin. Downers Grove, IL: InterVarsity Press.

"Johannine Fallacies: Ten Common Misconceptions Regarding John's Gospel." Pages 1–25 in *Rediscovering John: Essays on the Fourth Gospel in Honour of Frédéric Manns*. Studium Biblicum Franciscanum 80. Edited by L. Daniel Chrupcala. Milano, Italy: Editionizi Terra Santa.

2012

With David W. Chapman. "Jewish Intertestamental and Early Rabbinic Literature: An Annotated Bibliographic Resource Updated (Part 1)." *Journal of the Evangelical Theological Society* 55, no. 2 (June 2012): 235–72.

With David W. Chapman. "Jewish Intertestamental and Early Rabbinic Literature: An Annotated Bibliographic Resource Updated (Part 2)." *Journal of the Evangelical Theological Society* 55, no. 3 (September 2012): 457–88.

"*Invitation to Biblical Interpretation* and the Hermeneutical Triad." *Criswell Theological Review* 10, no. 1 (Fall 2012): 3–12.

"Excellence: The Character of God and the Pursuit of Scholarly Virtue." *Criswell Theological Review* 10, no. 1 (Fall 2012): 13–19.

"The Present and Future of Biblical Theology." *Themelios* 37, no. 3 (2012): 445–64.

"John's Transposition Theology: Retelling the Story of Jesus in a Different Key." Pages 191–226 in *Earliest Christian History: History, Literature, and Theology. Essays from the Tyndale Fellowship in Honor of Martin Hengel*. Edited by Michael F. Bird and Jason Maston. WUNT 2/320. Tübingen: Mohr/Siebeck.

"The Promises of God in the Mission of God." Page 736 in *The Mission of God Study Bible*. Edited by Ed Stetzer and Philip Nations. Nashville: Holman Bible Publishers.

"The Genre of the Fourth Gospel and Greco-Roman Literary Conventions." Pages 435–62 in *Christian Origins and Greco-Roman Culture: Social and Literary Contexts for the New Testament*, vol. 1: *Early Christianity in Its Hellenistic Context*. Texts and Editions for New Testament Study. Edited by Stanley E. Porter and Andrew W. Pitts. Leiden: Brill.

"New Testament Use of the Old Testament, Survey." *Lexham Bible Dictionary*. Bellingham, WA: Lexham Press, 2012, http://faithlifebible.com.

"Biblical Theology." *FaithLife Study Bible*. Bellingham, WA: Lexham Press.

2011

"Reading the Bible in Context." Pages 33–48 in *Read the Bible for Life: Your Guide to Understanding & Living God's Word*. Edited by George H. Guthrie. Nashville: B&H.

"Lifting Up the Son of Man and God's Love for the World: John 3:16 in Its Historical, Literary, and Theological Contexts." Pages 141–59 in *Understanding the Times: New Testament Studies in the 21st Century: Essays in Honor of D. A. Carson on the Occasion of His 65th Birthday*. Edited by Andreas J. Köstenberger and Robert W. Yarbrough. Wheaton, IL: Crossway.

"John's Gospel and Jewish Monotheism." Pages 69–84 in *Jesus, Salvation and the Jewish People: The Uniqueness of Jesus and Jewish Evangelism*. Edited by David Parker. Carlisle, UK: Paternoster.

"The Deity of Christ in John's Gospel," "The Deity of Christ in John's Letters," and "The Deity of Christ in the Book of Revelation." Pages 91–114, 151–67 in *The Deity of Christ*. Theology in Community 3. Edited by Robert Peterson and Chris Morgan. Wheaton, IL: Crossway.

"Love (John's Epistles)." *TableTalk Magazine* 35, no. 1 (January 2011): 20–23.

"Church Government," "Orthodoxy," "St. Peter," "Rudolf Bultmann," "Adolf Schlatter," "Bible Translations," "Kingdom of God," "Messiah," "Christian Publishing," "Titles of Christ," "Celibacy," "Discipleship," "Matrimony," "Tithe." Pages 543–51, 1735–43, 1813–14, 328–29, 2073–74, 247–48, 1277–79, 1491–93, 1909–10, 2388–89, 419–20, 694, 1451–52, 2387 in *The Encyclopedia of Christian Civilization*. 4 vols. Edited by George Thomas Kurian. Oxford: Blackwell.

2010

"The Glory of God in John's Gospel and Revelation." Pages 107–26 in *The Glory of God*. Theology in Community 2. Edited by Christopher W. Morgan and Robert A. Peterson. Wheaton, IL: Crossway.

"Is the Bible Today What Was Originally Written?" Pages 207–10 in *Evidence for God: 50 Arguments for Faith from the Bible, History, Philosophy, and Science*. Edited by William A. Dembski and Michael R. Licona. Grand Rapids: Baker Books.

"Hermeneutical and Exegetical Challenges in Interpreting the Pastoral Epistles." Pages 1–27 in *Entrusted with the Gospel: Paul's Theology in the Pastoral Epistles*. Edited by Andreas Köstenberger and Terry Wilder. NAC Monograph Series. Nashville: B&H Academic.

"Twelve Theses on the Church's Mission in the Twenty-First Century: In Interaction with Charles Van Engen, Keith Eitel, and Enoch Wan." Pages 62–70 in *MissionShift: Global Mission Issues in the Third Millennium*. Edited by David J. Hesselgrave and Ed Stetzer. Nashville: B&H Academic.

"John" and "Colossians." *Holman Christian Standard Bible Study Bible*. Edited by Edwin Blum. Nashville: B&H Academic.

"Was the Last Supper a Passover Meal?" Pages 6–30 in *The Lord's Supper: Remembering and Proclaiming Christ until He Comes*. Edited by Thomas R. Schreiner and Matthew R. Crawford. NAC Studies in Bible & Theology 10. Nashville: B&H Academic.

2009

"The Syntax of 1 Timothy 2:12: A Rejoinder to Philip B. Payne." *Journal for Biblical Manhood & Womanhood* 14, no. 2 (Fall 2009): 37–40.

2008

"The *Journal of the Evangelical Theological Society*: Retrospect & Prospect at the Occasion of the Fiftieth Year of Its Publication." *Journal of the Evangelical Theological Society* 51, no. 1 (March 2008): 11–17.

With Stephen O. Stout. "The Disciple Jesus Loved: Witness, Author, Apostle: A Response to Richard Bauckham's *Jesus and the Eyewitnesses*." *Bulletin of Biblical Research* 18, no. 2 (2008): 209–32.

"Do Jews Need to Be 'Perfected'?" *Global Missiology* (July 2008).

"The Gospel for All Nations." Pages 201–19 in *Faith Comes by Hearing: A Response to Inclusivism*. Edited by Christopher W. Morgan and Robert A. Peterson; Downers Grove, IL: InterVarsity Press.

"Is the Bible Today What Was Originally Written?" www.4truth.net.

"John." *ESV Study Bible*. Edited by Wayne Grudem. Wheaton, IL: Crossway.

"Albert Schweitzer," "Monogamy." https://biblicalfoundations.org/author/andreas-kostenberger.

2007

"Baptism in the Gospels." Pages 15–37 in *Believer's Baptism: Sign of the New Covenant in Christ*. Edited by Thomas R. Schreiner and Shawn D. Wright. Nashville: B&H Academic.

"Testament Relationships." Pages 350–52 in *Dictionary of Biblical Criticism and Interpretation*. Edited by Stanley E. Porter. New York: Routledge.

"Study Notes on the Gospel of John." *Holman Christian Standard Bible Harmony of the Gospels*. Edited by Steven Cox and Kendell H. Easley. Nashville: Holman Reference.

"Head." Pages 754–55 in *The New Interpreter's Dictionary of the Bible*. Vol. 2: *D–H*. Edited by Pheme Perkins et al. Nashville: Abingdon.

"Response: Progress and Regress in Recent Johannine Scholarship: Reflections upon the Road Ahead." Pages 105–7 in *What We Have Heard from the Beginning: The Past, Present, and Future of Johannine Studies*. Edited by Tom Thatcher. Waco, TX: Baylor University Press.

2006

With David A. Croteau. "'Will a Man Rob God?' (Malachi 3:8): A Study of Tithing in the Old and New Testaments," *Bulletin of Biblical Research* 16, no. 1 (2006): 53–77.

With David A. Croteau. "Reconstructing a Biblical Model for Giving: A Discussion of Relevant Systematic Issues and New Testament Principles." *Bulletin of Biblical Research* 16, no. 2 (2006): 237–60.

"Feminism, Family, and the Bible: A Biblical Assessment of Feminism's Impact on American Families." *Religion & Society Report (Online Edition)* 23, no. 1 (2006).

"The Moral Vision of John." *Midwestern Journal of Theology* 4, no. 2 (Spring 2006): 3–23.

"The Biblical Framework for Marriage." *Midwestern Journal of Theology* 4, no. 2 (Spring 2006): 24–42.

"The New Testament Pattern of Church Government." *Midwestern Journal of Theology* 4, no. 2 (Spring 2006): 43–56.

"Of Professors and Madmen: Currents in Contemporary New Testament Scholarship." *Faith & Mission* 23, no. 2 (Spring 2006): 3–18.

"Hearing the Old Testament in the New: A Response." Pages 255–94 in *Hearing the Old Testament in the New Testament*. Edited by Stanley E. Porter. Grand Rapids: Eerdmans.

"The Use of Scripture in the Pastoral and General Epistles and the Book of Revelation." Pages 230–54 in *Hearing the Old Testament in the New Testament*. Edited by Stanley E. Porter. Grand Rapids: Eerdmans.

"The Destruction of the Second Temple and the Composition of the Fourth Gospel." Pages 69–108 in *Challenging Perspectives on the Gospel of John*. WUNT 2/219. Edited by John Lierman. Tübingen: Mohr Siebeck.

2005

"'What Is Truth?' Pilate's Question to Jesus in Its Johannine and Larger Biblical Context." *Journal of the Evangelical Theological Society* 48, no. 1 (2005): 33–62.

"'Teaching and Usurping Authority: 1 Timothy 2:11–15' by Linda L. Belleville." *Journal of Biblical Manhood & Womanhood* 10, no. 1 (Spring 2005): 43–54.

"'Biblical Hermeneutics: Basic Principles and Questions of Gender'" by Roger Nicole and 'Hermeneutics and the Gender Debate' by Gordon D. Fee." *Journal of Biblical Manhood & Womanhood* 10, no. 1 (Spring 2005): 88–95.

"The Destruction of the Second Temple and the Composition of the Fourth Gospel." *Trinity Journal* 26 NS/2 (Fall 2005): 205–42.

"John's Trinitarian Mission Theology." *Southern Baptist Journal of Theology* 9, no. 4 (Winter 2005): 14–33.

"Introduction," "'What Is Truth?' Pilate's Question to Jesus in Its Johannine and Larger Biblical Context," and "Epilogue." Pages 9–17, 19–51, 131–36 in *Whatever Happened to Truth?* Edited by Andreas J. Köstenberger. Wheaton, IL: Crossway.

2004

"Jesus, the Mediator of a 'Better Covenant': Comparatives in the Book of Hebrews." *Faith & Mission* 21, no. 2 (Spring 2004): 30–49.

"'I Suppose' (*oimai*): The Conclusion of John's Gospel in Its Contemporary Literary and Historical Context." Pages 72–88 in *The New Testament in Its First Century Setting: Essays on Context and Background in Honour of B. W. Winter on His 65th Birthday.* Edited by P. J. Williams, A. D. Clarke, P. M. Head, and D. Instone-Brewer. Grand Rapids: Eerdmans.

2003

"Hermeneutical and Exegetical Challenges in Interpreting the Pastoral Epistles." *The Southern Baptist Journal of Theology* 7, no. 3 (Fall 2003): 4–17.

"Translating John's Gospel: Challenges and Opportunities." Pages 347–64 in *The Challenge of Bible Translation: Communicating God's Word to the World.* Edited by Glen G. Scorgie, Mark L. Strauss, and Steven M. Voth; Grand Rapids: Zondervan Academic.

"Marriage and Family in the New Testament." Pages 240–84 in *Marriage and Family in the Ancient World.* Edited by Ken Campbell. Downers Grove, IL: InterVarsity Press.

2002

"Jesus the Good Shepherd Who Will Also Bring Other Sheep (John 10:16): The Old Testament Background of a Familiar Metaphor." *Bulletin of Biblical Research* 12 (2002): 67–96.

"Diversity and Unity in the New Testament." Pages 200–223 in *Biblical Theology: Retrospect &Prospect.* Edited by Scott J. Hafemann. Downers Grove, IL: IVP Academic.

2001

"*Women in the Church*: A Response to Kevin Giles." *Evangelical Quarterly* 73 (2001): 205–24.

"The Identity of the ἸΣΡΑΗΛ ΤΟΥ ΘΕΟΥ (Israel of God) in Galatians 6:16." *Faith & Mission* 19, no. 1 (2001): 3–24.

2000

With David W. Chapman. "Jewish Intertestamental and Early Rabbinic Literature: An Annotated Bibliographic Resource." *Journal of the Evangelical Theological Society* 43 (2000): 577–618.

"Austria," "Consumerism," "Debt," "Economics and Missions," "Great Commandment," "Sociological Barriers." Pages 99–101, 224–25, 262–63, 297–99, 411–12, 889–90 in *The Evangelical Dictionary of World Missions*. Edited by A. Scott Moreau. Grand Rapids: Baker Academic.

"Women in the Pauline Mission." Pages 221–47 in *The Gospel to the Nations: Perspectives on Paul's Mission*. Edited by Peter Bolt and Mark Thompson. Downers Grove, IL: IVP Academic.

"Vielfalt und Einheit des Neuen Testaments." Pages 233–65 in *Das Studium des Neuen Testaments. Band 2: Spezialprobleme*. Edited by Heinz-Werner Neudorfer and Eckhard J. Schnabel. Wuppertal: R. Brockhaus/Brunnen.

"John," "Mission," "Nations." Pages 280–85, 663–68, 676–78 in *New Dictionary of Biblical Theology*. Edited by T. Desmond Alexander, Brian S. Rosner, D. A. Carson, and Graeme Goldsworthy. Downers Grove, IL: IVP Academic.

1999

"Schlatter Reception Then and Now: His *New Testament Theology* (Part 1)." *Southern Baptist Journal of Theology* 3, no. 1 (Spring 1999): 40–51.

"Preface: The Reception of Schlatter's New Testament Theology 1909–23." Pages 9–22 in *The Theology of the Apostles* by Adolf Schlatter. Grand Rapids: Baker Academic.

"Eine komplexe Satzstruktur in 1. Timotheus 2,12." Pages 89–113 in *Frauen in der Kirche: 1. Timotheus 2,9–15 kritisch untersucht*. Edited by Andreas J. Köstenberger, Thomas R. Schreiner, and H. Scott Baldwin. Translated by Andreas J. Köstenberger. Gießen: Brunnen.

"The Place of Mission in New Testament Theology: An Attempt to Determine the Significance of Mission within the Scope of the New Testament's Message as a Whole." *Missiology* 27 (1999): 347–62.

"The Two Johannine Verbs for Sending: A Study of John's Use of Words with Reference to General Linguistic Theory." Pages 125–43 in *Linguistics and the New Testament: Critical Junctures*. Edited by Stanley E. Porter and D. A. Carson. JSNTSup 168. Studies in New Testament Greek 5. Sheffield: Sheffield Academic Press.

"D. A. Carson." Pages 423–33 in *Bible Interpreters of the 20th Century: A Selection of Evangelical Voices*. Edited by Walter A. Elwell and J. D. Weaver. Grand Rapids: Baker.

1998

"Jesus as Rabbi in the Fourth Gospel." *Bulletin of Biblical Research* 8 (1998): 97–128.

"Aesthetic Theology—Blessing or Curse? An Assessment of Narrative Hermeneutics." *Faith & Mission* 15, no. 2 (1998): 27–44.

"Avoiding Fallacies in Interpretation: How Fallacies Distort Understanding of the New Testament Gender Passages." *Journal of Biblical Manhood and Womanhood* (1998): 1, 6–10. Abridged version of "Gender Passages in the New Testament: Hermeneutical Fallacies Critiqued." *Westminster Theological Journal* 56 (1994): 259–83.

"Mission in the General Epistles." Pages 189–206 in *Mission in the New Testament: An Evangelical Approach*. Edited by William J. Larkin Jr. and Joel F. Williams. Maryknoll, NY: Orbis Books.

1997

"The Crux of the Matter: Paul's Pastoral Pronouncements Regarding Women's Roles in 1 Timothy 2:9–15." *Faith and Mission* 14, no. 1 (1997): 24–48.

"What Does It Mean to Be Filled with the Spirit? A Biblical Investigation." *Journal of the Evangelical Theological Society* 40 (1997): 229–40.

"The Neutering of 'Man' in the NIVI: The Translation of *Anthropos* and *Aner* in the Inclusive NIV." *CBMW News* 2, no. 3 (1997): 8–13.

"Saved through Childbearing? A Fresh Look at 1 Timothy 2:15 Points to Protection from Satan's Deception." *CBMW News* 2, no. 4 (1997): 1–6.

"Ascertaining Women's God-Ordained Roles: An Interpretation of 1 Timothy 2:15." *Bulletin of Biblical Research* 7 (1997): 107–44.

"'We Plead on Christ's Behalf: "Be Reconciled to God"': Correcting the Common Mistranslation of 2 Corinthians 5:20." *Bible Translator* 48 (1997): 328–31.

"Translator's Preface." Pages 9–15 in *The History of the Christ* by Adolf Schlatter. Grand Rapids: Baker Academic.

1996

"Frühe Zweifel an der johanneischen Verfasserschaft des vierten Evangeliums in der modernen Interpretationsgeschichte." *European Journal of Theology* 5 (1996): 37–46.

"Economics and Mission." Pages 102–17 in *Missiology and the Social Sciences: Contributions, Cautions and Conclusions.* EMS Missiological Monographs 4. Edited by Edward Rommen and Gary Corwin. Pasadena, CA: William Carey.

1995

"Anguish over Austria: Rising Above Pragmatism." *Evangelical Missions Quarterly* 31 (January 1995): 64–70.

"The 'Greater Works' of the Believer According to John 14:12." *Didaskalia* 6 (1995): 36–45.

"The Seventh Johannine Sign: A Study in John's Christology." *Bulletin of Biblical Research* 5 (1995): 87–103.

"The Challenge of a Systematized Biblical Theology: Missiological Insights from the Gospel of John." *Missiology* 23 (1995): 445–64.

"Syntactical Background Studies to 1 Tim. 2.12 in the New Testament and Extrabiblical Greek Literature." Pages 156–79 in *Discourse Analysis and Other Topics in Biblical Greek.* Edited by Stanley E. Porter and D. A. Carson. JSNTSup 113. Sheffield: Sheffield Academic Press.

"The Contribution of the General Epistles and Revelation to a Biblical Theology of Religions." *Christianity and the Religions: An Evangelical Theology of Religions.* EMS Missiological Monographs 2. Edited by Edward Rommen and Harold A. Netland. Pasadena, CA: William Carey.

"Chapter Four: A Complex Sentence Structure in 1 Tim 2:12." Pages 81–103 in *Women in the Church: A Fresh Analysis of 1 Timothy 2:11–15.* Edited by Andreas J. Köstenberger, Thomas R. Schreiner, and H. Scott Baldwin. Grand Rapids: Baker.

1994

"Gender Passages in the New Testament: Hermeneutical Fallacies Critiqued." *Westminster Theological Journal* 56 (1994): 259–83.

1992

"Review Article: The Apostolic Origins of Priestly Celibacy." *European Journal of Theology* 1 (1992): 173–79.

1991

"The Mystery of Christ and the Church: Head and Body, 'One Flesh.'" *Trinity Journal* 12 NS (1991): 79–94.

EDITORIALS

Journal of the Evangelical Theological Society 63, no. 1 (2020): 1–4.
Journal of the Evangelical Theological Society 62, no. 1 (2019): 1–4.
Journal of the Evangelical Theological Society 59, no. 1 (2016): 1–4.
Journal of the Evangelical Theological Society 58, no. 1 (2015): 1–3.
Journal of the Evangelical Theological Society 57, no. 1 (2014): 1–3.
Journal of the Evangelical Theological Society 56, no. 1 (2013): 1–3.
Journal of the Evangelical Theological Society 55, no. 1 (2012): 1–5.
Journal of the Evangelical Theological Society 54, no. 1 (2011): 1–3.
Journal of the Evangelical Theological Society 53, no. 1 (2010): 1–3.
Journal of the Evangelical Theological Society 52, no. 1 (2009): 1–3.
Journal of the Evangelical Theological Society 50, no. 1 (2007): 1–2.
Journal of the Evangelical Theological Society 49, no. 1 (2006): 1–3.
Journal of the Evangelical Theological Society 48, no. 1 (2005): 1–3.
Journal of the Evangelical Theological Society 47, no. 1 (2004): 1–2.
Journal of the Evangelical Theological Society 46, no. 1 (2003): 1–3.
Journal of the Evangelical Theological Society 45, no. 1 (2002): 1–2.
Journal of the Evangelical Theological Society 44, no. 1 (2001): 1–3.
Journal of the Evangelical Theological Society 43, no. 1 (2000): 1–3.
Journal of the Evangelical Theological Society 42, no. 1 (1999): 1–2.

REVIEWS

2021

Review of Peter Stuhlmacher, *Biblical Theology.* https://www.booksataglance.com/book-reviews/andreas-kostenbergers-review-of-biblical-theology-of-the-new-testament-by-peter-stuhlmacher (June 20, 2021).

2019

Review of Judith M. Lieu and Martinus C. de Boer, eds., *The Oxford Handbook of Johannine Studies. Bulletin of Biblical Research* 29, no. 2 (2019): 264–66.

2018

Review of Cornelis Bennema, *Mimesis in the Johannine Tradition: A Study in Johannine Ethics. Bulletin of Biblical Research* 28, no. 3 (2018): 524–26.

Review of Francis J. Moloney, *Johannine Studies 1975–2017. Bulletin of Biblical Research* 28, no. 2 (2018): 328–32.

2017

Review of Lois Fuller Dow et al., eds., *The Language and Literature of the New Testament: Essays in Honor of Stanley E. Porter's 60th Birthday. Journal of the Evangelical Theological Society* 60, no. 3 (2017): 625–28.

Review of Armin Baum et al., eds., *Der jüdische Messias. Journal of the Evangelical Theological Society* 60, no. 2 (2017): 406–8.

Review of Craig Bartholomew, *Introducing Biblical Hermeneutics.* https://www.booksataglance.com/book-reviews/introducing-biblical-hermeneutics-comprehensive-framework-hearing-god-scripture-craig-g-bartholomew (January 18, 2017).

Review of Trevor J. Burke and Keith Warrington, *A Biblical Theology of the Holy Spirit.* https://www.booksataglance.com/book-reviews/introducing-biblical-hermeneutics-comprehensive-framework-hearing-god-scripture-craig-g-bartholomew (January 18, 2017).

2016

Review of *The Last Years of Paul: Essays from the Tarragona Conference. Journal of the Evangelical Theological Society* 59, no. 2 (2016): 416–18.

Review of N. T. Wright, *Paul and His Recent Interpreters.* https://www.booksataglance.com/book-reviews/leon-morris-one-mans-fight-love-truth-neil-bach-constantine-tischendorf-life-work-19th-century-bible-hunter-stanley-e-porter (September 21, 2016).

Review of Neil Back, Leon Morris, and Stanley Porter, *Constantine Tischendorf.* https://www.booksataglance.com/book-reviews/paul-recent-interpreters-contemporary-debates-n-t-wright (May 11, 2016).

2015

Review of Karl Weyer-Menkhoff, *Die Ethik des Johannesevangeliums. Bulletin of Biblical Research* 25, no. 1 (2015): 116–18.

2014

Review of Bill O'Reilly and Martin Dugard, *Killing Jesus.* https://www.thegospelcoalition.org/reviews/killing-jesus (October 9, 2013).

Review of Andrew Lincoln, *Born of a Virgin.* https://www.thegospelcoalition.org/reviews/born-virgin (February 17, 2014).

Review of Bart Ehrman, *How Jesus Became God.* https://www.thegospelcoalition.org/reviews/god-became-jesus (April 16, 2014).

Review of Michael Bird et al., *How God Became Jesus.* (April 16, 2014). https://www.thegospelcoalition.org/reviews/god-became-jesus

2013

Review of Stanley Porter and Eckhard Schnabel, eds., *On the Writing of New Testament Commentaries: Festschrift for Grant R. Osborne on the Occasion of His 70th Birthday. Journal of the Evangelical Theological Society* 56, no. 2 (June 2013): 411–14.

Review of Dorit Felsch, *Die Feste im Johannesevangelium. Bulletin of Biblical Research* 23, no. 3 (2013): 437–39.

2012

Review of Stanley Porter, ed., *Handbook for the Study of the Historical Jesus. Journal of the Evangelical Theological Society* 55, no. 3 (September 2012): 573–78.

Review of *The Oxford Handbook of the Reception History of the Bible. Southeastern Theological Review* 3 (2012): 99–100.

2010

Review of Hans-Ulrich Weidemann, *Der Tod Jesu im Johannesevangelium. Catholic Biblical Quarterly* 72, no. 1 (2010): 168–69.

Review of Richard Bauckham, *The Jewish World around the New Testament. Southeastern Theological Review* 2, no. 1 (2010): 74–75.

2009

Review of Michael Bird, *Jesus and the Origins of the Gentile Mission. Review of Biblical Literature* (2009).

2008

Review of Christopher Ash, *Married for God*. 9Marks.

Review of Christopher Ash, *Marriage: Sex in the Service of God*. 9Marks.

Review of Edward W. Klink III, *The Sheep of the Fold: The Audience and Origin of the Gospel of John. Journal of the Evangelical Theological Society* 51 (September 2008): 654–56.

2007

Review of Aquila Lee, *From Messiah to Preexistent Son. Faith & Mission* 24, no. 2 (Spring 2007): 84–86.

Review of Eckhard Schnabel, *Early Christian Mission. Review of Biblical Literature* 2 (2007).

Review of Eckhard Schnabel, *Early Christian Mission. Bulletin of Biblical Research* 17 (2007): 357–59.

2006

Review of Watson E. Mills, *Index to Periodical Literature. Faith & Mission* 23, no. 2 (Spring 2006): 86–87.

Review of Lewis Ayres, *Nicaea and Its Legacy. Faith & Mission* 23, no. 2 (Spring 2006): 81–82.

Review of Frey and Schnelle, *Kontexte des Johannesevangeliums. Bulletin of Biblical Research* 16, no. 2 (2006): 358–60.

Review of G. van Belle et al., *Theology and Christology in the Fourth Gospel. Faith & Mission* 23, no. 3 (Summer 2006): 78–79.

2005

Review of *Accordance. Journal of the Evangelical Theological Society* 48, no. 1 (2005): 196–97.

Review of Willis Hedley Salier, *The Rhetorical Impact of the Semeia in the Gospel of John. Trinity Journal* 26 NS/1 (Spring 2005): 137–40.

Review of Gary Manning, *Echoes of a Prophet. Journal of the Evangelical Theological Society* 48, no. 2 (2005): 389–90.

Review of Charles Hill, *The Johannine Corpus in the Early Church. Journal of the Evangelical Theological Society* 48, no. 2 (2005): 390–93.

Review of I. Howard Marshall, *New Testament Theology. Themelios* 31, no. 1 (2005): 91–93.

Review of Amy-Jill Levine, ed., *A Feminist Companion to John. Faith & Mission* 22, no. 2 (Spring 2005): 107–11.

Review of *Stuttgarter Elektronische Studienbibel. Faith & Mission* 22, no. 3 (Summer 2005): 107–8.

Review of Daniel Rathnakara Sadananda, *The Johannine Exegesis of God. Faith & Mission* 22, no. 3 (Summer 2005): 116–17.

Review of Tricia Gates Brown, *Spirit in the Writings of John. Themelios* 30, no. 2 (Winter 2005): 61–62.

Review of Han Young Lee, *From Historical Criticism to Narrative Hermeneutics. Faith & Mission* 23, no. 1 (Fall 2005): 99–101.

Review of Christopher Morgan and Robert Peterson, eds., *Hell Under Fire. Faith & Mission* 23, no. 1 (Fall 2005): 105–6.

Review of Wouter Hanegraaff, ed., *Dictionary of Gnosis and Western Esotericism. Faith & Mission* 23, no. 1 (Fall 2005): 121–22.

2004

Review of Craig Keener, *John. Journal of the Evangelical Theological Society* 47, no. 2 (2004): 350–53.

Review of John Lee, *A History of New Testament Lexicography. Journal of the Evangelical Theological Society* 47, no. 3 (2004): 485–86.

Review of Seán P. Kealy, *John's Gospel and the History of Biblical Interpretation. Faith & Mission* 22, no. 1 (Fall 2004): 105–6.

2003

Review of Reimund Bieringer et al., *Anti-Judaism and the Fourth Gospel. Themelios* 28, no. 2 (2003): 71–73.

Review of Christina Urban, *Das Menschenbild nach dem Johannesevangelium. Review of Biblical Literature* 2 (2003).

Review of W. F. Moulton and A. S. Geden, *Concordance to the Greek New Testament. Journal of the Evangelical Theological Society* 46, no. 1 (2003): 125–26.

Review of Eckhard Schnabel, *Die urchristliche Mission. Journal of the Evangelical Theological Society* 46, no. 3 (2003): 359–60.

Review of Lee McDonald and Stanley Porter, *Early Christianity and Its Sacred Literature. Themelios* 28, no. 3 (2003): 90–91 and 31, no. 1 (2005): 91–92.

Review of *The Holman Illustrated Bible Dictionary. Faith & Mission* 21, no. 1 (2003): 92–94.

Review of *The NET Bible. Faith & Mission* 21, no. 1 (2003): 96–97.

2002

Review of William Mounce, *The Pastoral Epistles*. *Journal of the Evangelical Theological Society* 45 (2002): 365–66.

Review of Marianne Thompson, *The God of the Gospel of John*. *Journal of the Evangelical Theological Society* 45 (2002): 521–24.

2001

Review of Linda Belleville, *Women Leaders and the Church: Three Crucial Questions*. *Journal of the Evangelical Theological Society* 44 (2001): 344–46.

Review of Jerome Quinn and William Wacker, *The First and Second Letters to Timothy*. *Journal of the Evangelical Theological Society* 44 (2001): 549–50.

Review of I. Howard Marshall, *Pastoral Epistles*. *Journal of the Evangelical Theological Society* 44 (2001): 550–53.

Review of J. M. Holmes, *Text in a Whirlwind*. *Review of Biblical Literature* (2001).

Review of Andrew Lincoln, *Truth on Trial*. *Trinity Journal* 22 (2001): 269–72.

Review of Konrad Haldimann, *Rekonstruktion und Entfaltung*. *Review of Biblical Literature* (2001).

2000

Review of Richard N. Longenecker, *Biblical Exegesis in the Apostolic Period*, 2nd ed. *Journal of the Evangelical Theological Society* 43 (2000): 136–37.

Review of Bruce J. Malina and Richard L. Rohrbaugh, *Social-Science Commentary on the Gospel of John*. *Journal of the Evangelical Theological Society* 43 (2000): 144–45.

Review of Craig Van Gelder, ed., *Confident Witness—Changing World: Rediscovering the Gospel in North America*. *Evangelical Missions Quarterly* 36, no. 1 (2000): 114–15.

Review of James LaGrand, *The Earliest Christian Mission to "All Nations" in the Light of Matthew's Gospel*. *International Bulletin of Missionary Research* 24, no. 2 (April 2000), 86.

Review of Johan Ferreira, *Johannine Ecclesiology*. *Review of Biblical Literature* (2000).

Review of C. Marvin Pate, *Four Views on the Book of Revelation*. *Faith & Mission* 17, no. 2 (2000): 86–89.

Review of Walter Schmithals, *The Theology of the First Christians. Faith & Mission* 17, no. 2 (2000): 89.

Review of Walter Weaver, *The Historical Jesus in the Twentieth Century 1900–1950. Faith & Mission* 18, no. 1 (2000): 111–12.

Review of Mal Couch (ed.), *An Introduction to Classical Evangelical Hermeneutics. Faith & Mission* 18, no. 1 (2000): 115–16.

1999

Review of Paul Anderson, *The Christology of the Fourth Gospel. Journal of the Evangelical Theological Society* 42 (1999): 150–51.

Review of Robert Gordon Maccini, *Her Testimony Is True: Women as Witnesses According to John. Journal of the Evangelical Theological Society* 42 (1999): 51–53.

Review of Ben Witherington, *John's Wisdom. Journal of the Evangelical Theological Society* 42 (1999): 153–55.

Review of Andreas Obermann, *Die christologische Erfüllung der Schrift im Johannesevangelium. Review of Biblical Literature* 1 (1999): 318–19.

Review of Richard S. Ascough, *What Are They Saying About the Formation of Pauline Churches? Faith & Mission* 16, no. 3 (1999): 90–91.

Review of Alister E. McGrath, *The Genesis of Doctrine. Faith & Mission* 16, no. 3 (1999): 117–20.

Review of David R. Beck, *The Discipleship Paradigm. Journal of the Evangelical Theological Society* 42 (1999): 749–51.

Review of D. A. Carson, *The Inclusive-Language Debate* and Mark Strauss, *Distorting Scripture? Journal of the Evangelical Theological Society* 42 (1999): 689–93.

Review of Albert A. Bell Jr., *Exploring the New Testament World. Journal of the Evangelical Theological Society* 42 (1999): 754.

1998

Review of Adolf Schlatter, *Romans: The Righteousness of God*, translated by Siegfried Schatzmann. *Journal of the Evangelical Theological Society* 41 (1998): 141–42.

Review of Gregory A. Boyd, *Cynic Sage or Son of God? Trinity Journal* 19 (1998): 110–14.

Review of Herman Ridderbos, *The Gospel of John. Trinity Journal* 19 (1998): 122–26.

Review of N. T. Wright, *What Saint Paul Really Said. Faith & Mission* 15, no. 2 (1998): 87–88.

Review of Bruce Winter, *Philo and Paul among the Sophists. Faith & Mission* 15, no. 2 (1998): 90–91.

Review of Martin Hengel and Anna Maria Schwemer, *Paul Between Damascus and Antioch. Faith & Mission* 15, no. 2 (1998): 91–92.

Review of Paul Barnett, *Jesus and the Logic of History. Faith & Mission* 15, no. 2 (1998): 95–96.

Review of Raymond E. Brown, *An Introduction to the New Testament. Faith & Mission* 15, no. 2 (1998): 97–98.

Review of Richard A. Muller and John L. Thompson, *Biblical Interpretation in the Era of the Reformation. Faith & Mission* 15, no. 2 (1998): 107–8.

Review of Hans-Joachim Schulz, *Die apostolische Herkunft der Evangelien. Journal of the Evangelical Theological Society* 41 (1998): 476–77.

Review of G. Van Belle, *The Signs Source in the Fourth Gospel. Journal of the Evangelical Theological Society* 41 (1998): 489–91.

Review of Stanley Grenz, *Women in the Church. Journal of the Evangelical Theological Society* 41 (1998): 516–19.

1997

Review of Teresa Okure, *The Johannine Approach to Mission. Book Notes for Africa* 3 (1997): 14.

Review of Morna D. Hooker, *Not Ashamed of the Gospel. Journal of the Evangelical Theological Society* 40 (1997): 315.

Review of Peter Head, *Christology and the Synoptic Problem. Faith & Mission* 15, no. 1 (1997): 76–78.

Review of Markus Bockmuehl, *This Jesus*; Peter Stuhlmacher, *Jesus of Nazareth—Christ of Faith. Faith & Mission* 15, no. 1 (1997): 80–82.

1996

Review of Horst Balz and Gerhard Schneider, eds., *Exegetical Dictionary of the New Testament. Journal of the Evangelical Theological Society* 39 (1996): 142–44.

Review of Martin Hengel, *Die johanneische Frage. Journal of the Evangelical Theological Society* 39 (1996): 154–55.

"Is there a 'Problem with Paul'? A review of Brian J. Dodd, *The Problem with Paul." CBMW News* 1, no. 4 (1996): 12–13.

"Women and Early Church Authority: A Review of Wendy Cotter, 'Women's Authority Roles in Paul's Churches: Countercultural or Conventional?'" *CBMW News* 1, no. 4 (1996): 14.

Review of Rudolf Schnackenburg, *The Johannine Epistles. Journal of the Evangelical Theological Society* 39 (1996): 491–92.

Review of Christian Welck, *Erzählte Zeichen. Critical Review of Books in Religion* 9 (1996): 302–304.

Review of Gerhard Maier, *Biblical Hermeneutics. Journal of the Evangelical Theological Society* 39 (1996): 636–38.

1995

Review of David Wenham, *Paul: Follower of Jesus or Founder of Christianity? Trinity Journal* 16 (1995): 259–62.

Review of Raymond F. Collins, *These Things Have Been Written. Journal of the Evangelical Theological Society* 38 (1995): 472–73.

1994

Review of Gary Burge, *Interpreting the Gospel of John. Trinity Journal* 15 (1994): 138–40.

Review of William Klein, Craig Blomberg, and Ronald Hubbard, *Introduction to Biblical Interpretation. Trinity Journal* 15 (1994): 251–52.

1992

Review of Ari Goldman, *The Search for God at Harvard. Trinity Journal* 13 (1992): 249.

Review of Eta Linnemann, *Historical Criticism of the Bible: Methodology or Ideology? Trinity Journal* 13 (1992): 95–98.

Review of Joel Green, Scot McKnight, and I. Howard Marshall, *Dictionary of Jesus and the Gospels. Trinity Journal* 13 (1992): 250–51.

EDITED SERIES

Evangelical Biblical Theology Commentary (EBTC, 40 vols.). Bellingham, WA: Lexham. Coedited with T. D. Alexander and Thomas R. Schreiner.

Biblical Theology of the New Testament (BTNT, 8 vols.). Grand Rapids: Zondervan.

Evangelical Exegetical Commentary (EEC, 17 vols). New Testament Editor. Bellingham, WA: Lexham.

Exegetical Guide to the Greek New Testament (EGGNT, 20 vols.). Nashville: B&H. Coedited with Robert W. Yarbrough.

CONTRIBUTORS

T. Desmond Alexander (PhD, The Queen's University of Belfast) is Senior Lecturer in Biblical Studies at Union Theological College in Belfast, Northern Ireland, UK.

Gregg R. Allison (PhD, Trinity Evangelical Divinity School) is Professor of Christian Theology at The Southern Baptist Theological Seminary in Louisville, KY.

Paul N. Anderson (PhD, University of Glasgow) is Professor of Biblical and Quaker Studies at George Fox University in Newberg, OR.

Darrell L. Bock (PhD, University of Aberdeen) is Executive Director of Cultural Engagement and Senior Research Professor of New Testament Studies at Dallas Theological Seminary in Dallas, TX, and elder emeritus at Trinity Fellowship Church.

Gregory Goswell (PhD, University of Sydney) is Academic Dean and Lecturer in Old Testament at Christ College in Burwood, New South Wales, Australia.

L. Scott Kellum (PhD, Southeastern Baptist Theological Seminary) is Senior Professor of New Testament and Greek at Southeastern Baptist Theological Seminary in Wake Forest, NC.

Michael J. Kruger (PhD, University of Edinburgh) is President and Samuel C. Patterson Professor of New Testament and Early Christianity at the Charlotte campus of Reformed Theological Seminary.

Quinn R. Mosier (MDiv, Midwestern Baptist Theological Seminary) is Pastoral Assistant at Wornall Road Baptist Church in Kansas City, MO, and doctoral fellow at Midwestern Baptist Theological Seminary.

Stanley E. Porter (PhD, University of Sheffield) is President and Dean, Professor of New Testament, and Roy A. Hope Chair in Christian Worldview at McMaster Divinity College in Hamilton, Ontario.

James A. Roh (PhD, Midwestern Baptist Theological Seminary) is Director of Global Outreach at McLean Bible Church in Vienna, VA.

Eckhard J. Schnabel (PhD, University of Aberdeen) is Mary French Rockefeller Distinguished Professor of New Testament at Gordon-Conwell Theological Seminary in Hamilton, MA.

Thomas R. Schreiner (PhD, Fuller Theological Seminary) is Associate Dean for the School of Theology and the James Buchanan Harrison Professor of New Testament Interpretation and Professor of Biblical Theology at The Southern Baptist Theological Seminary in Louisville, KY.

Alexander Stewart (PhD, Southeastern Baptist Theological Seminary) is Dean to the Faculty, Vice President of Academic Services, and Professor of New Testament Studies at Gateway Seminary in Ontario, CA.

Robert W. Yarbrough (PhD, University of Aberdeen) is Professor of New Testament at Covenant Theological Seminary in St. Louis, MO, and teaching elder in the Presbyterian Church in America.

Author Index

A

Alexander, T. Desmond 10, 11, 62, 63, 91
Allison, Gregg R. 10, 221
Ammon, C. F. 188
Anderson, Paul N. 65, 179
Aquinas, Thomas 221, 222, 227–239
Ashton, John 192
Augustine of Hippo 227, 233, 234

B

Bacon, Benjamin 162
Bailey, John 163
Bakhtin, Mikhail 81
Barker, James 164
Barrett, C. K. 50, 68, 86, 97, 133, 163, 245
Barth, Karl 191
Bauckham, Richard 53, 77, 136–139, 143, 164, 168, 178, 200, 218
Bauer, Bruno 188
Bauer, G. L. 188
Bauer, Walter 207
Baur, Ferdinand Christian 157–159, 162, 174, 175, 180, 184–190, 193, 199, 200, 204
Beck, David 171
Becker, Jürgen 164
Belleville, Linda L. 247

Bennema, Cornelis 171, 172
Bernier, Jonathan 169
Beyschlag, Willibald 187
Bieringer, Reimund 173
Blackburn, W. Ross 101
Blomberg, Craig 178, 204
Bock, Darrell L. 19
Boismard, Émile 164
Bond, Helen 70
Borchert, Gerald L. 245
Bousset, Wilhelm 160
Bratcher, R. G. 241
Brodie, Thomas L. 137, 138, 165
Brown, Raymond E. 62, 67, 77, 133, 135, 163, 167, 168, 169
Brown, Sherri 47
Brunson, Andrew 120
Bultmann, Rudolf 67, 86, 159–165, 175, 179, 183, 190–200, 204
Burridge, Richard A. 70
Byers, Andrew 140
Bynum, William 166

C

Carson, D. A. 47, 50, 178, 204
Cerinthus 211
Childs, Brevard 207
Clark-Soles, Jaime 97, 102

Author Index

Clement of Alexandria............... 66, 155, 209, 213

Climacos, John.................................. 255

Collins, Raymond F............................ 69

Conway, Colleen 171

Coutts, Joshua J. F............................ 113

Cullmann, Oscar............................... 167

Culpepper, R. Alan...... 68, 169, 170, 171

D

Daise, Michael A. 116, 166

Daly-Denton, Margaret,.................... 118

de Wette, W. M. L............................. 188

Didymus the Blind............................ 239

Dionysius bar Salibi 211

Dodd, C. H. 133, 165, 166, 175–178

Douglas, Mary 172

Dumbrell, William J............................ 48

E

Epiphanius................................. 211, 212

Eusebius of Caesarea.... 33, 155, 211, 218

F

Forster, E. M. 171

Fortna, Robert T................. 86, 163, 164

Freed, Edwin..................................... 166

Frey, Jörg........................... 168, 177, 204

G

Gabler, J. P. 184, 187, 188, 193

Gaius of Rome 210, 211

Gardner-Smith, Percival 133, 162, 163

Gathercole, Simon............................. 140

Gentry, Peter J........................ 45, 59, 60

Godet, Frédéric Louis........................ 189

Goodacre, Mark S. 135

Goppelt, Leonard.............................. 244

Goswell, Gregory........................ 10, 115

Gray, George Buchanan....................... 97

Grayston, Kenneth 30

Gunkel, Hermann..................... 159, 160

H

Hafemann, Scott J............................... 44

Hardy, Nicholas 203

Hatton, H. A...................................... 241

Heath, E. A. 48

Heidegger, Martin 160

Hengel, Martin 119, 168, 213, 216

Herrmann, Peter 36, 37

Hilary of Poitiers............................... 239

Hippolytus.. 211

Holmes, Stephen............................... 223

Holtzmann, Heinrich........ 187, 190, 193

Homer 262

Hooker, Morna D. 70

Hoskins, Paul M. 98, 99

Hoskyns, Edwyn 149

Howard, W. F. 162, 175

Hunter, Archibald M......................... 133

Hurtado, Larry......................... 122, 123

I

Ignatius 218, 219

Immer, Albert.................................... 187

Inge, W. R. 218

Irenaeus.............. 33, 209, 213, 214, 217

Iser, Wolfgang 170

J

Jobes, Karen H. 249

Just, Felix 179

Justin Martyr............................. 215, 216

Author Index

K

Kayser, G. P. C. 188

Keener, Craig S. 137, 178

Kelber, Werner H. 69

Kellum, L. Scott 43

Klink, Edward W. 44, 168

Koester, Craig 176, 177

Köstenberger, Andreas J. 9, 10, 29, 41, 43, 46, 62, 91, 103, 111, 115, 125, 131, 145–147, 171, 176–178, 183, 184, 192, 204, 207, 221, 240, 241

Kruger, Michael J. 10, 205

Kruse, Colin G. 250

L

Lang, Manfred 164

L. Calpurnius Piso Caesoninus 263

Levering, Matthew 227

Lierman, John 120

Lightfoot, Joseph Barber 158

Lightfoot, R. H. 162

Lincoln, Andrew 164

Lindars, Barnabas 69, 163

M

Malatesta, Edward 49

Malay, Hasan 36, 37

Malina, Bruce. 172

Marshall, I. Howard 183, 249

Martyn, J. Louis 163, 167, 168, 169

Meeks, Wayne 172

Menken, Maarten J. J. 166

Merk, Otto. 187

Michaels, J. Ramsey 69

Morris, Leon 144, 163, 178, 204

Mosier, Quinn R. 10, 11, 131

Moyise, Steve 92

N

Neander, August. 188

Neirynck, Frans. 133, 164

Neyrey, Jerome 172

Nicol, William 164

O

Oehler, Gustav 188

Origen. 30, 209

P

Papias of Hierapolis... 214, 217, 218, 219

Peterson, Norman 172

Petterson, Anthony R. 57

Petzl, Georg. 39

Phillips, Peter 171

Philodemus of Gadara 263

Photius of Constantinople 211

Pierce, Madison. 140

Piotrowski, Nicholas. 94

Plato. 263

Plutarch. 262, 264

Polybius. 262

Polycarp 214, 217, 219

Porter, Stanley E. 10, 99, 100, 155

Ptolemy the Gnostic. 209

R

Rainbow, Paul 177

Reim, Günter 165

Renan, Ernest. 158

Reuss, Édouard Guillaume Eugène 187, 188

Richards, I. A. 171

Ricl, Marijana 39

Author Index

Ritschl, Albrecht 190

Robinson, John A. T.... 69, 169, 175, 176

Roh, James A. 10, 103

S

Sallustius 244

Schlatter, Adolf 177, 178, 190,
193–196, 199

Schleiermacher, F. D. E. 190

Schmid, C. F. 188

Schmithals, Walther 161

Schnabel, Eckhard J. 10, 34, 196, 199,
200–203, 255

Schnackenburg, Rudolf 55, 164, 212

Schnelle, Udo 196–201, 204

Schreiner, Thomas R. 10, 44, 45, 241

Schuchard, Bruce 166

Scott, E. F. 162

Seneca 264

Shelfer, Lochlan 30, 31, 32, 34

Shepherd, David J. 51

Smalley, Stephen 252

Smith, D. Moody 133, 163

Staley, Jeffrey 170

Stevens, George 175

Stewart, Alexander 29

Stibbe, Mark 170, 171

Stovell, Beth 166

Strauss, David Friedrich ... 157, 158, 159,
162, 174, 179, 188

Streeter, B. H. 162

T

Tacitus 263

Tatian 215

Teeple, Howard 164

Tertullian 212, 213

Thatcher, Tom 179

Theobald, Michael 69

Thompson, Marianne Meye 95

Thucydides 262

Timaeus 262

Tischendorf, Constantine 158

Trummer, Peter 243

V

Vanhoozer, Kevin 145

van Oosterzee, J. J. 184, 187–190, 199

Vatke, J. K. 188

Voetius, Gisbertus 256

von Harnack, Adolf 190, 207, 208

von Wahlde, Urban 163

W

Waldstein, Michael 191

Weiss, Bernhard 187

Weiss, Johannes 159, 160

Wellum, Stephen J. 45, 59, 60

Westcott, Brooke Foss 158

Williams, Catrin H. 138

Williams, Peter J. 68

Witherington, Ben 204

Wrede, William 159

X

Xenophon 262

Y

Yarbrough, Robert W. ... 10, 11, 183, 252

Z

Zahn, Theodor 204, 207

Zeno of Sidon 263

SUBJECT INDEX

A

abiding 49, 50
Abraham 45, 50, 55, 79, 149
ad extra works of God 224
advocate
    legal context of 31
agency 85
ancient compositional norms............. 137
atonement 63

B

baptism 247
belief 83, 139
Beloved Disciple...................... 77, 86, 88
blessing 49
blindness 108
born again motif................ 241, 244, 248
bread of life 105, 117

C

Christ of faith....................................... 78
confession 75, 87
covenant... 48
    ANE 44, 51
    grant treaties...................................45
    new 44, 48, 55
    old 44, 45, 49
    renewal...51
    suzerain-vassal 45
cross 53, 114
curses 49

D

David 117, 126, 127, 242
devil 63
divine counsel 39
divine name... 101
divinity of Jesus 123, 148
double procession 231, 234
double sending 231

E

election 47
Enlightenment 156, 159
eternal life 55, 96, 99, 100, 125
Exodus 94

F

faith 252
farewell discourse................................. 44
feeding of 5,000 117
fictive kinship...................................... 46
filioque controversy 231
footwashing................................... 53, 62
forgiveness 61
futurist eschatology 47

G

gennaō 241
Gentile inclusion 58
glory......................... 112, 113, 125
God
    as begetter 252
Gospel traditions 135

315

Subject Index

H

Heracleon 209

Herodotus 262

Hesiod 262

high Christology 124, 174

historical criticism 156

history of religions 158

Holy Spirit
    as paraclete 31, 40, 57, 59, 64, 228
    eternal procession 221
    role in salvation 41, 55

I

"I am" statements 101

imperial cult 79

Israel 55

J

Jesus
    as Divine Son 118
    as eschatological prophet 85
    as Isaianic servant 113
    as judge 118, 123
    as King of Israel......107, 118, 120, 144, 195
    as Lamb of God................................63, 111
    as Messiah 54, 119, 139, 252
    as paraclete 40
    as Rabbi 46
    as revealer 85
    as sacrifice 97, 111
    as Son of David 120
    as Son of Man 123
    as wisdom 242
    death 53, 58, 61, 95, 122
    divinity..101
    of history..78
    resurrection 58, 195
    substitutionary death................................99

Jewish rewriting 138

Johannine authorship 157, 190, 198,
                                                    202, 208
    community hypothesis 166

Johannine dependence 142, 162

Johannine dualism 149, 175

Johannine idiom 138

Johannine independence 162
    form-critical foundations.......................136
    rise and retreat.......................................132

Johannine question........................... 177

Johannine school 198

Johannine studies 155
    Baur, F. C. 184
    Bultmann, Rudolf 160, 191
    conservative approaches........................178
    Johannine theologies 176
    Schlatter, Adolf......................................193
    Schnabel, Eckhard J. 200
    Schnelle, Udo..197
    social-scientific approaches 172
    van Oosterzee, J. J. 187

Johannine writings 72
    unity..190

John
    and Daniel 122–125
    and early church....................................205
    and Exodus 94
    and gnostics 206
    and hellenistic influences.......................194
    and history...................................179, 199
    and Judaism 173
    and Justin Martyr...................................215
    and missions..202
    and Nag Hammadi 210
    and New Testament theologies 184
    and Old Testament.................................139
    and Papias of Hierapolis 217
    and pentateuch..91
    and prophets 103
    and Psalms 115–122
    and Roman Empire.................................173
    and theology 141
    and writings 115
    authorial tendencies 139
    characters in 171
    date...169, 176

Subject Index

Fourth Quest 179
orthodox opposition to 210
Prologue.....65, 94, 245
reception in the early church 207, 212
sources 162
theology 174
use by heretics 209

John and Synoptics.... 131, 137, 142, 162
assumption.....143
form criticism.....134
interlocking tradition 144, 163
supplementation 144
theological transformation.....145

John the Baptist.....66, 70, 82, 97, 104, 149
as forerunner.....82

judgment.....117

K
kingship 119

L
lifted up 112, 113, 122
literary criticism 169
Livy.....263
Logos 80
Lord's Supper 53
Louvain school 133
love 54, 64, 72, 251

M
mandaeism 160
meal 62
memoirs of the apostles 216
Messiah 83, 119
miracles.....94
Moses.....51, 79, 85

N
narrative criticism.....170
new heaven and earth.....255

Nicodemus.....246
Noah.....45

O
obedience 48, 50, 55, 253
overture.....69, 88

P
passover.....46, 50, 53, 62, 95, 96, 111
people of God 55, 56, 79
preexistence.....148
prophetic allusion.....111
prophetic fulfillment 104
propitiatory inscriptions.....32

Q
quotation vs. allusion 91, 139

R
regeneration 248, 252
ritual meal.....50

S
sacrifice 52, 61, 96
salvation 55
sanctification 63, 250
Satan and Judas 147
sending motif.....27, 229
Shema.....48
signs.....93
signs and wonders 94
simplicity 223
single procession.....222
Son-Father relationship 50, 83, 242
Son of God.....100, 101
son of man 122
strophic design 78

317

Subject Index

T

tears
- and epistle to the Hebrews 271
- and James..273
- and Jesus..272
- and Paul..270
- and Revelation 274
- classification of.....................................255
- contrasted with weeping.......................269
- end of..275
- Hebrew and LXX translation................267
- in Greco-Roman world 262
- in Israel 267
- in letters and inscriptions 265
- in the New Testament 269
- semantic range 256

temple............................... 116, 126, 150

theological transposition.................... 145

throne of God 275

Torah 106

transfiguration............................. 87, 148

Trinity.. 222
- consubstantiality 237
- divine essence.......................................232
- divine life 223
- divine missions..............................221, 223
- divine processions.........................221, 231
- eternal generation.........................222, 225
- relations of origin 233

twelve disciples 64

V

Valentinians............................... 206, 209

W

water and Spirit.................................. 247

weeping of kings................................. 274

Z

Zeus... 34

SCRIPTURE INDEX

Genesis
1 ....79, 139, 159
3 275
3:8 277
3:16–19 275
6 45
12:1 47
17:1 46
18:19 47
21:16 ....257, 267
26:30 51
27 80
28:38 267
29:11 ....267, 269
31:54 51
32:30 277
33:4 269
42:24 269
43:30 269
45:2 267
49:11 107
49:25 246

Exodus
1–13 102
3:14 101
3–12 96
4:1 94
4:5 94
4:9 94
4:30 94
7:3 94
7:9 94
7:14–25 94
7–11 94
7–12 94
8:23 94
10:1–2 94
11:9–10 94
12 ....92, 96, 98, 111
12:5 96
12:8–11 98
12:22 100

12:46 ....92, 96,
 104, 110, 116
13:2 98
13:11–13 98
15:17 99
17 122
19:6 62
21:6 118
22:8 118
24:1–11 62
24:4–8 52
24:8 52
24:11 ....51, 277
29:1–37 63
29:31–34 98
33:11 277
33:20 277
33–34 79

Leviticus
8:1–36 63
8:31–32 98
21:18, 20 58
23:1–7 58

Numbers
3:13 97
8:7 97
9:12 ....92, 96, 104,
 110, 116
11:7–9 106
12:8 277
14:20–23 61
28:22 98

Deuteronomy
1:45 269
4:34 94
6:4–5 48
6:6 57
6:22 94
7:6 47
7:9 48

7:19 94
11:18 57
14:12 47
18:15–18 79
18:15–22 85
26:8 94
27 49
27:7 51
27:28 49
29:3 94
32:18 241
34:8 267
34:11 94

Joshua
3:16 246
8:30–35 51
9:4, 13 267
24 ....51, 52

Judges
4:19 267
13:22 277
14:16–17 269
20:23, 26 269
21:2 269

Ruth
1:9, 14 269

1 Samuel
1:7, 8, 10 269
10:3 118
11:4 269
15:27–28 122

2 Samuel
1:11–12, 24 269
3:32–34 269
13:36 267
15:23, 30 269
18:28 121

Scripture Index

1 Kings
11:29–31 122
22 80

2 Kings
8:11–12 269
11:17–18 51
20:3 .... 267, 269
20:5 .... 267, 268
23:1–3 51

1 Chronicles
25:1–3 127

2 Chronicles
14–15 51
24:4–14 126
30:1–27 126
34:29–33 51
36:22–23 127

Ezra
3:10 127
8:20 127
10:1 269
10:1–5 51

Nehemiah
1:4 269
3:16 127
8:9 269
8:10, 12 51
8:12 51
8–10 51
9:10 94
9:15 106
11:23 127
12:24, 36 127
12:24, 36, 45, 46 127
12:36 127
12:37 127
12:45 127
12:45–46 127

Esther
9:19–22 51

Job
3:24 257
14:17 267
16:2 39

16:16 267
32:8 231

Psalms
2 195
2:7 242
6:6 267
6:7 267
6:7–9 269
22 121
30:6 267
34:20 .... 92, 110, 122
35:19 121
39:13 267
41 121
41:9 121
42:3 268
42:4 267
45 118
45:6 118
46:10 60
55:12–14 121
56:8 267
56:9 267
58:1 117
69 .... 117, 121
69:4 121
69:9 .... 116, 126
69:21 122
78 117
78:16, 20 122
78:21–22, 31 117
78:24 106
78:24a 117
78:24b 117
80:6 267
82 117
82:6 .... 23, 117, 118
82:6b 118
89:3 47
95:6 269
96:13 120
98:9 120
100:3 60
102:10 267
103:30 229
105:27 94
110:1 79
116 271
116:8 267
118 .... 118, 120
118:25–26 118
119:136 260

126:5 267
126:5–6 269
132:1–10 126
135:9 94
137:1 .... 267, 269
137:4 125
138–145 125
145:21 126

Proverbs
8:22–30 79
8:22–31 242
8:25 242
26:24 267

Ecclesiastes
3:4 .... 267, 269, 277
4:1 267
12:5 269

Isaiah
5:1–7 111
6 148
6:1 .... 112, 113
6:9 109
6:9–10 108
6:10 ..... 103, 104, 108–110
9:1 112
9:6 276
11:2 112
15:2 274
15:2–6 269
15:3–4 267
15:3, 5 269
15:9 267
16:9 .... 267, 269
25:7–8 125
25:8 .... 255, 267, 269,
                        275, 276
25:8–9 275
26:19 125
27:2–6 111
30 50
30:19 269
38:5 267
40:3 ..... 103–105, 108, 111
40:5 112
40:9 107
41:4 112
41:10 107
42:1 112
42:1–6 54
42:6 54

Scripture Index

42:8 112
42:18–19 109
42:18–20 109
43:7 112
43:8 109
43:10 112
44:2 107
44:6 119
46:4 112
48:11 112
48:12 112
49:6 112
49:10 255
51:12 112
52:6 112
52:13 ....112, 113
52:13–53:12 ....110, 113
52:14 113
52:15 110
52–53 110
53:1 ....103, 104, 108
53:1a 108
53:2 113
53:4, 11–12 112
53:7 111
53:12 112
54:13 106
54:13a 103
54–55 106
55:1–3 106
55:1–5 58
55:10 106
55:10–11 106
56 58
56:1 58
56:10 109
60:1 112
63:16 276
64:8 276
65:17 243
65:19 269
66:22 243

Jeremiah
2:21 111
3:21 ....267, 269
4:13 274
5:20 61
6:9 111
8:23 ....267, 269
9:1 ....268, 269
9:17 267
12:10–13 111

13:17 ....267, 269
14:10 61
14:17 267
23:1–4 111
31:9 269
31:16 ....267, 269
31:23, 28 61
31:29–30 59
31:31 44
31:31–34 ....52, 58, 61
31:32 ....49, 267
31:33 57
31:34 ....59, 61
32:20–21 94
38:15 267
38:32 49
44:21 61
50:4 269

Lamentations
1:2 ....267, 268
1:2, 16 269
2:11, 18 267
2:18 ....268, 269

Ezekiel
8:6 55
8:14 268
11 55
11:13 56
11:19–20 56
11:26 56
15:1–8 111
17:5–10 111
18:31 56
19:10–14 111
24:16 ....267, 269
27:35 ....257, 267
34 111
36 248
36:22–36 56
36:24 56
36:25 247
36:25–27 247
36:27 ....56, 247
36:28 56
36–37 253
37 248
37:5 248
37:9–10 248
37:14 248
37:27 255
45:21–25 98

Daniel
6:26–27 125
7 ....122, 123, 124, 129
7:1 124
7:9 123
7:9–12 124
7:9, 13 123
7:13 124
7:13–14 123
7:14 124
7:21, 25 123
7:22, 24, 27 125
11:33, 35 125
12 125
12:2 125
12:3 125

Hosea
2:12 274
6:7 45
10:1–2 111
10:5 274
12:5 269
13:12 267
14:7 111

Joel
1:9–10 274
2:12–17 269
2:28–32 56

Amos
5:16–17 269

Micah
2:4 274
2:6 257

Zephaniah
3:15 118
3:16 107

Zechariah
2:10 120
7:3 269
8:3 120
9 107
9:9 ....103, 107, 118,
120, 121
11:4–17 111
12:9–13 110

Scripture Index

12:10 ...103, 104, 109, 110
14:5 120

Malachi

2:6 267
2:12 269
2:13 267–269
3:1 54

Matthew

3:3 104
3:7–9 149
3:11 71
5:4 272
5:8 277
12:34 149
13:14–15 108
13:15 109
16:13 122
16:27 124
17:1–8 148
19:28 .... 124, 242
21 120
21:5 118
21:9, 15 120
23:33 149
24:30 124
25:31 124
26:6–13 270
26:14–16 147
26:28 53
26:37 271
26:75 273
27:46 271
28:19 195

Mark

1 ....70, 88
1:1–5 71
1:1–15 70
1:1–20 67
1:2–3 104
1:7 71
1:8 71
1:13, 14 143
1:14 ....69, 71
4:12 108
5:38, 39 272
6:1–6 82
8:27 122
8:31 123
8:35 138
9:2–8 148

9:13 70
11:9–10 120
14:3–9 270
14:10–11 147
14:24 53
14:33 271
14:58 150
14:62 123
14:72 .... 257, 272
15:34 271

Luke

1:1–4 199
3:4–6 104
3:16 71
6:21 272
7:13 272
7:32 272
7:38 .... 270, 272
7:38, 44 257
8:10 108
8:52 272
9:18 122
9:28–36 148
19:38 119
19:41 272
22:3 147
22:19 53
22:20 44
22:62 273
22:69 122
23:28 273

John

1 ....78, 88, 186
1:1–2 74
1:1–3 71
1:1–5 ....69, 79
1:1–5, 14, 18 144
1:1, 14 25
1:1–18 ....65, 68, 79,
174, 205, 245
1:3 209
1:4 ....74, 94, 147
1:4–5 81
1:4, 7, 9 112
1:5 ....74, 147
1:6–3:36 69
1:6–7 71
1:6–8 70
1:6–8, 15 ....66–68, 70
1:6–8, 15, 19–23 71
1:6–8, 15, 19–28 105

1:6–8, 15, 19–42 70
1:8 71
1:9 ....74, 85
1:9–13 ....69, 83
1:9–14 ....69, 79
1:9, 14 121
1:10 74
1:10–13 68
1:11 ....63, 74
1:12 ....68, 74, 112, 245
1:12–13 ....46, 246
1:13 ....74, 245, 246
1:14 ....19, 66, 74, 78,
87, 112, 148, 218
1:14, 16 66
1:15 71
1:16 74
1:16–18 ....69, 79
1:18 ...19, 74, 85, 216, 277
1:19 ....68, 69
1:19–42 67
1:21 105
1:23 ....91, 103, 104,
108, 140
1:29 ....59, 63, 96, 112
1:29–34 143
1:33 71
1:35–51 217
1:35–4:45 143
1:36 ....63, 96
1:39, 46 148
1:41 ....117, 119
1:45 74
1:49 ....119, 144, 195
1:51 ....91, 122, 124
1–12 46
2:1–11 93
2:1–12 ....94, 143, 205
2:11 ....74, 93, 105, 112
2:13 96
2:13, 23 ....96, 111, 128
2:16 20
2:17 ....91, 116, 117,
126, 129
2:17, 22 108
2:20 19
2:21–22 150
2:22 116
2:23 ....82, 93, 96, 112
3 ....246, 253
3:1–2 246
3:1–8 246
3:1–21 205

Scripture Index

3:2 147
3:3 .... 216, 246
3:3, 5 119
3:3, 6 74
3:4 19
3:5 247
3:6 248
3:8 .... 218, 219, 248
3:9–10 .... 247, 248
3:11 .... 73, 74
3:13 124
3:13, 14 124
3:13, 31–36 144
3:14 .... 110, 112, 122
3:15–16, 36 73
3:16 .... 187, 216
3:16–17 59
3:16–21 123
3:18 112
3:19 112
3:24 .... 69, 71, 143
3:27–30 82
3:31 .... 121, 246
3:32 73
3:35 20
4:1–45 82
4:11–12 246
4:24 120
4:26 .... 112, 144
4:38 27
4:42 59
4:45 96
4:46 143
4:46–54 93
4:48 93
5 .... 24, 167
5:1 .... 96, 128
5:1–15 93
5:14 116
5:18–29 144
5:19 .... 218, 231
5:19–29 148
5:21, 26 73
5:23 20
5:24 .... 20, 73
5:25 73
5:26 222
5:27 .... 123, 124
5:28–29 125
5:30 20
5:36 20
5:38 20
5:39 106

5:41 112
5:42 85
5:43 .... 112, 229
5:46 .... 74, 105, 149
6 .... 67, 71, 106, 117
6:1–14 93
6:1–21 148
6:4 .... 96, 111, 128
6:5–7, 26–27 106
6:15–21 93
6:22–59 105
6:26 117
6:27, 53, 62 .... 122, 124
6:27, 55 106
6:29 20
6:31 .... 117, 129
6:31–33 106
6:31, 45 91
6:32 117
6:33 59
6:33, 38–44 106
6:35–37 20
6:35–58 117
6:38 20
6:40, 47 73
6:44 20
6:44–46 85
6:45 .... 103, 106
6:46 74
6:48 101
6:51 59
6:52 246
6:53–58 98
6:57 20
6:63, 68 73
6:64 73
6:65 48
7 167
7:2 128
7:12 21
7:14, 28 116
7:16 21
7:18 .... 21, 112
7:19 74
7:28 21
7:29 21
7:31 .... 82, 93
7:33–34 21
7:38 .... 91, 122, 140
7:39 247
7:40–42 117
7:42 91
8:12 . 72, 74, 101, 112, 147

8:12–13 21
8:16 21
8:17 .... 91, 121
8:18 22
8:19 22
8:21–29 148
8:24 112
8:24, 28, 58 101
8:26 22
8:26, 38 73
8:28 .... 110, 112, 113,
                124, 218, 236
8:28, 58 112
8:29 .... 22, 123
8:30–33 23
8:31 82
8:31–32 85
8:39 149
8:42 22
8:44 .... 73, 149, 150, 219
8:50 112
8:56 .... 105, 149
9 .... 24, 109, 167
9:1–41 .... 93, 205
9:4 .... 22, 147
9:5 74
9:15 112
9:16 93
9:22 .... 82, 109
9:25 23
9:34–41 123
9:35 124
9:38 82
9:39 109
9:41 .... 85, 109
10:7, 9, 14 218
10:7–18 111
10:9–10 101
10:11–15 101
10:22 128
10:23 116
10:25 112
10:28 73
10:30 .... 23, 74
10:31, 33 23
10:33, 36 118
10:34 ..... 91, 117, 121, 129
10:35–36 23
10:42 82
11:1–45 93
11:2 143
11:4 74
11:9 74

323

Scripture Index

11:10 147
11:17–44 205
11:25 96
11:25–26 95
11:27 ....95, 120
11:31 272
11:33 272
11:35 272
11:40 23
11:42 23
11:45 82
11:45–53 95
11:49–50 95
11:55 ....96, 111, 128
11:55–57 95
11:56 ....96, 116
11–12 95
12 ....108, 109, 113, 120
12:1 ....96, 111, 128
12:1–8 ....95, 270
12:3 91
12:7–8 95
12:12–15 144
12:12, 20 96
12:13 ..116, 118, 119, 120, 129
12:13, 28 112
12:14–15, 38, 39–40 91
12:15 ....103, 107, 118, 120, 121
12:15, 40 140
12:16 ....108, 116
12:23, 34 124
12:25 138
12:27 91
12:30–36 123
12:31 147
12:32 122
12:32, 34 ....110, 112
12:34 72
12:35 112
12:36 74
12:36–43 139
12:37 ....105, 108, 109
12:38 ...103, 104, 108, 109
12:38–40 .....104, 107, 110
12:40 ....103, 108–110
12:41 ....105, 109, 112, 113, 148
12:42 ....82, 109
12:43 113
12:44 24
12:45 24

12:46 74
12:49 24
12:49–50 236
12–19 96
13 53
13:1 ....50, 54, 85, 96, 111, 128
13:1, 2 50
13:1, 29 96
13:1–30 43
13:3, 31–33 53
13:6–11 53
13:8 ....54, 61
13:8–10 99
13:10 ....61, 121
13:12–20 53
13:16 ....24, 25
13:18 ....48, 91, 104, 117, 121, 129, 140
13:19 ....101, 112
13:20 24
13:21 73
13:26 121
13:27 147
13:30 ....47, 147
13:31 ....47, 124
13:31–16:33 43
13:34 72
13:34–35 ....58, 64
13:35 64
13:36 58
13:36–38 ....57, 58
13:37 58
13–17 47
14:1 60
14:1–4, 12, 19, 28 53
14:1–6 99
14:1–7 32
14:2–4 60
14:3 47
14:5–7 60
14:6 ....40, 55, 74, 85, 101, 227, 228, 231
14:7 60
14:8–14 60
14:9 149
14:10 236
14:13–14, 26 112
14:15 228
14:15–17 .....222, 227, 228
14:15, 21 55
14:15, 21–24 49
14:15–26 57

14:15–30 64
14:16 ....49, 227, 240
14:16–17 228
14:16, 26 ....29, 31, 226
14:21–24 49
14:23 73
14:24 24
14:26 ....24, 32, 41, 222, 227, 229, 231, 235, 240
14–16 ....227, 239
15:1 111
15:1–5 55
15:1–6 101
15:3 62
15:4–7 72
15:9–11 55
15:10 49
15:12 64
15:12–17 85
15:13–17 58
15:14 50
15:16, 19 48
15:16, 21 112
15:18 64
15:18, 19, 23, 24 121
15:21 25
15:22 64
15:24 64
15:25 ....64, 91, 104, 117, 121, 129
15:26 ....29, 31, 41, 222, 226, 227, 229–231, 235
15:26–27 .....32, 57, 64, 144
15:27 73
15–17 ....67, 71
16:2 ....64, 82
16:3 74
16:4 73
16:5 25
16:7 ....29, 31, 226, 229
16:7–11 64
16:7, 13–15 ..222, 227, 235
16:7–15 57
16:7, 16–17 53
16:8–9 59
16:8–11 ....32, 41, 235
16:9 31
16:12 235
16:12–15 236
16:13 ....41, 231
16:13–15 ....73, 236

Scripture Index

16:14 238
16:14–15 237
16:20 272
16:23–24, 26 112
16:26 59
17 ....26, 144
17:1 148
17:1–3 73
17:1, 11 53
17:1–16 205
17:1–26 43
17:2 59
17:3 ....25, 55, 60
17:5, 22, 24 112
17:6 64
17:6, 11–12, 26 112
17:8 25
17:9 48
17:11 26
17:12 ....91, 251
17:14 64
17:16 218
17:17 63
17:17–19 98
17:18 ....26, 59
17:19 26
17:20–23 ....25, 218
17:21 26
17:21, 23 59
17:22 26
17:23 26
17:24 26
17:25 74
17:26 26
18 43
18:5, 8 112
18:9, 32 104
18:18 57
18:20 116
18:28, 39 96
18:33, 37 119
18:33–38 144
19 100
19:3 119
19:7 119
19:13–42 99
19:14 96
19:14, 36 111
19:15 119
19:19–22 119
19:21 119
19:23–24a.....................121
19:24 ....117, 129

19:24, 28, 36, 37 91
19:24, 36 104
19:28 122
19:29 100
19:34–35 ...67, 72, 85, 219
19:35 198
19:36 ....92, 96, 110,
            116, 122, 140
19:36–37 ...100, 104, 107
19:37 ...103, 104, 109, 110
20:11, 13, 15 273
20:21 26
20:22 58
20:24–29 73
20:25, 27 216
20:28 ....46, 149, 195
20:29 196
20:30–31 .....68, 77, 93–95
20:31 ....9, 83, 112, 139
21 ....57, 58, 67, 71, 176
21:2 217
21:9 57
21:15–17 58
21:18–19 58
21:19 58
21:20–24 ....72, 75
21:20–25 77
21:22 58
21:24 ....66, 88, 105, 208
21:34 198

Acts

1:22 200
2:33 240
2:36 242
4:19–20 73
7:56 122
8:24 257
9:39 273
13:33 242
18:24–28 80
18–19 82
20:19 270
20:19, 31 257
20:31 270
21:13 273
28:26–27 108
28:27 109

Romans

8:9 ....228, 229
8:15 231
8:29 229

10:16 108
11:8 108
12:15 273

1 Corinthians

1:18–2:5 270
2:10–13 236
3:16 230
4:14–15 270
4:15 243
5:7 101
7:30 273
7:31 273
11:25 44
13:12 277

2 Corinthians

2:4 ....257, 270
2:5 270
3:6 44
6:13 270
12:14–15 270

Galatians

1:6 33
4:6 ....230, 231
4:9 246
4:21–31 243
4:23 243
4:24 243
4:29 ....243, 244

Ephesians

5:26 247

Philippians

2:6–11 ....79, 175
3:18 ....257, 273

Colossians

1:15–20 ....79, 176

1 Timothy

2:9–15 241
5:18 199

2 Timothy

1:4 ....257, 270

Titus

3:5 ....243, 247
3:9 243

Scripture Index

Philemon

10 243
16 243

Hebrews

1:1–4 ....79, 80
1:5 242
2:14 271
4:15 271
5:7 ....257, 271
5:8 272
8:8 44
8–10 44
9:15 ....44, 271
9:18–22 52
9:20 53
10:29 53
12:14 277
12:17 ....257, 272

James

3:15 246
4:9 273
5:1 274

1 Peter

1:3 244
1:18–19 101
1:23 244
3:21 247
5:1 198

2 Peter

1:16–18 87
3:16 199

1 John

1:1 ....73, 76

1:1, 3 73
1:1–3 ....66, 67, 70,
72, 75, 78, 200
1:1–4 ....73, 77, 88
1:2 ....73, 76
1:3 ....73, 76
1:4 ....72, 75, 76
1:6–7 72
1:8, 10 250
2:1 ....29, 30, 40
2:6 72
2:7 ....72, 73
2:9 72
2:13–14, 24 73
2:18–25 83
2:28 249
2:29 ....249, 250, 252
3:2 277
3:8 219
3:9 ....249, 250, 252
3:10 149
3:11 73
4:1–3 ....78, 84
4:2–3 219
4:7 ....251, 252
4:12 277
4:19 249
5:1 253
5:1, 4–5 251
5:4–5 253
5:13 9
5:18 ....249, 250, 252

2 John

7 ....84, 219
12 76

Revelation

1:1a...............................199

1:2–3 9
1:13–16 123
1:14 123
1:18 123
2–3 77
4:10 277
5:4–5 274
5:5 274
5:6 274
5:6, 9, 12 274
5:8 277
5:14 277
7:11 277
7:15–17 255
7:17 .....255–257, 275, 276
11:16 277
12 159
12:9 150
18:9 274
18:11 274
18:15 274
18:19 274
19 186
19:4 277
21:1–4 255
21:2 277
21:3 277
21:4 .....255–257, 275–277
21:5 277
21:6 277
21:7 276
21:23 277
22:1 230
22:2 277
22:3 277
22:4 277
22:16 199